SANGH
AUR
SARKAR

VAJPAYEE TO MODI : THE INSIDE STORY OF RSS-BJP RELATIONS

SANGH
AUR
SARKAR

VAJPAYEE TO MODI : THE INSIDE STORY OF RSS-BJP RELATIONS

SANTOSH KUMAR

PRABHAT
PAPERBACKS

Publisher
PRABHAT PAPERBACKS
Imprint of Prabhat Prakashan Pvt. Ltd.
4/19 Asaf Ali Road, New Delhi–110 002
Ph. 23289555 • 23289666 • 23289777 • Helpline/ 7827007777
e-mail: prabhatbooks@gmail.com • Website: www.prabhatbooks.com

Edition
2022

Price
Six Hundred Rupees Only

ISBN 978-93-5521-289-4

Printed at
Sanjay Printer, Sahibabad

SANGH AUR SARKAR
by Santosh Kumar

ISBN 978-93-5521-289-4

₹ 600/-

For all those curious readers,
who wish to know
the relationship between
Sangh** and the **BJP

Foreword

Renowned Journalist Santosh Kumar has written an excellent book on a very interesting topic i.e., the relation between "Sangh aur Sarkar" (RSS and Government). This topic naturally arouses curiosity. Those who are not much familiar with the working style of the Sangh or are not its members, they always wonder whether the government is run by the Sangh or the government influences the Sangh? Both these situations do not hold true. This is a matter of separate organic relationship and so, Santosh Kumar has accurately described the curiosity and interest regarding this subject with examples and contexts to make it meaningful. I congratulate him on this book.

During the United Progressive Alliance (UPA) government, there was the National Advisory Council (NAC). In a way, that advisory council influenced all the decisions of the government and also had the freedom to go through the files of various departments. In a way, we have seen a non-constitutional institution in the form of NAC apart from the Planning Commission. In such a situation, as people wonder if the Sangh also works like the National Advisory Council, the answer is clear – No, because although Sangh and BJP belong to one ideology family neither of them is an institution outside the constitution. What is the similarity between the Sangh and the Bhartiya Janata Party? The similarity is the idea of nationalism. The principle is Nation is Paramount. Nation comes first, then comes organization's interest whereas an individual's interest comes last. There are other ideas too such as the idea of broad Hindutva, along with that which unites all. Neither the Sangh ever taught nor the BJP ever thought of discriminating among the citizens of the country. Antyodaya—Empowering the last person in the last line; this is the foundation of both the organizations and this is what they operate upon.

It is true that after the ban on Sangh in 1951, the Swayamsevaks of the Sangh thought that this nationalist thought of the Sangh should effectively reach all areas, and so Jan Sangh, Bharatiya Mazdoor Sangh, Akhil Bharatiya Vidyarthi Parishad and later Vishwa Hindu Parishad and many new organizations were formed. In this, the common thread is that of thought and the common thread is that they are workers and taking inspiration from the thoughts of the Sangh, many workers started such activities. But it is also necessary to understand that there are many workers in the Bhartiya Janata Party who have come from the Sangh. But there is also a large number of workers who are not connected to the Sangh. It is the same in case of Vidyarthi Parishad, Mazdoor Sangh and other organizations. One thing we should understand about the Sangh Parivar is that no one controls anyone there. The Sangh does not run the government, or the BJP, or the Vidyarthi Parishad, or the trade union or any other affiliated organizations. But it brings about better coordination and there is an exchange of ideas; suggestions and information are received and if there is a difference of opinion, it is expressed. This is its form.

Those who did not understand this point or who did not want to comprehend it even after understanding it and wanted to play their politics had raised the issue of dual membership even during the time of Janata Party. It should be noted that the Sangh Parivar played a major role in the fight against Emergency. In the general elections of 1977, the Sangh and BJP leaders had the same idea that the entire party should come together and the Janata Party should be formed. Therefore, the Janata Party was formed by merging the Jana Sangh. It was imagined that this party would run very well as per the mandate of the people of the country. But some people deliberately raised the issue of dual membership. There was ruse that one should either leave the membership of the Sangh or give up the membership of the Janata Party. This led to dispute and finally, we saw that on 6th April 1980, the Bhartiya Janata Party was established by seceding from this issue because people of Janata Party created a ruckus on the issue of dual membership and forced Jan Sangh workers to leave.

Today, in the ideology family, there can be different opinions on any issue and different opinions are also expressed. But the way of expressing it is different within the organization and within the ideology family; express it when there is solidarity. I have experienced and seen many such open discussions. It happens. But if people think that democracy means to express the differences only through the newspaper or on television, then it is not true. The amount of discussion that takes place in the Sangh Parivar and the extent to which democracy is followed—I have rarely seen this happen anywhere else or in such a large organization.

In 2014, when the Bhartiya Janata Party came to power under the leadership of Modi ji and led the NDA, he said that this government is dedicated to the poor. He also said that the constitution is our scripture. When he entered Parliament for the first time, he bowed his head at its entrance. This is the sentiment of the Sangh towards the country. That's why he called himself the Pradhan Sevak (principal servant). This is very important and the core of the teachings of the Sangh. But it does not happen that the Sangh gives the order and the party or the government work according to that. The Sangh does not give orders. Yes, there is an exchange of ideas, we meet. When we take a decision related to an issue, we talk to the stakeholders, meet experts in that field, meet the NGOs working in that field, study the people and the documents related to that field. Similarly, there is also a vast system where all the people of the family give their opinions and also give suggestions and it paves the way. The same is true of the relationship between the Sangh and the Government.

Santosh Kumar had written another excellent book earlier – 'Bharat Kaise Hua Modimay'. It describes Modiji's journey in Gujarat;it describes in even more detail the surge of public wave that was created when he was declared the Prime Ministerial candidate and he toured the whole country for 10 months. After that the government was formed for five years and then came the 2019 general elections. The Bhartiya Janata Party achieved amazing success in that election which is described in detail in this book. In that too, all the issues related to the Sangh and the BJP have been covered. This is the second book –'Sangh Aur Sarkar'. I think that those who will read both the books will understand the bigger role and reality of the relationship between Bhartiya Janata Party and Sangh. Santosh Kumar is a freelance writer; but it is not as if his every word about the history or events will be correct. There can be a difference of opinion, but the author has that much liberty. He has written down the personal experiences that he had in all these relationships and what he saw based on those experiences. So, what he has written is his. But I am sure that this book will help us in our understanding.

– Prakash Javadekar

Member of Parliament, Rajya Sabha

Former Union Minister of Information and Broadcasting, Environment, Forest and Climate Change

INTRODUCTION
Contours of Collaboration

Once again, the country has got a stable government. This is the destiny of crores of Indians. It is a victory of the nationalistic powers. This election was between two different concepts of India. This ideological battle, which has been going on since the time of independence, has now reached a turning point. This election is an important stage in this battle. When the society started to unite, those who did the politics of division saw the ground slipping. So, all the divisive forces came together and tried to challenge this uniting force by supporting each other. But the well-informed and intelligent people of India have made the idea of development victorious by supporting a uniting and all-inclusive India. Hearty congratulations to the strong leadership which is on the side of India's interest and all the workers in this ideological fight.

This utterance on the day of the 2019 Lok Sabha election results expressed a feeling of satisfaction of the Rashtriya Swayamsevak Sangh which had completed 93 years working in the social sector. It had not only spent three generations in anticipation of this historic moment on the ideological front but it had also had a bitter experience during the rule of its own ideology. After forming a government for the first time in the year 1996 for 13 days and then a stable government from 1998 to 2004, the dilemma of BJP's distance from power for a decade and generational struggle seemed to end the justification of the battle of ideologies. After that, the Sangh brought about a generational change and laid down the blueprint for a big change in the Vichar Pariwar. It then weaved such a blueprint from social equation to pariwar coordination that it became a matter of research for some intellectuals, whether it was the victory of 2014 or of 2019 Lok Sabha elections. The way the Vichar Parivar had pulled the BJP out of the internal struggle and drawn the blueprint, both the results were not surprising.

But the question may arise that why it was not surprising for the Sangh? Before proceeding further, it would be appropriate to clarify two facts - first, the Sangh does not accept the word 'Sangh Parivar'. It prefers words like 'Vichar Parivar' for the affiliated organizations. But for understanding, it was necessary to do so and hence, the term 'Sangh Parivar' is often mentioned in the book. Second, the Sangh, which grew out of a long movement, was bound by the basic principles at the time of its establishment. But instead of venturing into politics itself, it supported the Jana Sangh and then the Bharatiya Janata Party (BJP) as an undertaking. Since the core of both the organizations is 'Volunteers' (Swayamsevak), it also creates an impression about the Sangh that it completely controls the government of its ideology and its agenda is implemented in the government or the BJP organization. But except for a few examples, it would not be correct. Whether it is the Jana Sangh or the BJP, whenever they have come to power, such people have occupied positions of power from leadership to policy-making who have been from the Sangh and whose thinking and working style naturally have the touch of the Sangh. Whether in government or in an organization, the leader is swayamsevak before anything else.

The book is completely based on the formation of its first ideological government to the mutual coordination between the BJP and the Sangh. But the coordination was not just about winning an election or running the government, but it was also about expanding the organization with a long-term vision in such a way that it could act as a pressure group whether its government remained or not in the future. But if the idea is to understand the importance of co-ordination in the family, then it becomes necessary to go through the bitterness during the government from 1998 to 2004 and then the bitter strife within the BJP from 2004 to 2013, because this experience became the cornerstone to make the BJP organization move like the flow of a river and avoid ideological conflict while in power. In a sequenced manner, the book narrates the story of the differences when the party was in power and then a decade-long leadership struggle in the BJP after the electoral defeat, which set the course and direction for the period after 2014. The story begins from the year 1998, when the BJP came to power at the centre for the first time under the leadership of Atal Bihari Vajpayee. Atal Bihari Vajpayee and LK Advani used to be synonymous with BJP then. But on economic issues, there was such a conflict with the affiliated organizations of the Sangh such as Bharatiya Mazdoor Sangh, Swadeshi Jagran Manch, Bharatiya Kisan Sangh etc that the organizations of the Vichar Pariwarstarted appearing in the role of opposition. Dattopant Thengdi of BMS had sat on a dharna, the example of which is still given as the Sangh-BJP conflict. From the change in the list of Ministers sent to Rashtrapati Bhavan to the RSS advising Vajpayee to become the President, there were many cases when the differences became public. In the year 2000, when KS Sudarshan became the RSS Chief after Rajju Bhaiya, the sourness increased and Sudarshan started targeting the government publicly. All the details will be found in the book chronologically. The book talks about the stand taken by the Sangh during the attempt to remove Modi from the post of Chief Minister after the Gujarat riots and how the impression was being created that 'Leader is the one whom Sangh chooses', leading to an internal conflict between the Sangh and the party with the Vajpayee government for a full six years. It went on to such an extent that even the cadre got confused and the result was that the BJP, which had registered a big victory in the assembly a few months ago, was removed from power in 2004 in such a manner that it took a decade for it to overcome the internal tussle.

After the unexpected defeat, Vajpayee, who went to Manali for a holiday in June 2004, again created a ruckus by calling the Gujarat riots as a major reason for the defeat; in response the Sangh Parivar opened a front against Vajpayee. In the end, Vajpayee had to bow down. After convening an emergency meeting of the parliamentary board, the party leadership had to announce that Narendra Modi would continue in his position. Then after the Lok Sabha elections, when the party lost the Maharashtra and Haryana assembly elections, the then BJP President Venkaiah Naidu resigned and the party reins were again in the hands of Advani. After that, the Uma Bharti episode and Sundar Singh Bhandari's publicly raised question about the party reins being handed over to Advani again had given rise to new discord. In April 2005, the interview of RSS Chief KS Sudarshan, in which he not only asked Vajpayee-Advani to retire but also refused to consider Vajpayee among the three best Prime Ministers or leaders of the country. The RSS Chief was a bit soft on Advani then; but the very next month, Advani enraged the Sangh Parivar by visiting Jinnah's tomb and calling him secular. The Jinnah that Advani had discovered by going to Pakistan exists in the books but not in the minds of Indian public and not at all in the books of the BJP-Sangh. Considering this as a drastic ideological deviation, the Sangh decided in a meeting of pracharaks from across the country held in Surat that Advani would have to give up the presidency. When the pressure mounted, Advani accused the Sangh of interfering in the day-to-day work and then announced his resignation in December 2005.

In the second generation, the command went to Rajnath Singh. RSS general secretary Sanjay Joshi got involved in the alleged sex CD scandal. But sensing the politics behind this CD, the Sangh did not appoint anyone in place of Joshi. Three months later, when Joshi got a clean chit from the Madhya Pradesh Police, the party reinstated him. By then Advani had regained his hold on the party and announced the Bharat Suraksha Twin Rath Yatra against the appeasement policies of the UPA government. Advani and Rajnath were to lead it from two directions and finally it was to end in Delhi on May 10, 2006. But in the midst of this journey, Pramod Mahajan who was considered BJP's trouble-shooter and big strategist was murdered, which was a huge shock for the party. In the same year, when Rajnath became the President for the entire term, Mohan Bhagwat as RSS Chief (Sarkaryavah) gave the mantra of ideological coordination. After that, Advani's campaign to become 'PM in waiting' intensified. Then the rebellion started raising its head at the time of UP elections. But the policies of the UPA government gave opportunities to the Sangh. Submitting an affidavit in the Supreme Court to deny the existence of Lord Ram on Ram Setu or the Vande Mataram controversy, Prime Minister Manmohan Singh's statement of minority's rights over resources—all these were issues that were favourable to the Sangh. But in such a situation, the question emerged - who should be the face of the party now and who can capitalize on these issues by moving forward on the path of Hindutva? Meanwhile, the Bhopal

Executive Committee meeting of September 2007 saw an uproar over the issue of 'who is the Prime Ministerial candidate'. But the time had also come when the Sangh was going to put a stamp on Advani's unfulfilled wish for decades albeit out of compulsion. Finally, at the Sangh's meeting in Dharwad, Karnataka between November 4-6, 2007, the issue of opportunity and fairness once again made the Sangh turn towards Advani. Eventually, Advani became the 'PM in waiting' after being declared the Prime Ministerial candidate on 10 December. Then the Gujarat assembly elections were going on. Modi made the headlines and his stature had also risen. Advani used all his might – he demanded a 'Bharat Ratna' for Vajpayee, wrote an autobiography, strategized in the Barack Obama style, met experts to set the agenda and indulging in the politics of symbols which is an important part of the BJP's strategy. He was tricking all the boxes of political game. The UPA government was also handing over issues; among them Amarnath Shrine Board land dispute and increasing terrorist incidents were important. Meanwhile, after the arrest of Sadhvi Pragya in the Malegaon blast case, the use of the word 'Hindu terrorism' by Congress was infuriating the Sangh. The BJP raised this issue vigorously on the advice of the Sangh. Then the Mumbai terror attack took place. Overall, the situation was in party's favour. But during the assembly elections, the party lost Rajasthan. The preparations for the Lok Sabha elections were in full swing. The Sangh advised the BJP not to indulge in favouritism and to distribute tickets based on the reports of the workers. It was then that Bhairon Singh Shekhawat who had retired from the post of Vice-President, opened the front. Rajnath advised him not to take dip in a well after bathing in the Ganges. Also, the term 'PM in waiting' became a topic of mockery in the party itself. Amid the tussle over the leadership in the second generation, with Arun Jaitley becoming the poll manager and his twelve-day confrontation with the national president over the Sudhanshu Mittal episode, the party's discord was out in the open. After the shoe (khadau) episode during Advani's meeting and then the demand to make Narendra Modi the Prime Ministerial candidate, it seemed that all the strategists engaged for Advani in the 2009 election for the 15th Lok Sabha were debating the leadership for the sixteenth Lok Sabha. In such a situation, Advani's fate was bound to hang in the balance and the party lost the election once again.

There was a change in the Sangh even before the 2009 election results and in March itself, Mohan Bhagwat, who was seen as a young leader, had taken the place of KS Sudarshan as the Sarsanghchalak. In such a situation, after the defeat in the Lok Sabha elections, it was certain that the BJP would get a new leadership as Vajpayee had retired from active politics on health grounds. Advani had also been tried. Now there was a need for a leadership that would not deviate from the path of Hindutva and the party workers could trust its ideology even with closed eyes; it was also reflected in the article written by the Sangh ideologue M. G. Vaidya in Marathi daily 'Tarun

Bharat' in June. There was a discussion in the BJP that now the party should reconsider the Mandal-Kamandal politics. But Vaidya wrote, "The BJP failed to convey the true meaning of Hindutva in the 2009 general elections. It would be better if the BJP distances itself from Hindutva. Doing so would automatically end its relationship with the Sangh and give the party an opportunity to adopt a modern approach." But the BJP President Rajnath Singh said that they could never leave the ideology of Hindutva because they had grown with the ideology. The new generation in the Sangh assumed that Hindutva would have to be used openly in the 2014 elections because the alliance would be possible only if the BJP which was leading it became strong itself first. But once again the discipline in the party was getting ruined. Arun Shourie even called National President Rajnath Singh 'Tom, Dick and Harry' and Humpty-Dumpty. Yashwant Sinha had also been vocal against making Arun Jaitley the Leader of the Opposition in the Rajya Sabha. There was the 'rotten pickle' statement of Manohar Parrikar and then the 'Letter Bombs' started erupting everywhere. In such a situation, RSS Chief (Sarsanghchalak) Mohan Bhagwat drew a clear line as to who would be the BJP president after Rajnath Singh. Advani did not agree to his farewell formula and went to the Swami Pejawara Matha so that he would get some time. In such a situation, Acharya Dharmendra, the leader of the VHP, said in an angry manner – "Without the Sangh, the BJP does not exist. If the instructions of the Sangh are not followed, the BJP will collapse like a castle of sand." In such a scenario, on December 18, 2009,

Advani's handing over the leadership of the party to Sushma Swaraj in the Lok Sabha, Arun Jaitley in the Rajya Sabha, and the next day, on December 19, Nitin Gadkari's - the choice of Mohan Bhagwat for party presidentship – entry into central politics directly from Maharashtra politics, was part of the party's transition period

On the other hand, Narendra Modi's rise to national leadership, the controversy surrounding Nitish Kumar's dinner meeting during Bihar's executive committee and Gujarat's development model seemed to lead him to becoming an alternative to Manmohan. Modi was rapidly emerging on the top in opinion polls. But the conflict started in the party again. Gadkari included Sanjay Joshi in the national executive committee while Modi also took a tough stand before the Mumbai executive meeting in May 2012. Finally, Sanjay Joshi departed. Then there were allegations of irregularities against Gadkari's company 'Purti' and the raids by the Income Tax Department before the nomination, which left the Sangh confused. The Sangh had to change its advice. In such a situation, once again Rajnath Singh was given the command. When there was a tussle for the presidency in the BJP, Narendra Modi was engaged in the mission along with his warlords. The voice in favour of Modi started emanating from every town and village. His third victory in the Gujarat Legislative Assembly elections in December 2012 and becoming the Chief Minister for the fourth time gave out the message of march towards Delhi; Modi started addressing people as 'countrymen' instead of 'Gujaratis'. The reason for this was a crucial three-and-a-half hour meeting he had with RSS Chief (Sarsanghchalak) Mohan Bhagwat, Bhaiyyaji Joshi and Suresh Soni on October 21, 2012 at Reshimbagh, Nagpur just before the assembly elections. This meeting gave a hint of the future. The importance of this meeting could also be gauged from the fact that Modi was constantly being attacked by the so-called secular brigade and in the same chain of events, in June 2012, Bihar Chief Minister Nitish Kumar had targeted Modi in an interview saying that the Prime Minister's post should have a secular face. In response to that, Sarsanghchalak Mohan Bhagwat, while addressing the Sangh workers in Latur, raised the question, "Why can't a Hindu leader be the Prime Minister of the country? The Prime Minister of the country should now be someone who propounds the Hindu ideology." The picture was quite clear. On the other hand, in the year 2014, there was a tremendous wave about Modi as the candidate for the post of Prime Minister. The Sangh also believed that leaving aside the hesitation regarding the style of his work, Modi was the BJP's trump card; the senior leaders of the Sangh believed that every person had a different style of working.

Modi too had started appearing different. Interaction with students in Shri Ram College of Commerce, campaign of saints in Allahabad Kumbh and dip in Sangam by Rajnath indicated the strategy of the Vichar Pariwar. Then Modi made Amit Shah general secretary and gave charge of Uttar Pradesh. However, from time-to-time, Advani played his cards. But the Sangh had decided and there was also a mindset that this time the issue of Hindutva ideology should be used all across. Finally, in June 2013, at the BJP National Executive meeting in Goa, Modi was handed over the command. To execute this campaign, Suresh Soni, the vice-general secretary (Sah-Sarkaryavah) of the Sangh, was also present in the same hotel where the strategy was being designed. The Sangh advised the party to employ the strategy of handing over the election campaign committee command to Modi first as a litmus test. But Advani created an uproar by resigning from all party posts. At that time, the Sangh's first public intervention was seen and finally, in September, by announcing Modi as the Prime Ministerial candidate the Sangh also rolled the last dice of a generational change. The full script of the events is in the book.

The entire Vichar Pariwar of the Sangh was now involved in Mission 2014 as a third defeat could put a question mark on its very existence. So, the matter was not limited to projecting only Modi. An important point was revealed during the discussions between the Sangh and BJP that despite the mobilization of all the forces of the party and the family, the vote share of the BJP would reach only 18 to 25 percent. In such a situation, a strategy was devised for additional 10 percent votes and an exercise was carried out to increase the social base through a new alliance. The results of the assembly elections in Madhya Pradesh, Chhattisgarh, Rajasthan and Delhi, which were considered semi-finals, proved to be favourable for this strategy. Ram Vilas Paswan, who had left the NDA after criticizing Modi over the Gujarat riots stood smilingly with the same BJP twelve years. Later In Bihar, Uttar Pradesh, Tamil Nadu, Haryana, Andhra Pradesh and Northeast, new alliance were ready to partner with Modi. New people were added on social basis and the rebellious attitudes were punished. Then the conflict on the tactics of Murli Manohar Joshi and Advani for tickets were contained and the moral advice of the Sangh contributed to the establishment of Modi's leadership. The full story will be found in detail in this book.

Finally, Narendra Modi after securing his place in the party and then launched such an election campaign which could not be called just election machinery in all fairness. The amount of distance that Modi travelled in nine months could be said to be equal to seven times the perimeter of the earth. Why was Modi so confident about his strategy as well as campaign that he made statement about the victory even before the results? What made him say that the Congress was not going to reach even three figures and that the BJP was going to get a majority on its own? In view of his experience in the organization, Modi had also placed the blueprint of the government and the BJP in front of the Sangh for advice. When the results came in on May 16, 2014, it was a moment of rejoicing for the BJP and comfort for the Sangh. The victory was described by the Sangh as the result of healthy democracy while the defeat of the years 2004 and 2009 was described by the Sangh as contrary to expectations. But this time in the statement, the Sangh made an important point, which was like a prelude to dialogue and coordination in the Vachar Pariwar. The then General Secretary (Sarkaryavah) Bhaiyyaji Joshi said, "We have to believe that the process of change has its own pace and change is possible only with the coordinated efforts of the government, administration, all political parties, public, social and religious institutions." The message of the Sangh was clear that there would be no conflict with the government on any issue. The Sangh was confident that the Narendra Modi government formed with the victory of ideology would not let the sacrifices of three generations go in vain. The Sangh also believed that the work which was not worthy of being done or could not be done by the government will mean that it was not possible for the government. This mantra became the basis of coordination between the Sangh and the Modi government. If the Sangh had faith in Modi, then Modi had also entered politics after fulfilling the role of a pracharak in the organisation. So, he was aware of the importance of the organization. Therefore, when he became the leader of the Parliamentary Party, in his address, he said that like India is my mother, BJP is also my mother and no son can be bigger than his mother. Modi's emotional speech was a sign of taking the organization into a new direction, which in the past decade had become known for flouting discipline. The conflict with the Vichar Pariwar during the Vajpayee government in 1998-2004 and then the organizational turmoil and lack of discipline in the BJP from 2004 to 2013 had taught a lesson. Narendra Modi had closely watched every incident and learn from them, he advised Amit Shah to prepare such a structure of the organization that government and organization would complement each other. At the same time, a complete mechanism was prepared for the Sangh Parivar too so that there would be no scope for any differences. In fact, the idea was to make the best blueprint for coordination in the family. Whether it was the appointment of Vice-Chancellors in universities or governors or other political appointments or policy matters, many small groups were formed for consultation with the concerned organizations so that decisions were taken by taking everyone into confidence. But that did not mean that there would be no controversy. Thoughts that were expressed or disputes that appeared on the streets during the Vajpayee government were now resolved in closed rooms within a few hours as if nothing had happened. There are many examples like reservation, demonetisation, making Yogi CM of UP, BHU vice-chancellor controversy, which tell the story of amazing coordination.

With the formation of the government, the Vichar Pariwar had made a blueprint for coordination in close consultation, but the government also had its own limitations. Firstly, the Sangh sent two pracharaks - Ram Madhav and Shivprakash to the BJP. Ram Madhav was the Sangh spokesperson during the Vajpayee government and he was aware of the bitterness of that period. As such, their important role in coordination was determined. But in the very beginning, there was opposition on many issues like land acquisition and Swadeshi. But how the Sangh gave a mantra in March 2015 to stop the conflict and suddenly the voices of allied organizations that were vocal against the Modi government were softened is mentioned in a separate chapter. There was an important meeting of the Sangh with the organization in-charges working in the BJP after a decade. In the coordination meeting of the Vichar Pariwar, a draft was prepared on six subjects and was shared as the thought of the Sangh. In the concluding session of this meeting, Modi had said, "The expectations of the public from the government are very high. We have to work at the same pace. But sometimes there is a rhetoric by the organizations (ideology family), which affects the mutual understanding." This coordination in the Vichar Pariwar was not only because of power, but whether it was the government or the organization, the leaders who were handling the responsibility knew its import. That's why everyone was wholeheartedly engaged in this work. In such a situation, whenever a dispute arose, there were many examples of how it was resolved. Only a fortnight after the coordination meeting, RSS Chief (Sarsanghchalak) Mohan Bhagwat's statement about reservation became a problem for the BJP in Bihar elections. However, behind the scenes, a wonderful exercise of damage control was undertaken, whose step-by-step information is part of the book. Then doubts were cast on Amit Shah regarding the defeat of Bihar elections and the post of president. But the Sangh, as always, confined itself to the role of moral guide. Similarly, during the Jaipur Literary Festival in January 2017, the issue of reservation again arose, which was resolved within a few hours so that it did not become an issue in the Uttar Pradesh elections. The Sangh also took a flexible stand at all times while the BJP also did not cross the limits.

The recurring controversy over reservation forced the Sangh to give impetus to the social harmony campaign launched under Vision-2025 and for which the slogan of 'One Temple, One Well, One Crematorium' was given in the 2015 All India Representative Meet. After this, a blueprint of harmony was also designed through symbols. As a part of this, first special issue of 'Panjanya' dedicated to Dr. Bhimrao Ambedkar was launched; many such events were organized, in which an attempt was made to give the message that if Ambedkar's words were read after removing his name, then they will look like the statements of sages. In the All-India Representative Meet at Nagaur, the Sangh dedicated the entire pavilion to Ambedkar, and had also kept a big portrait of former RSS Chief Balasaheb Deoras. Through the thoughts of Babasaheb to Balasaheb, the Sangh carried forward the messages of Ambedkar while on the other hand, the Modi government also worked speedily on the heritage related to Ambedkar. During the Nagaur meeting, the Sangh intensified its campaign of expansion and penetration among the youth by changing the uniform. But a change in dress would not be enough to attract them. The Sangh leadership knew that the contest to bring youth into the organization would have to be fought on the ideological front as well. In such a situation, it is important to know how the Sangh and the BJP strategized in a coordinated way and laid the ground for social expansion by weaving a blueprint for intellectual gathering. Modi had said during the 2014 election campaign itself that the coming decade belonged to the Dalit-backward. He had said, "BJP, which was called a party of Brahmins and Banias, has now become a party of Dalits and backwards. The future belongs to the Dalits and backward people only." But after coming to power, some anti-Dalit incidents in the society were also putting the Vichar Pariwarin a dilemma, which also led to a deadlock in the initiative of social harmony. In such a situation, along with making its entry into the society, the Sangh also intensified the work on creating a group of intellectuals, who play an important role in creating any kind of positive or negative concept.

The Sangh, from its inception till now, had a regret that though it had spread its branches in every section such as politics, society, students, labourers etc, it could not take 'roots' in the intellectual world. After the historic victory of the BJP in 2014, it was a key point of contemplation for the Sangh. The work on it started systematically. After the JNU incident, the top leaders of the Sangh-BJP held an important meeting of 14 people on the first day and 60 people on the second day at Haryana Bhavan and the leadership held the discussion; it is interesting from the point of view of understanding the future strategy. After this, a think tank inspired by the ideas of the Sangh was activated. About the marathon exercise of creating an intellectual pressure group, the ideologues of the Sangh then said, "The way the Sangh and its ideology have been systematically marginalized in the intellectual discourse of India has to be defeated by fact and logic today. That is an important aspect of the discussion." That is, the purpose of the Sangh Parivar was clear and the BJP and the government were also fully with it. Then in May 2016 itself, at the time of Ujjain Simhastha, the Vichar Mahakumbh was organized and the decision to take the Hindustan News Agency forward in a professional manner under the media strategy of the Sangh with far-reaching thinking was taken. The two-day 'Nationalist Writers' Meet' was also going on in terms of strategy for like-minded writers, bloggers, thinkers. The campaign was naturally criticized by opponents. But the Sangh had learned a lesson from the time of the Vajpayee government.

In an exercise for establishing intellectual roots, the Sangh developed a blueprint for change in education and the ideological body 'Prajnya Pravah' laid the foundation for organizing events like Lok-Manthan . The Sangh had made its intention clear by having a secret meeting with the education Ministers of the BJP-ruled states for uniformity in the education blueprint and converting the 'Shiksha Sangam' in Delhi into an intellectual Mahakumbh. For the first time, there was a gathering of 721 academicians, including professors, assistant professors, associate professors and 51 vice-chancellors (from 20 central universities and 31 state universities), in which RSS Chief

Mohan Bhagwat himself held a meeting with intellectuals in different groups. Krishna Gopal also held a meeting with the Vice Chancellors. Mohan Bhagwat, while sharing the cricketing experience at the event, said that when team members played with the spirit of playing for India, India is bound to win. While talking on Indian history and its writings, Dr Krishna Gopal, the Vice-General Secretary (Sah-sarkaryvah) said that everything was done under the design of Christian missionaries and churches. So now there was a need to explore history because Indian history has been written by hunters, not by lions themselves. The mantra given by the Sangh for this was the basis for giving impetus to the intellectual movement. A group called 'Udaan' was also formed in the theatre to counter the Leftists. There was also a strategy to answer the challenge to the Modi government posed by the left intellectuals through its intellectuals. Apart from this, the Sangh's strategy was also to include more and more books related to its ideology in universities and schools with a favourable atmosphere. But the Sangh also indicated that there would be no discrimination in the campaign to connect intellectuals by holding a meeting on 26-27 August, 2018 in remembrance of Gandhi at Rajghat. It said that if someone wanted to move away from other ideology and join our side, he should be welcomed.

Later, a coordination meeting of the Sangh Parivar was held in Mathura. But after a few days, the controversy of Banaras Hindu University deepened. Being Prime

Minister Modi's parliamentary constituency, it naturally made headlines. Therefore, a decision to remove Vice Chancellor Girish Chandra Tripathi was taken at the top level in the government. But when he did not agree, the Sangh took the initiative; it is one of the examples of coordination between the Sangh and the government. Demonetisation and making Yogi CM in UP are also some examples of this. After that, the visit by former President and veteran Congress leader Pranab Mukherjee must have riled the congress deeply. But the Sangh's strategic invitation to Pranabda for an address at the Sangh headquarters dimmed the tag of 'untouchability' that some intellectuals attached to the Sangh. Suddenly the number of people joining the Sangh increased, especially from West Bengal where Pranabda belonged. It is also a fact that west Bengal played an important role in BJP's victory in the 2019 general elections.

It was a pleasant feeling for the Sangh as the acceptance of the Sangh increased during the favourable government and ideological environment. In such a situation, an idea came up in the Sangh Parivar that the confusion or false propaganda about the organization among the opponents or some of the media should be removed by the Sangh itself. That is, instead of the third party, the Sangh itself decided to clear the confusion. There was confusion about issues like the role of the Sangh in the freedom movement, the tricolour flag, Dalits etc. This was probably the first time in the 93-year history of the Sangh that such an event was held. About six months before the Lok Sabha elections, the opposition had raised eyebrows at such an event. A three-day program 'Future India: Union's Vision' was organized from 17-19 September, 2018 at Vigyan Bhawan, Delhi. At this event, over two days, the Sarsanghchalak explained in detail various issues right from the establishment of the Sangh to the life of Dr Hedgewar, Hedgewar's dialogue with communist Ruikar, the working style of the Sangh, nurturing a Swayamsevak, Hindutva, the discipline of the Sangh, Tricolour vs. Saffron Flag, remote control on allied organizations, women's participation etc. Speaking directly on reservation, the Sangh Chief said, "Some statements are made from time to time and some sort of meaning is derived from them. But keep in mind that the reservation given in the constitution to remove social disparity is and will be fully supported by the Sangh." There was also an unambiguous opinion on the twisted questions like NOTA, the naturalness of the Sangh-BJP relationship and the lack of democracy in the election of the Sarsanghchalak. Then 'Prajnya Pravah' organized an intellectual fair in Ranchi and reiterated its thought of reviving the idea of nationalism.

The effect of the BJP government at the centre and the leadership of Narendra Modi were visible on the people of the country. Therefore, in this environment, the Sangh also succeeded to a great extent in establishing social and intellectual roots, the benefit of which was that the branches of the Sangh also started spreading rapidly. Between 2009 and 2014, on one hand the Sangh's branches increased by close to 5,000, on the other hand, the figures also decreased several times during that period. But after the formation of the Modi government, more than 6,000 branches were added in the first year itself. Comparative picture will be found in this book. But in the meantime, the BJP suffered a setback in the assembly elections of Madhya Pradesh, Chhattisgarh, Rajasthan, which were considered to be semi-finals. But Amit Shah did not stop the movement of the organization and the Sangh Parivar also threw the dice of upper caste reservation based on the feedback of the Swayamsevaks. The Modi government approved it in the cabinet on January 7, 2019; it was passed by the Lok Sabha on January 8 and Rajya Sabha on January 9 and got the President's recommendation on January 12. The stakes for giving reservation to the poor upper castes were taken after the Supreme Court's decision on the SC-ST Act was overturned in Parliament and its political losses in the elections in three states. Once again, the Vichar Pariwar was involved in Mission-2019 with enthusiasm. Now the time had come to repay the power which had given the Sangh benefit of changed situation. Swayamsevaks were given the task of ensuring 100% voting. A group of teachers was sent to different areas. In the intellectual world also, a group had been formed which was ready to respond to any attack from the opposition immediately. To respond to any campaign against Modi, 'Academics for NaMo' was started with the inspiration of Dr Krishna Gopal, the Vice General Secretary (Sah-Sarkaryavah) of the Sangh, who created an atmosphere through articles and ideas. Apart from this, the way the Sangh expanded its 'Vasudhaiv Kutumbakam' (the world is one family) spirit in the world through Hindu Swayamsevak Sangh and increased its work in 39 countries of the world, the BJP also got its benefit naturally.

On March 8-10, 2019, just before the announcement of the election dates, the Sangh did not ask for votes by taking the name of the BJP according to its principles. Rather it launched a voter awareness campaign by raising issues related to the nation, which concerned the Modi government. This included all the schemes of the government, which directly benefited the voter. In such a situation, call it nationalism if you will, the Sangh and the entire Vichar Pariwarcreated a sponge-like ground by setting an example of wonderful coordination which absorbed the BJP's other issues including the retaliatory action in Balakot after Pulwama. It created such a wave that the BJP under the leadership of Narendra Modi created a new record by winning more seats than in the year 2014. As part of its campaign, the Sangh had prepared the ground in more than 3.5 lakh villages by directly contacting more than 40 crore voters, that is, under the strategy, the Sangh Swayamsevaks had contacted 60 percent of India. Certainly, the proper management of the Sangh Parivar along with the coordination once again witnessed the historic victory of the BJP under the leadership of Narendra Modi in the year 2019 and the lack of coordination in the Vichar Parivar during the BJP government between 1998 and 2004 was left behind forever. There was coordination during Vajpayee rule too, but his government was not experienced, so the Sangh had to be vocal on some issues. The oppozition sometimes went to such an extent that it became prestige issued leading to hotility. But this time, it was kept under control and since 2014 till now, such a wonderful thread of coordination has been created from the first day of the reign of Narendra Modi that in the last seven years there has never been a discord. This trend is continuing and its length keeps increasing. In such a situation when I was covering the BJP and the Sangh Parivar, I am reminded of an important point in the addresses given in the national executive-sessions of some top leaders like Atal-Advani-Rajnath etc., in which they used to say, "Destiny desires a strong BJP for a strong India. If the Congress got the credit for independence in the twentieth century, then destiny has reserved the credit for India's greatness in the twenty-first century for us."Perhaps this was not possible until the BJP looked strong. Modi also made his blueprint keeping Amit Shah in mind. In today's politics, perhaps even opponents will agree that what the BJP used to say in principle, Modi transformed into reality. Only the strong BJP laid the foundation of strong India in the true sense, which is an integral part of the Sangh Parivar. The result of the 2019 general election was a sign of realizing the ideological issues, then within six months Article 370 was nullified and the historic decision of the Supreme Court paved the way for the construction of Shri Ram Janmabhoomi temple. In the true sense, since its birth, the BJP has been moving ahead in the light of its mother organization Sangh. But the Sangh too, taking lessons from the past experiences, retained its role as a 'moral guide' rather than a 'political guide'. On the Sangh-BJP relationship, Bhaiyyaji Joshi, the then Sarkaryavah of the Sangh, once said in a conversation with me, "Why was the BJP formed? It was on the issue of the Sangh that the Jana Sangh separated from the Janata Party. That's why some relationship remains. Discussions are definitely held with the Sangh on ideological-intellectual issues. We meet each other as Swayamsevaks. But advising the BJP does not mean ordering."

That means the basic mantra of 'dialogue' and 'cooordination' is the cornerstone of the strong relationship between the Sangh and the BJP.

Note: *This book was written during the tenure of the then office bearers of the Sangh-BJP. But there were some changes during the Bangalore Representatives meeting just before its publication. The designations should be read in that context.*

❑

Acknowledgements

Many a times in life, the things that you have not thought about happen suddenly. Circumstances emerge in such a way that thoughts also begin to flow. When I was writing the book 'Bharat Kaise Hua Modimay: The Story of a Historic Victory' which was about the inside story of the 2019 Lok Sabha election victory, I did not think that I would have to move to another book anytime soon. The book which has become a best seller received many types of feedback and one of my interviews about the book reached more than 1.5 million readers. There was important feedback in this episode that the role of the Sangh should also be mentioned in detail. While writing a book on the election victory of Lok Sabha in the year 2019, it came to my mind many times that the role of Sangh and Vichar Parivar should also be included in it. But to cover the work done by the Vichar Parivar silently in the atmosphere of that big victory in just a few chapters might not have done justice to the strength of the organization. But the compulsion or preoccupation with the profession or whatever one may say, caused a constant delay in completing the research for this book. But when I was free from the daily compulsion of the profession during the global pandemic of Corona, I was determined to make good use of it.

But while working on any news, it has become a habit to find every detail about it, record it and store it in the form of a document. Newspaper or magazine has its own limit in terms of words. But the old tendency to write down the remaining portions and save them has proved to be helpful in giving the shape to this book. I actively started working as a journalist on November 3, 2003. In such a situation, a dilemma occurred at the very first stage when the form of the book had taken shape in the mind and brain. When I sat down to write the book, there was no direct and in-depth insight of Atal Bihari Vajpayee's reign from 1996 to 2004. Though there was definitely a study on it a book could not be written based on it. In such a situation, a blueprint for writing a book was made in three phases. In the first phase, the details of the Sangh-BJP and government coordination between 2014 and 2019 were collected. In the second phase, the BJP's internal struggle from 2004 to 2014 and the role of the Sangh in it was covered. In the third phase, the first chapter was brainstormed upon, during which I had a long discussion with many well-known journalists of the time, especially Vijay Trivediji who is a senior journalist and who wrote a book on Atal Bihari Vajpayee. He shared many facts which generally suited my style of work. Therefore, I express my special gratitude to Vijayji for his contribution in writing this book. My own reporting came in handy in preparing the rest of the parts. The daily column 'India Gate Se' in the daily 'Navjyoti', the research report during my tenure in 'India Today' and the experience of working in other institutions became the basis for writing the book and gathering facts. The book contains the same things which I had briefly published there and have now been comprehensively included in the book. I would like to express my special gratitude to Shri Deenbandhu Choudharyji, the whole and sole of Dainik Navjyoti Group, all the seniors, colleagues and editors who guided me during my time in India Today.

Certainly, the role of the family becomes crucial in any such project as it is not easy to create an environment at home conducive for writing a book when everything comes to a standstill in the midst of a disaster like Corona. But parent's blessings and wife Nalini's support constantly inspired me and helped me write the book from morning till late at night. During this time, I also used to watch TV broadcasts of historical epics like 'Ramayana' and 'Mahabharata' with family to refresh the mind and prepare for hard work again. During this, daughter Vaishnavi and son Vaibhav also gave their full cooperation so that I could concentrate on writing the book. This expression of gratitude may not be necessary for the family, but they also have a natural right on it for the record. I am also grateful to colleague and friend Vibhor Sharma for his cooperation in editing the book. I also thank my colleagues Divya Talwar, Ravindra Sharma and Shyam Shankar Tiwari for their cooperation in designing the cover of this book.

We have been able to bring this book to this point because of my style of working—while doing any work, I tend to delve deeply into it and then bring out every aspect in front. It is a moral responsibility as a journalist to understand politics and bring out its true form, whether it is positive or negative.

❑

Contents

PART -1

From Struggling Opposition to Power

(1996-2004)

As the opposition, the image of first Jan Sangh and then BJP was that of a fighting and rational party. But when the government was formed for 13 days for the first time in 1996 and then in 1998 for 13 months, followed by a government from 1999 to 2004, it had a fierce confrontation with the mother organization Sangh, especially on economic issues. At that time, the affiliated organizations of the Vichar Parivar played the role of a strong opposition rather than establishing co-ordination. The differences had increased to such an extent that there was confusion among the workers and eventually, the Vajpayee government was out of power. There was a complete lack of coordination between the leaders in the Pariwar as well as in the government. After the Gujarat riots, differences also emerged between Atal-Advani regarding Modi. But in the present era, the lessons learnt in the past became the cornerstone for creating a new path of coordination.

❑

1

CHAPTER

Power and Public Conflict

When the BJP came to power for the first time, the conflict in the Vichar Pariwar also came to the surface. In the BJP, when there was a difference of opinion between Atal and Advani too, then the message went out – the leader is the one that Sangh decides. Why was there a lack of coordination even after coming to power and then what was the lesson learned from the results?

At the very outset, it would probably be appropriate to clarify the notion, where it is said that the Sangh completely controls the government of its ideology. Had it been so, then during the government of 1998-2004, such a conflict might not have come to the fore. But why is the matter of Sangh's control discussed? There is also a reason for this - whether it was Jana Sangh or BJP, whenever they were in power, people who occupied the policy-making positions came from Sangh's background and so their thinking and working style naturally reflected that, which in turn was perceived as the Sangh's influence. However, the fact is that the government and the system have their own style of functioning, with which the thinking of the organization sometimes does not match. And whenever this happens, the confrontation between the people who have nurtured the organization and the government also comes to the fore. When the experience of forming and running the government is relatively less and the mutual ambitions of the leaders start to clash, then the conflict or differences may increase even more.

Something similar happened during the government led by Atal Bihari Vajpayee between 1998 and 2004. Although the previous 13-day government was formed in 1996 Vajpayee had resigned with his historic address due to not being able to prove the majority. Then when the United Front government which was surviving on the crutches of the Congress became a victim of its infighting and was out of power in a few months, the country had to face the mid-term elections. On one hand, the Congress and the Third Front parties had strong regional ambitions and on the other hand, there was Atal Bihari Vajpayee who was a gentle person, eloquent orator and skilled strategist, for whom even the opponents had respect. The election of the Eleventh Lok Sabha (April-May 1996) was described as a desperate election as there was no established major party or leader. But at that time, the BJP stressed its position as the largest party. As BJP president, Advani had issued a manifesto promising that his government's goal was Ram-Rajya. It said that the 50 years of Congress' misrule had ruined the country, which they would change and bring about a revolution in the political-socio-economic field. But after the experiment of the 13-day government in 1996, the BJP and the Sangh put in full effort. Apart from issues like Ram Mandir, Article 370, electoral reforms in the twelfth Lok Sabha i.e. 1998 elections, the most important part was its slogan of 'stable government and qualified Prime Minister'. This slogan broke the general perception of voting in the election and the result of this election with Vajpayee's face was that the BJP emerged as the single largest party in 1998 with 182 seats and a rainbow-hued coalition of 26 parties (known as NDA – the name given by Vajpayee) came into existence. Vajpayee took oath for the second time. But 13 months later, then Tamil Nadu AIADMK leader Jayalalithaa went to Congress leader Sonia Gandhi's house and had tea. That gave rise to such a storm that Vajpayee's government fell with just one vote in 1999. There was an uproar in the Lok Sabha over this one vote as the Congress Chief Minister of Odisha, Girdhar Gomang had not resigned from the membership of Parliament after becoming the Chief Minister and played a decisive role by participating in the vote. But Vajpayee's popularity grew and public sympathy also worked. Mid-term elections were held again in September-October 1999. But before that, two big issues had made Vajpayee extremely popular. Vajpayee gave a befitting reply to Pakistan in the Kargil war, due to which the feeling of nationalism was strong. On the other hand, Sharad Pawar, PA Sangma and Tariq Anwar revolted against Congress President Sonia

Gandhi on the issue of foreign origin. The issue of foreign versus indigenous Prime Minister became important in the election. NDA in its manifesto promised to bring a law banning people of foreign origin in high positions in the legislature, executive and judiciary. This election was completely fought with the face of Vajpayee and was considered an election of 'Atal Lehar'. 'India Today' wrote - "As soon as the decade (1990) began, the Congress family's rule ended and the era of coalition politics began. The BJP understood the urgency of the times and after the rule of the Third Front with the outside support of the Congress, the BJP became the basis of the new alliance in 1998. The BJP had also learned to hold on to both ends of the rainbow alliance by subverting the saffron ideology." After this, the government of Atal Bihari Vajpayee ran with complete stability till the year 2004. But a change in the thinking of the government was indicated by Advani in the National Council meeting of the BJP in Chennai on 28-29 December 1999. The 'Chennai Manifesto' said that keeping all controversial issues aside, the government will move forward on the agenda of the NDA.

Perhaps this manifesto was not suitable for the Sangh. It felt that Vajpayee was moving in the direction of building his own image. The talks of differences between the affiliated organizations of the Sangh Parivar and the BJP government led by Vajpayee had started to surface. The controversy was due to some initiatives, especially on economic issues, of the government. But some disputes became a matter of personal prestige between senior

Sangh leaders and Vajpayee, which manifested after the party was out of power when even the Sangh Chief began attacking Vajpayee-Advani publicly. It will be discussed in the next chapter. But the discussion here is about the government of the year 1998-2004, when there was a lack of coordination between the government and the Sangh and the differences started spilling out of the closed rooms on the streets.

Case of Pramod-Jaswant

In 1998, senior BJP leaders Jaswant Singh and Pramod Mahajan lost the elections. The Sangh was angry and said that the losers should not be made Ministers. Both these leaders were not liked by a particular lobby of the Sangh. At 6 pm, Vajpayee called his colleague Shakti Sinha, handed him a hand written slip and asked him to prepare it and send it to Rashtrapati Bhavan. The first list had reached Rashtrapati Bhavan. But at around 9.30 pm when Vajpayee was at the dinner table with his daughter Namita, a message arrived saying that Sudarshanji, who was then the Vice General Secretary (Sah-Sarkaryavah), had arrived. The two leaders met at the table and after a 20-minute conversation, Sudarshan left. Vajpayee called Shakti Sinha and asked him to send the list to Rashtrapati Bhavan again - it did not have the names of Jaswant and Pramod. At that time, Vajpayee accepted Sangh's demand. But after taking oath as Prime Minister, he made Jaswant Singh and Pramod Mahajan his advisors. A few days later in July 1998, Pramod Mahajan resigned and was elected an MP for the Rajya Sabha. Vajpayee inducted him in his cabinet in December 1998. Vajpayee constantly gave important ministries to Pramod Mahajan. But he got the communication ministry, which was his choice, in 2001. After that, there were some disputes regarding policy issues and once again there was pressure from the Sangh. His resignation was demanded by the opposition, which Vajpayee did not accept. However, when the cabinet was reshuffled in 2003, Mahajan was sent to the BJP organization as the national general secretary. This change was also described in the media as the result of the scuffle between Vajpayee and Advani.

Opposition on Economic Issues

During the NDA government, differences started to emerge between Prime Minister Atal Bihari Vajpayee and the Sangh. The Sangh protested the amendment to the 'Indian Patent Act', which was favourable to the international environment and indicated that the ruling party MPs would also oppose it. The government stuck to its stand and finally, the Sangh had to back down. Yashwant Sinha, who was the finance and foreign Minister in the Vajpayee government, told me in a conversation after the announcement of 'Bharat Ratna' for Vajpayee, "Atalji used to stand firmly by his Ministers." It was clear that Vajpayee did not want anyone to dominate his government. Sinha recalled that period in this way, "In the government, there was an initiative to reform the insurance sector which was not part of the BJP's thought process at that time. When the proposal for its approval was brought to the cabinet, there was fierce opposition in the cabinet and it seemed that the proposal would not be passed. But Atalji did not reject the proposal on the basis of majority. On the other hand, he found a middle way and then formed a Group of Ministers (GoM) under the leadership of Jaswant Singh. After deliberation in the group, when I again went to the cabinet with the proposal, it was passed without any opposition." Regarding the differences with the Sangh, he also said that before the formation of the government, there were several rounds of discussions between the party and the Sangh regarding economic policies, of which he was also a part. According to Sinha, some differences had also emerged in this conversation. Sinha summed up the conversation, "Despite some differences in the discussion on economic policies, both the Sangh and the BJP had agreed to try to bring about uniformity in policies as far as they could. But if there is a difference of opinion even after that, then they should go ahead." But according to Sinha, after forming the government, there were a lot of differences on the issues and it seemed that they were working against each other. Atalji was constantly in touch with the Sangh, trying to convince them. He also gave me the responsibility of explaining to the people of the Sangh many times. As I recall, during the Vajpayee government, we had decided to allow 26 per cent foreign investment in the production of defence material. The Sangh was very angry with this decision. Atalji sent me to talk to the leaders of the Sangh. When I talked with the Sangh leaders, my argument was whether it was better to spend thousands of crores of rupees in foreign currency and import defense material from outside or it was right to get some foreign investment in the country and produced the material in the country itself? After this meeting, the Sangh understood the point and withdrew its protest. According to Sinha, "The talks always gave some results. But there were times when there was no conclusion." There was a tremendous tussle not only within the Vichar Pariwar but also among the cabinet Ministers. On the issue of disinvestment of oil companies, Arun Jaitley and Petroleum Minister Ram Naik had a confrontation with Disinvestment Minister Arun Shourie.

Dattopant Thengdi's Displeasure became an Example

Dattopant Thengdi, a skilled organizer and who laid the foundation of allied organizations like Bharatiya Mazdoor Sangh, Kisan Sangh, Swadeshi Jagran Manch, Akhil Bharatiya Vidyarthi Parishad, was in the limelight during the six years of Atal Bihari Vajpayee's government. When it comes to coordination between the Sangh and the BJP, Thengdi's activities during 1998-2004 government are not only presented as examples but they are also used as a basis for comparative studies. The Vajpayee government was busy with the preparations for its first anniversary celebration. Meanwhile, the Bharatiya Mazdoor Sangh was vocally protesting against the Insurance Regulatory Authority Bill. As soon as the bills were introduced in the Parliament, Dattopant Thengadi and S Gurumurthy sat on a dharna outside the Parliament. This was seen and publicized as a direct and harsh attack by the Sangh on Vajpayee. Dattopant Thegadi's opposition to the government's economic policies occupied most headlines at that time. Thengadi had called Vajpayee anti-farmer, anti-labourer and Yashwant Sinha as criminal, anti-people and even anti-national. Not only that, Thengadi also politely refused to accept the Padma Bhushan award saying that there were more deserving people than him. The displeasure with the policies was such that he even described Vajpayee as a 'frivolous person'. Before his visit to Tehran in April 2001, Vajpayee called the then Labour Minister Satyanarayan Jatiya and asked about the rally to be held by Bharatiya Mazdoor Sangh in Delhi. Later, on behalf of the government, an important Minister had also asked a leader of the trade union whether they had decided to make the government fall. Sangh Chief Sudarshan had also given his consent to the rally. But later the intensity of the protest was reduced.

Senior journalist Vijay Trivedi, who has written a book on Vajpayee and who closely watched the events of that time, says that in November 2001, the Sangh and its allies were not happy with some of the economic policies of the government. Dattopant Thengadi of Bharatiya Mazdoor Sangh had even said that such decisions were like sedition. It was interpreted in the media that Thengadi called Vajpayee a traitor. It was natural for Vajpayee to be angry. Vajpayee's relationship with the Sangh was worsening due to these reasons though some people also took the initiative to improve the relationship. Seshadri Chari, who was the editor of the Sangh's mouthpiece 'Organiser', had good relations with the Sangh Chief Sudarshan. He took the responsibility of arranging a meeting between Vajpayee and Sudarshan. The meeting was fixed for lunch time. But later it came to light that on the day of the meeting it was Ekadashi and that Sudarshan kept a fast. In such a situation, it was decided that special food would be prepared for Sudarshanji. When they sat down for lunch, Vajpayee said to Sheshadri Chari that since he was not fasting, he would eat Sudarshanji's share. In the end, there were mangoes and ice cream. Sudarshan did not want to eat ice cream either. So, Vajpayee insisted that Chari should eat that too. After the meal was over, the two leaders talked for half an hour and people believed that that meeting normalized the relationship between the two.

Sangh wanted Vajpayee to become the President and Advani to be the Prime Minister

The effect of Sangh's displeasure was also visible in the BJP because there were many such issues when important leaders and Ministers started clashing with or opposing each other. However, Vajpayee who had a grip on the pulse of politics graciously found a middle ground in such a way that at least a consensus was reached within the government. Vijay Trivedi said that one such episode took place in the year 2000. Sushma Swaraj used to be one of the harshest critics of the then Finance Minister Yashwant Sinha. When the BJP's National Council meeting was held in Nagpur that year, Yashwant Sinha was not going to attend it due to ill health. But Vajpayee called him and told him that they were going together. Vajpayee and Sinha reached Nagpur together. Murli Manohar Joshi was on the stage, who came down on seeing Vajpayee and said that Sushma Swaraj had expressed her displeasure with the economic policies of the government. Vajpayee asked Sinha whether he wanted to answer the questions then or later. Sinha responded that he would reply the next day after knowing reason for Sushmaji's displeasure. Vajpayee was aware of the possible anger of the leaders in the National Council and therefore took Yashwant Sinha with him. But the presidential election was a good example of how Vajpayee and senior RSS leaders understood each other's political messages. LK Advani himself writes in his autobiography – I would like to mention here an interesting incident that happened at that time. One day I received a call from Prof Rajendra Singh (Rajju Bhaiya), the former Sarsanghchalak of the Sangh. He said that he wanted to talk to me on an important subject. I invited him home the next morning. Over breakfast, he recounted the meeting that he had had with Atalji last evening, "I visited the Prime Minister to discuss the issue of Presidential election. I suggested to him that he could become the President. I gave the reasons behind this suggestion. He would not have to do much running with the responsibility of Rashtrapati Bhavan since he has knee problems. Moreover, people will accept him as an ideal President in terms of personality and experience." I asked him about Atalji's answer. Rajju

Bhaiya said, “Atalji kept quiet. He didn’t say ‘yes’ or ‘no’. So, I think he hasn’t rejected my suggestion.” Then I told Rajju Bhaiya that a meeting was held to discuss the issue of Presidential election and that in this meeting three days ago, the Prime Minister was unanimously and formally authorized to finalize the name of a suitable and nationally acceptable candidate on behalf of the NDA leaders.

But about this meeting, senior journalist Vijay Trivedi says, “It was the year 2002. The President was to be elected. The Sangh wanted Vajpayee to become the President and Advani to be given the reins of the Prime Ministership. Advani had the same wish. Rajju Bhaiya and Madandas Devi called on Prime Minister Vajpayee. They talked about the candidate for the presidential election; then the Sangh leaders talked about Vajpayee becoming the President and handing over responsibility to Advani. In his typical style, Vajpayee neither refused nor agreed with the Sangh leaders. Vajpayee only smiled. Thereafter, the Sangh Chief met Advani. Advani asked the leaders of the Sangh about Vajpayee’s answer. When both the leaders told him about the discussion that they had, Advani understood that Vajpayee did not agree to it. It was only after this that the formula to make Advani the Deputy Prime Minister came out and, respecting the wishes of the Sangh, Vajpayee made him Deputy Prime Minister on June 29, 2002, which was a few days before the formal election for the post of President.

But on the day that the Sangh Chief had met Vajpayee, Vajpayee called Chandrababu Naidu and told him that he wanted to talk to APJ Abdul Kalam. At that time, mobile facility was not easily available like today and Kalam was in the university. It is necessary to mention here that even in 1998, Vajpayee wanted to make Kalam a Minister in the central government. But as he was working on a particular project, Kalam had declined. But now Vajpayee was trying to make him the President. Vajpayee's conversation with Kalam could not take place during the day. They spoke around 11.30 pm and Vajpayee talked about making him the President. Finally, Kalam said that he was ready if all the parties agreed. Vajpayee's had a far-reaching vision in wanting to make Kalam President. Riots had broken out three-four months earlier in response to the burning of kar sevaks in the Godhra train fire in Gujarat in February 2002. That riots had become big. Prime Minister Atal Bihari Vajpayee went to Gujarat and advised the then Chief Minister Narendra Modi of 'Rajdharma'. Vajpayee had made up his mind to remove Modi. But there was a huge tussle in the party on this issue and Advani as well as the Sangh did not agree with the arguments for Modi's removal. After the tense meeting of the Goa Executive in April 2002, the idea of giving a different political message had struck Vajpayee, which he realized by electing APJ Abdul Kalam to the post of President. It is important to know the reason for that difference because the matter kept raging for a long time.

Differences over Modi's Removal after Gujarat Riots

Advani has written about this in detail in his book 'Mera Desh, Mera Jeevan'. He gave two examples of his differences with Vajpayee. One is about before coming to power at centre and the other is about Modi. Advani writes that a lot of differences arose between Atal Bihari Vajpayee and him because Vajpayee did not agree with the direct involvement of the BJP with Ayodhya movement. But Advani further states that Atalji, being democratic by belief and nature and always willing to bring about consensus among his peers, accepted the collective decision of the party. But the second episode is related to Gujarat. When kar sevaks were burnt in the Godhra train fire in February 2002, communal violence broke out in Gujarat. After the riots, the opposition parties demanded Modi's resignation. Although some people in the coalition government of the BJP and the ruling NDA began to think that Modi should step down, Advani had a completely different view on the matter. After interacting with people from different sections of the society in Gujarat, he believed that Modi had been made a victim of politics and it would be unfair to remove Modi, who had become Chief Minister less than a year ago. According to Advani, "I knew that Atalji was deeply hurt by the events in Gujarat. We were proud of the fact that since the formation of our government in March 1998, we had been able to dramatically reduce the incidences of communal violence in the country. Before 2002, our work was contrary to the allegations of opposition parties, which said that after the BJP came to power at the centre, there would be widespread communal attacks on Muslims and Christians. In fact, Atalji's government won the goodwill of not only Muslims in India but also of Muslim countries across the world. The party and the government at the centre were harmed by the sudden eruption of communal violence in Gujarat and the bitter condemnation by ideological opponents. Vajpayee was hurt by this and was in favour of Modi's resignation. In the second week of April 2002, the National Executive of the BJP met in Goa. Due to the prevailing atmosphere, the focus of the media was on how the party would discuss Gujarat and what would be the decision about Modi's fate. Vajpayee asked Advani to accompany him on his journey to Goa. Advani, the then External Affairs Minister Jaswant Singh and Communications and Information Technology Minister Arun Shourie were also in the special aircraft in the space earmarked for the Prime Minister. The discussion during the two-hour visit remained Gujarat-centric. Vajpayee knew that Advani was not in favour of removing Modi. Vajpayee became meditative for some time. There was silence in the special plane. Then Jaswant Singh asked, "Atalji, what are you thinking?" Atalji replied, "At least he could have offered to resign!" Advani then said, "If the situation in Gujarat improves with Modi's resignation, I would like him to resign. But I don't think that it will be of any help. I do not believe that the party's national council or executive will accept this proposal." As soon as everyone reached Goa, Advani spoke to Modi and asked him to propose to resign to which Modi readily agreed. When the discussions started in the National Executive, many members started giving their views. After hearing their views, Modi rose to speak and gave a detailed account of the Godhra incident and the events that followed. He gave an insight into the historical background of the communal tension in Gujarat and explained how riots have been raging frequently over the past decades. He ended his speech by saying, "Nevertheless, as the head of the state government, I take the responsibility of this incident in my state. I am ready to resign." The moment Modi said this, hundreds of executive members started saying, "Don't resign, don't resign." Advani said, "I separately inquired about the views of senior party leaders on this subject. Invariably each one of us said, "No, he should not resign." Some leaders like Pramod Mahajan said, "There is no question of resignation." Advani also writes, "Politics often makes difficult choices. This difficulty lies in the complexity of the issues and situations that we have to deal with. The difficult choice is sometimes distasteful or unpleasant. But I believe that when one considers a decision to be right, then one should not hesitate to stick to that decision. In fact, history has justified the party's decision of not seeking Modi's resignation at that time."

However, according to journalists of the time, the Goa incident was entirely based on a script written by Advani so that the Atal Bihari Vajpayee's dignity would be maintained and Modi also would not have to resign. At that time, the Sangh was also not in favour of removing

Modi and Advani tried to find a respectable path by taking the Sangh along. But perhaps Vajpayee had a twinge about the episode, which was reflected after the 2004 election results. But another biggest and historical event of this term was the mask episode, when KN Govindacharya, who was preferred by Sangh and Advani, had to leave the position first, then the BJP headquarters and finally the party itself. Govindacharya had a strong grip on economic matters and his standing as the organization general secretary of the ruling party was such that it took him an hour to reach the main gate from the back of 11 Ashoka Road (then the BJP headquarters). Crowds of workers and leaders used to wait for him. But what happened that Govindacharya had to resign? Vijay Trivedi has mentioned this in detail in his book on Vajpayee and I understood the situation at that time after having a long conversation with him.

Similarly, the Kandahar plane hijacking case and the release of terrorists in return followed the BJP for a long time as Advani continued to say that he had lodged his dissent against it in the cabinet. But the manner in which the dharna-demonstration took place at the house of Prime Minister Vajpayee at that time also tarnished the image of the government. Overall, the situation during the Vajpayee government was unfavourable, both from the Vichar Pariwar and the opposition sides. But the mask dispute became the cause for prolonged internal tussle in the party.

Mask Controversy

This incident is from the year 1997. Usually, foreign ambassadors or high commissioners meet people from different political parties and take their opinions on some issues. This is quite common. On September 16, 1997, two representatives from the British High Commission met the then BJP's organization general secretary Govindacharya and had long discussion with him on many issues like Ram temple, foreign investment, foreign policy. At the end of the conversation on all the issues, they asked as to who could be the next president of the party. Govindacharya took many possible names, but Vajpayee's name was not among them. The delegates asked with surprise as to why Vajpayee's name was not mentioned. So, Govindacharya said that Vajpayee is their Prime Ministerial candidate and was most popular. The conversation was over. But three weeks later, on October 6, 1997, a syndicate article by RSS ideologue Bhanupratap Shukla was published in 11 Hindi and English newspapers simultaneously, in which Govindacharya was quoted as saying – 'Vajpayee is a mask.' So, there was a ruckus because on the basis of that meeting, the article claimed that Govindacharya had called Vajpayee a mask. Advani immediately called Govindacharya and asked about it. Govindacharya said that no such thing had happened. Advani asked Govindacharya to issue his rebuttal. In the evening, Govindacharya also received a call from the British High Commission that since such a conversation had not taken place, then how it was printed. Govindacharya also asked the High Commission to refute the news. The next day, Govindacharya's and High Commission's rebuttals were published in the newspapers. But it left a mark against Govindacharya in Vajpayee's mind. When Vajpayee returned from abroad on October 10, he called Saha-Sarkaryavah Sudarshan to express his displeasure. Sudarshan called Govindacharya and said that Vajpayee had the tape of his conversation, to which Govindacharya responded saying that it was very good indeed and that it would clear the whole situation. Well, the tape did not come out, but Vajpayee's displeasure with Govindacharya went on increasing. Then the BJP government was formed and instead of Advani, Kushabhau Thackeray became the BJP President. Vajpayee asked him to show the list of office bearers before releasing it. That gesture was enough for Kushabhau. He visited Vajpayee. As they took a stroll on the lawn, he told Vajpayee that he (Govindacharya) would be made the vice-president only in the name and that there would be no special responsibility. Vajpayee said, "Kushabhau, why don't you understand?" Certainly, this decision was not liked by the Sangh as Govindacharya was one of the most loved and powerful pracharaks of the Sangh. Confrontation with the government over economic policies continued, and in August 2000, Bangaru Laxman became the BJP president.

An incident took place on July 30, 2000. Senior Sangh leader Madandas Devi informed the BJP leadership that Vajpayee had asked Govindacharya to be taken back in the Sangh. After this call, Kushabhau Thackeray, Bangaru Laxman and Pyarelal Khandelwal met Madandas Devi at the Sangh's Delhi Headquarters. Devi conveyed that Vajpayee had said that he would resign from the post of Prime Minister if his words were not listened to. When this was conveyed to Govindacharya, he said that he had been asking for study leave for a long time and that they should give it to him and that it would make it easy for everyone. Later, due to the Tehelka episode, Bangaru Laxman had to resign and K Jainakrishnamurthy became the president of the party. Later in the year 2002, he was made Minister of State for Law and the command of the party was handed over to Venkaiah Naidu. So, after making a list of his team, Venkaiah went to meet Vajpayee and asked him whether to keep Govindacharya's name or not. Vajpayee left the decision to him. Then he went to Advani and conveyed Vajpayee's signal to him. Advani also gave his consent. But when this information was received by the Sangh, it reached Madandas Devi who was handling the responsibility of coordination in the BJP on behalf of the Sangh. He asked Venkaiah Naidu why Govindacharya's name was not there. Naidu told him that Vajpayee and Advani had rejected. Devi said that Govindacharya's name should be added to the list by making amendments. But Venkaiah said that it would only make the news of Vajpayee-Advani clash more prominent. Devi then spoke to Vajpayee-Advani and finally Govindacharya was dropped.

'The Leader is the one that Sangh Decides'

However, there is a perception about the Sangh that it interferes in and controls politics. But the reality has been mentioned in the beginning itself. However, after the formation of the NDA government under the leadership of Atal Bihari Vajpayee, that was also the reason for the relationship to come out in the open. The situation was not like this till Rajju Bhaiya was the Sarsanghchalak of the Sangh. The main reason for this was that earlier the party was not in power. Till the year 2000, though Rajju Bhaiya remained in command KS Sudarshan was vocal as Sah-Sarkaryavah. Till Rajju Bhaiya was in command, the discord in the family did not come out. But after the hardliner KS Sudarshan became the Sarsanghchalak on March 10, 2000, direct interference in the affairs of the BJP started whereas earlier there would be consultation and guidance. The BJP used to accept the advice of the Sangh. But the message did not go out that the decision had been imposed. When Sudarshan became the Sarsanghchalak, the BJP was facing burning issue of Tehelka at the time. Sudarshan publicly said on March 18, 2001 that there were some incapable people sitting in the Prime Minister's Office and that if there had been capable people, the crisis would not have happened. At the time of presidential election, the Sangh thought of sending Vajpayee to Raisina Hill so that Advani could get the command. But Vajpayee's masterstroke did not give that chance to the Sangh. The Sangh could not persuade

Vajpayee to become the President. But it ensured that Advani was made the Deputy Prime Minister of the country, thus showing its power. It was then that senior journalist Vijay Trivedi, who covered the BJP, was at the dinner table with senior party leader Pramod Mahajan. In the midst of political discussions, Vijay Trivedi asked Mahajan in an informal atmosphere, "There is so much uproar as to who is the bigger leader in the party? Vajpayee or Advani?" Mahajan, a mature political player who had a good sense of the strength of the organisation, smiled in a tactful manner and said, "Our leader is the one whom the Sangh chooses."

But it was also not that the relationship between the Sangh and Vajpayee was bitter. It fluctuated as the BJP, which was becoming the political face of the Sangh, was going facing transition right from leadership to issues to reach power. During his visit to the US in September 2000, Vajpayee had declared at a meeting of Vishva Hindu Parishad sadhus that no one could take away his right to be a swayamsevak. Similarly, in 1991, when the Sangh replaced Vajpayee as the leader of the opposition, Prime Minister Narasimha Rao asked him to leave the party. Vajpayee was given the same offer in the year 1980, when he parted ways with the Janata Party. It was always said about him that the right person was in the wrong party. But Vajpayee had said even then, "I have a 25-year-old association with the Sangh and I was in the Janata Party for only two years. My relationship with the Sangha is similar to that of the umbilical cord." Vajpayee used to recite Dev Anand's song for people many times in private conversation- 'Jaayein toh jaayein kahan?'

Certainly, the conflict between the Sangh and its own ideological government from 1998 to 2004 was such that it did not send a good message to even cadre. Irrespective of who was responsible for that, the effect of the gloomy atmosphere was that the workers stayed home and the BJP lost power in the 2004 general elections, whereas it had won a big victory in the assembly elections held a few months ago. But this confrontation prepared such a path of coordination with the Modi government formed in the year 2014, which constantly kept the cadre upbeat and energetic. This is necessary not only at the level of the government, but also the power of the organization is a life-saver for any government. After losing power in 2004, the party had to go through a decade-long organizational struggle so that the story of subsequent coordination could be realized.

❑

PART-2

A Decade of Learning from Defeat

(2004-2014)

When the Atal government lost power, the Sangh Parivar opened a public front and asked Atal-Advani to retire. It then made a blueprint for an ideological return and handed it over to the BJP. When Advani called Jinnah secular during his visit to Pakistan, the Sangh opened the front and advised to hand over the command to the new generation. But in the second generation, the battle for leadership broke out in such a way that General Advani's dream of the 2009 General Elections remained unfulfilled and it seemed as if the BJP was contesting for the sixteenth Lok Sabha instead of the fifteenth Lok Sabha! For the ideology family, this struggle during the years 2004-09 and then 2009-14 became the decade of learning from defeat, improving and drawing strategy for 2014, which helped BJP not only in strengthening the government but also in strengthening the organization.

❑

2

CHAPTER

Struggle while Remaining Out of Power

When the Vajpayee government lost power in 2004, the Sangh became vocal. The Sangh Chief's 'Sudarshan Chakra' was used on Atal-Advani. What was the stand taken by the Sangh Parivar when there was an attempt to sacrifice Modi?

The 2004 election results were unexpected for both the BJP and the Congress. As a journalist at that time, I used to cover all the parties of the Third Front apart from the national parties. Congress President Sonia Gandhi meticulously prepared the roadmap for the alliance and there was a gathering against the BJP. The BJP targeted Sonia by raising the issue of foreign origin, while the Congress attacked the BJP and the Sangh. When the BJP mentioned about bringing a law on the issue of foreign origin, Kapil Sibal, as the spokesperson of the Congress, gave a statement on March 30, 2004. He said, "If the Congress government is formed, it will bring a bill to keep the leaders of the Sangh Parivar away from the constitutional posts of the country. The Sangh has not contributed to the freedom struggle of the country."

BJP gave slogans like 'India Shining and Feel Good'; this move had backfired. The election ended amid accusations and counter-allegations, and the BJP-led NDA was voted out of power in the May 2004 election. A new coalition was formed which was led by the Congress and supported from outside by the Left; it was called the United Progressive Alliance (UPA). In the midst of high voltage drama, Sonia Gandhi was elected the leader of the Parliamentary Party and then she stepped down and handed over the command to Manmohan Singh. From the BJP, leaders like Sushma Swaraj and Uma Bharti came out with a strong protest against Sonia Gandhi becoming the Prime Minister. Eventually, Manmohan Singh took the oath of office on 22 May 2004. The Speaker's chair in the Lok Sabha was given to Somnath Chatterjee of the Left Party.

A new governmental group was formed under the leadership of Sonia Gandhi, which was named 'National Advisory Council' (NAC). It was the advisory body for the new government which was headed by Sonia Gandhi. The Congress which seemed to be headed for defeat in the late 1990s rose again. In terms of seats in the Lok Sabha, the Congress (145) had won only 7 seats more than the BJP

(138). But it formed the government with the support of the Left by forming the UPA. But this unexpected defeat brought to the surface the disputes in not only the BJP but also the Vichar Pariwar and the Manmohan Singh government of the Congress tried to trigger it further by targeting the Sangh. The first thing that Home Minister Shivraj Patil did as soon as he formally took the charge in June was that instead of asking the Governors with the Sangh background to resign, he had them removed from the Raj Bhavans by sacking them. Congress leader Vayalar Ravi had said that the Raj Bhavans have been made the offices of the Sangh. Against this, Advani along with a delegation met President APJ Abdul Kalam and lodged a protest.

Modi Blamed for the Defeat

What was Sangh's Argument?

After the defeat in the Lok Sabha elections, former Prime Minister Atal Bihari Vajpayee went to Manali for rest as an important meeting of the party's national executive was to be held in Mumbai on June 22-25, 2004 to review the defeat. But in Manali itself, Vajpayee gave an interview to a private TV channel on June 13, which created a ruckus not only in the party, but in the entire ideological family of the Sangh. The interview given in Manali tried to blame the Gujarat riots for the defeat. Vajpayee had said, "After the Gujarat riots, I was in favour of removing Modi, but I could not take a hard decision due to two views in the party. But now it can be considered in the Mumbai Executive Meeting." But the very next day, the then BJP President

Venkaiah Naidu first spoke to Vajpayee on the phone and then gave a statement that there would be no discussion on Gujarat in the Mumbai Executive Meeting. Vajpayee's statement had caused an upheaval. On June 15, VHP leader Ashok Singhal opened a front defending Modi. Singhal said that the BJP had lost the Lok Sabha elections because of Atal-Advani and not because of Narendra Modi. Instead of making Modi the scapegoat for the defeat, Atal and Advani should boldly take the responsibility of defeat and retire because the Lok Sabha elections were fought under the leadership of Vajpayee-Advani. Therefore, they should honestly take the responsibility of defeat. Singhal, who had always been vocal against Vajpayee on behalf of the VHP during the 1998-2004 government, had termed Vajpayee's statement as derogatory to the Hindu society of Gujarat and the whole of India. Singhal had also said that the reason for the defeat was being attributed to no action taken against Narendra Modi after the events in Gujarat, while Sarsanghchalak KS Sudarshan bluntly replied that if Modi was responsible for the defeat in the elections, then how did the party get huge victory in Rajasthan, Madhya Pradesh, Chhattisgarh assembly elections? Singhal said, "Not addressing the main issues of the Hindus and the repressive policies adopted on the Ayodhya issue had sunk the BJP. Its present policies proved fatal for it and it must consider the future. If it continued with its current policy, the consequences would be even more dire in the coming times. The BJP must return to the matter of Hindutva, only then it can regain its lost mass base. Singhal further said, "The BJP grew from two MPs and became a ruling party using the Ram Janmabhoomi issue." He said that the contradictory statements by Vajpayee were also the reason for defeat because in the election campaign, Vajpayee adopted the policy of Muslim appeasement and gave a statement about recruiting two lakh Urdu teachers, which was understood by our people. He said that, by adopting this policy, BJP went one step ahead of its rival party Congress. VHP president Vishnu Hari Dalmiya also said, "The Congress-led UPA government has displayed wisdom in its Common Minimum Programme. Regarding Vajpayee's statement in Manali, leaders like Sangh Chief Sudarshan, VHP leader Giriraj Kishor, Praveen Togadia used many indecent words against him like power-hungry etc.

But the altercation continued. In an interaction with workers in Manali on June 17, Vajpayee reiterated that the issue of Gujarat would definitely be discussed in the Mumbai Executive Meeting. But even then, the Sangh said that it was not ready to accept that the BJP was defeated because of the Gujarat riots. Ram Madhav as a spokesperson of the Sangh said, "It is an internal matter of the BJP to discuss Gujarat. The argument that BJP lost because of Gujarat riots is not acceptable to us." Within a month of the election results, such uproar had created a dilemma and media headlines were adding to the confusion among the workers. The Sangh wanted this issue to be resolved quickly. But the leaders of the VHP and Sangh did not agree with the opinions being voiced about Gujarat and Modi. Amidst the rhetoric and the growing controversy, on June 18, Vajpayee took responsibility for the defeat and talked about atonement. It meant that he considered Gujarat riots among the reasons for defeat, which in turn meant that after his atonement statement, there was increased pressure to remove Narendra Modi from the post of Chief Minister of Gujarat. Seeing Atal's intentions, the BJP leadership called a meeting of the Parliamentary Board on June 20. Venkaiah Naidu immediately met Advani and held discussions. Advani then spoke to Vajpayee over phone, where Venkaiah Naidu, Jaswant Singh and Pramod Mahajan were also present. Advani, who was preparing to crack down on the Gujarat issue at the Parliamentary Board meeting, sat in a long silence after Vajpayee's statement. The Sangh was uncomfortable with the skirmish that was happening on this issue. Mahajan said that Vajpayee was not under any pressure from the Sangh as he was a tall leader, and he had taken the responsibility of defeat as a commander. Advani also had talks with Madandas Devi, who was coordinating on behalf of the Sangh. He also met Vajpayee on June 19 and said that removing Modi or not was an internal matter of the BJP. But he said that the party would also have to keep in mind the upcoming elections before taking any decision. It was then clear that the Sangh was not in favour of removing Modi in any case. Vajpayee also understood that. So, he also indicated that Modi would not be removed and said that they would face new election in the new year, terming the Modi episode as the past.

The Parliamentary Board meeting began at the residence of BJP President Venkaiah Naidu two days before the executive meeting. It was during that meeting that Sangh leader Madandas Devi reached Naidu's house. Finally, in this emergency parliamentary board meeting, Modi got the protection. After the meeting, Naidu said, "The issue of Narendra Modi was discussed, but there is no proposal to remove him." In that meeting, it was decided to form a committee to review the defeat in the Lok Sabha elections, but the names of the members were not decided that day. Looking at the kind of atmosphere that was created after the 2004 defeat, the Sangh began working on a strategy to break the myth that the BJP would not be able to lead without Vajpayee. Then three months later, Venkaiah Naidu resigned as the party president taking responsibility for the defeat. The transition period began in the party and when Venkaiah left on October 18, once again LK Advani took over as the leader of the opposition in the Lok Sabha as well as the party president.

Advani again in Dual Role

In October 2004, LK Advani again took over as the party president. In the meeting of the National Council on October 27, Advani again raised the issue of Ram temple. He said that all the preparations had been made and if the Vajpayee government had returned to power, the work of building the temple would have started. But despite the good work of the Vajpayee government, the party lost the Lok Sabha elections due to the negative temperament of the MPs, neglect of the workers and overconfidence. He said that earlier BJP believed that there were three paths for the construction of Ram temple. But later the party came to conclusion that making a law in the Parliament would not be the right way. Therefore, the only way out would be through negotiations or court decisions. He said that in the last year, the talks were going in a positive direction. But the decision was not taken because of the elections. When Ramlala's slogan reverberated in the auditorium, he spoke about focussing on special preparations for the silver jubilee year of the BJP i.e. 2005.

Advani was still very precious for the Sangh. So, that point was clear from his speech as well. Advani hit hard on the criticism that party faced due to Hindutva. He said that those who do so insult the basic concept of the Constitution and that they call themselves secular and BJP communal. However, Hindutva is not a religion, but a system of life, which had been made very clear by the Supreme Court in its judgment on 11th December, 1995. He told the workers that there should be no shame in speaking about the ideology of Hindutva. Even on differences with Vajpayee while in government, Advani said that there were differences on many issues, but there was no discord. Advani said that the most important thing was to understand what BJP was and how many dimensions it had. Advani said that there were three important parts of the BJP- first workers, second Sangh Parivar and third identifying the masses associated with the party after its inception. And most importantly, it was important to remember that BJP was the only nationalist party. Vajpayee also took a jibe during his speech. On Advani becoming the President, Vajpayee said, "Even when Advaniji was not the President, his position was same as the President. He has the ability to resolve any complicated situation. Vajpayee said, "This time even those who have lost the elections cannot understand how they lost and the winners also cannot understand how they won!" Vajpayee said, "One should not lose courage after losing the elections. We can have another chance. One more shot will be played. We lost due to negligence, but now it will not happen again."

Then the Discipline Started Turning into Discord

Meanwhile, the attack of the Manmohan Singh government on the Sangh and its people continued. When the Congress held its session in Delhi on August 21, 2004, the target was the Sangh Parivar. Sonia Gandhi said that the nationalism of the Congress was secular and harmony-based, whereas the nationalism of the Sangh and BJP was based on hatred and communalism. The Congress described its fight with the BJP as not just an electoral one but as an ideological one. Later, there was an uproar when film actor Anupam Kher was removed from the post of Censor Board Chairman by the UPA government because he was removed after being called 'Sanghi'. Harkishan Singh Surjeet called him a man of RSS. Kher strongly opposed it and said that the government was kneeling before the Left. The then Railway Minister Lalu Prasad Yadav targeted Narendra Modi by making the interim report of the UC Banerjee Commission on the Godhra issue public. Meanwhile, in Tamil Nadu, there was an uproar over the arrest of Kanchi Kamakoti Peeth Shankaracharya Jayendra Saraswati and the entire top leadership of BJP, including Vajpayee and Advani, arrived at Sansad Marg to stage a dharna. Former Prime Minister Chandrashekhar, former President R Venkataraman also reached the venue of that dharna. After this episode, on November 10, 2004, when Uma Bharti opened the front, Advani made the meeting of the office bearers live and Uma boycotted the meeting making allegations against Pramod Mahajan, Arun Jaitley and Mukhtar Abbas Naqvi. By late evening, Advani suspended her from the party. Uma had left for Karnataka for the Tiranga yatra and had resigned from the post of Chief Minister of Madhya Pradesh, which she had also tried to realize. During that time, she met Madandas Devi, Mohan Bhagwat and other Sangh leaders, where she was advised to maintain discipline and refrain from public rhetoric.

Meanwhile, film actress Smriti Irani, who had recently joined the BJP at that time and had lost the Lok Sabha elections from Chandni Chowk announced a fast demanding the resignation of Narendra Modi. The winter session of Parliament was going on. Pramod Mahajan immediately spoke to Vinod Tawde in Mumbai. When the possibility of strict action by the party increased, Irani withdrew her statement with an apology by late evening. That statement was also a part of the internal tussle in the party, which she had given at the behest of a prominent party leader. When that leader realized that the Sangh would not tolerate such a statement, his statement was withdrawn.

Babulal Marandi had threatened to topple the party's government in the state on issue of appointment of party president in Jharkhand. In Gujarat, Keshubhai Patel camp was continuously active against Modi. In Rajasthan too, there was a conflict between the organization's general secretary and Vasundhara Raje. So, in the meeting of the National Council, the then party president LK Advani expressed concern. He advised the workers, "Try to settle the dispute within the party and not through the media." The discipline of the party was beginning to fray. Sangh Chief KS Sudarshan himself was so vocal that he had now started advising both Vajpayee and Advani to give up the leadership and prepare the way for the new generation. Pramod Mahajan also called the Gujarat riots a blot, while Sunder Singh Bhandari, the senior most leader of the BJP who was the Governor of Gujarat, also targeted Vajpayee-Advani. Bhandari raised a question, "What is the point of handing over the command of the party from Advani to Advani?" There were no signs of the upheaval in the BJP calming down which was further fanned by the 'Walk the Talk' interview of Sangh Pramukh KS Sudarshan by Shekhar Gupta, the senior journalist.

'Sudarshan Chakra' on Atal-Advani

The Sangh, especially the Sarsanghchalak, usually stays away from the media. But the way KS Sudarshan, who had been vocal against BJP's policy and leadership since its government in 1998, attacked Vajpayee in a 'Walk the Talk' interview with journalist Shekhar Gupta was nothing short of a 'Sudarshan Chakra'. About the experience of the government from 1998 to 2004, the Sangh Chief said that there was a demand for a charter regarding education and students from all over the country were reaching Delhi with 74 demands. On November 26, 2002, a rally of about 75,000 students took place, that too against the ruling party of their ideology.

At that time, Dattatreya Hosabale was the organization head of ABVP. The Sangh Chief had written a letter saying that some of the demands of the students should be accepted so that the students would be happy. Vijay Goel, the Minister of State in the PMO, had gone to meet the students. Sudarshan said that when he spoke to the Human Resource Development Minister Murli Manohar Joshi about it, he accepted four or five demands, but he formed a committee for the rest of the demands and nothing happened further. Similarly, when we asked to take steps against atrocities on Hindus in Bangladesh, Prime Minister Vajpayee did not do anything. He was then asked whether the Ministers who were not from the Sangh background were doing a better job? Sudarshan took the name of Sushma Swaraj. Regarding Arun Shourie, he said that the only thing they wanted from him was that the enterprises which were in profit should not be disinvested and only those which were in loss should be disinvested.

Sudarshan said that if the BJP wanted to grow, then new people would have to be taken; but all those who joined should have an ideological commitment. Sudarshan had also objected to the government's communication policy. He said that foreigners or those whose allegiance to the country was doubtful should not be allowed in this area, but that the communication sector should remain completely under the government. But the government didn't accept that either. He was asked out of all the leaders in the country in the last 60 years, who were the two or three prominent leaders, whom he considered to be the best. In response, Sudarshan said that even after the Congress was divided, Indira Gandhi was such a leader who did not succumb to any pressure whether it was Russia or anyone else. That was her speciality. But she was self-centred and stubborn. Still, from the point of view of the nation, she was a great leader. She knew and understood people. If she had taken all the decisions with nation in mind, then the country would have got another Chanakya. The second leader was Narasimha Rao who became Prime Minister by circumstance and was from outside the Nehru-Gandhi family. But the question arose that both these leaders belonged to Congress. He was asked about leaders from his party or group. Sudarshan took the name of Advani instead of Vajpayee. He said, "Advaniji has the administrative efficiency. But he always kept in mind that there should never be an alternate centre of power. That's why he never opposed Atalji. We used to tell him that he should speak. There are decisions which are not in our interest, like in the case of Bangladesh. What did he think about the Hindus there? He said that we had got power for the first time. That's why we should not lose it." But why did he not put Atal Bihari Vajpayee in the category of prominent leaders? Sudarshan responded bluntly, “We do not believe that has done enough that I should take his name. Alright, he did take some big decisions. But Atalji did not maintain the dialogue with everyone the way he should have. That’s why people got angry with him.” He was asked how will Atal’s name be written in history? Sudarshan replied, “The historians will write it. Contemporary history does not give a correct depiction. But Atalji did some good work that brought prestige to the country; he made it a nuclear country. But he could have done many things that he did not do. E.g., he could have given the acquired land for the Ram temple, but he did not do so. On the question of change in leadership, Sudarshan said, “We used to say at that time that raise new people. You people are too old. If the BJP has to sustain for a long time, then new people will have to be brought forward. But we only give advice, BJP has to decide who will become Prime Minister or leader.” But with whom did Vajpayee not communicate? Sudarshan said that he did not keep communication with many organizations and there was anger among the volunteers working in different organizations. Regarding Brijesh Mishra, Sudarshan said that Vajpayee had given him the task of national security and foreign policy as well. It was not fair to give both the profiles to one person. Sudarshan had objected to this and spoken to Vajpayee. He said that on one hand, Mishra worked for Vajpayee and on the other hand, he was in collusion with Sonia Gandhi. Vajpayee had also objected that why he was speaking like that. In that interview, Sudarshan also said that Vajpayee had also been asked to stop his son-in-law Ranjan Bhattacharya from interfering in the PMO. But Vajpayee had said that it was difficult. Sudarshan said that Vajpayee used to listen to everything, but he did not say anything. While on the other hand, Advani had set an example and did not allow his son and daughter to take any advantage. But Vajpayee did not do that. Sudarshan even said that the Leftists could never be loyal to the country. Therefore, even the Sangh-BJP-Congress could come together against the Left at some point because there was no untouchability in politics. He said that though today the BJP had become the focal point he did not consider the Congress to be untouchable because a Swayamsevak of the Sangh could go to any party provided that the allegiance of that party was not against the country.

But Sangh Chief Sudarshan praised Narendra Modi's work. On the question of Gujarat and Modi, Sudarshan said that re-elections were held after the riots and he came back to power with a two-thirds majority. He said that Modi had done a lot of work in Gujarat and took proper decisions. Sudarshan, however, said that Modi's style was not about taking the party along. His suggestion was that though he did good work he should take everyone along. When Sangh Chief K.S. Sudarshan advised Vajpayee-Advani to give up the leadership through that interview, on April 19 Vajpayee said that he did not hold any post. He himself and the party should decide about Advani. After this statement, there was a stir in the BJP again. Sudarshan had put the function of the NDA government in the dock. About that, Vajpayee said, "I have also read the statement of Sudarshanji. This is his own opinion. Everyone has the right to have their opinion. I'll answer it when the time comes." But everything does not necessarily go as planned in politics. Destiny also decides a lot. The same happened in the case of the Sangh and BJP. In the midst of this stir, Advani went on a tour of Pakistan and what he wrote and said at the tomb of Muhammad Ali Jinnah brought new shocking waves to the party, which scripted the end of the Atal-Advani era and the transition to a new generation. After that, there was a competition among the leaders of the second generation. Everyone started trying to prove himself close to the Sangh. It was at this time that an article by Arun Jaitley appeared, in which he spoke about himself, Venkaiah Naidu and Pramod Mahajan being associated with the Sangh since the time of Emergency; he did not mention Sushma Swaraj. That was the beginning of the quest - who would be the leader in the second generation after Advani?

Politics and elections have their own compulsions. Even though Vajpayee tried to pin the blame for the 2004 defeat on Modi, he also understood the political compulsions very well. That is why during the Gujarat riots, when he was the Prime Minister and Congress leaders in opposition used the word 'genocide' about Gujarat without hesitation, Vajpayee said in Parliament, "I will say to the Leader of the Opposition that the use of the word 'genocide' about Gujarat is not correct. The scope of genocide is different. This word is used when a race or nation is destroyed. Both Hindus and Muslims died in Gujarat. People on both sides were killed by the bullets of police. I am speaking about the word. Try to understand its meaning. This word can be used against India in international forums." But when the BJP was going through a period of upheaval after being voted out of power, the Sangh could not leave it in limbo.

That did not mean that the Sangh wanted to control the BJP. In fact, the way the BJP was formed, it has to look towards the Sangh for everything - from its ideological-policy matters to every major issue. The reason for this is the huge cadre of the Sangh and also it acts as a machinery indirectly at the time of elections. A representative of the Sangh is always present in the BJP. The organization in-charge of the party is the pracharak of the Sangh and is appointed by the Sangh. The states also have the similar structure. Therefore, when Advani's Jinnah episode sent a message of ideological disorientation among the volunteers, the Sangh had to take a tough stand.

❑

3

CHAPTER

Jinnah Case and Sangh

How the Sangh directly intervened from behind the scenes and Advani was forced to step down... But it was not easy for the Sangh to give command to Rajnath Singh in the new generation after effecting the BJP's ideological comeback.

This is a historic episode in the relationship between the BJP and Sangh. In June 2005, LK Advani went to Pakistan. On 4th June, he visited the tomb of Muhammad Ali Jinnah and called him secular on the basis of Jinnah's address to the Constituent Assembly of Pakistan. On June 5, 2005, he reiterated in a meeting that Jinnah had strongly advocated the creation of a secular state in his speech to the Constituent Assembly on August 11, 1947. This statement immediately made headlines everywhere – 'Advani has called Jinnah secular'. No prominent leader in the party came to Advani's rescue. His statement was targeted by the Sangh. Advani was hurt that without knowing the background, an atmosphere was created as if he had committed an ideologically heinous crime! He mentions that in his autobiography, "Even before boarding the Pakistan Airlines flight to Delhi on the morning of 6 June, I had decided with a heavy heart that I would resign as the President of the BJP." He resigned as soon as he reached Delhi on June 7, and wrote a letter to the then General Secretary Sanjay Joshi, in which he seemed very hurt. He wrote that if my colleagues do not have faith and trust in me, then I would not like to work as the party president. The BJP's parliamentary board and central office bearers did not accept his resignation. In a meeting on June 8, they unanimously passed a resolution asking Advani to continue to lead the party as before. Advani's contribution to the nation and ideology were praised in this resolution. Also, in this resolution, the objectionable statements made by the leaders of Vishwa Hindu Parishad against Advani were refuted and such statements were termed against the practices of Hindu religion.

But Advani was unwilling to withdraw his resignation; he was clearly seeking support from the party for his statements on Jinnah. In such a situation, the party's strategists were preparing a way for intervention on June 9. The Parliamentary Board meeting was to be held on June 10. A draft was prepared and it was written in it that the BJP criticizes Jinnah's two-nation theory on the basis of religion. It also said that Advani's visit to Pakistan had led to the beginning of improvement of relations between the two countries during the Vajpayee government, especially with the laying of the foundation stone for the restoration of the Katasraj temple. Through this proposal, there was an attempt to preserve Advani's as well BJP's stand. But the Sangh probably did not agree. It was not even in favour of Advani withdrawing his resignation. However, this news was refuted by the Sangh. But before there could be any discussion on the proposal, Murli Manohar Joshi opened the front. The Parliamentary Board meeting was to be held on June 10 and Venkaiah Naidu, Pramod Mahajan, Sanjay Joshi were working on the proposal. Murli Manohar Joshi disagreed with it and felt that the motion was proceeding without his consent. He publicly opened the front. Joshi and then Babulal Marandi opened the front in BJP for calling Jinnah secular. Joshi said, "Jinnah got India divided on the basis of two-nation theory. Therefore, he cannot be considered secular on the basis of one speech. I agree with the Sangh's stand and completely disagree with Advani." But on June 10, a meeting of the Parliamentary Board was held, in which the Chief Ministers of the party-ruled states were also present. A statement was issued, which read – "BJP appreciates the unprecedented visit of its President LK Advani to Pakistan. The party is happy that Advani raised the issue of cross-border terrorism with the President of Pakistan. BJP welcomes Pakistan's move to invite Advani for the revival of Katasraj Temple. BJP reiterates that whatever Jinnah's vision of Pakistan may be, the state founded by him is religious and non-secular. The mere idea of two separate nations for Hindus and Muslims is against the principles of the BJP. The BJP has always condemned the partition of India on communal lines and will continue to do so. The party will continue to strongly reject the two-nation theory propounded by Jinnah and supported by the British colonialists. There is no denying the fact that Jinnah led a communal movement to achieve the goal of creating Pakistan, in which thousands of innocent people were killed and lakhs were rendered homeless and unemployed." Advani finally withdrew his resignation, putting an end to the BJP's political storm.

But the Sangh was still not satisfied and the ideological storm was not over yet. The Sangh and its affiliated organisations, especially Vishwa Hindu Parishad, had made up their mind to remove Advani from the presidency. Sangh Chief KS Sudarshan had already advised Vajpayee and Advani to retire in an interview on April 17, 2005; but at that time, mainly, Vajpayee was the target. Now the Jinnah episode forced the Sangh to open a front even against Advani, who at that time was cherished more by the Sangh than Vajpayee. Sudarshan had praised Advani in an interview two months back. But the Sangh considered the Jinnah episode as a blow to its ideological standing. So, Advani was sent a message to resign before the closing ceremony of the party's silver jubilee year.

The Script of Farewell from the Post of President

The controversy over the Jinnah episode had subsided, but the extent to which the ideological storm was on rise was reflected in a four-day vital meeting of the

Sangh's state pracharaks in Surat, Gujarat in early July 2005. India Today writes in its July 18, 2005 issue, "The Sangh's regional pracharaks cautioned that a heavy price would have to be paid for the BJP's unstable and weak leadership and if it condoned cases like BJP President LK Advani's of deviating from the ideology, then the entire Sangh Parivar would have to bear its brunt" The pracharaks argued that they were unable to answer the questions of the swayamsevaks on the Advani-Jinnah episode. There was a clear message in the meeting that action should have been taken on the Advani issue by then because the organization could not be run by statements of ideology alone.

Although a section of the Sangh was also in favour of giving time to Advani leaders like Sangh Chief Sudarshan, VHP's Ashok Singhal, Praveen Togadia, MG Vaidya—who had openly demanded Advani's removal during the Jinnah episode—believed that only with the removal of Advani, the ideological confusion that had arisen within the Sangh Parivar could end. At that time, in an interview, Ashok Singhal had said, "Advani has cut himself from the foundation of the Sangh Parivar and the BJP by deviating from the ideology. If he had the heart of a common worker of the Sangh or BJP, he would not have done all that he did in Pakistan." Singhal also said - the wheel of the Sangh Parivar works for the BJP during the elections and helps in taking it forward. Hence there is harmony in the Sangh Parivar. The problem lies in the BJP, especially at the level of its leadership, which requires reform measures.

It was decided in this meeting that the ideological position of the Sangh should be clearly explained to the BJP on four points-Jinnah, Akhand Bharat, Ram Mandir and Gujarat riots. There was a clear indication that Advani would have to step down from the presidency. Advani had already been given a hint, but he was unsure. Advani writes in his autobiography – "I was in a dilemma. What should be the reaction? Because such a situation had never arisen in my political life." This situation continued for about a month and a half and the leaders of the second generation, who were once loyal to Advani, had started leaving one by one. In such a situation, Advani sought help from Vajpayee on July 16, 2005. When he went to meet Vajpayee accompanied by Venkaiah Naidu and Jaswant Singh, he suggested to Advani that he should talk to Sudarshanji. Advani said that Sudarshan was not talking to him. So, Vajpayee spoke to him on the phone and later Advani spoke to him after coming home. Sudarshan sent Mohan Bhagwat and Suresh Soni to Delhi to talk to Advani. Bhagwat conveyed the message of generational change in allied organizations during that meeting. The Sangh wanted the new leader to take over at the end of the Silver Jubilee year and Advani to resign before the Sangh's Diwali meeting. For a moment, Advani was in a mood to clash with the Sangh, but Vajpayee advised him not to do so.

Advani's cogitation over his resignation continued. In the meantime, a meeting of the BJP's national executive was held in Chennai on 16-18 September 2005, and the

Sangh conveyed that Advani should announce in the very executive meeting that he would tender his resignation from the post of President at the closing ceremony of the party's silver jubilee year in Mumbai. Through that announcement, the Sangh wanted to buy time to identify suitable new leadership so that the new generation could be formally handed over the command in December. Finally, at the Chennai executive meeting, Advani was forced to announce that he would step down as BJP president in December. But while addressing the executive, Advani accused the Sangh of interfering in the party's day-to-day affairs. He said, "Recently, the perception is becoming stronger that no political or organizational decision can be taken without the consent of the Sangh officials. Neither the Sangh nor the party will benefit from this perception." Advani called on the Sangh to redefine relations and limit it to symbolic relationships. Ram Madhav, then the official spokesperson of the Sangh, said, "We have always believed that our relationship is based on principles and we have an umbilical relationship. This has been our approach, which will not change." But Sangh did not make any public statement about the allegations of interference in party's day-to-day work. However, in 2012, when I interviewed Sangh's Sarkaryavah Bhaiyyaji Joshi for India Today, he admitted, "Leaving aside one occasion (Jinnah episode), I don't see Sangh interfering in the day-to-day affairs of the BJP. " Finally, at the end of the Silver Jubilee year, the National Council of the BJP met in Mumbai from 28 to 30 December 2005, which was the last session presided over by Advani. It was in this meeting that the two-and-a-half-decade-old party ushered in a new era under a new leadership when Advani was succeeded by the new generation represented by Rajnath Singh, who was then General Secretary in Advani's team. As always, the veteran BJP leader Pramod Mahajan was in-charge of this grand event. When Vajpayee delivered the concluding address, he called Advani Ram and Mahajan Lakshman from the stage. But the confrontation was not over and the leaders' egos kept clashing, which resulted in the controversial sex CDs making headlines from Mumbai and questioning of the Sangh's morality instead of the news of new generation taking over the party's reins.

Leadership Change and the Sanjay Joshi Case

But in event of such conflict, how could the transfer of power take place smoothly? The result of the internal conflict within the party was that the alleged sex CD of the Organization's General Secretary Sanjay Joshi who was Sangh's representative in the BJP reached the media, which meant that the Sangh was directly targeted. Sanjay Joshi had become a very powerful Sangathan mantri . He had taken a tough stand during the Jinnah episode and was emerging as a flamboyant leader with a distinct image. Sanjay Joshi immediately resigned and filed a case with the Madhya Pradesh Police because the CD had arrived from there by post. After this episode, the Sangh did not appoint anyone in his place. It was decided to keep the post vacant till the police investigation was over as RSS too saw a conspiracy in the CD case. It was a tough time for Rajnath Singh, too. But on January 13, 2006, the Madhya Pradesh government gave a clean chit. Kailash Vijayvargiya as the spokesperson of the Madhya Pradesh government said, "The investigation so far indicates that Sanjay Joshi has been framed and is innocent. The police are now looking for the conspirators." The Madhya Pradesh Police also gave a clean chit to Joshi on March 30 by terming the CD as "manipulated and truncated". After Joshi was given the clean chit by the police, VHP leader Praveen Togadia termed the CD case as a conspiracy by some BJP leaders and said that Joshi had passed the ordeal and should be reinstated on the post. The Sangh had also sent a message to the BJP by reinstating him as a pracharak, and finally, within 24 hours of his reinstatement as a pracharak, on April 3, Joshi was reinstated as the general secretary of the BJP.

Three days later, that is, from April 6, the day of the party's foundation, the twin Rath Yatra of Advani and Rajnath from two directions was also going to start. But Sanjay Joshi remained in this post till Rajnath was re-elected as the president and in March 2007 he announced his new team. The Sangh also did not argue.

When Rajnath's team was formed in March 2007, Ramlal was appointed the General Secretary of the organization. The Sangh wanted removal to be treated as a normal process and not as a fallout of the CD scandal. Removing him earlier would have meant allowing doubts about one's own pracharak to grow stronger. The Sangh maintained its position and in the December

2006 Lucknow session, the BJP President was given the right to appoint some more sangathan mantri s through an amendment to the party's constitution. As per the RSS formula, Rajnath Singh added four sah-sangathan mantris in March 2007, two of whom were given territorial responsibility directly with Ramlal. Remaining two were given responsibilities in Andhra Pradesh and Tamil Nadu after establishing centres there.

The Sanjay Joshi episode was a double blow for the BJP and the Sangh because a few days ago on December 12, eleven MPs were caught in a TV channel's sting 'Operation Duryodhana' taking bribe for asking questions. Six of them were BJP MPs. As a party president, Advani immediately suspended them. But later, on 23rd December, the parliamentary committee decided to sack all the MPs. But then the BJP opposed it saying that the parliamentary committee did not follow due process and rules. Then in 'Operation Chakravyuh', the sting about commission in lieu of MP fund also came to light, in which the names of three BJP MPs were also included. That kind of evidence was not found in this case, so much strict action was not taken. But soon after the corruption scandal, the alleged CD where question mark was put on the character created trouble in the Silver Jubilee year and the opposition started attacking by talking about 'Chaal, Charitra, Chehra'. But the clean chit received in the CD scandal gave strength to the Sangh-BJP. Anyway, the BJP was getting vocal against the Muslim appeasement policy of the UPA government.

Bharat Suraksha Yatra...Pramod Mahajan's murder

There were many issues like the head count ruckus in the three wings of the army by the Sachar Committee, recognition of minority commissions, the exercise of Muslim reservation in government jobs, the formation of a minority ministry, a separate fund for the development of Urdu and Prime Minister Manmohan Singh's statement that the minority had the first right on the resources of the country, which gave an opportunity to the BJP and Sangh to sharpen the edge of Hindutva. Suddenly Advani took initiative. On March 10, a meeting of the Parliamentary Board was called, after which a nationwide Rath Yatra 'Bharat Suraksha Yatra' (similar to that of Ayodhya) was announced by the BJP. Advani started the 'Bharat Suraksha Yatra' from Gujarat and Rajnath Singh started from Odisha on April 6, 2006, which was party's foundation day. The yatra against UPA government's policy of Muslim appeasement started from two directions and was to end in Delhi on May 10. The political buzz was that Advani, who had been isolated since the Jinnah episode, scripted the journey to re-establish himself. In the same yatra, Advani also revealed his disagreement in the then Vajpayee cabinet on the Kandahar episode, which created a ruckus.

Meanwhile, the yatra left Mumbai and went ahead. After that, Pramod Mahajan went home and rested. On the morning of 22 April, he had an argument with his younger brother Praveen Mahajan at his house in Mumbai and within 15 minutes Praveen opened fire. Mahajan fought for life for 13 days at Hinduja Hospital in Mumbai. His popularity was visible at that time. He finally died on 3 May. He was a promising BJP leader about whom Advani had said, "Pramod was the youngest in the Parliamentary Board, but we used to give him a chance to speak at the end because no matter how many differences there were among all the members of the Parliamentary Board on an issue, when Pramodji spoke in the end and whatever he said, everyone agreed in an instant." Mahajan was considered BJP's trouble-shooter and Chanakya. Although a faction within the Sangh and BJP was critical of him due to the five-star culture, he was a friend of friends. On the main gate of his official residence 7 Safdarjung Road in Delhi, it was written – 'Friends are welcome at all times. Relatives should take appointment.' When Rajnath Singh became the president for the first time, Pramod Mahajan had simply said, "I want to be Sachin Tendulkar of the BJP. Whoever is the captain, I always find a place in the team to play." Such was the simplicity of Mahajan. His demise was a big setback for the BJP.

Bhagwat's Path of Harmony, Rajnath Leads Again

Mohan Bhagwat was appointed as Sarkaryavah for the third time in Nagpur's Pratinidhi Sabha. He followed the path of coordination and generational change. He believed that all affiliated organizations, including the BJP, should think about ideology. This step was taken under the policy of co-ordination as coordination between the organizations is a well thought out arrangement of the Sangh. In December 2006, Rajnath was unanimously elected the national president for a full three-year term. Till now for the last 11 months, he was completing the remaining tenure of Venkaiah Naidu and then Advani. After becoming the President, a meeting of the National Executive and Council was held in Lucknow. Instead of holding the meeting in a hotel, it was held in a school run by Sangh. Rajnath's presidential address to the meeting held on December 22-24, 2006 was a clear indication that the ideology for which the Sangh was struggling for the last one and a half years, the BJP had started entering that path. Firstly, in the executive, Rajnath admitted that the party's reputation had been tarnished because of backtracking on its agenda when it was in power. He said that now a mechanism had to be developed in the party to restore the example of political uprightness. When Rajnath spoke in the meeting of the council, the headlines said- 'Rajnath completely Sangham saranam gachami' ('Rajnath completely surrenders to Sangh). He reiterated his resolve to build Ram temple in Ayodhya and also threw a challenge to build Babri Masjid at the disputed site if anyone had the courage. He also mentioned the plight of Kashmir Pandits, atrocities on Hindus and Sikhs abroad, Afzal Guru, Vande Mataram, returning medals by martyrs' families, politics of religion under the guise of Sachar Committee etc and asked for a mandate for only ten years of rule. He described the politics of Congress as making the majority Hindu society second class citizens.

But Rajnath knew how difficult his responsibility was. So, he said, "Uttar Pradesh will be witness to the turning point of future history. To change history, I have worn a necklace of embers, chosen a path full of thorns, and I will rest only after turning history." Rajnath may not have been able to make it a reality during that tenure, but when he again took over the responsibility in 2013, his words at that time became the writing on the wall. Rajnath also spoke about the core of discipline in that meeting in Lucknow, "Discipline will not come from being expelled from the party, but discipline needs to be rooted within." Atal Bihari Vajpayee also expressed concern over the party's factionalism and declining influence and once again emphasized on creating a lively atmosphere in the BJP. He had said, "There should be no place for factionalism in the BJP. I want the same atmosphere in the party again. Get rid of your fatigue, the future is waiting for us. Praising Rajnath, Vajpayee said that within a few months, new confidence had been instilled in the party with the appointment of the person who had experience of both organization and administration. After this meeting, there was a stir about the next Prime Ministerial candidate because when Rajnath described himself as the groom of the ruling beauty, the news spread that he also was in the race for the post of PM. In response to a question, Vajpayee also said that his blessings were with Advani.

When Rajnath Singh announced his team, the Sangh handed over the command to Ramlal in place of Sanjay Joshi. Rajnath went to the Sangh Headquarters in Delhi on 6 February 2007 and met Saha-Sarkaryavah Suresh Soni. Then in March, the meeting of the Akhil Bhartiya Pratinidhi Sabha of the Sangh was also held in Lucknow; it was being held in this city after 15 years. Vajpayee also gave the message of a new beginning in the December meeting splitting the word Lucknow as 'Luck-Now'. Under the Presidentship of Rajnath, the party won the Bihar Legislative Assembly, UP-Mumbai civic elections and Punjab-Uttarakhand assembly elections. Now it was the turn of Uttar Pradesh assembly elections. But before the election, a tremendous uproar started. Yogi Adityanath was so angry that he announced the candidates by forming a separate party. Uma Bharti, who was running a separate party also said that BJP would lose 40 seats because of her. The separation of the saffron robe wearing leaders was not a good sign, so efforts to persuade them started. Earlier on March 12, 2007, Yogi had cried bitterly in the Lok Sabha and accused Mulayam Singh Yadav of fabricating false cases. But in UP, factionalism drowned the party. On behalf of the Sangh, Ram Madhav warned, "BJP should learn a lesson from UP. Anti-incumbency should not prove expensive in Rajasthan, Madhya Pradesh, Chhattisgarh and Gujarat." The BJP had pushed ahead by sharpening the issues related to Hindutva. But the result was disappointing. The BJP could not save a single seat in the by-elections for the seats of the sacked MPs.

❑

4

CHAPTER

Advani's Unfinished Journey

The Sangh expressed confidence again. The UPA government also handed over the issues of Hindutva. Time appeared favourable. But the fight in the second generation was so dominating as if the battle ad begun for the sixteenth Lok Sabha instead of fifteenth!

Seeing the ups and downs in the BJP, the Sangh felt that unless a leader in the second generation was trained thoroughly, LK Advani could not be side-lined completely. However, by April-May, Advani was again seen getting closer to the Sangh. On the other hand, the presidential election had been announced. Bhairon Singh Shekhawat was contesting it on behalf of NDA. Meanwhile, on May 15, Mamta Banerjee proposed to make Vajpayee the President. She was a part of NDA then. The Sangh wanted to make Vajpayee the President in the year 2002. If he had wanted to, he would have been willing at that time. During the time, the name of APJ Abdul Kalam came up again. But there was no consensus. Finally, Vajpayee had to declare that after Rajendrababu, there was no tradition of electing the same person to the post of President twice. In such a situation, the Congress threw the bet of the first woman President and announced Pratibha Devisingh Patil who was then the Governor of Rajasthan as its candidate. Pratibha Patil became the President. There was cross voting from the BJP, especially the anti-Modi camp in Gujarat. So, on July 23, two days before the oath taking ceremony of the President, Rajnath Singh suspended five Gujarat MLAs, including Govardhan Jharmaiya, from the party. An interview of Rajnath's in August again sparked a controversy, claiming that the proposal for removing Narendra Modi from the Parliamentary Board had 70 per cent of Rajnath's opinion and 30 per cent of the Sangh's opinion whereas both had 50-50 percent contribution for the removal of Arun Jaitley from the post of spokesperson.

Meanwhile, the Congress government gave another issue to BJP and Sangh, when they denied the existence of not only Ram Setu but also of Lord Ram by submitting an affidavit in the Supreme Court. In para 20 of the affidavit, it was quoted on behalf of the Archaeological Survey of India - 'There is no historical record of the characters of Valmiki Ramayana and Tulsidas' Ramcharitmanas.' The government's culture department and its Minister Ambika Soni came under attack. On September 12, the Vichar

Pariwar of the Sangh organized a nationwide strike. A fight also broke out in Congress over Ramayana. Jairam Ramesh, a Minister in the Manmohan Singh government, demanded Ambika's resignation, and on 14 September, Ambika immediately offered resignation to Sonia Gandhi instead of Prime Minister Manmohan Singh. Two officials of the Archaeological Department were suspended.

Controversy on Vande Mataram, Muslim appeasement etc. were such issues that were driving the sangh to a Hinauvadi face and in the present situation, Advani was the most suitable choice for it. It meant that there was an issue as well as atmosphere. So, Advani again focussed on being 'PM in waiting'. The National Executive meeting was held in Bhopal from 21 to 23 September and this was the first meeting in which Vajpayee was not present due to health reasons. Rajnath said in his address, "There is the same atmosphere in the country again. So, let's take a pledge that the purpose of the lamp which will be lit here today will be to establish our rule in the centre." But Advani wanted the Prime Minister's candidature for the year 2009 to be announced in this meeting itself. So, Jaswant Singh, Shatrughan Sinha, Venkaiah Naidu, Yashwant Sinha–everyone started public lobbying in front of the media. The agenda of the meeting revolved around Advani.

But when Rajnath Singh read Vajpayee's letter, the controversy ended. It was written in it - 'I am still around. I will be able to join you soon." He also wrote in the poetic style – 'The sacrifice remains, the sacrifice is incomplete, the obstacles of loved ones surround, to make the weapon for the last victory, nav dadhichi melts the bones. Come, let's light the lamp again.' But at the Bhopal rally, Advani told Sangh that his goal was the beloved Ram Mandir, which changed the course of his life, too. In the same meeting, the BJP took a historic decision that the party would give 33 per cent reservation to women in the system. After returning to Delhi, Advani also said that Atal was their leader.

But since the Sangh was also aware, consensus started building on Advani. He too got the hint and he started his work on 'Vision-2009', in which Narendra Modi emerged as an important man of Advani's. The excitement of Gujarat elections had increased. When Sonia Gandhi called Modi 'maut ka saudagar' (merchant of death), the political terminology stooped to a new low. On the other hand, even in the UPA government, battle had broken out on the nuclear deal and the Left parties supporting from outside had opened the front. In the BJP too, there were signs of the doubts regarding the Prime Ministerial candidate ending. November 8 was Advani's birthday. So, the way Chief Ministers and political leaders thronged his house indicated that Advani was going to be the Prime Ministerial candidate. The announcement was not made that day, but Rajnath Singh gave a hint by saying that Advani was undoubtedly a great leader and his 50-year-old career had no blemishes. But Sushma Swaraj said that some things also happen unannounced. Finally, on December 10, the moment came which Advani had been awaiting since decades and when he had had the opportunity, he had proposed Vajpayee's name. Eventually, Advani became the BJP's official 'PM-in-waiting', the script of which was drawn at the Sangh's annual meeting held in Dharwad, Karnataka on November 4, 2007. As a result, on Advani's birthday, his home environment was different. At that time, it was an unofficial sign. But after taking consent from the unwell Vajpayee, it was finally announced on 10 December. The excitement of Gujarat elections was high. So, Prime Minister Manmohan Singh said that it was an announcement made out of fear of Modi. A few days later, on January 22, 2008, the NDA also approved Advani's candidature.

Modi and Mission Advani

Advani had become the Prime Ministerial candidate in the middle of the Gujarat elections. When the results came out in December 2007, Modi's image also changed. Modi prepared to take oath as the Chief Minister for the third time. So, after the meeting of the Legislature Party, Modi who was hurt by the politics and media troll expressed his sentiments. Getting emotional, Modi said, "BJP is my mother. No son can become bigger than his mother. Those who do not know the history of Jana Sangh and BJP are calling me bigger than my party. But my image looks bigger because your lens is limited. If you increase your focus, you will see thousands of workers who have carried me on their shoulders." Modi was the focal point of that election and now his focus was also on the horizon of national politics and he was also part of Advani's Vision 2009. So, the preparation started. Modi had become a brand. Also, a movement as to who would take over after Advani became 'Atal' had also started in BJP, in which Modi was seen at the forefront. Changes also started to take place in the Sangh and on December 28, 2009, I wrote in my 'From India Gate' column of the daily 'Navjyoti' - "After the Gujarat elections, it is being discussed as to why should not the team of Vichar Parivar be such that it should run in one line and occupy the power at the centre, that is, in the Sangh too, there was a churning going on to change the face and handing over the command of the Sangh to Mohan Bhagwat in place of Sudarshan." It was Bhagwat who had argued for Advani to be given the last chance in 2009, that is, the mission and vision for the BJP was the general election of 2009, for which preparations started in full swing.

On the day of Modi's swearing-in, there was a discussion between Sangh leaders Suresh Soni and Rajnath Singh and a strategy was made to improve the organization in the states where elections were coming up. It was discussed at the organization level in the meeting on December 29, in which Modi was also present. After that, a strategy was made to hand over the command of Rajasthan BJP to Omprakash Mathur considered close to Modi, on January 1, 2008, instead of Mahesh Sharma. But it seemed that the confrontation had become a part of the BJP's strategy. First, Vasundhara Raje protested and then news started coming in that Advani was also against the removal of Mahesh Sharma. About that, Rajiv Pratap Rudy said on 3 January, "It is a fictional piece of news. Advaniji is our PM candidate and Rajnath Singh is the head of the organization. There is no confrontation between the two leaders." But apart from the confrontation, in the same meeting, a committee of Sushma Swaraj, Arun Jaitley, Ananth Kumar and Vinay Sahasrabuddhe was formed, which was to make a future action plan for the year 2009. The five members met on 2 January and submitted the report to Advani and Rajnath on 7 January. The plan was implemented immediately and on January 9, 2008, a 19-member election management committee under the leadership of Rajnath Singh was also announced. Apart from Rajnath Singh, the committee consisted of Murli Manohar Joshi, Jaswant Singh, Venkaiah Naidu, Sushma Swaraj, Arun Jaitley, Vijay Kumar Malhotra, Bal Apte, Ananth Kumar, Gopinath Munde, Thaawarchand Gehlot, Vinay Katiyar, Yashwant Sinha, Ramlal, Mukhtar Abbas Naqvi, Arun Shourie, Ravi Shankar Prasad, Balbir Punj and Vinay Sahasrabuddhe.

As part of the strategy, on the same day, Advani also made public a letter he had written to Prime Minister Manmohan Singh on January 5, on which Manmohan had remained silent. In that letter, Advani had demanded 'Bharat Ratna' for Vajpayee. If Vajpayee had been conferred 'Bharat Ratna', the credit would have gone to Advani. But if that did not happen, it would have been natural to implement the strategy of surrounding the government by projecting his ideal image. Every strategy was being executed. On the occasion of Pongal, Narendra Modi reinforced the future possibilities by meeting Jayalalithaa in Tamil Nadu. Then the first meeting of the election management committee was held on January 15 as soon as the sun was in Uttarayan, in which manifesto, advertisement-posters, media, team to prepare blueprint of state-wise meetings, team to implement the plans, i.e., several teams were formed. The party had also identified that 297 seats where the lotus had blossomed at some point from 1989 to 2004. The target of Mission 297 had been fixed internally. NDA meeting was held on 22nd January and resolution was passed which consisted of three important things - NDA will mobilize for a decisive mandate in the upcoming Lok Sabha elections; it will fight with a common strategy and programme under the leadership of Advani; and Vajpayee will remain the chairman of NDA. But the way the NDA moved the proposal indicated that the core agenda of the BJP would have to be kept aside as in 1999. Sushma Swaraj said in an interview, "Even if BJP wins 272 or 291 seats, we will form the government of the NDA and not of the BJP." The NDA's circle, including the BJP, was reduced to five parties—JDU, Shiv Sena, BJD and Akali Dal. In such a situation, the exercise of expanding the scope of NDA in terms of the year 2009 went ahead.

Modi again dominated the BJP executive meeting on January 27. Rajnath even called Modi a role model and also advised other Chief Ministers to learn from him. After this, a two-day meeting of the National Council was to be held at Ramlila Maidan in Delhi. In this meeting, Vajpayee sent best wishes for Advani. When Modi addressed the council, his style was that of a national leader. He also praised Vajpayee saying, "The right leader is the one who appoints his rightful successor." That is, Vajpayee had made Advani the successor and now it was Advani's turn. It seemed that Advani was holding meeting for election strategy now, but Modi seemed to be his successor. That is why Advani had termed the victory of Gujarat as 'victory of good governance' more than that of Hindutva.

Advani's 'My Country, My Life'

Advani took every step for the year 2009. On February 21, the BJP held a massive rally especially for women at Ramlila Maidan, where the party proudly mentioned the achievement of providing 33 percent reservation or women. The following month, on March 19, Advani's autobiography hit the market. Advani wrote autobiography to explain his personality in the right contexts, whereas one usually writes an autobiography after retirement. In the foreword of the book, Vajpayee wrote – 'Advaniji is a very sensitive person, so he is unable to express the thoughts that keep coming to his mind properly. But now everything has been told through the book. Now people will be able to understand him better." Since that was his last bet to become the Prime Minister after the Lok Sabha elections, he kept the autobiography like a passport to reach the PMO and waited for the visa in the form of vote of the people.

Advani had written a 1,010-page book, which was a subject of curiosity. But the controversy could become a barrier in his way. So, he wrote his words with caution. Advani's autobiography 'My Country, My Life' was released on March 19, 2008, for which former President APJ Abdul Kalam reached a short distance on foot in a traffic jam. Celebrities from all walks of life including politics to Bollywood and social organizations were present at the launching ceremony. All the prominent leaders of NDA, Chief Ministers of BJP-ruled states, corporate figures, Sarkaryavah Mohan Bhagwat from Rashtriya Swayamsevak Sangh (ideology family) and Ashok Singhal from VHP were also present. About the aim of the book, Bhairon Singh Shekhawat said, "Everything is written in it is fool proof. So, there is no room for improvement." But Mohan Bhagwat said something significant, "Swayamsevak means the one who makes his own way while living in the present times. Advaniji proved this as a true swayamsevak, account of which is in this book. Advaniji transformed the circumstances the way he wanted, which is a source of inspiration for the swayamsevaks of the Sangh." That is to say, the essence of Advani's autobiography was that he was dedicated first to the country, then he was a worker, then came the ideals of the party and ideology family. In the end, Advani himself said, "Now the book should tell whatever I want to say." Through his strategy of including everyone in the book which was written to establish his identity as a sensitive, thoughtful and visionary leader, Advani tried to bring back the leaders who had turned away from the

BJP. Madanlal Khurana, who spoke against the party had left. So, he returned on 4 April. Khurana had been ousted earlier as well during Advani's tenure as a president. But then Vajpayee had intervened. By late evening Advani had revoked the suspension in a dramatic fashion and Khurana had apologized.

Shaheed Dhuli Kalash Yatra

In politics, the art of binding people through symbols is very important, which Narendra Modi mentions in today's era. But this art was tried even before the 2009 elections. At that time, Advani did not want to leave any stone unturned. That campaign was handled by the Sangh behind the scenes. The entire blueprint of that campaign was made in Mumbai. In it, a strategy was made to keep Bahadur Shah Zafar and Rani Lakshmi Bai in the centre. BJP started praising Bahadur Shah Zafar. The reason was - the Mughal dynasty had become a symbol of political unity during the revolution of 1857. The party was trying to make place among the moderate Muslims through Bahadur Shah Zafar. At the same time, there was also the occasion of the 150th anniversary of the revolution of 1857. On this occasion, BJP started 'Shaheed Dhuli Kalash-Yatra' on 8th April. The 'Naman 1857' programme was held at the Parade Ground of the Red Fort. BJP took out a rally of 1857 motor cycles. Soil was collected from 290 locations in the country where martyrs belonged and started the Kalash Yatra, the purpose of which was to carry the Kalash made of clay taken from the birthplaces of the martyrs across the country so that new energy of nationalism could be infused in the party cadre. In this yatra, Bahadur Shah Zafar's 'Roti' and 'Kamal' were attached to the party's election symbol lotus and started the Yatra on the 'Martyrdom Day' of Mangal Pandey. On May 10, on the occasion of completion of 150 years of revolution, BJP organized a unique tribute to the martyrs by observing 57 seconds of silence at 6.57 minutes in every street. In fact, the entire campaign of the 150th anniversary of 1857 Revolution was conducted under the guidance of the Sangh. The Sangh had held a meeting and given instructions to all its organizations regarding this campaign. Letters were prepared in all the languages of the country and sent from Mumbai to the whole country. This was also carried forward by the BJP in a strategic way. Events related to this were especially organized in higher numbers in tribal areas because tribal leaders were more involved in the revolution of 1857.

'Head Start' Formula and from Trust Vote to Betrayal

However, on April 14, when the BJP core group was holding talks regarding coordination with the four big leaders of the Sangh - Madandas Devi, Mohan Bhagwat, Bhaiyyaji Joshi and Suresh Soni - Jaswant Singh raised the issue of corruption against the Vasundhara Raje government. But the Sangh asked to end the internal factionalism. The rebellion of MLAs against Sushil Modi in Bihar was not pacified. Meanwhile, Gopinath Munde resigned from all posts including that of the General Secretary of the BJP. The reason for his displeasure was that without taking

Munde into confidence Nitin Gadkari had appointed Madhu Chavan as Mumbai BJP city president, who was anti-Munde. The exercise was done in a hurry. Advani called them to Delhi and a reconciliation was reached on 22 April. Munde's point was accepted. But party discipline was once again in shambles. At that time, Munde also expressed regret. But after resolving the matter, the party turned its attention to the year 2009. The 'head start' formula, which was used for taking the lead in the election campaign before the opposition parties during the Gujarat and Karnataka elections, became the blueprint for the execution of the Lok Sabha's strategies, under which the election material and the process of candidate selection were decided. The strategy was that the names of all the candidates should be announced by August-September.

On the other hand, BJP had an eye on young voters. So, a strategy for Advani's yatra amongst youth in October was planned. To prepare the ground for that, an exercise of describing Advani as a strong leader with a strong will began. Yuva Morcha prepared the blueprint for Advani's campaign titled 'My Dream for Young India', which was to be held in ten cities. It was to have 1,500 youth with Advani on stage. For this, a campaign was launched to engage the youth from June itself and questionnaire was distributed among 25-30 thousand youth, which was made by assessing their interest and awareness in politics. There was also a discussion in the executive meeting of June about making a strategy for youth penetration and ticket distribution. But the BJP, which was busy making Lok Sabha strategy, suffered a setback when the differences between the UPA government and the Left over the nuclear deal led to a withdrawal of support and Manmohan Singh had to move a trust vote in the Lok Sabha to save the government.

On July 22, 2008, Manmohan Singh managed to save the government, but there was a lot of cross-voting. Manmohan government would not have survived if there had been no cross voting. The 'cash for vote' incident took place. Bundles of notes were waved in the Lok Sabha. Eleven MPs from the NDA cross-voted, including seven from the BJP. Advani regretfully said, "The BJP is emerging, so such people are also joining the party." The betrayal by one's own party members during the trust vote had shaken the party. So, the party postponed the meeting of the Central Election Committee convened on July 28 for the selection of candidates and issued a new directive to the states to send the list of candidates who were 'trustworthy' rather than who were 'winnable' so that they could not be 'bought' in future. The party also decided to conduct a fresh survey at the top level.

'Har Har Mahadev' after 'Jai Shri Ram'

This was the time, when the spark that had been lit for two and a half months had now flared up. When the Amarnath Shrine Board was first given the land and then was withdrawn due to the protest by the separatist organizations, the 'Amarnath Sangharsh Samiti' opened a front. Jammu flared up in early August itself. Its flames started spreading across the country. Advani had advised the Manmohan Singh government to talk to the people of 'Amarnath Sangharsh Samiti' and return the land. The government gave land in Baltal for some temporary construction for the Amarnath Yatra. But the PDP then withdrew support to the Ghulam Nabi Azad government and when the separatists applied pressure, the government succumbed. There was a reaction from Jammu. There was a separatist versus nationalist conflict. Eventually, the 'Amarnath Sangharsh Samiti' fought for 63 days. During this period, Jammu came to a standstill. More than 18 people died. The then Home Minister Shivraj Patil had to go there and talk to the people. The BJP tried to give its direct support to the movement and a rally was also organized. However, the Sangharsh Samiti cancelled it at the last moment. But after the agitation ended, a felicitation ceremony of the leaders of the Sangharsh Samiti was held on September 10 in the Constitution Club in Delhi where senior leaders of the Sangh and BJP were present. At this event of 'Jan Abhiyan Sanstha' in the Constitution Club, BJP's National President Rajnath Singh, Regional Sanghchalak of the North Zone of the Sangh Dr Bajrang Lal Gupta and Kshetriya Pracharak Dinesh Chandra were especially present. Rajnath and Bajrang Lal felicitated Advocate Leelakaran Sharma who was the convener of Shri Amarnath Yatra Sangharsh Samiti, and two senior members - Dr. Jitendra Singh and Chandramohan with shawls. Dr. Jitendra Singh was a well-known doctor of Jammu. But during the movement that lasted for more than two months, he kept aside everything and stood with the people of Jammu on the question of faith and identity. On this occasion, Rajnath said that the government will have to decide whether it will go ahead with the mindset of appeasement or with secularism in the true sense. But the point to note was that when this movement gained momentum and the BJP directly targeted the Manmohan Singh government, the BJP had coined a new slogan. During the General Elections of the year 1996, the slogan 'Bharat Mata Ki Teen Dharohar, Atal-Advani-Murli Manohar' was very popular. But now when the Amarnath issue was found, the party started a new slogan - 'Atal-Advani-Rajnath, save Amarnath'. On the other hand, the BJP was aggressive against the UPA government regarding the incidents of terrorism. As a part of the strategy, it was decided to make Narendra Modi, the then Chief Minister of Gujarat, the face to speak on the issue.

Modi - The Aggressive Face against Terrorism

Politics was being played on the rising terrorist incidents. The way the bomb blasts took place in Bangalore-Ahmedabad after the trust vote, senior BJP leader Sushma Swaraj described it as a conspiracy of Manmohan government instead of a coincidence. On July 28, Swaraj said, "Such an attack took place only four days after the trust vote. Is there anything in the world called circumstantial evidence or not? It has never happened that two BJP-ruled states have had similar serial bomb blasts in 24 hours. There have been attacks to divert attention from the 'cash for vote' and to show the BJP's fear to the lost Muslim vote bank as it shunned congress due to its pro-America stand." Then on 29 July, 18 live bombs were found in Surat. There was a rumour of bombs in Delhi and Meerut. It was as if the whole country was sitting on a pile of gunpowder. On the third day, Prakash Javadekar shrugged off Sushma's statement and called it her personal statement. After 45 hours of making the statement, Sushma also said that it was her personal opinion. Narendra Modi was becoming the face on behalf of the BJP in the vocal fight against terrorism. After meeting Prime Minister Manmohan Singh on August 29, Modi came out and advised him not to play any politics in the war against terrorism and to adopt a practical approach. On September 3, he raised questions about the non-approval of Gujarat's law against terror - 'GUJCTOC'. Whether the incidents of terrorism took place in Bangalore or Rajasthan or anywhere else, Modi was pushed forward to speak; this strategy was devised by Arun Jaitley. When questions arose, Modi said, "I am speaking on behalf of everybody." In fact, Modi had become such a face on which the Hindu vote could be united and for that Modi was being brought to the fore to speak against terror and SIMI. After that, the BJP's national executive meeting started in Bengaluru on September 13 and on the same day there were serial bomb blasts in Delhi and the capital was shaken. Earlier in the day, in the executive, Modi spoke especially on internal security. He took an aggressive stand on a range of issues like GUJCTOC not given approval,

Ram Setu, Amarnath controversy, infiltration, politics on SIMI network, conversion law, Sachar committee report, religious reservation and so on. On September 25, there was good news for Modi - he had been given clean chit by the Nanavati Commission on the Godhra incident. But the so-called secular brigade was not ready to accept it. The National Integration Council (NIC) meeting was held on 13 October, in which the Chief Ministers of all the states along with the Prime Minister were present. But the issue of terrorism was not on the agenda of the meeting. So, the BJP planned a walkout strategy from the first meeting. However, Modi argued that they should attend the meeting and by protesting put the government on the back foot. And that is what happened. Manmohan Singh spoke of not targeting a particular community in the name of terrorism. In response, Modi proposed that the feeling of equal security should be increased among all sections without any discrimination of minority or majority and again demanded the implementation of GUJCTOC. The meeting had been especially called after the conversion related incidents of violence in Odisha. But after the meeting, BJP leaders believed that Modi's strategy brought the government under pressure, otherwise the UPA government would have been successful in banning Bajrang Dal.

Controversy Over the Term 'Hindu Terrorism' and 26/11 Mumbai Terror Attack

Whether it was about Hindutva or terrorism, a semi-final battle had been declared amid all the issues. On October 14, the Election Commission announced assembly elections in Delhi, Madhya Pradesh, Rajasthan, Chhattisgarh and Mizoram. The challenge for the BJP was to regain power in Madhya Pradesh, Chhattisgarh and Rajasthan. The semi-final election was very important for both the BJP and the Congress. But then on October 24, the so-called secularists seemed to have got their wish fulfilled. In the Malegaon-Modsa terror blast case of September 8, 2006, three people of an Hindu organization were arrested, including Sadhvi Pragya. The term 'Hindu terrorism' was coined by Congress and terrorism became an institutional issue in this election. Then the Congress-ruled Maharashtra's ATS also took the name of ABVP and 'Hindu Jagran Manch'. Sadhvi Pragya was arrested on Friday and initially BJP leaders were seen shunning her. Meanwhile, on October 30, when there were 14 serial bomb blasts in Assam, Congress spokesperson Manish Tewari raised the question – when the security agencies did not know, how did Advani know that HUJI was behind it? How do BJP leaders get information first? The allegations and counter-allegations on terrorism became very sharp. On the other hand, Pragya's case had taken a political hue. Hence a meeting of BJP President Rajnath Singh and LK Advani with Sarkaryavah Mohan Bhagwat at Jhandewalan took place and from 3rd November entire party came to the defense. After that the entire team of legal experts of the party got busy with fact-finding on the legal aspects, which revealed the role of SIMI in the investigation conducted in the year 2006 and the evidence of buying a cycle from a Hindu shopkeeper to divert the investigation. Riyaz Bhatkal was also arrested in this case. After these facts, the BJP raised the question that if the ATS found the role of SIMI in 2006, then why did the investigation not proceed on the same? BJP said that ATS was not working impartially. BJP demanded proof against Pragya. As the election campaign progressed, the entire Sangh Parivar stood with Pragya. Pragya filed an affidavit in the Nashik court alleging harassment from ATS and the words she wrote sparked emotions. Advani said in a meeting in Chhattisgarh in November, "I was stunned to read Sadhvi Pragya's affidavit. In a country where sages and saints are respected and people take pride in the rule of law, how can an investigating agency behave in such a barbaric manner?" When the declaration of the 'PM in Waiting' increased the momentum, Prime Minister Manmohan Singh called Advani and talked to him. When Advani reiterated his opinion which he had voiced in the meeting, the PM asked him to wait till the completion of the investigation. The then National Security Advisor MK Narayanan made a statement that Pragya's allegations would be investigated. After the Manmohan-Advani talks, on November 21, the National Security Advisor and IB Chief met Advani. Advani made it clear that the allegations made by Sadhvi Pragya in the affidavit could not be tolerated by a civilized society. But then the Mumbai ATS played a new trick and imposed MCOCA on all the ten accused of Malegaon blasts, which meant that the police could keep them in custody for six months without court's approval.

Meanwhile, a major terrorist attack took place in Mumbai, which can be called the biggest terrorist attack. On the late evening of 26 November, terrorists from Pakistan took people hostage at Hotel Taj, Nariman House, Oberoi and other places and opened fire on railway stations. There was an orgy of death on the streets of Mumbai. After the operation that lasted for three days, the terrorists were killed and Ajmal Amir Kasab was caught alive. This terrorist attack has once again laid the security system bare. The country was shaken and the people silently sat in front of the TV for three days. Hundreds of people were killed and injured. 14 soldiers engaged in security were also martyred in this operation. Advani immediately reached Mumbai, where he gave a statement, "The terrorists have made it a pattern to attack on 13th or 26th of every alternate month. All the major attacks took place on these dates. Godhra, Jaipur, Ahmedabad, Delhi and Mumbai are examples." Politics also started on the biggest terrorist attack in the midst of election fervour.

The Semi-final Match Ended in a Draw

After the Mumbai incident, the exercise of tightening the security system in the country started. The command of the Home Ministry was handed over from Shivraj Patil to P. Chidambaram. A bill to set up a National Investigation Agency was passed by convening a special session of Parliament. As the Indian government's global campaign to isolate Pakistan on the issue of terror started, the country also awaited the election results on December 8. Congress's

Sheila Dikshit won for the third time in Delhi, BJP's Shivraj Singh Chouhan won in Madhya Pradesh and Raman Singh won in Chhattisgarh. But Rajasthan was snatched from the hands of the BJP and Congress was the winner. Excluding Mizoram, the semi-final match ended in a draw. Despite this, losing Delhi and Rajasthan was a setback for the BJP. Vasundhara Raje's supporters argued about the defeat of Rajasthan saying that they lost due to the indifference of the Sangh. In fact, Raje's confrontation with Prakashchandra, the Sangathan mantri in Rajasthan, was well-known and Raje's attitude was no less responsible for it. The situation worsened so much that on December 15, the then state president Om Prakash Mathur and Sangathan mantri Prakash Chandra reached the Sangh headquarters at Jhandewalan and discussed the reasons for the defeat with Sah Sarkaryavah Suresh Soni. He first met Prakashchandra and then met Mathur. The power was already lost and now there was a conflict over the post of Leader of the Opposition. It was clear from the results of the semi-finals that the politics on the issue of terrorism was not accepted by the public. Therefore, Rajnath Singh argued that since the voters had already made up their mind, the Mumbai attack had no effect on the election. But the Advani-Rajnath duo was still hopeful of putting the government on the back foot on the issue of terrorism in the Lok Sabha elections. Venkaiah Naidu had then admitted that there was some mistake due to which they lost Delhi and Rajasthan. On December 19, Rajnath Singh constituted a two-member committee of Thawarchand Gehlot and Yashwant Sinha to review the defeat of Rajasthan. But the review did not fix the responsibility on anyone. But the year 2008 gave another shock to the BJP. Suddenly on December 30, there was a news that Rs 2.6 crore had been stolen from the party headquarters.

Advani's Obama Style

On the other hand, the victory of Barack Obama in the US presidential election gave impetus to Advani's campaign. Advani had followed Barack Obama's formula. He first made his website, then met industrialists to deal with the economic downturn in 2008. He had a meeting with fifteen industrialists on 20th November at his official residence 30 Prithviraj Road. He said, "There is insecurity, uncertainty and despair in the country. The NDA government will end this environment and restore hope and confidence in the country." When UPA announced a package for farmers, he had a meeting with agriculture experts. In this way, he started organizing such meetings with people from all walks of life and also started briefing them in the same manner when a Prime Minister forms the government. But this strategy created a circle of people around him who were less concerned with the ground reality and more with statistics. Advani gave this responsibility to Sudheendra Kulkarni, who was once an influential figure in the PMO during Atal Bihari Vajpayee's tenure. Kulkarni ran the 'Advani for PM' campaign and continued it with slogan on the website, T-shirts just like Barack Obama did in the US election.

Like Obama, Advani started communicating with people through the Internet and even addressed several rallies during the election, for which the entire team worked continuously. Advani talked to experts on every issue – foreign, security, farmers. But Congress made fun of it. Congress' Manish Tewari had said that Advani was trying to become Obama at the age of John McCain.

Sangh's Advice and Shekhawat's Declaration of War

2009 was the year of decisions. It was decided in the meeting of the Parliamentary Board that the tickets would be announced in January. From Sangh, Mohan Bhagwat, Madandas Devi, Suresh Soni reached Advani's house and had a meeting with the leaders of BJP's core group. The Sangh advised that instead of favouritism regarding tickets, they should ask for the opinion of the workers for each seat and then select candidates. At the same time, the Sangh also planned to amend the constitution of the BJP, in which there could be liberty to become the party President more than once and Rajnath Singh could get the benefit of it after the election. So, there was a discussion about differences between Advani and Rajnath once again. On January 5, a news appeared in two prominent newspapers that Advani was BJP's sole decision maker. The tone of the news said a lot. But on the same day in Ahmedabad, Advani had to refute it. The next day, i.e. on January 6, Bhairon Singh Shekhawat, who had retired from the post of Vice President gave a surprise. In Rajasthan, he targeted Vasundhara Raje by alleging corruption in the party and indicated to the central leadership that if action was not taken, he would contest the Lok Sabha elections, which meant that Shekhawat started challenging Advani. Shekhawat gave a statement in Kota, Jaipur and there was a stir at Advani's house in Delhi. After the meeting, on January 7 Rajnath Singh refused to give ticket to Shekhawat saying that there was no tradition of contesting elections by those who had already held constitutional posts. He even said that after bathing in the Ganges, they should not bathe in a well. On this, Murli Manohar Joshi quipped, "I take bath with a mug from a bucket filled with water."

Shekhawat was incensed by Rajnath's statement and cited the example of C. Rajagopalachari, who was the first Governor General of independent India and later became a union Minister and Chief Minister of Madras State. The next day, i.e. on January 8, Shekhawat gave vent to his anger regarding Rajnath Singh's statement about Ganga and well in this way, "When I entered politics, Rajnath was not even born. It will take time for Rajnath to understand me and the BJP." In true sense, Shekhawat's target was like the saying in the villages - 'Goli chali ram par, lagi shyam ko aur mar gaya ghanshyam' (The bullet was fired at Ram, it hit Shyam and Ghanshyam was killed). When Jaswant Singh and Rajnath Singh met and spoke with him, Shekhawat said, "I am not harming the BJP, rather I am seeking purification so that the party becomes stronger. I am angry with the circumstances. The disease of corruption has increased in the party and now there is a need to deal with it strictly; otherwise, the party will be destroyed." But when things did not work out in the party, Shekhawat showed political skills, after which NCP leader DP Tripathi said that Shekhawat's candidature should be supported by all parties.

The Word 'PM in Waiting' became a Joke

On the other hand, there was a demand to project Modi as PM

The 'Advani for PM' campaign started on 13 January. With this campaign, a blueprint for Yuva Morcha was made wherein they would campaign door-to-door with the slogan - 'Father, Mother, Brother and Sister, Advani for PM'. But how could the bridegroom proceed if the relatives in the marriage procession started to get angry? That was the situation in BJP, that too when the election had come to a head. Even the people in the party started making fun of Advani's catchphrase 'PM in waiting'. On the occasion of Makar Sankranti on 14th April, a Khichdi Bhoj was organized at the BJP headquarters and many people participated. Advani, Joshi, Sharad Yadav, Rajnath – they were all there. Murli Manohar Joshi had come before Advani. So, the question arose that those with waiting tickets had not arrived yet. On this Joshi also quipped, "I always carry a confirmed ticket. Well, nowadays there is also the facility of tatkal service." That meant that even if Advani became the PM, Joshi's position was confirmed. On the other hand, on April 14, there was a 'Vibrant Gujarat Global Investors Summit' going on in Gujarat, where industrialists Sunil Bharti Mittal and Anil Ambani presented a new election weapon. Ambani not only praised Modi's leadership but also lobbied for Modi to be projected as the next Prime Minister. Anil Ambani recalled the words of his father Dhirubhai Ambani, "My father used to say – Modi is the long-haul player." Mittal also said similar things. The Congress even started reprimanding the industrialists. But a new front in the leadership battle opened up in the BJP. However, the BJP said that whichever BJP-ruled state the industrialists would visit, they would become fans of the BJP Chief Ministers after seeing the work done there. Since Modi was not speaking on this issue, the opposition was getting the chance. Four days later, Modi said, "This time as well as next time also, Advani will be the PM." The matter did not end there. When voting was going on, on April 27, i.e. 20 days before the results, Arun Shourie, a member of Advani's election management team, also talked about making Narendra Modi the Prime Ministerial candidate after Advani. Elections were being held in 2009, but the focus on Advani, the current leadership, was constantly changing due to the talk of future leadership.

Election Command and Dispute (Mahabharat) on Tickets

The BJP's National Executive Council meeting was to be held in Nagpur in February, just before the Lok

Sabha elections. But before that, there was uproar in the party. Venkaiah Naidu wanted Arun Jaitley and Sushma Swaraj to contest the election so that he would be given the command of election management. But Advani had already refused Sushma. Jaitley also started saying that Naidu was from Nellore in Andhra Pradesh; that seat was reserved earlier and now it was a general category and so he should contest from there. In the end, it was decided that Sushma Swaraj would contest from Bhopal. But Jaitley played the trick, after which Advani asked Naidu to contest from Nellore. So, he immediately asked to be the in-charge of elections in the southern states. In this way, Jaitley got the job of election management and Advani said, “None of us have the kind of intelligence that Jaitley has. That’s why I have stopped him from contesting elections.” Reminiscing the Emergency, the BJP released its first and indicative list of candidates on June 26, 2008, which had the names of six candidates, including Advani. By January 19, 2009, the names of 36 candidates were announced through four lists. The fourth list released on January 19 also had only 18 names. That means the path of tickets was not as easy as Advani and Rajnath had thought. Kalyan Singh protested openly about the nomination of Ashok Pradhan from Bulandshahar. Eventually, he left the BJP again on 20 January and declared that he would not return to the BJP till his last breath. He said in harsh words that there was no place for grassroot leaders in the BJP and that the party will be ruined.

On 7 February 2009, the issue of Ram Mandir came up again in the National Council in Nagpur. BJP made it clear that it was looking for an opportunity and that Ram temple would definitely be built in Ayodhya. Rajnath remembered Vajpayee in this way, "May God bless Atalji with a speedy recovery. He should see his colleague and younger brother Advani hoisting the flag from the ramparts of the Red Fort." There was a commotion not only in the party but also in the NDA regarding the seats. The command of Maharashtra was in the hands of Modi. So, Shiv Sena's Uddhav Thackeray was upset. By March, it was felt that Shalya had boarded Advani's chariot. In Odisha, Naveen Patnaik was also unwilling to stay with the NDA as his advisor Pyaremohan Mohapatra had reported that aligning with BJP might hurt. In such a situation, when Chandan Mitra reached Bhubaneswar on March 9 as Advani's emissary, Naveen Patnaik proposed to give BJP 5 out of 21 seats in the Lok Sabha and 37 out of 146 seats in the Assembly, which the BJP could not accept at any cost. Hence, the alliance with the BJD broke down. The NDA had started to disintegrate in the midst of the electoral atmosphere.

When the Battle between the Election Manager and the President Lasted for 12 Days

Perhaps Advani was right. "Only BJP can defeat BJP," he told leaders at the National Executive of Bengaluru on September 12-14, 2008. He had indicated the internal tussle then and the situation was still the same, which seemed to be making Advani's prophecy come true. The election manager of the BJP i.e. the poll manager was

Arun Jaitley and president was Rajnath Singh. But when the leaders on two important positions start clashing after the announcement of the Lok Sabha elections on March 2, what could be the result? The same thing happened in the 2009 elections as well. There was turmoil in the party, the alliance was crumbling. Rajnath Singh was also busy in forming his own special team. Just before Holi, he attached Muralidhar Rao, who had come from Swadeshi Jagran Manch on March 9, with him i.e. the president and made Sudhanshu Mittal the co-in-charge of the Northeast. Jaitley did not like both of them. But his displeasure was especially with Mittal, who used to be very close to the late Pramod Mahajan. In such a situation, on March 13, Jaitley spread the rumour of boycotting the Central Election Committee which selected the candidates and offered to resign. Jaitley was discussed for an hour in the meeting. Sushma and Joshi objected to the manner of protest. Advani remained silent.

The fight was not simple. When Advani gave the list of election managers to Rajnath, Rajnath had added Ramlal on behalf of the organization. Then at the behest of Jaitley, Advani also added Swapan Dasgupta, who in his article had called Rajnath Singh a fool, dumb etc. Rajnath's wound opened up. So, he showed his strength by appointing Mittal. The Sangh was trying to reason, but Jaitley was not agreeing. It seemed that even time was not ready to support BJP now.

Before the election committee meeting on March 17, the organization general secretary Ramlal called Jaitley and gave a formula that he should go to the meeting and protest and recommend removal of Sudhanshu Mittal in writing. But when Jaitley did not agree, Advani admitted that day that there was a difference of opinion, but he called it a minor issue. One could predict the outcome if those on the frontlines fought among themselves like that. In the end, a formula was designed that Mittal would resign, but first Jaitley would come to the meeting and there would be discussion in the forum. But Jaitley did not reach. In such a situation, a strategy was also being planned that instead of holding the election committee meeting, Rajnath should announce the rest of the names in consultation with Advani. Meanwhile, a controversial provocative statement by Varun Gandhi became a major problem for the party. An FIR was registered and an arrest was made under the National Security Act. The matter also went to the Election Commission. On March 21, Rajnath went to Nagpur to seek advice of the Sangh officials so that dispute with Jaitley would end. But before that there was a joint rally with Shiv Sena in Mumbai. On the other hand, the meeting of the Akhil Bhartiya Pratinidhi Sabha of the Sangh was going on in Nagpur, where the Sangh had made a big change and Mohan Bhagwat was going to occupy the post of Sarsanghchalak. KS Sudarshan, who had campaigned for a change in leadership in the BJP and had forced Vajpayee and Advani to go on the back foot with his public statements had retired. But the new generation and new leadership was now a significant signal for the BJP as well.

When a Sandal was thrown in Advani's Election Meeting

Till then the BJP was running a campaign to describe a strong leader and decisive government and Manmohan Singh as a weak PM, due to which Manmohan Singh was hurt. On March 24, Manmohan Singh asked, "Now let the nation decide who is weak," recalling the attack on Parliament, the Kandahar episode, the Jinnah episode and how Advani was isolated in the BJP. The BJP made a blueprint for the formal election campaign with the beginning of Navratri. The blueprint was made for the beginning from five directions simultaneously, according to which Rajnath in the north, Venkaiah in the south, Arun Jaitley in the east, Advani himself in the west and Sushma Swaraj in the centre were to hold public meetings. Then on the occasion of Ram Navami, BJP released its election manifesto. Advani then said that the NDA did not agree on making a law regarding the Ram temple in the Parliament. But the manifesto had glimpses of theology, sociology and economics. It meant that the BJP in its manifesto made a commitment to keep all options open, like talks on Ram temple, making laws including in courts and Article 370 and Uniform Civil Code for the Sangh Parivar, but the alliance declared that it would follow the 'Common Agenda for Governance'. However, it took a direct stand on the issue of Ram Setu, Gau Raksha and Ganga. Promises were made to provide facilities to the economically backward people of all sections of the society and to bring minorities also in the main stream of development. From the economic point of view, the party made announcements like a budget, which included schemes like raising the tax exemption limit to 3 lakhs, giving 35 kg of food grains at the rate of Rs 2, loans to farmers at 4 per cent interest per annum, exempting army from tax, bringing back black money, making POTA-like laws, education policy, one rank one pension, Ladli Laxmi, Bhamashah etc. The Congress was irritated and called it their copy.

Meanwhile, a journalist Jarnail Singh threw a shoe at Home Minister P Chidambaram at a Congress briefing against giving tickets to anti-Sikh riots accused Jagdish Tytler and Sajjan Kumar. There was an effect and Congress cancelled the plans to give them tickets. But that sparked a new debate about the mode of protest. Varun Gandhi was also released from jail on 16 April after the first phase of voting. But the shoe throwing incident started gaining momentum. Advani had a meeting in Katni, Madhya Pradesh on April 16, where Pavas Agarwal, a district youth wing leader of the BJP, tossed a khadau and not a shoe or slipper. The sentiment behind tossing the khadau as described by Pavas was certainly an indication of the results—"I threw my father's khadau and not chappal at Advani. I did this due to divine inspiration because Advani is a fake Iron Man. There is a difference between his words and deeds. He talks about Ram, but goes to Jinnah's tomb. BJP should change its Prime Ministerial candidate." Then eleven days later, Arun Shourie also talked about making

Narendra Modi the Prime Ministerial candidate after Advani. Then Arun Jaitley and Venkaiah immediately agreed to Shourie's opinion, but what Sushma Swaraj said also openly expressed the contradiction within the party. Sushma said, "The authority is not given to the son when father is alive." But in an informal discussion, Jaitley also replied, "Even after death, the father's authority is passed on to the son and not to the daughter." In this way, the leaders were making the mutual enmity public. But Modi was judicious saying that he was not in competition and kept busy with his mission throughout.

Election for the Fifteenth Lok Sabha, Debate for the Sixteenth Lok Sabha

It was strange situation - BJP leaders were fighting election for the 15th Lok Sabha with Advani as its leader, but the new generation leaders were more interested in establishing themselves than Advani's victory. Therefore, the debate during the elections would constantly turn towards the sixteenth Lok Sabha. Narendra Modi also kept ruling the headlines continuously. On May 1, he had double relief from the Supreme Court. It ordered that the trial of the cases related to the Gujarat riots be resolved by setting up a fast-track court; it dismissed the petition for trial outside Gujarat and removed the ban imposed from November 2003 on ten cases related to the riots. The SIT was asked to submit report every quarter and everything was brought under the supervision of the High

Court. Teesta Setalvad and Congress's intentions were in vain and Congress's Veerappa Moily raised doubts about the Modi administration. But on the same day, the then international president of Vishwa Hindu Parishad, Ashok Singhal also showed confidence in Modi in this way, "Narendra Modi has all the qualities to become a Prime Minister. If Modi becomes the Prime Minister, the dispute over Ram temple in Ayodhya will be resolved." Modi had become the focal point of that election, whether willingly or unwillingly. The opposition also continuously attacked him.

The election campaign was nearing its conclusion and to give the message of NDA's unity as part of the strategy, a rally was held in Ludhiana, Punjab before the last phase, in which all the Chief Ministers and leaders of NDA parties were present. That was the historical picture of the rally, in which Narendra Modi and Nitish Kumar were seen expressing their lofty intentions with folded hands. Both the alliances now had hope only from manipulation. Modi had also reached Delhi before the results and was laying the strategy for Advani because he had spoken to Jayalalithaa. On May 15, a day before the results, Nitish Kumar played a card saying that the one who gave special status to Bihar would get his support. The Congress immediately agreed. Hence Rajnath had to make a statement, "Advani has already supported Nitish Kumar's demand for special status for Bihar in the rally itself." The strategy was being laid from both the sides because this time the situation was different from the year 2004 as the Left parties were fighting outside the UPA.

Everyone was waiting for the results that were going to be declared the next day.

May 16, 2009—Advani in Limbo

Then the expected happened. The BJP embroiled in a leadership debate for the sixteenth Lok Sabha lost the battle for the 15th Lok Sabha and Advani's position became like that of Bhishma Pitamah, for whom it was necessary to strengthen the BJP from all sides before retiring. BJP's internal squabbles kept it out of power for the second time in a row despite perfect preparations on the strategic front. In fifteen states including Union Territories, BJP did not even open the account. Three general secretaries, two vice presidents, two Front presidents and many secretaries had lost the election. It seemed that the new generation did not want Advani to come to power. On May 17, the next day after the results, Bhaiyyaji Joshi - new Sarkaryavah of the Sangh, Madandas Devi - Sah-Sarkaryavah and Suresh Soni met Advani and advised that with the change in the BJP, the new generation should be given full command and senior leaders should remain limited to the role of guides. Before the swearing-in of the Manmohan Singh government on 22 May, Yashwant Sinha opened the front on the responsibility of defeat in the BJP on 21 May. One important thing that he said was that by December, Advani would hand over the reins to the second generation. The same thing happened. But before that Sinha had said, "Like Pramod Mahajan had taken responsibility for the defeat in 2004, this time also the responsibility should be fixed. Not only Arun Jaitley, everyone involved in election management is responsible."

Certainly, the BJP was shocked by the defeat in the Lok Sabha elections for the second time in a row. But now a real transition had begun as Advani's age did not fit the Sangh's formula for the 2014 elections. In such a situation, it was necessary to bring forth not only a leader who was acceptable to everyone but also someone who in coordination with ideology could infuse new energy among its workers and end the BJP's exile. The Sangh believed that the third successive defeat would weaken the ideological battle and then it would not be possible to rise for a long time. In such a situation, the thinking of the Sangh was that before a strong NDA, a strong BJP would have to be built and a leadership whose ideological commitment was free from doubt would have to be brought in. To a large extent, the 2009 Lok Sabha elections had indicated the direction of leadership because Modi had already entered national politics due to the plan of making Advani the Prime Minister and who had become the Hindu heart throb of the workers. Now there was a need to actualize it; it is also an example of how the Sangh and Modi carried forward it in a strategic way. The Sangh was doing this not because it wanted to control the BJP but because BJP was the political face of the Vichar Pariwarwhose image created an impression about the entire family. After becoming the Sarsanghchalak, Mohan Bhagwat had prepared the complete script of this change, whose glimpse will be clearly visible in the subsequent chapters. But this decade-long internal struggle was undoubtedly a lesson for giving a new direction not only to the leadership but also to the organization. Narendra Modi had watched this entire decade very closely and as a pracharak of the Sangh, by accepting its advice, he had brought the party to this point, which set a tremendous example of coordination in the vichar Pariwar.

❑

PART-3

Generational Change

(2009-2014)

The defeat in two consecutive general elections had weakened the ideological struggle. In such a situation, the Sangh made the blueprint of the new generation not only for the BJP but for the entire ideology family. After the struggle within, the BJP had to go through a phase of major transition for a new leadership to emerge. What should the leadership be like - RSS Chief Mohan Bhagwat publicly drew a line or it. How the Sangh planned the strategy of strengthening the BJP before the alliance and chose a leadership dedicated to the ideology of Hindutva, about whom the workers did not have the slightest doubt. But in the important battle of the year 2014, how the party worked for 10 percent vote in the mass base by connecting with social, intellectual and professional people. When Narendra Modi became the leader, the results also started showing and along with the people, the parties also joined. How Ashok Singhal saw the soul of Lord Rama in him! The result was that for the first time, the BJP got a majority on its own and destroyed all the records and remembering lessons learnt during Vajpayee's reign, the vehicle of coordination galloped on the highway.

❑

5

CHAPTER

Generational Change: Transition Period

The youth got the command in both Sangh and BJP. But instead of generational changes taking any shape, the BJP and Sangh Parivar were entangled in squabbles from 2009 to 2012. Then how did the BJP and Sangh Parivar overcome it?

The year 2009 was a turning point in the generational change in the Sangh and BJP. On March 21, 2009, the then Sarsanghchalak KS Sudarshan announced the name of Mohanrao Madhukarrao Bhagwat as his successor. Bhagwat became the Sarsanghchalak of the Sangh at the youngest age after Dr. Hedgewar and Guru Golwalkar. He was 59 years old. There were a lot of allegations of political interference on the Sangh at the time of Sudarshan. In such a situation, the challenge of Bhagwat was to refine the position of the Sangh. The Sangh had to be brought back to basic, that is, to do its work in the society instead of direct involvement in politics. At the same time, there was also a feeling that the BJP would also be heading towards a big change. But that would not be as smooth as a change in the Sangh. At that time, senior BJP leader LK Advani was playing his last bet as the Prime Ministerial candidate, whom the Sangh had also consented to give a chance in the 2009 elections though out of compulsion after the bitter experience of the Jinnah episode.

But the real game began when the results of the Lok Sabha elections came out on May 16, 2009, and the BJP was badly defeated for the second consecutive general election. In such a situation, the Sangh avoided direct intervention, but it also considered a change in the BJP necessary. But Advani was not ready to give up at all. The Sangh was also reluctant to say anything outright. On the other hand, the effect of the frustration of the results was clearly visible in the BJP. No one was ready to bear the responsibility of defeat nor was there any discussion about review. Meanwhile, on May 20, Rajasthan BJP president Om Prakash Mathur submitted his resignation to the then national president Rajnath Singh, taking responsibility for the defeat in the state. But no decision was taken on that either. 13 days after the result, the message of the Sangh was clearly expressed in what the then editor Prabhat Jha wrote in the BJP mouthpiece 'Kamal Sandesh'. The text of this editorial went like this - 'BJP needs a leader who will work at the ground level like a seed; one who talks less and does more because without sowing seeds and cultivating them, a farmer cannot harvest the crop. The land will remain fallow. BJP should decide with what mindset it wants to contest the elections – we have to we are winning again? To turn ideology into a social current, such personality, activist and such leadership are needed, in whom the society has complete faith. The common citizen does not expect bigotry from the BJP, rather it expects the leadership of the BJP to be natural, ordinary and simple.' This editorial directly targeted Advani and his team, who ran the Lok Sabha election campaign like a parallel organization. The ruckus escalated when Arun Jaitley, who had taken over the management of this general election on June 3, was made the leader of the BJP in the Rajya Sabha and given the status of Leader of the Opposition. Advani became the leader of the opposition in the Lok Sabha and Sushma Swaraj became his deputy. The decision of giving authority to Jaitley after a major defeat angered many leaders, including Yashwant Sinha, Jaswant Singh and Arun Shourie. On the other hand, journalists like Sudheendra Kulkarni, Swapan Dasgupta, who were part of Advani's team in the elections, went back to journalism and started criticising the party through their articles. Kulkarni wrote in an article – 'Sangh and BJP should brainstorm on their ideology regarding Muslim, Hindutva and poor people'. It was Kulkarni's opinion as a freelance journalist. There was such a ruckus in the party that when Sushma Swaraj who was on a tour of Madhya Pradesh during that time, was asked about it, she said, "The volcano has erupted in the party now. So, if I say anything, it will become a spark."

The process of fixing the responsibility started, but it was at the level of states. On 23rd June, BC Khanduri, the then Chief Minister of Uttarakhand, had to pay the price for losing all the five Lok Sabha seats – he had to resign. Mathur's resignation which he submitted on May 20 was also accepted. On 10th August, Vasundhara Raje was asked to step down from the position of the Leader of Opposition. But she was so adamant on not resigning that the matter remained unresolved for more than two and a half months after Diwali. Advani also insisted on the parliamentary board to save her. But then Rajnath Singh rejected the demand for reconsideration in view of the dignity of the presidency.

Meanwhile, letter bombs also started detonating. Yashwant Sinha wrote a letter which was leaked. Same was the case with Jaswant Singh. On August 24, Arun Shourie, who was a Minister in the Vajpayee government, targeted Rajnath Singh in a TV programme 'Walk the Talk'. The bitterness was apparent in Shourie's words - he first called Rajnath Tom-Dick-Harry. He also called him Humpty-Dumpty and 'Alice in Blunderland' title. He said that there was neither enthusiasm nor vigour in the BJP. Shourie appealed to the Sangh to take over the reins of the BJP and asked for the removal of the current central leaders. Shourie was the leader who had given the formula of making Narendra Modi the Prime Minister right in the middle of the election.

The Press Conference of Sarsanghchalak that Drew Lines

Overall, there was an uproar in the BJP and five days after Shourie's statements, the pre-scheduled press conference of Sarsanghchalak Mohan Bhagwat was held on 28 August 2009 at Jhandewalan, the Sangh headquarters in Delhi. In his opening address, the Sangh Chief denied any interference in BJP as per the principles of the organization and also exhorted it to decide its own future. He also refused to accept the mother-son relationship. He also reiterated the opinion of the Sangh regarding the age limit for leadership. The message was clear, yet there was a consideration. He also said, "The Sangh does not hesitate to give advice, but it is considerate." Later, when there were questions and answers about the BJP, Bhagwat said that BJP would rise from the ashes and if there was a need for chemotherapy, it would also be given. However, there was a clarification about this statement later, in which he said, "I had said that the BJP will rise from the ashes, I did not say that it has becomes ash. However, if it at all it has, it will rise out of it, too." He also indicated that D-4 (four prominent leaders sitting in Delhi) did not get the command of BJP. As soon as the press conference was over, four prominent leaders of BJP - Sushma Swaraj, Arun Jaitley, Venkaiah Naidu, Ananth Kumar - reached Keshavkunj. The meeting went on for three hours and with the formula given by the Sangh, the four leaders reached Advani's house late in the night and gave a message. The Sangh had indirectly signalled to Advani to also leave the post of Leader of the Opposition and pave the way for the new generation. The bitterness had grown so much that Manohar Parrikar, the then Chief Minister of Goa and who was in the race for the new national president, compared Advani to rotten pickle, which led to a lot of controversy. Sensing pressure from the Sangh to retire from politics, Advani went to Pejavar Swami's Math in late September (possibly on 28-29 September 2009). Advani did not want to leave the post till December and insisted that Swamy make a statement to that effect. After Swamy's revelation, VHP leader Acharya Dharmendra had made a very sharp remark, "Without the Sangh, BJP does not exist. If the instructions of the Sangh are not followed, the BJP will collapse like a castle of sand." But Advani seemed to be getting a breather because times were such that disputes continued one after another in BJP.

'Gadkari' becomes the Guard and Advani Bids Farewell

The announcement by the Sangh Chief of a president from outside Delhi had quelled the hopes of some, while the hopes of some regional leaders had stirred. There was also speculation about Advani's departure from the post of Leader of Opposition. But Sushma Swaraj announced that Advani would remain in this post for full five years. This statement further added to the inner turmoil. On the other hand, when Bhagwat was in Delhi in November, on November 11 Rajnath Singh met him in the morning and Arun Jaitley met him in the evening. At that time, too there were reports that Narendra Modi's name had also emerged. So, the eyebrows of the opponents were raised. A request was made to appoint someone else, which meant that the situation could not be said to be very good. But by then the Sangh had decided who would be the next president of the BJP, about which Bhagwat had conveyed to Rajnath Singh a day earlier in the form of an advice during the meeting. Nitin Gadkari suddenly reached BJP headquarters (11 Ashok Road) in the afternoon on 12th November. His meeting with the then Sangthan Mahamantri Ramlal lasted for about two hours. But when he came out, he said, "I am not in the race for the presidency." However, as the week ended, everything became clear. On November 18, the then BJP national spokesperson Prakash Javadekar, who himself hails from Maharashtra, explained the literal meaning of the name 'Gadkari' from the stage – Gadkari means the defender of the fortress, one who strengthens the fort!" Actually, this word was used a lot during the time of Shivaji Maharaj. Shivaji used to conquer the fort and the soldier who was posted to protect it was called 'Gadkari'. So, the word spread that Gadkari would be the party President and the next day Sushma Swaraj interpreted the D-4 formula of the Sangh Chief. She said that among the four leaders that the Sangh Chief talked about, it was Ananth Kumar and Narendra Modi. According to her, when the process had started three months ago and her (Sushma Swaraj's) name had come up, she had decided to succeed Advani in the Lok Sabha. Jaitley was ruled out due to his excellent performance in the Rajya Sabha. Venkaiah Naidu was ruled out as he was President earlier and Modi was ruled out as he was the Chief Minister of Gujarat. In the end, the name of Nitin Gadkari was agreed upon. Now how much truth was there in this argument will never be known now. But then Sushma Swaraj had explained the issue in this way and I had mentioned it in my daily column 'India Gate Se', which was published in the November 21, 2009 issue of the daily 'Navjyoti' newspaper.

But since Sangh was trying to avoid the allegation of direct interference, a statement was issued on the night of November 19, in which it was said that the D-4 leaders would join the race for the post of President. The next day, Venkaiah Naidu issued a statement, in which the important point was that the Sangh and BJP had only ideological relationship and both did not interfere in each other's work. He said that he was not in the race for the president's post and that Sangh had neither suggested nor rejected any name as BJP had not yet decided on its president. He further stated that the new president would be announced only after the process of consensus was completed. This meant that even after the decision had been made, an atmosphere of uncertainty was being created. It seemed as if the entire script was written and it was being worked upon with time. On December 18, 2009, Advani was bade farewell in an honourable manner. As per Sangh's wish, he had to finally give up the post of Leader of the Opposition in the Lok Sabha within a few months. Two points were added to Article 6(a) of the BJP Constitution. First, there shall be a Chairman of the BJP in Parliament, who shall be elected by the MPs of both the Houses. Second, the chairman will nominate the leader, deputy leader, Chief whip in both the houses. In this meeting held in the Parliament Annex, Yashwant Sinha proposed Advani's name for the chairman of the parliamentary party, Advani nominated Sushma Swaraj as the leader in the Lok Sabha and Arun Jaitley in the Rajya Sabha. Advani also indicated that he had been a charioteer from the age of fourteen and would never leave the rath yatra. Advani's message was that he had left the post but he had not retired. Gadkari, who was celebrating his twenty-fifth wedding anniversary on the same day, reached Delhi on Saturday and declared that he was taking the charge as BJP's national president. On December 19, 2009, Nitin Gadkari was formally appointed as the President of BJP. Regarding turmoil in the party, he said, "If there is a will, there is a way." He described his appointment as Advani's choice rather than Sangh's. He also said that two months ago he had first received this offer from Advani and then he was asked by Rajnath Singh. That meant that Gadkari was already busy in managing the citadel. But despite the backing by the Sangh, the road was not so easy.

It is very important to mention some incidents of that time because it will be easy to understand that way of discipline in the present era. When Gadkari called a meeting of BJP Chief Ministers in Mumbai, Advani did not go. Arun Jaitley also did not reach and Yashwant Sinha returned from the airport. Rajnath Singh was not even invited. In fact, before that, ticket distribution in the Rajya Sabha elections had put the party back from where Gadkari had taken over. When Ram Jethmalani was given a Rajya Sabha ticket from the party, many leaders like Vasundhara Raje and Yashwant Sinha got angry. Rajnath and Yashwant were not even consulted regarding Jharkhand ticket. The big question was raised by Sheshadri Chari, who had come to BJP from Sangh background, through a letter bomb. Seshadri Chari objected to Tarun Vijay being given ticket from Uttarakhand. In a letter to Gadkari, he said, "It is now clear that ever since the party lost the elections, the central leadership has been deviating from the ideology and vision." Pointing to Tarun Vijay, Sheshadri Chari wrote- 'In Uttarakhand, ticket was given to a person whose honesty has been questioned. It is not proper for the party to give ticket to a person who has been forced to step down by the party's commission of inquiry on the basis of financial misconduct."

Meanwhile, Jaswant Singh who was very close to Advani had returned. When Jaswant was expelled from the party ten months ago, let alone prominent leaders, even small leaders spoke against him. After the defeat in the Lok Sabha elections, there was an upheaval in the BJP. It was decided that by holding a contemplation meeting in Shimla, the worries would be removed. But then Jaswant Singh's book 'Jinnah: India in the mirror of Partition' was launched. In his book, Jaswant had written the same thing about Jinnah that Advani had said in Karachi on June 5, 2005. But questions regarding the role of Sardar Patel were also raised in Jaswant's book. Therefore, BJP ended the Jaswant chapter on August 19, 2009 before the contemplation meeting in Shimla.

Modi begins to be Mentioned as 'National Leader' in Headlines

Bihar assembly elections were to be held in 2010. BJP decided to hold its national executive meeting on June 12-13 in Patna. Earlier, Bihar had suffered a lot due to floods in Kosi. Bihar had received help from all over the country. As the Chief Minister of Gujarat, Narendra Modi also gave a cheque of Rs 5 crore. Just a day before the executive meeting in Bihar, a full-page advertisement was published in the newspapers of Bihar courtesy of 'Friends of Bihar' thanking Narendra Modi for giving an assistance of Rs 5 crore. Similar hoardings were also put up in Patna. In the picture in the advertisement, Modi and Bihar Chief Minister Nitish Kumar were seen holding each other's hands and raising them upwards. Nitish was repelled with this. As an ally party, BJP leaders were invited for dinner by Bihar Chief Minister Nitish Kumar. Invitations had been distributed. In anger, Nitish cancelled the dinner. He was with the journalists at Chanakya Hotel for lunch on the same day. He was angry and said that when you give charity, even your other hand should not know about it. He said that it was not the right way and that he was returning the check of 5 crores to Gujarat. Naturally, it was a humiliating situation for the BJP. The alliance seemed in trouble. But the irritation was clearly visible among the BJP leaders. Here too there were two factions in the party – one was in favour of Nitish and the other was in favour of Narendra Modi. However, Gadkari decided to continue the alliance after brainstorming at the top-level. But Nitish Kumar put forth a condition that Modi would not campaign in Bihar. Narendra Modi was watching everything closely and was also learning in the process, the benefits of which he is experiencing in the current political scenario. But at that time, BJP had to surrender for the sake of alliance in Bihar. Then on June 23, 2009, Shivanand Tiwari who was close to Nitish bluntly declared that since Nitish was the CM of Bihar, he would decide who would visit Bihar and who won't. BJP spokesperson Prakash Javadekar also made a similar statement, "Narendra Modi goes where he is invited. He is our star campaigner. But as far as Bihar is concerned, Nitish is the CM and everywhere the CM is the star campaigner."

But Narendra Modi's spirits were high. In September, just a week before the Allahabad High Court's decision on the Ayodhya dispute, Narendra Modi's name resounded and from Gandhinagar Gadkari set the ball rolling. Lotus blossomed for the first time in the by-election held or the Kathlal assembly seat. Modi said in his trademark way, "The Congress and CBI have been rejected by the people." In Delhi, Gadkari had spokesperson Nirmala Sitharaman read the script which Modi had written in Gandhinagar. But the next week, i.e. on 30 September when the Ayodhya verdict came in, Sangh and BJP made a cautious statement. Sarsanghchalak Mohan Bhagwat left the matter to the Sant Uchchadhikar Samiti as to what action to take on the court's decision to divide the land into three parts. But both Bhagwat and Advani tactfully expressed their happiness, "The rights of the Hindus have been proved. So, now a grand Ram temple should be built on the sanctum sanctorum. The High Court's verdict is a new chapter of national unity and a new era of communal harmony." Mohan Bhagwat described happiness over the verdict as natural. But appealing for restraint, he said, "No one should do anything that hurts the sentiments of another." The Sangh Parivar appealed to the Muslim community to let bygones be bygones and also invited them to get involved in the construction of the temple. In an official statement issued by the Sangh, it also referred to the sacrifices of those martyred in the temple movement.

But the year 2011 was remembered in the country especially because of the Anna movement. Inflation, corruption, terrorism were many such issues related to the UPA government, which were naturally giving Narendra Modi an opportunity to attack. On inflation, Modi had given such a report that even Congressmen were in trouble. The UPA government and Congress had always tried to put the blame of inflation on the states. In such a situation, a group of some Chief Ministers was asked to submit separate reports. Narendra Modi was responsible for consumer affairs and along with him the CMs of Maharashtra, Andhra Pradesh and Tamil Nadu were also made members. That meant that Modi was the only BJP CM in the team of UPA ruled states.

The Working Group was formed on April 8, 2010. Prime Minister Manmohan Singh made Modi the head of this group. The 'Modi Committee' finalized its report in January 2011, which was submitted to the government on March 2, 2011.

Now just look at Modi's touch in that report! Modi recommended an immediate ban on futures trading in commodities of general necessity. He suggested the Government of India should set up a Price Stabilization Fund to help states in procurement and distribution of food grains. He advised Ministerial-level coordination mechanisms at the central and state levels so that policies could be formulated in a coordinated manner. He also advised government to prepare a ten-year long-term plan for infrastructural development for the backward areas in the agriculture sector and link the top sector with the market in production. He emphasized on making the offense under the Essential Commodities Act non-bailable and prosecution by a special court. To crack down on black marketeers, it was suggested to increase the period of six months of detention to one year. Modi committee suggested 20 recommendations and 64 points for action, that is, overall Modi proved that the central government was responsible for inflation and that it was capable of controlling it. Meanwhile, there was a relieving news for Modi that the SIT of Supreme Court had declared Modi innocent in the case related to the Gujarat riots. It was a nail in Modi's feet which was hurting him since 2002. Around this time, Anna movement had started in Delhi regarding the Lokpal Bill. The difficulties of the government were on rise. The atmosphere in the country started to look disordered. The Sangh was also active in this movement. Sangh's Sarkaryavah Bhaiyyaji Joshi later told me in an interview, "We did not take any decision keeping Anna's movement in mind. We had a meeting before that in

Puttur, in which the Akhil Bharatiya Pratinidhi Sabha decided in 2011 that Swayamsevak will participate in any movement against corruption. When Anna gave a call, our people also joined him."

Modi's incessant roar and Gujarat's 'development model' were leading him to an alternative to Manmohan. In India Today: Mood of the Nation in January-February 2012, Modi was not only at the top of the list of all the Chief Ministers of the country, he also became the choice of 24 percent of the people for the post of Prime Minister; 17 percent people wanted Rahul Gandhi on this post. According to the survey, 48 per cent people wanted BJP to project Modi as the Prime Minister while 24 percent chose Advani and 10 percent chose Sushma Swaraj. This meant that, step by step, Modi was moving towards Delhi.

'Decisive' Confrontation on Sanjay Joshi Issue

Modi was writing his destiny with firm steps. But an initiative by Nitin Gadkari in BJP soured his relationship with Narendra Modi. In August 2011, ahead of the Uttar Pradesh assembly elections, Gadkari brought Sanjay Joshi, who was considered to be an eyesore by Modi, in the national executive and handed over the charge of Uttar Pradesh. The bitterness of the relationship between Modi and Sanjay Joshi was well-known. Nevertheless, giving him such responsibility opened a new front in the party. Modi had rejected it even then. Modi had conveyed his point to the top leadership of the Sangh through the local leader of the Sangh.

The Modi-Gadkari rift came to the fore when Gadkari did not reach Ahmedabad for Modi's three-day Sadbhavna fast in September 2011, which was attended by almost entire leadership. Gadkari's surgery was then cited as the reason and Modi did not attend the national executive meeting in Delhi in October 2011 saying that he would be fasting for Navratri. But Modi was playing for a bigger stake because he knew it would yield good results in the long run. The result was that even at the behest of the Sangh, Narendra Modi kept himself away from the campaign for the Uttar Pradesh assembly elections. The bitterness grew when Nitin Gadkari started saying in some interviews that Modi is a leader like other Chief Ministers of the party. In a conversation with India Today in April 2012, Gadkari had said something like this on the question of the post of Prime Minister, "We have many capable leaders who are eligible for the post of Prime Minister and Modi is also one of them." In the same interview, Gadkari had also said, "RSS does not impose anything on the BJP. Times have changed and so has the Sangh. The way of saying it may change, but the basic sentiment will not change." The problem was that there was no communication link between Gadkari and Modi. In fact, Modi was seen as a leader who could be the bridge between modernization and tradition and was perceived as a market-friendly Hindu nationalist. Sangh knew his importance and Modi, who had been a pracharak, was also aware of the importance of the organization. When Sangh made up its mind to appoint Nitin Gadkari as President again, Modi made his sense of importance about the Sanjay Joshi episode feel in this way.

The National Executive meeting was being held in Mumbai on 24-25 May 2012. Modi laid a condition that he would not attend the meeting until Sanjay Joshi was removed from the executive. The message had reached the top leadership of Sangh and BJP that Modi and his team could resign from the executive and national council if Joshi was not removed. To break the deadlock, a meeting of the party's core group was held and after consultations with the Sangh, a middle way was found. Sangh's Saha-Sarkaryavah Suresh Soni played an important role in this and Gadkari himself spoke to Sanjay Joshi. Only after that, Modi went to Mumbai for the National Executive meeting. In fact, the Sangh Parivar had a strategy in place to pass the blueprint of the necessary constitutional amendment to give Nitin Gadkari a second term during this executive. Initially, Modi was not in favour of this amendment. But then he agreed to it in lieu of Joshi's resignation. Joshi wrote in his resignation – 'I have always learned to rise above personal interest. To end the deadlock, I am resigning.' To understand the context, it may be necessary to state the reason behind the feud between Modi and Joshi. The Sangh had engaged Sanjay Joshi for training in Gujarat with the then organization secretary Modi. The duo laid the party's roots and in 1990 BJP was in such a position that the Janata Dal needed it to form the government. In 1995, the BJP government was formed under the leadership of Keshubhai Patel. From there, the direction of Gujarat's politics changed. There was a period of bitterness in the relationship between both pracharaks of Sangh - Modi and Joshi. Modi was made

BJP's Rashtriya Mantri in the same year and given charge of Himachal Pradesh and Haryana. But his centre was kept Chandigarh instead of Delhi. Modi felt that Joshi was behind that because he believed that Joshi behaved nicely with him in front of others, but he complained about him to the Sangh behind his back. After the year 2005, the two had neither a face-to-face nor a phone conversation. But by leaving this controversy behind in Mumbai, Modi moved forward towards his destination.

Modi's Rising Graph, Sangh worried about Gadkari

Meanwhile, the Anna movement in the country was going towards its culmination in August 2012. On August 3, 2012, it was announced from Jantar Mantar in Delhi that a new party would be born (which later became the Aam Aadmi Party). The presence of former Chief of Army Staff General VK Singh along with Anna on this platform was important. On the other hand, Swami Ramdev was also leading an agitation in Ramlila Maidan on the issue of black money. In this foggy atmosphere of the country, Modi was bursting like a cloud, due to which his popularity was increasing day by day. Just six months later, i.e. in August 2012's India Today: Mood of the Nation, the number of people who wanted Modi as Prime Minister increased to 21 per cent, and Rahul Gandhi's popularity dropped from 17 per cent to 10 per cent. Modi was leading in all the surveys as well. Modi was now focussing on the eye of the fish like Arjun, which was going to open the way for him in the year 2014. Elections to the Gujarat assembly were to be held in December 2012 and before that such an atmosphere had built in the country that if Modi won for the third time in Gujarat, he would be the Prime Ministerial candidate. He maintained his first position among all the Chief Ministers in this survey as well. Meanwhile, on September 26-28, a national convention of the BJP was held at Surajkund, Faridabad, Haryana, in which the constitutional amendment that would give Gadkari a second term was approved. Now anyone could be the BJP President for two terms of three years each, which was earlier for one term only, i.e. Gadkari's path was clear on part of the organization. But there were allegations of irregularities on his company 'Purti'.

BJP MP Ram Jethmalani opened a front against Gadkari. This concern was visible in the Akhil Bhartiya Executive Board meeting of the Sangh held in Chennai on November 2-4, 2012 as the Sangh was in favour of giving a second term to Gadkari. When Sarkaryavah Bhaiyyaji Joshi was asked a question after that meeting, he clearly said, "How can we say that he (Gadkari) is wrong on the basis of mere allegations? A fair investigation is needed." The Sangh got it investigated informally by its special and professional chartered accountant S Gurumurthy and took the intervention route. India Today in its November 21, 2012 issue writes – 'Gurumurthy met Advani on 6 November and explained to him that there is nothing immoral or legally wrong in Nitin Gadkari's business activities. But instead of understanding his point, Advani demanded Gadkari's resignation before the completion of his term on December 17. The message was sent to Sangh. But Sangh also made it clear that Gadkari would complete his term. Later, Gurumurthy also met Ram Jethmalani, who had written to Advani saying that retaining Gadkari as the president would be a cause of ruin for the country and BJP." But in the meantime, Gadkari met Sushma Swaraj and Arun Jaitley. Sushma told Gadkari, "As long as Sangh is with you, I will be with you." The Sangh appointed a ten-member team to control this fight for ambition in the BJP, which would keep an eye on the activities of the party. Apart from Bhagwat, Bhaiyyaji Joshi, all the four Sah-Sarkaryvah -Suresh Soni, Dattatreya Hosabale, Krishna Gopal and KC Kannan and executive members Madhubhai Kulkarni, prachar pramukh Manmohan Vaidya, sah-prachar pramukh Arun Kumar, member Shrikant Joshi and VHP's Ashok Singhal were included. On the other hand, Modi was fully prepared for the conquest of Gujarat because Delhi could only be claimed with victory in Gujarat.

Modi's Hat-trick and Eye on the Future

Gadkari or a new president for BJP - BJP and Sangh were dealing with this turmoil while in Gujarat Narendra Modi was writing the script for the future. The noise of the Gujarat Assembly election campaign came to an end and the results were declared on 20 December 2012. By achieving a hat-trick of victory in Gujarat, Modi made the opposition including the Sangh aware of his growing influence and importance of this Gujarat election. But for

Modi it was only a short stop as his real battle was 2014. He also said in the Ahmedabad meeting, "The eyes of the voters are on the future." There was a reason for this, too. Modi, who had faced the heat of the Gujarat riots and hatred of a certain intellectual group, presented Gujarat as a model and India as the miserable country plundered by the UPA-Congress-rule during the entire 2012 election campaign. Swapan Dasgupta wrote in an article – 'Modi has emerged as a leader whom you can either love or hate, but you cannot ignore him under any circumstances.' He also wrote- 'Modi is not going to beg to BJP. The pressure coming from below in the party will force BJP to put him forward. Only then will the war for India formally begin." This time instead of Gujarati, Modi gave speech in Hindi and spoke on national issues. Even before this victory, in October, Modi had gone to the RSS headquarters in Nagpur and had had a long conversation with Sangh Chief Mohan Bhagwat which gave an idea of the future. Perhaps even the Sangh realized the growing influence of Modi and the importance of the Gujarat elections. But there was still a state of indecision as the Sangh was unable to take a final call on Gadkari.

When Gadkari left the fort, Rajnath was given the Responsibility of 'Empire'

The Sangh was in a state of indecision, but sticking to an advice is not its policy nor principle. Bhaiyyaji Joshi told me in an interview in January 2013 in an answer to a question as to why Gadkari shouldn't be put to test in view of the allegations, "Sure, he should be. But I think he will try to pass the test. " Then a member of the Akhil Bhartiya Executive Board of the Sangh informally told me, "It has become clear in the discussions within the family that there is no face other than Narendra Modi who has the capacity to lead the party to power in 2014. By bringing in Modi, the alliance also seems to be strengthened and the lost Hindu vote bank can be unified." However, there was confusion about Modi's working style in a section of the Sangh. There has been an atmosphere of cogitation in the relationship between the BJP and Sangh. According to Govindacharya, who had been the think tank of the BJP, Sangh intervenes only when the party cannot think of a way. According to him, Bhagwat's comments about the BJP in 2009 were an example of excessive interference. But the extent to which Bhaiyaji expressed his candid opinion on Gadkari in that interview, he was not clear on Modi's leadership in 2014. He said that the question of leadership of 2014 was still untimely. However, on the Sangh-BJP relationship, he said, "I don't see Sangh interfering in the day-to-day affairs of the party, leaving aside Jinnah episode. But going back to history, why was the BJP formed? The Jana Sangh separated from Janata Party only on the issue of the Sangh. That's why some or the other relationship remains. Discussions are definitely held with the Sangh on theoretic-ideological issues. We meet each other as Swayamsevaks. Advising BJP does not mean ordering."

At last, that day arrived. The election for the post of BJP's national president was to be held on 23 January 2013. Nomination proposals were ready in the name of

Nitin Gadkari. The Advani camp was also adamant and Yashwant Sinha had taken the nomination form for himself. On January 22, the Income Tax Department raided the premises of Gadkari's 'Purti Group' and Advani's stand became stronger. That day he was in Mumbai attending an event with Bhaiyyaji Joshi. Seeing the conspiracies, Gadkari declared that he would stay away from the elections. The Sangh also felt that defending Gadkari now would raise questions about the credibility of the Sangh for the time being. In such a scenario, after much brainstorming, it was decided that the command would be handed over to Rajnath Singh who had been the president during 2005-09. Gadkari's name on the nomination paper was replaced with that of Rajnath Singh by applying whitener. After this election an important round of transition period was completed. That year In January again, in 'India Today: Mood of the Nation', Modi became the choice of 36 per cent of the people as the best Prime Minister, compared to 21 per cent six months ago, which meant that the script for the Modi-era's unveiling was being prepared.

❑

6

CHAPTER

Sangh Policy and Modi 'The Best' among Counterparts

Leaving aside the hesitation of working style, the Sangh also agreed that Modi was the trump card of the BJP. But how did Narendra Damodardas Modi become the leader of the second generation despite Advani's altercation?

"Today, after many days, meeting was planned with Bhagwatji. There was a discussion for three and a half hours on various topics with respected Bhaiyyaji Joshi, respected Sureshji Soni and respected Mohanji Bhagwat. It was very enjoyable. I am also a swayamsevak and this is a place of worship for the Sangh. So, it is natural that there is a heart-to-heart talk." These words spoken by the then Chief Minister Narendra Modi after meeting the top leadership of the Sangh at Reshambagh in Nagpur on October 21, 2012 just before the Gujarat Assembly elections were a sign of the future. That was when the news that Modi's relations with the Sangh were not good was floating in the media market. But Modi himself being a pracharak knew the importance of the organization. When there was a change of leadership in the BJP and Rajnath Singh took over the reins of power in the year 2014 in place of Nitin Gadkari, Narendra Modi in a Twitter message from Gujarat wrote about the benefits of Rajnath Singh's organizational and administrative experiences while congratulating him. On January 27, he visited Rajnath Singh at his official residence and had lunch with him. By hugging Rajnath Singh, Modi gave a message that the party was paramount and that for the year 2014, both of them were going to work as a strong team. Two days before this meeting, workers had raised slogans of 'PM-PM' at a meeting organized in honour of Modi at the BJP headquarters on January 25.

When I interviewed Rajnath Singh two-three days after this meeting, he gave clear indications regarding Modi. Rajnath said, "Modiji met me. We had a good discussion for one and a half or two hours. But he did not present his claim. We are the same age in politics. I have an old relationship with him and we understand each other very well. But I would emphatically say that Modiji is one of our decent workers." During his first term, Rajnath Singh had removed Narendra Modi from the Parliamentary Board who had been included in the as Chief Minister. But now he said that at that time some people had told him that

CM should not be in the Parliamentary Board. But he further said that from what he had understood so far, he thought that he could be and that the possibility of Modi being included could not be ruled out. In a way, he also rejected Gadkari's statement, in which Gadkari had said in December - As party president, I say with full authority that we will not project a Prime Ministerial candidate before the elections. We will announce the name of the Prime Minister at the right time. But Rajnath said that it will be decided by the Parliamentary Board. On the demand to project Modi, he said that Narendra Modi was their most popular leader and that he was very happy that they had a leader like Modi. He also spoke about talking to Nitish Kumar who avoided Modi in NDA, at the right time. This showed that overall, the stage was being set for Modi.

A Changed Modi, Nitish in Trouble and the Sangh is also Strict

Narendra Modi also expressed his desire to be on the national stage when he delivered a message to the youth on February 6, 2013 in an interaction with students at the prestigious Shri Ram College of Commerce (SRCC) in Delhi. He was presenting himself in a different avatar. Before this event, he also got rid of diplomatic untouchability by having a meal with the ambassadors of European countries. But the student interaction at SRCC was historic, which gave strong support and attention to his changed image. Talking about hope and despair, Modi said that Gujarat had the same employees, files and system, but Gujarat was progressing rapidly while there was such atmosphere in the country as if everything was over. He gave a notable example that was appealing to the people. Holding a glass of water which was half filled, he said, "There are different perspectives of looking at the same thing. Those who are optimistic will say that the glass is half full and those who are pessimistic will say that the glass is half empty. But I think differently from these two paths. I would say that this glass is full - half with water and half with air." Showing a ray of hope, Modi indicated towards turning around the situation. Modi said that the challenge was that how the 65 percent youth who were below 35 years utilized that opportunity. Presenting Gujarat's model of development, Modi said that their focus was on one-third agriculture, one-third industry, one-third service sector. During this student interaction, Modi gave them the mantra of his personality, philosophy, development model, modernity, minimum government-maximum governance, internal security, global agenda, education, skill, scale, speed, i.e. Modi put forth the agenda of his possible future government. On the other hand, Sant Samaj led by Vishwa Hindu Parishad started demanding to make Modi the Prime Ministerial candidate at Allahabad Kumbh in February 2013. In this Kumbh, the demand for construction of Ram temple again started gaining momentum. On the day when Modi was presenting the agenda of development while interacting with the students in Delhi University, at Allahabad Kumbh, party president Rajnath Singh was taking a dip of Hindutva. That is, the Sangh-BJP did not intend to leave out any strategic aspect. On January 31, in a meeting of the leaders of the Sangh-BJP-VHP at the house of BJP leader Shripad Yeso Naik in Delhi, it was decided that the BJP would move on the agenda of development and VHP should organize an agitation for temple.

But Modi's growing influence and changed style put Bihar Chief Minister Nitish Kumar in the most difficult situation. He also opened a political front and organized 'Adhikar Rally' on March 17, 2013 at Ramlila Maidan in Delhi to demand special status for Bihar. Through that, Kumar gave a message to both BJP and Congress that everything was fair in politics, i.e. Nitish was not in favour of BJP making Modi its Prime Ministerial candidate. But the Sangh did not find such threats justified. In the words of Sangh's Sarkaryavah Bhaiyyaji Joshi, "I think that BJP will decide on the merits of the situation in this context. But NDA is needed by everyone and everyone has to consider it. One person cannot decide." That means Sangh had also started believing that this time they would not relent whether Nitish Kumar or other allies remained in the NDA or not.

At the end of March, the new team of Rajnath Singh was also announced. On March 31, Rajnath tried to get Advani's consent on this team, but it had already got Modi's approval. Modi had already become a part of the Parliamentary Board, the highest policy-making body of the BJP, as Chief Minister. But Advani was also in favour of bringing in then Madhya Pradesh Chief Minister Shivraj Singh Chouhan so that he could play his cards. He also objected to the names of some general secretaries. But consent was also taken from the Sangh regarding the team. The most important appointment of all was that of Amit Shah as the national general secretary, whom Modi had brought under 'Mission Uttar Pradesh'. He was also again made in-charge of UP. Muralidhar Rao, a former leader of the 'Swadeshi Jagran Manch', considered to be Sangh's favourite, also became the General Secretary. Varun Gandhi was made general secretary, Uma Bharti and Smriti Irani were appointed vice-president. In this team of Rajnath's, there was a combination of Sangh and Modi, which also marked the beginning of the best coordination. Modi was becoming influential with his ability and the indirect support of the Sangh and his impression was clearly visible on the entire team. Meanwhile, on May 8, 2013, the BJP suffered a setback, when it lost power in Karnataka. The separation of BS Yeddyurappa from the BJP in the assembly elections might not have brought much benefit to Yeddyurappa, but it did harm the BJP. Advani had dismissed Yeddyurappa from the party. Therefore, as per the strategy for the year 2014, preparations to bring back Yeddyurappa started and Yeddyurappa also had no other option.

The popularity of Narendra Modi was increasing continuously and all the surveys tilted in favour of Modi. The Sangh also realized that Modi was BJP's trump card for forming government at the Centre. But till now BJP was not able to give any clear direction because a leader like Advani was not ready to surrender and he also played his trump card. Advani was addressing the concluding session of the state executive meeting in Gwalior, Madhya Pradesh on June 1, 2013. He first described Chief Minister Shivraj Singh Chouhan as a humble person like Atal Bihari Vajpayee and then said, "I tell Narendra Bhai that Gujarat was healthy before and you have made it excellent. But Shivraj not only made BIMARU Madhya Pradesh healthy, but he has also turned it around so much that you would want to rate it number one not only in India but also in the world. I have the figures and if these are distributed then people will wonder about the achievements made in the state after the arrival of Shivraj! It is like a miracle happens." Advani's announcement came at a time when Modi's Gujarat model against the Manmohan Singh government was the subject of research for anti-Modi people. So, the opponents got a chance because at that time no one in the party targeted Modi even indirectly. But when the patriarch of the party spoke like this, it was natural for the anti-Modi opponents to make the most of it. But now the time had come that the condition and direction of the BJP should go with clarity instead of indications. And finally, that time had come.

When Modi became the Chairman of the Election Campaign Committee

At that time, three theories were being put forth in the BJP's internal circles - first, this time the Prime Ministerial candidate would be decided from the grassroots level and only the parliamentary board of the party including the Sangh Parivar would give approval for it. Second, the election campaign would be completely on the lines of the election of the US President. Third and most important, the real race for the post of Prime Minister would start after reaching the Golden Line and who would reach the finishing line would be decided at that time. Two of the theories were put forth by Modi's well-wishers while the third theory was put forth by the faction that would block Modi's path. In BJP, Arun Jaitley was involved in the advocacy of Modi with a tight strategy, while some writers like journalist Swapan Dasgupta started saying in their articles that Modi had become bigger than the Sangh and BJP and he was moving far beyond the Atal Bihari Vajpayee situation of 1996 and with an organized force. Finally, on June 9, 2013, in a very dramatic manner, during the Goa National Executive meeting, Narendra Modi was handed over the command of the campaign committee for the 2014 Lok Sabha election campaign. But its announcement was not easy. The national president Rajnath Singh also had to operate the chariot like a clever charioteer of Modi.

On the midnight of 8-9 June, there was a tremendous churning going on at the Marriott Hotel in Goa as to how the announcement about Modi should be done. Sangh was preparing the full script. Then Saha-Sarkaryavah Suresh Soni, who was looking after the coordination in the BJP on behalf of the Sangh, stayed in the hotel in Goa till all the meetings were over. Rajnath Singh constantly met with different leaders regarding this matter. But knowing that Modi was to be given the command of the election campaign in Goa, Advani had boycotted the Goa Executive. Sangh also did not want to leave any stone unturned in pacifying

Advani so that later there would be no charge of imposing the decision. When Advani did not reach the executive meeting on the first day, the next day on the morning of June 8, Sangh Sah-sarkaryawah Dattatreya Hosabale and Suresh Soni went to his official residence in Delhi and told him that the decision had been taken to make Modi the chairman of the election committee and that he too should now accept that and give his blessings. But hurt Advani took a tough decision and made up his mind to stay away from the executive. On the same day, he also expressed his anguish through a blog- 'Bhishma Pitamah is lying on his bed with arrows and preaching to the Pandavas...' However, it was formally stated that he was ill and therefore, he did not go to Goa.

On the other hand, till around 3.30 at night on June 8-9, there was tension in the hotel in Goa as the party was completely divided into groups with two thoughts. Soni was often seen strolling in tension. The Advani camp wanted that the decision to hand over the responsibility to Narendra Modi should be taken only in the presence of Advani after reaching Delhi. But the leaders in favour of Modi did not want any delay. Suresh Soni who was strict in the matter of organizational discipline was keeping a constant watch on the whole activity. After racking the brain whole night, he took the top leadership of the Sangh into confidence in the early hours of the morning and then even before breakfast on the morning of June 9, he told Rajnath Singh to go ahead and make the announcement. Rajnath Singh did not delay and it was announced that the party would contest the Lok Sabha elections under the leadership of Narendra Modi.

But it is necessary to mention an incident here that when BJP won the municipal elections in Delhi in May-June 2012, Venkaiah Naidu was in charge of Delhi BJP. When I interviewed him at his residence on the evening of June 26, 2012, at the end of the informal discussion he had said that the country's politics had become personality-oriented and the party must project a face for the year 2014. But on the fight regarding ambition in the second generation, Naidu had said that everyone had a different personality. But Narendra Modi was the most suitable face. But would everyone agree? Venkaiah had said, "It is all about making a decision. Once the decision is taken, everyone will agree and it will be done easily." His first point was right. But the point about it being easy turned out to be wrong because at that time BJP was going through a phase when every leader who had ambition wanted to be Atal Bihari Vajpayee. No one was ready to be a charioteer like Advani. Though Vajpayee was resting and was away from politics Advani was in the field. So, how could someone else become 'Advani'! Modi received the legacy of Atal, but with this announcement, a new short-lived Mahabharata also started in the party, which ultimately went in favour of Modi.

Advani's Resignation and Sangh's First Direct Public Intervention

When Advani's boycott didn't work and Modi got the reins despite his reluctance, Advani finally resigned from all important posts in the party–the National Working Committee, the Parliamentary Board and the Election Committee. Earlier, Modi had tweeted saying that he had spoken to Advaniji and he had given his blessings. But the very next day, Advani's letter to Rajnath Singh became public, in which he wrote - 'Given the direction in which the party has been going for some time, I am finding it difficult to adjust with the current working style of the party. Now I do not think that this is the same idealistic party that was formed by Dr. Shyama Prasad Mookerjee, Pt. Deendayalji, Nanaji and Vajpayeeji, the main objective of which was the country and its people. Now the main objective of our leaders is their own personal agenda. I have decided to resign from the National Executive, Parliamentary Board and Election Committee of the party. This letter of mine should be treated as resignation.' In response, Modi tweeted that he had spoken to Advaniji and requested him to reconsider the decision. Rajnath Singh spoke about rejecting the resignation and asking Ram Madhav and Sushma Swaraj to convince him. But Advani's heart did not melt for dear disciple Modi despite the leaders' pleas.

Advani did not agree. Finally, on the evening of June 10, Rajnath Singh called an emergency meeting of the Parliamentary Board, in which apart from Narendra Modi, Murli Manohar Joshi and Thaawarchand Gehlot, the other six members were present. Rajnath put forward the board's proposal after talking to the three members who were not in Delhi. He said that Advani was a respected leader, a guide and his resignation would not be accepted under any circumstances. With this proposal, Rajnath and other leaders met Advani again. But Advani flatly refused to withdraw his resignation. The Sangh was extremely upset with the entire episode and called it an unfortunate move. The next day, i.e. on 11th June, the efforts to resolve this situation continued throughout the day. Rajnath Singh was to go to Banswara, Rajasthan in the morning for the unveiling of the statue of Maharana Pratap. So, he talked to Modi. Then on June 11, when the sun was setting in the midst of marathon meetings and sweltering heat, the BJP was inching closer to a formula to pacify its patriarch, LK Advani, who had reached the slope of politics. In the presence of the media, BJP President Rajnath Singh read out a written statement of three paragraphs at Advani's house at exactly 6.07 pm. First para-"Shri LK Advaniji had resigned from three important posts of the party-National Working Committee, Parliamentary Board and Election Committee, which was rejected by the Parliamentary Board of BJP in yesterday's meeting and Advaniji was urged to remain on all these posts." Second para- "The National President of the party, Shri Rajnath Singh assured to consider all the implementation-related concerns of the party raised by Shri Advaniji and the National President will discuss the process with Advaniji." But the third paragraph of this statement was not only the most important, it was also going to be historic- "This afternoon the Sarsanghchalak of the Rashtriya Swayamsevak Sangh, Shri Mohan Bhagwatji had discussion with Shri Advaniji and he urged to him to accept the decision of the Parliamentary Board of the Bharatiya Janata Party and continue guiding the party in the interest of the nation. Shri Advaniji has decided to follow this advice of Shri Bhagwatji." It was not just a 'Bhagwat medicine' to stop the earthquake. That was the first time in the history of the Sangh Parivar that its interference in the BJP (which the Sangh had publicly denied) had been engraved on paper for the first time. Now it did not remain just a document, but Bhagwat had become an important link between Advani and the party in every important decision of the BJP.

Nitish Breaks Ties, NDA's Litmus Test

As soon as Modi got the command, Advani gave the first blow and the second big blow was given by Bihar Chief Minister Nitish Kumar. On June 16, 2013, Nitish severed his alliance with the BJP to show that he could not compromise on principles. Instead of giving time to resign, he dismissed all the eleven Ministers from the BJP quota and also fixed June 19 as the date for proving the majority. Then in the 243-member assembly, JDU had 118 MLAs and BJP had 91 MLAs. Nitish needed only 4 MLAs, whom he easily found. Sharad Yadav, who was a JDU leader, also tendered his resignation from the post of NDA convener. The NDA was shrunk and only Shiv Sena and Akali Dal were left along the BJP. The Sangh and BJP were aware of Nitish Kumar's thought process. So, by giving command of the election campaign committee to Modi, the party's strategy was to settle some of the remaining infighting. It was also NDA's litmus test because it was necessary to guess how the sentiments of other parties about Modi would take shape.

After this, the Sangh Parivar moved towards issues. But to maintain peace in the BJP, RSS Sarsanghchalak Mohan Bhagwat invited LK Advani to the Nagpur headquarters on July 5 and after talking to him assured him of respect. The Sangh was aware that even if Advani could not stop Modi's path, his displeasure could harm the game. In such a situation, the Sangh was working on the strategy of taking everyone along. Then, ten days later, on July 16, Modi had a meeting with Bhagwat, in which all these issues must have naturally been discussed as no formal information ever came out. Modi reached Nagpur via Jagannathpuri in Odisha and had a conversation with Bhagwat for about two and a half hours. But in order to increase the scope of the alliance, regional parties were identified state-wise in terms of political advantages and disadvantages. Modi was moving ahead with the agenda of development, while on the other hand BJP and Sangh had made up their mind to try Hindutva this time while taking forward the battle of ideology, that is, Hindutva was present along with development in the dual strategy of ideological battle.

Kedarnath Disaster Amidst Political Stir

The disaster that struck Kedarnath in Uttarakhand on June 16 shook the entire country. There was such a scene of devastation that the soul trembled. Thousands of people, houses, businesses, cattle—all were washed away in this natural calamity. Narendra Modi, as the Chief Minister of Gujarat, showed courage and took the initiative to rescue people trapped in the disaster. However, a lot of questions were also raised on the news of the rescue of 15 thousand people. But apart from this controversy, Modi wanted to visit the areas affected by the disaster in Kedarnath, which was not allowed by the Congress government at that time. Modi was the first person who proposed the reconstruction of the Kedarnath temple to the then Congress government so that the experience of reconstruction after the earthquake in Bhuj, Gujarat could be used to rehabilitate the devastated areas of Uttarakhand. This was rejected by the Bahuguna government. Actually, Modi has a different kind of faith towards Kedarnath Dham. He spent some important days of his life in this area. That is why even after becoming the Prime Minister, he visited Kedarnath Dham many times and even after campaigning for the last phase of the 2019 Lok Sabha elections was over, he visited Kedarnath Dham and got rid of fatigue through meditation in a cave.

Exactly a year after the disaster, i.e. on the night of 15-16 June, I was also in Kedarnath. Due to bad weather, the helicopter could not come back to take me back. So, the night was spent in a tent made by the government. Food was arranged in the camp because even at that time the reconstruction work was going on. Even after a year, the soul trembled at the sight of the devastation. On the basis of that experience, I can say that the devastation of Kedarnath could be gauged only by going there because the devastation was more frightening than it could be imagined. After the disaster, efforts of rescue relief and reconstruction where taken by different states.

In his Hyderabad rally, Modi gave an idea of keeping a 5-rupee ticket to help in this disaster. When a rally was to be held there on August 11, Modi gave this formula to support Uttarakhand. Then Congress leader and Information and Broadcasting Minister Manish Tewari had mocked Modi saying, "Rs 100 to 1,00,000 tickets for Baba's discourse! Despite being a flop at the box office, Rs 200-500 for a cinema ticket and Rs 5 for listening to a Chief Minister! The market has given the real price." Modi's strength and Congress's weakness were paving the way for the BJP. While Modi was connecting people on the issue related to sympathies, Congress was trying to describe Modi as a leader worth 5 rupees. But regardless of that, Modi was marching ahead as per the strategy.

84 Kosi Parikrama of Hinduism

When Singhal called Modi Lord Ram

On one hand, Modi talked about the reconstruction of Kedarnath Dham, while on the other, VHP was raising the slogan of the construction of Ram temple. The issue of Ram temple had arisen from the Allahabad Kumbh in February, when the saints passed a resolution and talked about the construction of the temple through law. Till then Modi was not formally handling the election command of BJP. In this Kumbh, a strategy of 84 kosi parikrama had been made from 25 August to 13 September to assert Hindutva. The Vishwa Hindu Parishad (VHP) was playing a smooth game. About two months before the date of this parikrama, Modi's Chief warlord Amit Shah, who was in-charge of Uttar Pradesh, had visited Ayodhya where he had also said that the temple should be built. But then he got involved in the election work and the rest was taken over by the VHP. But from a strategic point of view, Modi was completely silent on this issue. At the same time, the then SP government of the state was intent on stopping this 84 kosi parikrama and it was banned even before the 25 August journey. The VHP's strategy seemed to be successful whether parikrama took place or it was stopped by the government because it was going to have an effect on the public psyche. A detailed conversation on this whole issue with Ashok Singhal, the patron of Vishwa Hindu Parishad who was the leader of the movement while I was with 'India Today', which was very interesting and indicated the strategy of the Sangh and BJP.

What was the purpose of organizing it in an environment of election? Singhal said, "The decision of 84 Kosi Parikrama was taken on the occasion of Kumbh in the month of February itself. It was discussed in it that the construction of Ram temple will be done only through Parliament. It is no longer a matter of court. Ram Lalla had also said, "My child, the law will be made and everyone will support it." But it was alleged that VHP is aggressive in pushing BJP and Modi forward in the 2014 elections. Singhal said, "It is a programme of saints. Rambhakts want such a government which can also build Ram Janmabhoomi temple. If Ram Bhakts believe that BJP will give us benefits then who can stop Ram Bhakts!" His answer to the third question was filled with tremendous confidence. "Do you expect that if the government is formed under the leadership of Modi, he will bring a resolution in the Parliament?" The answer was, "Why not! I believe that when the Lord Himself has entered him as the power of Lord Rama, let's see what will he get him to do." Singhal had also prepared for the non-permission of the yatra, "200 saints will join it every day and 250 teams have been made for that." Singhal had said, "The authorities might stop the yatra in Ayodhya, but the yatra is enclosed in its five districts. Where all will they stop it? Every day 200 saints will come. Stopping the saints will not end the pilgrimage."

Meanwhile, an incident of molestation took place in Kawal village of Muzaffar Nagar in Uttar Pradesh, which was purely a law-and-order issue. Within a week, the issue took the form of a communal riot. When this riot caused displacement on a large scale, then the matter of Hindu-Muslim unity became a victim of politics. When the then SP government worked on the strategy of capitalizing it to its political advantage, then in response the right-wing ideology also retaliated, which had a natural effect on the sections of the society.

Sangh's Eye on Youth

The Sangh had given its indirect support to the Anna movement. 'Youth Against Corruption' was playing an important role in the atmosphere being created against the UPA government. In such a situation, the Sangh under a strategy created a movement of youth across the country. The responsibility of keeping ABVP, an ideological organization active among the students and Sangh-BJP together in this campaign and sharpening the movement, was entrusted to Sunil Bansal who was Sah-Sangathan mantri of ABVP.Bansal, who worked by creating a network among youth and students, carried out the strategy of jam, dharnas and demonstration across the country simultaneously. Cartoons/pamphlets/leaflets were distributed in schools and colleges. In this, all the issues were listed against the UPA government, due to which the youth was disappointed in the Manmohan Singh government and there was new hope in the form of Narendra Modi. It was a massive campaign, which was carried out in a phased manner by the Sangh Parivar. That's why Sunil Bansal was made the national convener of this campaign.

Certainly, Narendra Modi, with his diligence, put forward patient strategies in such a way that he emerged as the 'best' leader among his peers and completely dominated the BJP by garnering the affection of the Sangh. But he was still a step away in the party because not only a section of the party but also a section of the media was unable to digest the rise of Modi. So, some theories kept going around, ranging from BJP not getting majority to the discussions on a possible alliance, in which predictions were also being made that Advani's role would be important. But Modi and his team were busy making a dream come true, away from these intellectual and journalistic interpretations. Modi, as the head of the election campaign, was constantly roaring against the Manmohan Singh government in the election public meetings. In every rally or meeting, he used the terminology to connect with the public. Each initiative was being carried out according to the strategy, the natural effect of which was visible. Eventually, the moment came when Modi's popularity had grown to such a degree that the Vichar Pariwar made up its mind to remove the dark clouds of doubt regarding the leadership issue which Modi's opponents in the party as well as in the media were apprehensive about because a third defeat after two consecutive defeats in Lok Sabha elections could hurt the ideology. Therefore, the decision was taken to end whatever little strategic hesitation about Modi.

❑

7

CHAPTER

Full Fledged Modi Era

Amidst all the turmoil, how did Modi become the main hero of the 2014 Mahabharata even before the semi-finals, and the Sangh Parivar worked in a co-ordinated manner to increase the vote share by 10 percent!

Before the final, the hustle and bustle of the election semi-finals had intensified. Election boards were in full swing being laid in Delhi, Rajasthan, Madhya Pradesh, Chhattisgarh. In the states where the party had Chief Ministers or where there were none, person who was the face was out travelling. Narendra Modi was also holding rallies. Modi had a rally in Ambikapur, Chhattisgarh on September 7, 2013. The entire stage was prepared as if it was a real Red Fort. The Congress had started making fun of the design of the stage. BJP President Rajnath Singh was also present on this stage. While Modi was roaring against the then Prime Minister Manmohan

Singh from that fake 'Red Fort', the script was being written to take him to the real Red Fort at the Rashtriya Swayamsevak Sangh headquarters in Jhandewalan, Delhi. On the stage, Modi received a message, 'Do not go to Ahmedabad, come to Delhi first.' After every day's meeting, Modi used to go to Ahmedabad and leave from there in the morning.

There was a sudden change in the schedule after the message from Delhi. The then Chief Minister Raman Singh carried out the arrangement according to this message. Modi and Rajnath flew to Raipur from Ambikapur by helicopter and then flew to Delhi from Swami Vivekananda airport in Raipur in a special plane at exactly 5.25 pm. On reaching Delhi, both of them went to Jhandewalan directly, where they met Sarkaryavah Bhaiyyaji Joshi and other office bearers of the Sangh. Simultaneously, it was decided that now there would be no hesitation as the issue of development was being left behind by confusion over leadership. So, BJP will march towards Mission-2014 under the leadership of Modi only. Meanwhile, RSS's Akhil Bharatiya Prachar pramukh Manmohan Vaidya's also issued a statement, "We have informed the BJP about the sentiment of the Sangh and the demand of the people. Now party has to decide." The BJP was advised as per the Sangh's policy. The next day on September 8-9, the coordination meeting was a mere formality, with no need for discussing Modi's candidature as the decision had already been taken.

Modi's 'Party Victory', Advani Furious Again

But in the coordination meeting, informal discussions were held in small groups about how the Sangh and BJP leaders should work on the future strategy. In view of the bitter experience of June, the Sangh also suggested to Rajnath Singh that this time the message of isolating LK Advani should not go like in Goa. As a part of this strategy, all the exercises were done to take Advani into confidence. After the coordination meeting, top leaders of the Sangh and the party, including Sarsanghchalak Mohan Bhagwat, met Advani separately. But hopelessness prevailed. Seeing Advani's persistence and the intention of registering a formal protest at the Parliamentary Board meeting, Rajnath Singh had once made up his mind to declare Modi as the Prime Ministerial candidate without a meeting of the Parliamentary Board. But he was instructed not to do so by the Sangh because doing so would send a message of division of the BJP which was not good for the future.

Like Goa, this time too Advani did not participate in the announcement of Modi's name. But this decision was not as smooth as in Goa. The round of meetings had started from the morning of 13 September. Ananth Kumar met Sushma Swaraj, and Nitin Gadkari and Murli Manohar Joshi went to meet Advani. In the afternoon again Gadkari, Sushma, Ananth Kumar visited Advani's house and met him. Rajnath Singh also went and pleaded with him. The media persons, including me, continued shuffling between 30 Prithviraj Road and 11 Ashok Road. Meanwhile, Advani's convoy was also ready to go to the

BJP headquarters for the meeting. But after reaching the gate, Advani suddenly stopped and went inside the house on foot. But before leaving, he told the security personnel that he was not going to the meeting. After this, Advani wrote a letter to Rajnath Singh - 'Dear Rajnath Singhji, this afternoon when you came to inform me about today's Parliamentary Tribunal (Board) meeting, I expressed anguish in my heart and said something about despair regarding your working style. I had asked you at that time whether I should come to the meeting and speak to all the members or not? Now I have decided that it would be appropriate not to attend the meeting.'

By 5 pm, Narendra Modi had also reached Delhi. At 6 pm, Rajnath Singh announced that BJP will now march towards victory under the leadership of Modi and that parliamentary board had decided to make him the Prime Ministerial candidate.

As soon as the formalities were completed, there was a wave of enthusiasm not only from Delhi to Gujarat but among all BJP workers across the country. NDA constituent Shiv Sena's Uddhav Thackeray described the decision as being in line with expectations and like Amrit after the churning of sea. Akali Dal's Parkash Singh Badal had already extended support to Modi. After this responsibility, Modi reached Advani's house directly and touched his feet and Advani also embraced him. Regarding the responsibility, Modi said, "The BJP leadership has entrusted a huge responsibility to a small-town worker like me who comes from a normal family.

I am grateful to the leadership. I pledge to work hard to ensure BJP's victory in the 2014 elections."

Just before his birthday on September 17, Modi was given such a 'birthday gift' by his own Vichar Parivar that was not going to be limited to just winning power as the Sangh Parivar had had a bitter experience of power. In such a situation, it was indicated that the coordination of the Sangh Parivar with Modi was going to be amazing in the times to come. Sarkaryavah Bhaiyyaji Joshi had already given an example of the relationship between the Sangh and the BJP, which is mentioned in the previous chapter. In fact, this time Advani wanted that the Prime Ministerial candidate should not be announced till the election results of Madhya Pradesh, Rajasthan, Chhattisgarh and Delhi because instead of inflation and corruption, Modi's controversial image would become an issue for the opposition causing damage to the party. But the Sangh Parivar was aware of the ground realities and also of Advani's future strategy. Therefore, considering all the aspects and the Muhurta, the Sangh declared a decisive ideological battle by advising to make Modi Prime Ministerial candidate before the Shraddh Paksha. Narendra Modi had finally conquered the Delhi headquarters of the BJP and the patriarch of the party had moved to *Kop Bhavan*. The only hope left for the opponents was that if the party did not win in the assembly elections, Modi could be cornered again. But perhaps it was a mistake of the Advani camp.

If Advani had shown a big heart like the year 2009, the party would have run under his shadow like a banyan tree. It is worth noting here that two days before the 2009 election results, Narendra Modi was camping in Delhi. He was not only Advani's core team but also his favourite Chief Minister. At that time, Prem Kumar Dhumal was the Chief Minister Himachal Pradesh and he was also present in Delhi. He had said one thing then, which I also quoted in my daily column 'India Gate Se' of the daily 'Navjyoti' newspaper. Dhumal had said, "Advani himself will put forward the name of Modi as PM candidate in the year 2014." Had Advani proven what Dhumal had said five years ago true, then perhaps this stalwart of politics would not have had to leave the land which he himself had nurtured.

Sangh's 'Vijaya' Dashami Message

In his new role, Narendra Modi started holding public meetings according to the new strategy. To change his image, Modi gave indications of a syncretic and all-inclusive image by inducting some Muslims into the party on his birthday on September 17. We will talk about it later. But in this Mahayagya the Sangh was ready to sacrifice fully. When Modi became the 'PM in waiting' on September 13, the Sangh called for 'confirming' this 'waiting' in its 'Vijayadashmi address', which coincidentally was exactly a month later on October 13. Sarsanghchalak Mohan Bhagwat called for the 'Victory' of the year 2014 from the grounds of the huge Smriti Bhavan of Reshambagh, Nagpur like this, "There should be hundred percent voting." The traditional address, which was going on among about 5,000 volunteers, was being heard and watched live across the country. With a sense of resolve, Bhagwat also elaborated on the misrule of the Congress-led UPA government. He listed all the issues like growth rate, decline in the value of rupee, dependence on imports, excessive foreign direct investment, China policy, internal security lapses, women's insecurity, anti-communal violence bill and said, "Now the time has come to change this government." The Sangh's call was a direct call for ideological victory under Modi's leadership. But the need was to broaden the social base with Brand Modi. Certainly, the Sangh was a major contributor to the big victory of the party. But Narendra Modi's own projection as Brand Modi was also important. But after this victory, Modi's challenge now was to make party victorious in the assembly elections as well as increase the scope of NDA in future and connect allies in states like Uttar Pradesh, Bihar, South India. In Uttar Pradesh, Modi's favourite Amit Shah was working hard; he had often been called 'Modi's Hanuman'. He had already formed the network in this state when he had been forced to stay out of Gujarat due to a legal battle.

This is How Work was done on the Plan of Additional Target of 10 percent

Although Sangh was advising the BJP, its basic work was to promote social interests in the areas of forest dwellers' welfare, education, service, medicine etc. so that the nation remained paramount. Through this work, the Sangh was giving a base to the BJP, which was going to give birth to new possibilities in the social, intellectual and spiritual fields. The Vichar Pariwar was in no mood to leave out any page of warfare in preparation for the 2014 battle. On the basis of a comprehensive analysis, the Sangh-BJP realized that despite the full force applied by the party and the ideology family, the vote share of the BJP had gone up to only 18-25 percent. If we look at it from the beginning when the BJP was born out of the Janata Party, then in the first election, i.e. in the year 1984, the party had won only 2 seats with 7.4 percent votes whereas in 1989 it won 85 seats with 11.4 percent votes. But when the 1991 elections were held in the midst of the Ram Mandir agitation, the party won 120 seats with 20.1% votes. Then five years later, in 1996, the BJP emerged as the single largest party with 20.3% of the vote, when it secured 161 seats. Being the largest party, the President had invited Atal Bihari Vajpayee to form the government, accepting which Vajpayee took oath as the Prime Minister. It was a historic moment even though the government fell after 13 days as the party could not collect the majority figures. But public sympathy for Vajpayee increased. In such a situation, the United Front government fell untimely, and in 1998, the Lok Sabha elections were held again. But the seats and votes won by the BJP that time were the pinnacle of its politics so far. In this general election, BJP won the highest number of seats i.e. 182 seats with highest i.e. 25.6 percent votes. Vajpayee ran the government by forming an NDA. But the government collapsed in 1999 due to a vote because of Jayalalithaa's withdrawal of support. Mid-term elections were held in the country again and this time under the leadership of Vajpayee, the BJP returned with 182 seats. But the vote share did not increase. This time it got 23.8% of the votes. After this, in the year 2004, the BJP lost the election, but it got 22.2 percent of the vote and 138 seats. In 2009, even when Advani was in command, the party got 18.8 per cent votes with 116 seats. That is, despite the full strength of the ideology family, the BJP was able to go up to 25 percent of the vote and even in the worst case it remained up to 18 percent. That is, the vote share of the BJP on an average was close to 20-22 per cent; by adding an additional 10 per cent to it, the party was planning to win the power.

The arithmetic of the BJP's electoral political journey from its birth till that time formed the basis of its strategy for the year 2014. In such a situation, both the Sangh and the BJP had to expand beyond their original scope, for which programmes were carried forward as part of the strategy. Narendra Modi's first rally took place in Haryana's Rewari on the third day after he was declared the Prime Ministerial candidate. The presence of former Army Chief General VK Singh on this platform was important from the point of view of political signal. At that time there was a tremendous movement of ex-servicemen in the country for the demand of 'One Rank One Pension'. Since the year 2009, drastic steps like return of medals were being taken by going on a gradual hunger strike and by that time more than 30 thousand medals had been returned to the President. One and a half lakh former soldiers had tried unsuccessfully to hand over the signatures done in blood to the President. The reason for this fight of the army was the policy of the government under which the soldiers are retired at a young age to keep the army young. About 85 percent of soldiers retire at the age of 38 years, 10 per cent at 46 years and only 5 per cent at the age of 56 to 58 years, whereas in civil the retirement age is fixed at 60 years. Lt Gen (Rita) Raj Kadyan, who was then commanding the army movement, told me, "A soldier of the army usually retires at an age when he has more responsibility. The government should also keep us in the job for 60 years, we will not ask for 'One Rank One Pension." Kadyan had declared, "Before the next general election, the government will have to give the rights of soldiers. Our struggle will continue till we get our rights under the ambit of law and military discipline." Then the government was not rejecting it, but was not accepting it either as it was being argued that it would burden the exchequer. Its discrepancies started after the Third Pay Commission and were further aggravated by the Sixth Pay Commission. The number of retiring soldiers then was about 65 thousand annually and according to estimates, there were 23 lakh ex-servicemen and 3 lakh ex-servicemen widows in the country, which was a part of the ongoing battle part of the three decades of the 'Indian Ex-Servicemen Movement' to remove the pension discrepancies.

So, when the Sangh-BJP saw the scope to increase their base here, they took General VK Singh on their side whereas a few months ago, when Anna Hazare announced Arvind Kejriwal's new political party while ending his fast at Jantar Mantar, the General was sitting on that platform. But this time he was on stage with Modi, where a group of retired commissioned officers were also present. Along with them, shooter Rajyavardhan Singh Rathore, who had won a silver medal in the Olympics for India was also present with Modi on stage. So, on September 15, 2013, the rally in Rewari was in honour of the ex-servicemen. "If Atal Bihari Vajpayee had become the Prime Minister again in 2004, the issue of 'One Rank One Pension' of the Army would have been resolved," Modi told the forum.

Modi's roar at the ex-servicemen's rally had a clear message that he stood with the soldiers and their families who gave their all for the security of the country. Meanwhile, Modi's rallies continued to take place in different parts of the country. A security-related issue came up during the October 27 rally in Patna, when several bomb blasts took place at Gandhi Maidan. BJP attacked Nitish government. In the same rally, Modi said, "I have sold tea in the train. I know how difficult it is to make a living." In this rally, a message was sent out by taking out the asthi-kalash yatra of the victims of the bomb blasts and Narendra Modi later met the families of all of them. The Patna rally proved significant in two ways - the crowd remained calm despite the bombings and the 'Chaiwala' slogan, which became an unbreakable bond between the poor and Modi. Every address of Modi used to be on the path of soft Hindutva, of which nationalism was bound to be part. But his entire focus was to corner the Manmohan Singh government on the issues of inflation, development, corruption, and as an alternative, to give a message of adopting the development model of Gujarat across the country.

Swami Ramdev had also jumped in the fray for Modi. At that time, the assembly elections were going on and Ramdev declared that he would not return to Patanjali Peeth until the Nehru dynasty was completely destroyed and the Congress was ousted from power. Ramdev called Narendra Modi as Lord Ram and himself Vishwamitra. He gave impetus to his campaign through 'Bharat Swabhiman Trust'. By including this yoga guru with a spiritual hold, the Sangh Parivar closed the rift in Hindutva vote. It also contacted former IPS officer Kiran Bedi who was with Kejriwal in the Anna movement. She was sympathetic to the party and joined during the mid-term elections to the Delhi Assembly in January 2015.

At its level, Sangh took all the possible rebel leaders like Yashwant Sinha, Arun Shourie etc. The family realized that even if these people did not have the power of votes as such, they could create such an adverse environment through media rhetoric that the opposition would try to create problems in the path of the 2014 battle. After this, the era of alliance started, a message had already been given to the soldiers guarding the borders of the country, VHP was working for a hold in the spiritual field so that it could influence voters with its impact through religious places. Initiatives were also being taken for access to the intellectual world. The lateral entry of MJ Akbar was part of the strategy; he was the country's renowned journalist and Congress MP in the year 1989-91.

The Sangh and BJP needed to move beyond their current base, which was stuck around 18 to 25 percent, for electoral victory. It was achieved with these strategies. In 2014, the party secured 31.3% of the vote with 282 seats. It was after 30 years that any party got majority at the centre on its own. In order to achieve this goal at its level, the Sangh did many programmes of discussion with the journalists. In the election strategy from tickets to nomination filing also, symbols were used to target a specific group of voters. For example, I will mention a case here. When Anurag Thakur filed his nomination for the Lok Sabha elections from Hamirpur in Himachal Pradesh, the central leadership sent General VK Singh, the former Chief of the Army Staff because there is a large number of soldiers posted in the army from Himachal and ex-servicemen, while VK Singh himself was a candidate from Ghaziabad in Uttar Pradesh. Rally in Rewari, Hunkar rally in Patna, Gelisi rally in Bangalore, Bharat Vijay rally in Amethi, Fatah rally in Jagraon, Bharat Vijay rally in Varanasi, Chennai rally, Mahajagaran rally in Assam, Mahagarjana rally in Mumbai, Vikas rally in Delhi—each rally was planned with a specific thought and a whole team was involved in completing it with commitment, that is, each strategy and symbolic places and words were being selected according to the strategy.

The Victory of the Semi-finals... the Parties Started Joining... the Wave Named Modi

The BJP registered big victories in the assembly elections of four states considered to be semi-finals - Madhya

Pradesh, Rajasthan, Delhi and Chhattisgarh. Although Arvind Kejriwal's new Aam Aadmi Party did not allow the BJP to win power in Delhi, it did emerge as the single largest party. In the rest of Madhya Pradesh and Chhattisgarh, the BJP made a comeback whereas it snatched Rajasthan from the hands of the Congress. The acceptance of Modi was now stamped upon by the public as a section in the party was waiting for this result. But the results spoiled the plans of the opponents. At the same time, a section of the media and politics was still not able to digest the growing stature of Modi. So, many theories were being given. Meanwhile, in January 2014, the results of 'India Today: Mood of the Nation' came out, in which it was clear that under Modi's leadership, the BJP was heading towards a historic victory and the Congress towards a historic defeat. The number of people who wanted to see Modi as the Prime Minister had now reached 47 per cent, while Rahul Gandhi was far behind with a choice of 15 per cent. Meanwhile, Modi's stormy tour was on and his core team was busy in its work in the backyard of the Chief Minister's residence in Gujarat. The work and scope of each team was divided in such a way that no one could interfere in another's area. After the rallies, Modi used to reach Ahmedabad directly and give directions till the night after taking a complete report.

Initiatives to increase the social base had already started. The most important in this was the Dalit segment. The Dalit policy of the BJP had always been guided by the Sangh and efforts had always been made to implement it through symbols. In this, the Sangh-BJP got a big success when exactly twelve years after the Godhra incident, that is, on February 27, 2014, Lok Janshakti Party supremo Ram Vilas Paswan joined the NDA. In 2002 also, Paswan was part of the NDA and was a Minister in the Vajpayee government. But he broke ties with the NDA by resigning from the post of Union Coal Minister against the post-Godhra riots in Gujarat. Now the arrival of Paswan was a subject of discussion not only for Dalit vote but also for the political pundits as he is said to have mastered the art of listening to the voice of conscience in times of political instability. Wherever they went, the political pundits could sense the direction of the wind of election. This happened when Paswan walked to 10 Janpath through the back of his official residence and met Congress President Sonia Gandhi. He was also in talks with Lalu-Rabri's RJD in Bihar. There was Paswan's political turmoil there. But on February 27, four hours before dusk, he along with his political successor Chirag Paswan reached the residence of BJP President Rajnath Singh and then at sunset, a new alliance for Modi emerged.

For Bihar Chief Minister Nitish Kumar, it was a 'bizarre, but true' move. But the gleam on Paswan's face as he held the bouquet that he received from the BJP president seemed to suggest that Gujarat riots were a closed chapter and the issue of so-called secularism could be kept aside for the time being. Paswan had earlier contested the 2009 elections in alliance with the RJD against the NDA and also lost from his traditional seat, Hajipur. Later, with the help of Lalu Yadav, he went to the Rajya Sabha. But the BJP saw an advantage in Paswan as he was supposed to hold 7 per cent of the vote, and more importantly, strengthen Modi's candidacy as well as increase the leadership's acceptance among potential allies.

The Sangh had already made up its mind that first BJP will become strong, then it will think of NDA. The RSS's strategy was fitting in with Paswan's entry, and it was reflected in the words of BJP leader Arun Jaitley, "When Modi was declared the PM candidate, it was being said that the BJP would be politically isolated. But from the beginning, I have believed that only a strong BJP can lead a strong NDA."

The Sangh believed that it would not be right to rely solely on the Modi wave, social engineering would also have to be done. It believed that if the Modi wave had to become the end of power, then social engineering is also necessary through understanding the reality of the social fabric of the states.

Before this alliance, Modi had announced in a meeting in Kerala that the coming decade would be of Dalits and backwards. In this episode, Upendra Kushwaha's Rashtriya Lok Samta Party from Bihar was also made a part of NDA. There was an alliance with Apna Dal in Uttar Pradesh and MDMK in Tamil Nadu. The Haryana Janhit Congress in Haryana had already joined. In Maharashtra, Ramdas Athawale's party RPI (A) and Raju Shetty's 'Swabhiman Paksha' had also joined the alliance. The

'Gujarat Parivartan Party' formed by Keshubhai Patel in opposition to Modi in Gujarat was merged with the BJP. At that time, efforts were on to woo Asom Gana Parishad in Assam and Chandrababu Naidu or Jaganmohan Reddy in Andhra Pradesh. Later, Chandrababu Naidu joined Modi, which he benefited from in the assembly. PA Sangma had also stood with the NDA in Meghalaya. The former Chief Minister of Arunachal Pradesh, who had once joined the BJP with a full cabinet and then returned, also joined the BJP. Talks were on with AJSU in Jharkhand. Then, along with General VK Singh, they worked on the strategy of connecting Kiran Bedi with the party, which I had mentioned in my 'India Today' story then. Mumbai Police Commissioner Satyapal Singh was brought into the party and fielded in the election from Baghpat to remove possible resentment in the Jat community due to the Muzaffar Nagar riots.

About this rise of leadership and social base, political analyst Ram Bahadur Rai said that this phenomenon resembled Indira Gandhi's election in 1971. He believed that after Jawaharlal Nehru, Narendra Modi was the only leader during whose speeches every venue seemed small. In his opinion, in view of the circumstances in the country, Modi had ignited a ray of hope among the 10-crore new young voters who were joining for the first time. He summed up the growing circle of the alliance in this way, "The image of the BJP has always been that it is a communal party of Brahmin-Baniyas. Modi has changed both these images and now he is moving towards inclusive politics." So, overall, the election now belonged to Modi where Rahul Gandhi was the opponent. The Sangh and BJP had left the traditional way and brainstormed on leadership and strategy with a new thinking. In such a situation, it was natural for the people belonging to traditional politics to be uncomfortable, which was reflected in the distribution of tickets.

New Strategy for Ticket and Controversy

There was not much controversy over tickets in the Lok Sabha elections as Modi completely dominated the election. On March 5, the Election Commission formally announced the Lok Sabha elections. Uttar Pradesh was most important for the BJP in its strategy to convert Modi's rising stature into a wave, with Purvanchal being the weakest link. Modi's charioteer Amit Shah was constantly working in Uttar Pradesh and he had decided that if Narendra Modi contested from Varanasi, then Purvanchal as well as entire UP could be won with Modi's wave. When RSS Chief Mohan Bhagwat undertook his five-day winter tour in Varanasi from February 14, it was indirectly decided that Modi would fight from Varanasi. But then the MP from Varanasi, Dr. Murli Manohar Joshi was also adamant and he also started his election office on 20 February. When news of some differences over tickets in the Central Election Committee meeting of March 8, 2014 came out, Murli Manohar Joshi was still not ready to give up his claim from the seat.

When Joshi called a press conference on March 9, it was suspected that there would be some ruckus. But he had called the press conference as the chairman of the election manifesto committee to share some details of the interaction with the farmer representatives. But he expressed his pain in this way, "I am a disciplined soldier. The decision about the ticket is to be taken by the election committee. There will be Narendra Modi, our Prime Ministerial candidate. I don't think there will be any decision which will dent his reputation or affect the party's chances of winning maximum seats." Dr. Joshi was giving the message in gestures. The three-day annual meeting of the Rashtriya Swayamsevak Sangh's Akhil Bharatiya Pratinidhi Sabha had begun in Bengaluru on 7 March, even before the election committee meeting, from where the BJP had received a message that it was necessary to quell the voice of the emerging differences in the party. The Sangh also gave a message that everyone in the family should bow down to the wishes of the people for change in the country. Later, Joshi blamed the media for the news of revolt. Eventually, the Sangh had to talk to Joshi and he was given a Lok Sabha ticket from Kanpur. Similarly, there was some controversy over the Lucknow seat where Lalji Tandon was in no mood to give up the claim. But BJP's national president Rajnath Singh staked his claim on this seat that had been held by Atal Bihari Vajpayee. LK Advani also started indicating that he would move away from Gandhinagar in Gujarat and expressed his desire for a ticket from Bhopal with the help of his dear disciple Shivraj Singh Chouhan. But from a strategic point of view, this move of Advani's did not seem to suit Modi's strategy. That would keep Advani's displeasure in the headlines till the end of the elections and it won't not send a good message to Gujarat as well. In such a situation, the Sangh had to intervene and Advani agreed to contest from Gandhinagar.

Modi worked on a dual strategy by strategically deciding to contest from Vadodara in Gujarat and Varanasi in Uttar Pradesh. He kept his association with Gujarat and gave the message of making Uttar Pradesh his new land of work. Whenever there was any dispute or difference of opinion in the battle of Mahabharata, Sangh always kept the family together by becoming a trouble-shooter like Lord Krishna. So, the Sangh gave a message for the Lok Sabha elections from the Akhil Bhartiya Pratinidhi Sabha in Bangalore from 7 to 9 March, 2014, "There is going to be an election to the Lok Sabha in the near future. This is an opportunity for the countrymen. The credibility, honesty, commitment to the nation of the present government (UPA) is under question. Today the country wants change. In such a situation, there is an important role for enlightened voters, who are going to shape the future destiny of the nation. As such, it is our duty to assess our role properly so as to bring about a change that will reflect the wishes and aspirations of the people."

RSS has Full Faith in Modi

In fact, the Sangh's confidence in Modi's leadership had grown so much that now it had no hesitation even with his style of functioning. During the Lok Sabha election campaign, Rajnath Singh also denied the interference of the Sangh in this way, "If the RSS does not control our party, then why would it control our government? It works in the socio-cultural field and does not force anything." That is, the blueprint of coordination had started so that discipline in the family was not called control. Meanwhile, in an interview to the 'India Today' magazine, Sangh's Sarkaryavah Bhaiyyaji Joshi said, "People of the country believe that change will come with Modi because Modi has been successful in Gujarat and we hope to do good work at the Centre. " But Sarkaryavah gave a very practical answer to the question raised about Modi's style of functioning, "All Sangh workers cannot be cast in one mould. Everyone has their own style of work and their own way of doing things. The important thing is that Narendra Modi will do his job honestly." He also hinted at the coordination blueprint that Modi would be under no time limit pressure on contentious issues, which had also been decided before the results. Bhaiyaji had said, "Issues like Article 370, Ram Mandir, Uniform Civil Code are mentioned in the manifesto of BJP. These may take some time. We hope that one day all these goals will be achieved. It is not right to tie them down to a time-limit."

Expedition as if Seven Revolutions of the Earth in Nine Months

The election campaign continued with allegations and counter allegations, personal attacks and objections.

'India Today' writes in the May 2014 issue - 'After being declared the Prime Ministerial candidate, Narendra Modi toured all over India in about nine months and during this time has travelled about 3 lakh kilometres or say he circled the earth seven times. He attended 5,187 meetings and addressed 477 rallies in 25 states. During this, he gets only five hours of sleep every day. An estimated 23 million people have been contacted by internet-mobile telephone. Modi's election campaign and machinery is such that even Obama's 2012 US Presidential election would be embarrassed. Believe Modi or reject him, but the way the country's most controversial leader has built his image within a year has changed the way of contesting elections forever." There were more than 700 3D meetings and every campaign echoed with 'Namo-Namo'. Modi's leadership had now turned into a wave. When I roamed in the mountains of Uttarakhand and visited areas close to Kedarnath, I did not find a single person who had taken the name of any other leader or party other than Modi. During rafting in the Ganges in Rishikesh, the life saver took the name of Congress's Harish Rawat according to the politics of the state. But it was the ground reality and not the bias, regarding which the head of the ostrich could not be buried in the sand as the echoes of 'Namo-Namo' were continuously heard on the mountains. There is also an example of how important strategy is in everything - after becoming the Prime Ministerial candidate, he started the rally on September 15, 2013 by addressing the ex-servicemen's conference in Rewari, Haryana whereas after the announcement of the election dates, he held the first meeting on March 26, 2014 in Jammu with the blessings of Maa Vaishnodevi and concluded in Ballia, Uttar Pradesh, the birthplace of the great hero of the 1857 revolution, Mangal Pandey. This campaign of Modi, driven by the wonderful use of modern technologies, transformed the concerns of the poor and middle class by assuring them into a new political electorate.

Modi Confident of Victory and Sangh's Stake

Modi was convinced by his visits and the feedback from the machinery that his government of absolute majority was going to be formed. He had said in many of his interviews that Congress was not going to reach triple digits and this time the strongest government in the last 25 years was going to be formed. He also started talking about the agenda and blueprint of the government in his interviews. He was so sure that he had already discussed with the Sangh the complete blueprint of the next government. One important thing in this blueprint was the appointment of his favourite Amit Shah as the national president of the BJP. About 10-15 days before the election results, Modi had talked about giving the command of the Sangh president to Shah and taking Rajnath Singh in the government. But the Sangh was a bit uncomfortable because both Modi and Shah come from the same state, Gujarat. The CBI case against Shah was also going on. The Sangh felt that the hold of the government and the organization by the same person could weaken the organizational structure. So, after this proposal, at the behest of the Sangh, Rajnath Singh made a statement that he would like to remain the president of the organization. But Modi asked to be trusted, referring to the lack of coordination and experimentation in the organization during the Vajpayee government. Seeing the experience of the Vajpayee government, the Sangh also expressed full confidence in Modi and agreed to hand over the command to Shah. Modi proved through Shah how important it is for the organization to move like the flow of a river for the success of the government.

The Country Expressed its Trust in 'Chaiwala'

Congress and opponents were making fun of Modi being a chaiwala. But when the election results came on May 16, 2014, it was as if Modi had become a thought and not a person. BJP bagged 282 seats with 31.3 per cent of the votes and NDA had an overall tally of 335 (38.3 per cent votes). It was unexpected for the country, but for Sangh and Modi these results were expected, which was clearly visible in many pre-poll statements. This grassroot worker of the Rashtriya Swayamsevak Sangh had travelled from being a skilled organizer of the BJP to four-time Chief Minister of Gujarat and then to the chair of the Prime Minister. The sharp arrows of criticism, the poisonous words and the storm of hatred in the eyes of a large section of the intellectual class could never deter Modi. He laid the track of politics with a goal and running on it became Alexander. In Uttar Pradesh, out of 80 seats, BJP won 71 and ally Apna Dal won 2, i.e. history was created by winning 73 seats and for this, Modi gave the title of 'Man of the Match' to his favourite Amit Shah. The Congress was reduced to 44 seats in the worst performance in history and could not even fulfil the criterion to have a Leader of the Opposition which required membership of 10 percent of the total strength of the Lok Sabha.

The Sangh-BJP had devised a strategy to broaden the social base, as a result of which it won 40 of the 84 seats reserved for the Scheduled Castes. In this way, BJP won 47 per cent of the SC seats and in many seats, Dalit women were elected while it won 27 of the 47 seats reserved for Scheduled Tribes, which was 69 per cent. That is, if we look at the NDA, it won 62 percent of the seats reserved for SC and 70 percent of the seats reserved for ST. Narendra Modi not only gave the BJP an unimaginable victory, but he achieved this success riding on a wave of expectations which the BJP had never been able to do before. Narendra Modi's BJP broke all political stereotypes that were associated with the Vajpayee/Advani era and the then Jan Sangh in the 1980s. The social nexus that Narendra Modi forged was unique in terms of its demographic profile, geographical spread, gender equality and its mandate. About this victory, Narendra Modi's personal website says: "This mandate marks the beginning of an era of change in the wider political movement that gave birth to Jana Sangh in the 1950s and the BJP in the 1980s. If its first generation was Dr. Shyamaprasad Mookerjee and Pt. Deendayal Upadhyay, then the second generation was the era of Atal Bihari Vajpayee and LK Advani. Now the third generation has started under the leadership of

Narendra Modi. Along with having a national mandate for the governance of India, he now also has a political mandate, so that he can give a new look to this movement and display his philosophy of good governance. A billion dreams and hopes are now looking towards Narendra Modi."

Sangh's Sigh of Relief

The results of the Lok Sabha elections were not only in line with the expectations of the Sangh, but there was a victory on the ideological front, which was giving comfort to the Rashtriya Swayamsevak Sangh as the time had come to fulfill the issues for which the three generations of the Sangh had sacrificed. On May 17, the formal statement of the Sangh came out about this victory. Sarkaryavah Bhaiyyaji Joshi said, "In the recently concluded Lok Sabha elections, all the countrymen have set an example of healthy democracy in front of the whole world. It is commendable. It is a matter of great happiness for all of us that the election process was generally conducted with restraint, calmness and awareness. Thousands of workers of all the political parties participating in this, hundreds of candidates of all the parties participating in the election, media, administration and security system-the role of all these has been satisfactory. During the election period, there must have been rebuttal of views, personal accusations and counter-allegations. We believe that with the completion of the election process, everyone will make a positive effort to create a general cordial atmosphere. There was restraint shown by all the countrymen till date. It is our humble prayer that everyone will play their part in creating a harmonious environment in the same way. Crores of countrymen have expressed their desire for change. We are confident that the newly elected government will prove successful in fulfilling the public sentiments and expectations. We hope that with the cooperation of all of us, rising above ideological, social and religious differences, free from discriminatory and unequal behaviour, the newly elected government will prove successful in maintaining unity towards building an exploitation-free and harmonious society. The role of the government in a democracy is certainly important. We have to believe that the process of change has its own pace and change is possible only with the coordinated efforts of the government, administration, all political parties, public, social and religious institutions. Hearty congratulations to the newly elected government and all the countrymen."

The message of the Sangh was very clear that there would be no conflict with the government on any issue. The Sangh was confident that the Narendra Modi government formed with the victory of ideology would not let the sacrifices of three generations go in vain. The Sangh was also convinced that whatever work was not done or would not be done in the government would mean that it was not possible for the government. This mantra became the basis of coordination between the Sangh and Modi government. Therefore, Sarkaryavah clearly said in his message that the government had its own pace. In such a situation, for any kind of change, along with the government, people from all walks of life related to social concerns would have to join together. If the Sangh had faith in Modi, then Modi had also entered politics from the role of a pracharak in the organization. So, he realized the importance of the organization.

When Modi said - like India is my mother, BJP is also my mother

The symbols and words are very effective in politics and Narendra Modi seemed to have become adept at using them. When Modi reached the Parliament House for a formal meeting of the Parliamentary Party to be elected the leader of the BJP, he expressed his faith in the temple of democracy by paying obeisance at the entrance inside the complex. After the formality of being unanimously elected leader of the Parliamentary Party, Modi's sentiments flowed. First of all, he expressed gratitude. He remembered Atal Bihari Vajpayee saying that if his health had been good and he had been here today, it would have been like icing on the cake. The things he said about his election campaign showed his seriousness about the organization. In his address, Modi said, "On September 13, 2013, the responsibility of the Prime Ministerial candidate was fixed for me. I started my work from 15th September. When the organization gives responsibility completely with the spirit of a worker in the mind, then every particle of the body, every moment of time, should leave no stone unturned in fulfilling the responsibility of the party. We have got these values from the organization. So, the hard work which started from 15th September and when the campaign ended on 10th May, I called up the President (Rajnath Singh). I said that I want to come to Delhi to meet you before going to Ahmedabad. He said you are not tired now? I said that I have to report to you because I have to tell my president about the work that he had given to me. Rajnathji was hesitant, he even laughed. I said that I am coming. Then I was in Eastern Uttar Pradesh. So, I reached Delhi and went to him and reported to my President like a disciplined soldier. I told him that from September 13, 2013 to May 10, 2014, I tried to do the work that you had given me. Only one programme could not take place. He kept looking at me. I've been running for so long. But on May 9, in the midst of all the hustle and bustle, only one programme had to be postponed, that too of Ghosi because there our district president Sushil Rai, who was worrying about the rally, died suddenly. But as a worker, I report to you on this holy earth, too." Modi said, "I have come to the Parliament for the first time in my life. It had happened earlier in life that I saw the CM's chamber and assembly hall after becoming the Chief Minister. A similar opportunity has come today. But we are sitting at this historical place. It is the strength of the Constitution that a person from a poor family is standing here today."

But when Modi started mentioning some words from Advani's address, his emotions burst out and he started crying. Advani had said that Narendra Bhai had kindly brought the party up to this point. Modi said emotionally, "Can serving mother ever be a favour? It can't be so at all. Just like India is my mother, BJP is also my mother. And therefore, the son can never do a favour to the mother. The son can serve the mother only with devotion. The country became independent. All the governments that ruled, tried to take the country forward in their own way. Those governments and those who led them deserve to be congratulated for the good that has happened. It is our responsibility to move forward with goodness and try to do good. If this feeling remains in the mind, then the countrymen will not be disappointed." Modi also tried to prove the possible interpretation about the outcome of the Lok Sabha elections as baseless, in which it was being said that the anger against the Manmohan Singh government made Modi successful. But the implications of this mandate were pointed out by Narendra Modi himself, "I don't watch much TV and newspapers. People will evaluate the election differently. If the countrymen had had chosen a Hung Parliament, had given a fractured mandate, then we could have said that anger towards the government was the only reason or there was an anti-establishment atmosphere. But giving an absolute majority to the Bharatiya Janata Party means that the people have voted for hope and faith. This entire mandate is for hope." Modi reminded MPs and party leaders in a philosophical manner like Vajpayee, "You will remember, when our National Council met at the Talkatora Stadium in 2013, I said that this election is an election of hope. I had said one thing that day. I want to remind everyone that I had said that day whether we move or not, the country has started moving. Today when we are in such a large number, the Central Hall is full of dedicated BJP fighters. The reason for that is that the country has started to move whether we move or not. This enthusiasm, this fervour will continue. The era of responsibility begins. There will be many people like me in this auditorium, who were born in independent India. For the first time, the government is being formed under the leadership of a person born in independent India. We could not fight for the freedom of the country. But now we have got the privilege of living for the country. This election was an election of a new hope."

Modi had also reiterated the resolution of the year 2019 for himself from this platform. He said, "With the cooperation of the people of the party and the guidance of the seniors, I have fulfilled my previous duty. Today I assure you, in 2019 I will give my report card again, I will live for the country. This government is dedicated to the poor. We are here with an intent of working. This Modi that you see is not because he is great. You can see him because senior leaders of my party have carried me on their shoulders. Let us never make the mistake of saying that see, I got the ticket and so I won; if he had got it, he would not have won. Whatever we have got today, we have got it after five generations of penance. People did not understand Jana Sangh. They wondered who they were - religious or social? Families sacrificed so that lamps could be lit on the walls. Today, I bow down to all those generations. We are not here today because of us, we are here because of their penance." Modi made it clear that it was not the victory of the individual, rather it was the effort of the organization. Remembering the sacrifice of the Sangh and Jana Sangh, Modi once again gave the message of coordination of the Vichar Parivar in the future.

Finally, ten days after the election results, when the blueprint for coordination with the government-organization and the Vichar Parivar was fully prepared, Narendra Damodardas Modi took oath as the Prime Minister of the country on May 26, 2014. Incidentally, that day was also the fiftieth death anniversary of Pt. Jawaharlal Nehru, the first Prime Minister of the country. By forming a team of 45 Ministers, Modi carried forward the mantra of 'Minimum Government, Maximum Governance'. Not only did the Ministers have the thought process of the organization, the Sangh, but Modi also gave preference to professionalism, which had been a part of his style of functioning since the time of Gujarat, in which he joins them all to make a bouquet. On the third day itself, the 100 days agenda was asked from the Ministers. There was an agenda to start work straightaway, there was no time to get rid of electoral fatigue. A team of experts had been deployed. By connecting ideological professionals who were working behind the scenes in elections, along with Ministers, Modi accelerated the system by coordinating with the bureaucracy and professionals.

Lessons Pane the way to Wonderful Coordination

The conflict with the Vichar Pariwar during the Vajpayee government in 1998-2004 and then the organizational turmoil and lack of discipline in the BJP from 2004 to 2013 had taught a lesson. Narendra Modi had watched every incident closely and taking lessons from it, he advised Amit Shah to prepare such a structure of the organization so that the power and the organization could complement each other. At the same time, a complete mechanism was prepared for the Sangh Parivar too so that there would be no scope for any differences. Considering economic issues, taking family related organizations into confidence, appointment of governor, discussion on cabinet appointments, discussions on appointments in educational institutions - it had become a strategy to move forward with dialogue on all issues. A strategy was made that before any kind of process that was related to the Vichar Pariwarwas taken to the government level, all the parties would brainstorm on it and form an opinion and present it to the government. The most important thing in this dialogue and coordination was that the government would do all those things that were possible. Regarding the things that could not be done, it should be assumed that it was not possible to do them rather than being adamant about them. Call it a lesson from the times of the Vajpayee government or Modi's own organizational experience, such wonderful coordination has been seen with the Vichar Parivar from 2014 to 2019 that even the media let alone opponents could not find the negative side. But it wasn't as if there was no possibility of difference of opinion on any issue. There were differences, the possibilities of dispute also prevailed. But the Modi government had created such a mechanism for the Vichar Parivar that the differences or disputes within the organization were resolved before coming out as if nothing had happened. The core of this coordination was dialogue and coordination, the examples of which will be seen in detail in subsequent chapters along with issues.

❑

PART-4

Coordination in the 'Parivar'

(2014-2015)

With the formation of the government, a blueprint was made for the coordination among family. But there were many issues like land acquisition, Swadeshi, on which there was a conflict situation. But seeing the issue getting heated, Sangh Chief Mohan Bhagwat took cognizance and gave a message to the affiliated organizations that they must speak about it but should not insist on it government to make it into a situation is no return. After this, continuous meetings for coordination were held so that there was no complaint. How the Sangh gave mantra for the first time to all its pracharaks working in BJP so that the organization would not be stagnant and deviate from the ideology and coordination was done in the same practical way not only at the power level but also at the level of the organization.

❑

8

CHAPTER

Sangh and Government: Disagreement-Agreement

In the first year, there was a conflict between the affiliated organizations with the government, then how did the strength was achieved through unmatched coordination and constant meetings

In the 2014 general elections, the BJP had won the electoral battle. The challenge was to pursue the ideology, on which the Sangh became active. With the expansion of ideology, the big challenge was to coordinate the Sangh-BJP government in such a way that there was no conflict like it was during the Vajpayee government (1998-2004). A blueprint was drawn, in which the government and Vichar Pariwar were seen moving together in coordination. But it was not as if this coordination did not allow any differences or bitterness to emerge! There were many occasions when the BJP-Union-

Government contradiction was politically disturbing. But it is also a fact that whenever a subject or issue came up, on which there was a situation of contradiction between the BJP government and Sangh, there was a coordination with immediate solution, which we will understand further with some examples. On July 24, 2014, within two months of the formation of the government, Prime Minister Narendra Modi gave indications of better coordination by inviting the top officials of the Sangh to dinner. Modi has come from Sangh and joined BJP, so he is well aware of the strength and importance of the organization. According to those close to him, Modi had advocated a strong rapport with the Sangh from the very beginning. An informal meeting of Sangh-BJP leaders took place at the official residence of Nitin Gadkari on the same day before the dinner with Prime Minister Modi. In this meeting, National President Amit Shah, former BJP President and the then Home Minister Rajnath Singh and Gadkari himself were present on behalf of BJP. Except Sarsanghchalak Mohan Bhagwat from the Sangh, all senior officials were present, including Sarkaryavah Bhaiyyaji Joshi of the Sangh, Sah-Sarkaryavah Suresh Soni, Dattatreya Hosabale etc. In this meeting, apart from better coordination in the family, ideas were also exchanged regarding organizational appointments, the criteria for the deployment of their people in the government and the upcoming Maharashtra, Haryana and Jharkhand assembly elections.

But the first thing the Sangh did after Narendra Modi became the Prime Minister was to send two of its special pracharaks, Ram Madhav and Shivprakash, to the BJP. The entire script of coordination had already been prepared, under which Shivprakash was given the responsibility of Rashtriya Sah-Sangathan Mahamantri and Ram Madhav was given the responsibility of General Secretary. But he was the only general secretary who was assigned the entire area instead of being given the charge of a particular state, like Sah-Sangathan Mahasachiv are assigned. He was assigned the Northeast and Jammu and Kashmir regions. Madhav's work was to coordinate the Sangh-Government-Organization, which he initiated on November 25, 2014, when the coordination meeting was held in Delhi for the first time after coming to power. But the first coordination meeting did not last very long. On the evening of December 29, 2014, when the Modi government brought the Land Acquisition Ordinance, its opposition started. Meanwhile, the BJP also suffered a political setback. It was during this period that BJP President Amit Shah embarked on his ambitious campaign to enroll 10 crore members and the party was fighting a crucial battle in the assembly elections in Delhi and Jammu and Kashmir after forming its government in Maharashtra, Haryana and Jharkhand. For the first time in Jammu and Kashmir, two opposite poles - BJP-PDP formed the government by preparing a common agenda, but the condition of BJP in Delhi became very pathetic. The newly launched Aam Aadmi Party won 67 out of 70 seats and the BJP got only 3 seats. Sarsanghchalak Mohan Bhagwat held a meeting with Sarkaryavah Bhaiyyaji Joshi and the three Sah-Sarkaryavahs on the third day of the results when the Delhi defeat was reviewed. Then the next day Bhaiyyaji and Saha-Sarkaryavah Krishna Gopal, who was playing the role of coordinator with the BJP, Suresh Soni, held a meeting with the then BJP's organization general secretaries Ramlal, Ram Madhav and the then Union Health Minister JP Nadda. In this meeting, Bhaiyyaji expressed strong displeasure. He said that what was the use of the membership drive on which so much emphasis was being put when the party was not getting votes at all? Bhaiyyaji even said that the membership of BJP was increasing as if a wrestler increases the number of his push-ups every day! Such a massive defeat in the country's capital within nine months after the big victory in the Lok Sabha had forced the BJP and the Sangh Parivar to introspect. But the Sangh ensured that this defeat did not derail the coordination. But one also has to understand the extent of collision before coordination took place.

Confusion over Land Acquisition and Economic Policies

Except for the election year since the formation of the Modi government, the first budget of 2015 was about to come out. But before that, the government was facing opposition from allied organizations of the Sangh more than the opposition on the land acquisition bill. The extent of bitterness could be gauged from the fact that when on 28 December, in front of the then Union Finance Minister Arun Jaitley and some other Ministers, including people from the Finance and Agriculture Ministry, allied organizations of the Sangh, Mohini Mohan Mishra, the then Rashtriya Mantri of the Kisan Sangh, had said in a stern tone, "Why do you have to ask everything? Don't you eat food? Don't you wear clothes? Everything is clearly visible. Then why are farmers looked at differently?" But the government had made up its mind to bring an ordinance on land acquisition. In such a situation, the organization of Vichar Parivar suggested that it would not be right to remove the 'Social Impact Assessment' (SIA). Before any land acquisition, its impact on the society must be assessed.

Against its own government, the 'Bharatiya Mazdoor Sangh' (BMS) along with all other trade unions had announced a nationwide satyagraha on 26 February 2015 for their demands. On the other hand, organizations like Swadeshi Jagran Manch, Bhartiya Kisan Sangh added to the difficulties in the budget session by stalling the government's efforts to legalize the Land Acquisition Ordinance and demanding release of a white paper on the issue of FDI. The issue of confrontation between the BJP and other affiliated organizations of the Sangh over economic policies has always been in the headlines during the party's government at the Centre. When the Vajpayee government went ahead with bringing FDI in the insurance sector during the first NDA rule, Dattopant Thengdi, the founder of Swadeshi Jagran Manch (SJM), sat on a dharna. SJM co-convener Ashwini Mahajan told me then, "We may work under the inspiration of the RSS, but whoever runs the government doesn't matter. The DNA of Swadeshi Jagran Manch is such that it will not survive without raising its voice if any government undermines economic freedom or displays exploitative tendencies." Then the talk of the Sangh giving two years' time to the Modi government this time on these issues was rejected outright by the three organizations.

In fact, when the Bharatiya Janata Party reached the house of power in Delhi, the organizations associated with the Sangh Parivar had also readied themselves for a siege on economic front. The Modi government wanted to take steps towards labour reforms, but Bharatiya Mazdoor Sangh's general secretary Virjesh Upadhyay said, "We have put a 10-point demand in front of the government and on February 26 we will sit for a satyagraha for the same. If the government does not accept it, then we are also free to take to the streets." Regional organization head of BMS Pawan Kumar said, "We believe in positive cooperation. Recently, bank employees had announced a week-long strike, but later it was postponed."

Upadhyay plainly said, "A difference of opinion occurs when the party and government come to power, but we will not compromise on labour interests." At that time, the government was constantly discussing economic issues with the affiliated organizations associated with the Sangh Parivar. But as Pawan Kumar told me then, "The meetings are going on continuously, but the result is zero." The Sangh organizations even started opposing Prime Minister Modi's 'Make in India' slogan that he gave from the ramparts of the Red Fort. BMS said that it had strong objection to this slogan. It said that it should be made in India by Indians and instead of 'Make in India', there should be talk of 'Make in India'. But we do not agree with 'Make in India' and working on the issue of workers. If the government will move forward despite our opposition, then we will also move forward by taking to the streets. BMS's Virjesh Upadhyay said that 'Make in India' was not a new concept. But many foreign companies are working in India, which neither apply the law of India nor of their country to the workers. In this way Swadeshi Jagran Manch raised issues like demand for ban on foreign direct investment and e-commerce.

But more than economic policies, there was a dispute over the Land Acquisition Ordinance. RSS-affiliated Bharatiya Kisan Sangh and Swadeshi Jagran Manch had put a condition in front of the Modi government to change some of the provisions of the ordinance and for this, they started mobilization by writing letters to all the MPs outside the party line so that pressure could be put on their own government. Prabhakar Kelkar, general secretary of the Bharatiya Kisan Sangh, had then said, "We may be one from the point of view of ideology family. But if there is any issue related to the farmers, then we cannot backtrack. Our basic issue is what kind of system and policy is there for the farmer who gives 60 percent employment to the country and is being forced to commit suicide?" The biggest objections of the Bharatiya Kisan Sangh and the Swadeshi Jagran Manch were the neglect of provisions such as the consent of the Gram Sabha, Social Impact Assessment (SIA) and food security in the Land Acquisition Ordinance. Regarding this ordinance, the National Secretary of the Indian Farmers Association, Mohini Mohan Mishra, commented, “If the government acquires land in matters like infrastructure, railways, defence, then farmers may not even object to it. But why does the government want to acquire and give land to private companies for industrial corridors?” He said that the industry should take land on lease from the farmer, which will also reduce the cost of investment and also eliminate litigation. Mishra was even demanding reintegration of the provision that mandated SIAs in government acquisitions. Kelkar and Mishra had also objected to the word ‘land acquisition’ and advocated for making a land utility planning law in the country and adding a provision in it that if an industry did not start the project within five years, then the land would automatically be given to the farmer.

The Modi government was trying to coordinate with the Sangh Parivar on economic issues, taking lessons from the experiences of the NDA government headed by Atal Bihari Vajpayee from 1998-2004, But the dual challenge before it was how to move forward on the agenda of development with coordination

The Message of Coordination Emanated from Reshambagh

Five Ministers of the Modi government - Steel Minister Narendra Singh Tomar, Agriculture Minister Radha Mohan Singh, Environment Minister Prakash Javadekar,

Energy Minister Piyush Goyal and Minister of State for Agriculture Sanjeev Balyan were present in a meeting with senior officials of the Sangh - Suresh Soni, Krishna Gopal, Dattatreya Hosbale, Bajrang Lal Gupta at Madhya Pradesh Bhawan in Delhi in October 2014 with the aim of building coordination within the Vichar Pariwarregarding the economic policies of the Modi government. In this marathon meeting, the Sangh Parivar discussed all the economic issues like FDI, GM crop, land acquisition. Officials of Swadeshi Jagran Manch, Bharatiya Kisan Sangh and BMS were also present. But the coordination was not working out. Meanwhile, the political defeat in the Delhi Assembly elections gave more opportunities to these organizations, after which the top leadership of the Sangh took over the command.

After the defeat of Delhi, the meeting of the Akhil Bhartiya Pratinidhi Sabha, held every third year at Reshambagh, Nagpur, was held on March 13-15, 2015. Even before this, the opposition had targeted the Modi government over the Land Acquisition Ordinance and allegations of it being a suit-Boot's Ki Sarkari were made. Due to this ordinance, the affiliated organizations of the Sangh-Bharatiya Mazdoor Sangh, Swadeshi Jagran Manch, Bharatiya Kisan Sangh had also opened a front against the government of their ideology. In such a situation, when the Representatives meeting took place, the Sangh, as the parent organization, instructed, "The affiliated organizations should speak on the issues, but should be adamant about it." This meant that the disagreement should not be so strong that there was no room to retreat from there. This message emanating from Reshambagh immediately after the budget session of the year 2015 softened the attitude of these organizations and the attitude of the Swadeshi warriors became soft. The tone of leaders of these three organizations who had opened the front suddenly changed from the way they spoke till some time ago. For example, after the Land Acquisition Ordinance, Virjesh Upadhyay, the General Secretary of the Bharatiya Mazdoor Sangh, had threatened the government with Satyagraha saying, "We will carry out satyagraha against the government. 'Make in India' is not new. We can teach government a lesson." But after this meeting with Sangh, Upadhyay suddenly started praising the Modi government saying, "Modi government is doing better work than UPA. It hasn't done anything which is against the labourers." Similarly, Swadeshi Jagran Manch co-convenor Ashwini Mahajan used to say earlier, "Social impact assessment on land acquisition bills should be studied. 'Make in India' is wrong, e-commerce should be banned." But later he started saying, "Land Acquisition Bill is right for development, but first the SEZ land should be audited. The Modi government has created a positive atmosphere in the country." Similarly, Mohini Mohan Mishra, the then Rashtriy Mantri of the Bharatiya Kisan Sangh used to say, "The Land Acquisition Bill is not acceptable. Take land on lease from farmers and the provision of SIA (Social Impact Assessment) should be added." The Bharatiya Kisan Sangh had even threatened that it would write to the MPs of all parties to bring down this ordinance in the Parliament. But later Mishra started saying, "Modi is a leader who understands the pain of the poor and farmers because of his background. The Land Acquisition Bill should be passed in the Parliament and after its implementation, if any problems are seen, then the organization will come forward to make changes accordingly."

These organizations were clearly instructed by the Sangh that they should not contest on any issue. However, freedom was definitely given to talk about the issues related to their organizations in such a way that the opposition would not take advantage of it, that is, staying within the limits, these organizations were given freedom to speak to save their existence. Ram Madhav, who was then made the national general secretary of the BJP directly from the Sangh, told me, "Due to some propaganda, there was doubt in the minds of the leaders of the affiliated organizations, which we have tried to clear by sitting together. It is because of these efforts that our relations are continuing in a good environment." Ram Madhav, who served as the spokesperson of the Sangh during the Vajpayee government, said that this time the emphasis was on better coordination from past experience. He said, "I was the spokesperson of the Sangh during the previous government. Talks were going on with the government on many issues. Some organizations had different views on certain issues. That's why there was a lot of tussle during the previous government, this is not true. But with the experience of the previous government, efforts were started from day one on how to have more coordination this time. There is an effort from our side and also from the side of the Sangh, so that family understands what we are doing and we also understand their concerns and thoughts. This effort will go on continuously."

Modi and Sangh in 'Madhyaanchal'

The co-ordination efforts resulted in a change in the tone of the affiliated organizations, which were sharp before the 2015 budget, after the meeting of the Akhil Bhartiya Pratinidhi Sabha in Nagpur on March 13-15, 2015. But by then the image of the Modi government had become that of a pro-corporate. The first year of the Modi government was completed in May. But the land ordinance had created the image of the government as being pro-corporate; it was decided to break it. After bringing an ordinance on it thrice since December 29, 2014, the government found it difficult to get it passed in Parliament. So, finally on August 30, 2015, Prime Minister Modi said with a heavy heart in the radio program 'Mann Ki Baat', "We had brought ordinance in the interest of the farmers, but confusion was spread, the farmers were intimidated. But I want my farmer not to be confused and never to be afraid. Therefore, I am restoring the old position on land acquisition."

Earlier, in a conversation with me, former RSS pracharak Suryakant Kelkar also said that if the government had broadened the process of discussing the land acquisition bill, then there would not have been so much opposition. Initially, even the organizations associated with the Sangh Parivar were not consulted, so there was opposition from the family as well. Later, when organizations related to the subject were called and held discussions with and their suggestions were added to it, then the opposition of the Sangh was weakened.

But the problem wasn't one sided. The 2nd Annual Coordination Meeting of the Sangh began on 2nd September 2015 at Madhyanchal Bhawan, Delhi. It was attended by 93 prominent people from 15 important affiliated organizations of the Sangh. In the concluding session on the last evening of this three-day marathon coordination meeting, Prime Minister Narendra Modi's said, "The expectations of the public from the government are very high. We have to work at the same pace. But sometimes there is a rhetoric from the organizations (Vichar Parivar) itself which affects the mutual understanding." His reference was clearly to the initial opposition of the affiliated organizations of the union on issues like Land Acquisition Ordinance, Labor Reforms, FDI in Retail, GM Crop, which was made political weapon by the opposition parties and this ordinance created a negative image of the government and which forced the government to step back. In the presence of Modi, Rashtriya Swayamsevak Sangh (RSS) Sarsanghchalak Mohan Bhagwat also gave the essence of the three-day meeting in the form of a message. Bhagwat said, "All the organizations of the Sangh, we are all one Vichar Pariwar and the views of all should continue to be exchanged in this way. This benefits both the government and the people sitting in the organization. Together we should take this process forward. Dedication to ideology and organization is essential."

'Draft Policy' of Coordination on Six Subjects

Apart from the stage at Madhyanchal Bhavan, there was a deep discussion in 'Mukt Chintan' with senior officials of the Sangh and Modi during the snack. Neither the BJP nor the Sangh was in a mood to repeat the mistakes committed during the Atal Bihari Vajpayee government since the result of lack of coordination was visible on the streets at that time. But this time the Sangh had prepared a draft policy on six important topics-economic policy, foreign policy, internal and external security, education policy, social initiative, cultural policy in a meeting of Vichar Parivar even before the Modi government was sworn in at the Centre. It was called the family's own contemplation. But in the first year of the government, the message of coordination was not clearly sent down to the lowest rung , there were many occasions when affiliated organizations did not refrain from publicly attacking the government on issues related to ideology, raising questions about the credibility of the government. Therefore, the Sangh informally advised these organizations to exercise restraint and on the other hand the BJP and the government had also started the process of consultation with other organizations of the family like Bharatiya Mazdoor Sangh, Swadeshi Jagran Manch, Bharatiya Kisan Sangh. A group of Ministers was formed for discussions with different organizations. In such a situation, when a three-day coordination meeting was held at Madhyanchal Bhawan, various Ministers gave their presentations in separate sessions - Union Finance Minister Arun Jaitley on economic policy, External Affairs Minister Sushma Swaraj on foreign policy, Home Minister Rajnath Singh on internal and external security, then HRD Minister Smriti Irani on education policy. Irani, Union Social Justice and Empowerment Minister Thaawarchand Gehlot and Tribal Minister Jual Oram on social initiatives and Water Resources Minister Uma Bharti and Culture Minister Dr. Mahesh Sharma on cultural policy, in which they gave possible details of the steps taken and goals set by the government. In this, suggestions were also given by the Sangh because the Sangh did not want to keep its role limited to a mute spectator. Therefore, the meeting was extended and all the concerned parties were invited so that there would be direct talk in front of the government and representatives of the affiliated organizations and the top leadership of the Sangh woud be present there. The entire marathon process had only one goal - coordination of the Vichar Parivar with the Modi government.

Mohan Bhagwat specially mentioned in this meeting that the Sangh had spent three generations on its ideology. In such a situation, without waiting now, the Modi government would have to move forward with a strong will-power. The then BJP President Amit Shah also made a special mention of the contribution of the Sangh Parivar in the 2014 general elections. Shah said in that meeting, "We are here (in governance) today, because of Modiji's image, wrong policies of Congress etc. But the biggest thing is that the whole Vichar Pariwarstood behind us.

That's why BJP had such an amazing victory." The result of this meeting was also seen immediately. Be it Vijesh Upadhyay of the Bharatiya Mazdoor Sangh or Prabhakar Kelkar of the Bharatiya Kisan Sangh or Kashmiri Lal of the Swadeshi Jagran Manch—all expressed satisfaction with the work of the government in unison.

Taking lessons from the past, the Sangh played the role of a guardian. When the Sangh placed its blueprint on economic, educational, cultural and security in front of the government, the government also wrote a new script of coordination with the ideology family, gaining the confidence of not taking a stubborn stand on controversial issues, due to which for the first time the coordination between the government formed by its own majority ideology and its affiliated organizations at the centre was initiated. But power has its own character and influence, which the Sangh realized well since the Vajpayee regime (1998–2004), when the organization was dwarfed by the presence of leaders like Vajpayee-Advani in government. In such a situation, when the Modi government was celebrating its first year, the Sangh also took precautionary measures behind the scenes and in this way, after almost a decade, the Sangh called an important meeting of the organization Ministers working in the BJP.

❑

9

CHAPTER

A New Attempt to Establish Roots

After a decade, the Sangh held a meeting of 43 pracharaks who saw direct work in the BJP and gave a mantra not to forget the organization amid the affair of the government so that the path of coordination would be smooth.

The Narendra Modi government was celebrating the first year with the slogan 'Saal Ek, Shuruaat Anek' (One Year, Many beginnings). For this celebration, the organization also took the responsibility of taking the work of the government to the public by stopping some of the work going on in the organization; it was named 'Janakalyan Parv'. This was to go on for a whole month. Soon after the annual celebrations were over, the Sangh called all 43 pracharaks working in the BJP for a three-day brainstorming on June 26-28, 2015, to discuss the experiences of the government for one year and pracharaks also had to be alerted for the coming times. It was a highly confidential and informal meeting, which was kept away from the media spotlight. But when I inquired about this meeting while working for India Today, it brought to the fore the doubts of the Sangh, which it had felt under the Vajpayee government. The Sangh wanted to completely eliminate the apprehension that the Modi government, after coming to power, might follow the path of so-called secularism and its core issues would be left behind! Keeping these things in mind, 43 pracharaks working in all the state and central units of BJP, organization Ministers and working in other roles were called for 'Rambhau Mhalgi Prabodhini Sabha' in Mumbai.

The importance of this meeting could be understood from the fact that after a long time, on the instructions of the Sangh, only and only the pracharaks who were looking after the direct work of the BJP were called for the meeting, in which Sarkaryavah Bhaiyyaji Joshi on behalf of the Sangh was present along with saha-Sarkaryavah Dr. Krishna Gopal who played the role of coordinator with the BJP. The message of this meeting went like this - 'While working in the Bharatiya Janata Party, we have to keep in mind that it is a political organization. So, you not only have to work keeping in mind the thoughts of the Sangh, but also ensure that the methodology of working as a team is developed in the party." That is, the responsibility of upholding the principle of 'organization paramount' lies with the sangathan mantri s and they have to pay special attention to it. Ram Madhav, the pracharak and national general secretary of the BJP, who attended the meeting, told me, "The meeting of 43 pracharaks working in the BJP took place after a decade, in which there was no political discussion. The meeting was inspiring as it explained how pracharaks should live; Referring to the life of pracharaks like Deendayalji, Shyamaprasadji, Nanaji Deshmukh etc. they were told how to carry forward the values in the party that they learned in the Sangh." Though he did not state it clearly, but it was clear from the words of Ram Madhav that the Sangh advised its pracharaks working in the BJP not to deviate from the 'principles of the Sangh' and for this they also gave examples of those ideals.

However, Ram Madhav also admitted in the conversation that there was an information session on the BJP's Mahasampark and Mahaprashishan Abhiyan. In fact, the Sangh was concerned that the speed with which the BJP had crossed the target of 11 crore members and set the record of being the largest party in the world, somewhere due to the slowness of the organization, the programme of contacting all those people should not be weakened. Therefore, the Sangh made a strategy to connect its network with the party for the Maha Sampark Abhiyan (Grand contact campaign). The Sangh believed that the agenda of the government should not affect the activities of the organization. After this meeting, there was a change in the blueprint of the Maha Sampark Abhiyan, where earlier the party had made a blueprint for a big meeting at its conclusion. But after the meeting with the Sangh pracharaks, a strategy was made to divide the entire country into seven zones and hold meetings of BJP national president Amit Shah and then general secretary Ramlal from July 5 to 12 in every zone. Feedback regarding electoral states like Bihar was also discussed in this meeting.

But the important objective of this meeting was to give preference to ideology in view of the way the power equation and environment had changed. Although the Sangh did not draw any Lakshman Rekha in front of the pracharaks for this, but it had moved forward towards its long-term strategy because this kind of meeting of Sangh pracharaks working in BJP were not in the routine. The mention of this informal discussion did not come out formally, but the Sangh leadership reminded the pracharaks of the sanskars, mentioning their role as Sangathan mantri and told them to learn from and follow the biography of the old pracharaks. Along with this, they were also advised to review BJP's campaigns and pay attention to their behaviour and character. Sarkaryavah Bhaiyyaji Joshi gave the mantra of giving priority and importance to ideology in the battle of politics and ideology and Saha-Sarkaryavah Dr. Krishna Gopal gave the idea of Hindu philosophy. He talked about Hindu philosophy instead of Hindu religion in this way, "We have to try to see the influence of Hindu philosophy in the political field also because Hinduism is not religion, but philosophy." In the same episode, the cleanliness mission and the campaign of Yoga Day, held in just one year of the Modi government, were also described as a part of Hindu philosophy. The Sangh also gave a message of coordination and said that giving importance to ideology did not mean that disputes should be raised immediately on subjects like Ram Mandir, Article 370. One should work under a strategy on these subjects.

The Sangh also made up its mind to make some important changes through the meeting of pracharaks, which included increasing the number of pracharaks in the BJP by posting sah-sangathan mantri s in some states and changing those in-charges of some states where the sangathan mantri s had been posted for more than seven years. The then national organization general secretary Ramlal was excluded from this criterion because the Sangh believed that his work was satisfactory in the coordination of power and organization.

Certainly, the strategy of the Sangh was to carry out the coordination of the Vichar Parivar in the best way under the Modi government, as well as a strong strategy to expand the ideology, which was started in a phased manner, a glimpse of which will be seen in the next chapters.

❑

PART-5

Controversy on Reservation and Harmony

There was a ruckus on the reservation statement of Mohan Bhagwat at the time of Bihar elections. Despite the possibility of political damage, he did damage control in a dignified manner and resolved a similar dispute that took place in Jaipur in a few hours. But after repeatedly investigating the reasons for the dispute, the Sangh took the initiative to reach out to every Segment under the 'Vision-2025' by taking forward the already initiated social harmony campaign. The idea of 'one temple, one well, one crematorium' and through symbols to reach out to the Dalit community was further carried forward. What steps did it take to maintain the role of a moral guide rather than a political driver in the context of the BJP?

❑

10

CHAPTER

Confusion over Reservation

At the time of Bihar elections, after the political ruckus on the reservation statement of the Sangh Chief, he prepared his ground through coordination.

The strong cord of co-ordination was tied. Both the BJP and the Sangh were busy executing their script. An extended meeting was held on 2-4 September 2015 on coordination in the Vichar Parivar . But only after about a fortnight, a statement came from the Sarsanghchalak Mohan Bhagwat that made party very uncomfortable. But to keep the record straight, it is important to know what Sarsanghchalak had said in that interview and if he was really a victim of vote bank politics or he actually said something like that? Whatever he had said in 'Panchjanya', it would be appropriate to present it here as it is. He was asked, "You said that authenticity is the criterion. Any policy which you feel is right and such policies implemented with sincerity can lead to the realization of an integral human philosophy? Do you see a single policy that may or may not have been implemented? What's your idea?" To this Bhagwat's reply was, "If our constitution talks about reservation policy on the basis of social backwardness, then instead of politics, if we had run it as it was in the mind of the constitutionalists, then all these questions would not have arisen today. Ever since this provision came into the constitution, it has been used in the form of politics. We say that form a committee, which should also have the representatives from politics, but only those people who are service-oriented and who have the idea of the interest of the whole country in their mind should decide. Let them decide for how many people reservation is necessary, for how many days it will be needed? The full authority to implement all these things should be in the hands of that committee. It has to be kept in mind that all these things are applied with authenticity.

In fact, in an interview to the RSS mouthpiece 'Panchjanya' and 'Organiser', Bhagwat may not have commented directly on the existing reservation system, but in view of the voices being raised regarding the demand for reservation in the backward classes, Bhagwat made a statement about carrying out a review by forming a committee. This naturally created a political storm and in the Bihar assembly elections and the BJP which was weaving the blueprint of social equation, got worried. The Nitish Kumar and Lalu Prasad Yadav camp, who had formed a grand alliance, immediately made it an election issue. BJP national president Amit Shah, who was busy in a fight for prestige in Bihar felt that it could cause electoral damage. So, he appealed to the Sangh for immediate relief.

While working in India Today at that time, I observed this development very closely and wrote about it. Since the statement on reservation came from the head of an organization whom the BJP considered its inspiration and guide, it was not easy for any BJP leader to dismiss the remark. Hitesh Shankar, the editor of the magazine, who interviewed Bhagwat for Panchjanya-Organizer, told me bluntly, "The Sangh never speaks according to the weather or elections." The seriousness of the matter can also be gauged from the fact that none of the party leaders spoke directly to Bhagwat and Sarkaryavah Bhaiyyaji Joshi. On September 21, 2015, when political attacks started regarding Bhagwat's interview, Amit Shah first expressed the possibility of loss in the Bihar assembly elections by talking to Krishan Gopal, the Sangh's Sah-Sarkaryavah, who was handling the responsibility of coordinating with the BJP on behalf of the Sangh. After that, Shah brainstormed with national organization general secretary Ramlal, Bihar's Sah-sangthan Mantri Saudan Singh, general secretary in-charge Bhupendra Yadav. But the difficulty was that if the BJP shied away from the stand of Sarsanghchalak Mohan Bhagwat, then a new ruckus would have arisen in the Vichar Pariwar. Therefore, it was decided that first the Sangh's clarification should be issued and later the party should give a statement. In such a situation, Shah requested the Sangh leadership to give an explanation so that the dignity of the Sarsanghchalak was also maintained and the party also would not suffer political losses. Therefore, he gave the responsibility of contacting the Sangh to BJP General Secretary Ram Madhav. On September 21, Ram Madhav landed at the Delhi airport at around 1.30 am. At the same time, they received a message from Shah, after which Madhav and Ramlal discussed with Krishna Gopal the format of clarification to be issued by the Sangh and the BJP. Shah wanted the dispute to be resolved by the late evening of 21 September. Also, the first line of the Sangh's explanation should be such that it gave the message that no comment had been made on the current reservation system. Bhagwat's consent was obtained on the final draft. But even the signing of the statement was delayed by half an hour as the Akhil Bharatiya Prachar pramukh Manmohan Vaidya was busy with another programme. That's why the BJP also had to delay the press conference. Late in the evening, first the Sangh and then the BJP issued the statement.

According to the strategy, the Sangh's statement issued late in the evening said, "In this interview, the Sarsanghchalak of the Sangh, Mohan Bhagwatji has not made any comment regarding the reservation being given to the various weaker sections of the society at present. Rather, according to the thoughts in the minds of the framers of the constitution, the benefit of reservation must reach all the weaker sections of the society, which should be considered by all the people together." In the last line, the Sangh talked about seeing this interview in the context of the integral human philosophy, that is, it argued that the last person also should get the benefit of it. BJP in its statement bluntly said, "BJP has been in favour of reservation for Dalits, Adivasis, Backward and Extremely Backward since its inception and Jan Sangh era. The BJP is not in favour of a constitutional rethinking of the current reservation policy." The BJP's fear was evident from the statement as the party, in its three-sentence statement, had twice mentioned that it did not support a reconsideration of the existing reservation system.

Finally, late in the evening, the operation to crack down on the reservation dispute took place in a hurry as the cord of co-ordination in the Vichar Pariwarwas firmly tied, the comfort of which was clearly visible on the faces of the strategists engaged in the Bihar elections. When some leaders were interacting in an informal conversation, one said, "The timing of Bhagwatji's statement was not correct." And another said, "Don't look at it from the point of view that the timing was not right, but say that we responded in time."

...but the responsibility for Bihar's defeat fell on the Sangh

The first phase of polling for the Bihar Assembly elections was to be held on October 12, 2015. Just a day before polling, Sarsanghchalak Mohan Bhagwat who was in Gorakhpur, Uttar Pradesh looked very worried. When a leader considered very close to Amit Shah saw him worried, he asked the reason out of courtesy. Bhagwat said, "My reservation statement was misinterpreted." That leader also agreed, saying, "The wrong message has gone down to the bottom in Bihar and there has been a lot of back-lash." When the election results were declared on November 8, Prime Minister Narendra Modi had reached LK Advani's house on the same day to wish him a happy birthday. The result was troubling for the BJP. Then party MPs like BJP MP Hukamdev Narayan Yadav, Ashwini Choubey and Shanta Kumar blamed the defeat on Mohan Bhagwat's reservation statement just before Diwali. Hukamdev Narayan Yadav, then MP from Madhubani, had said, "Some people do not know the soil of Bihar. Bhagwat's reservation statement is largely responsible for the defeat." Although Choubey argued that Bhagwat's statement was misinterpreted he said that Bhagwat's statement was used by the opponents to create an adverse atmosphere.

Amit Shah had probably sensed the statements of the MPs and the possible opposition of leaders like LK Advani, Murli Manohar Joshi, members of the Margdarshak Mandal. Therefore, he met Sarsanghchalak Mohan Bhagwat present in Delhi and spoke regarding the statements of the MPs. Instead of making any statement on behalf of the Sangh, Shah was asked to clarify the position on the entire issue at the party level. But at that time the Sangh too had gathered its arguments in response to Bhagwat's reservation statements being blamed for the defeat. The Sangh clearly believed that though BJP could not win in the Bihar assembly elections its vote percentage had increased while the vote share of the RJD-JDU alliance and Congress had decreased as compared to past. The Sangh's argument was that it was due to the unification of non-BJP votes that the Mahagathbandhan (Grand Alliance) got more seats. The Sangh also said that if the BJP's vote share was even slightly lower, it could be linked to the RSS Chief's reservation statements. But this did not appear to be the case in terms of vote share. But it was Diwali on 11th November and just a day before that, on 10th November, the Margdarshak Mandal detonated the bomb. LK Advani, Murli Manohar Joshi, former Union Minister Yashwant Sinha and Shanta Kumar issued a joint statement questioning the working style of Prime Minister Narendra Modi and Amit Shah. That statement said, "The party leadership did not learn any lesson from the defeat of the Delhi Assembly elections. In such a situation, to say that everyone is responsible for the defeat in Bihar means that no one wants to take responsibility. But the responsibility of defeat should be fixed. Those who were responsible should review the defeat. There should be an honest review of the humiliating defeat of Bihar elections." The statement from its senior leaders was uncomfortable for the BJP leadership. But on the advice of Bhagwat, the party leadership adopted a restrained approach.

After the discussion at the top level, the party issued a statement saying, "We welcome the suggestions of senior leaders. The party has always had a tradition of taking collective responsibility. We are serious about the defeat and the reasons for this have been discussed in the party's parliamentary board. The reasons for the defeat will be discussed at other levels as well."

RSS on Shah - Political Operator or Moral Guide?

After the defeat of Bihar, questions were raised on Amit Shah's style of functioning. The discussion even started as to whether Shah would be given a new term as the president or not? However, during his tenure of 18 months, Shah had become the source of the BJP of Modi's dreams. Shah started with a bang. First of all, he separated Atal-Advani-MurliManohar who were once counted among the three legacies of the BJP. He gave a clear message of taking the organization into a new stream by separating them from the parliamentary board, the highest policy-making body of the party, and forming a guiding board. Then, he not only cashed in on the enthusiasm of the workers who were caught in the Modi wave but also realized many plans for the grand expansion of the party. On the other hand, with the successful decision of breaking the alliance with Shiv Sena in Maharashtra and winning power alone, forming government in alliance with PDP, which was totally opposite, in Jammu and Kashmir or bringing the party to power in Haryana, Shah made party's dreams soar in true sense. But the crushing defeats in Delhi and Bihar forced Sangh to introspect on the organizational front. Before the Bihar results, on 7 November, when the top leaders of the Sangh were brainstorming in Delhi, it was discussed that whatever be the results of the Bihar elections, there should be a change of leadership in the BJP as the party had become over-centralised and the message is going that the party's power had been concentrated between Modi-Shah-Arun Jaitley (all three from Gujarat). But in the same meeting, the opinion of some other office bearers of the Sangh was different. They believed that if Shah was removed now, the image of Narendra Modi, who had emerged as a strong leader in the country and the world, would be questioned and it would also be said that after the defeat of Bihar, the faith of the Sangh Parivar in Modi had diminished and so the Sangh had tightened the noose on the organization. Not only this, the brigade, which was running the award-return campaign alleging intolerance at the time of Bihar elections, would also get a new opportunity to attack Modi. But even then, the Modi-Shah duo was confident. A close aide of Shah told me, "The Bihar-Delhi defeat was not a good enough reason for a change of leadership. Had there been a defeat in the BJP-ruled states, Shah's reconsideration could have been affected. But Shah was the only party president who knew that the social equations in Bihar were in favour of Nitish-Lalu. Still, he put the party's entire reputation at stake and fought elections so that the morale of the workers was not weakened.

But the Sangh gave some suggestions to Modi-Shah to change the processes of the organization and it was decided that Shah would continue on the post of President and Modi-Shah pair will lead the campaign for 2019 Lok Sabha elections. On January 24, 2016, Shah assumed the responsibility of his first full-time presidential term. Earlier, he was completing the remaining 18-month term of Rajnath Singh. After the defeat of Bihar, the party intensified the exercise of taking forward the local leadership instead of contesting elections only in the name of Modi. After being elected to the presidency, Shah began to advance his strategy rapidly. Firstly, Shah decided to make and declare Sarbananda Sonowal Chief Ministerial candidate for the Assam assembly elections. That is, the Sangh, in view of the experiences of the Vajpayee government and the changed circumstances, decided that instead of becoming a political driver, it would continue to play the role of a 'moral guide'.

Again, the same controversy: Now Via Jaipur Literary Festival

When and which statement would create trouble in politics - it is often realized later. This was the biggest irony of the BJP was that it got caught in the tangles of reservation time and again and incidentally that trap came from the party's mother organization - Sangh. They would want to say something else; the effect would turn out to be something else. As a result, 'Operation Damage Control' had to be run every time. The BJP had suffered the brunt of reservation in the Bihar elections. There was also a brainstorming in the family about this. But on January 20, 2017, a dispute arose again regarding reservation. Actually, 'Sahitya Mahotsav' was going on in Jaipur. Sangh's Sah-Sarkaryavah Dattatreya Hosabale and the then Akhil Bharatiya Prachar pramukh (now Sah-Sarkaryavah) Manmohan Vaidya attended a session there. During the festival, a question was asked about Muslim reservation, linking it to caste-system, reservation and Sachar report. In response, Vaidya called Muslim reservation against the basic spirit of the Constitution and promoting separatism. But the controversy was caused by his statement, in which he quoted Dr BR Ambedkar in the context of SC-ST reservation and said that it was not proper to have the provision of reservation forever and its need should be abolished at the earliest and the time should be created to give equal opportunities. Hosbale called the varna system irrelevant and declared caste-based reservation as per the constitution. But after taking out a part from the whole quotes, it was circulated in the media. Manmohan Vaidya was quoted saying that the Sangh advocated the abolition of reservation. This news spread like wild fire.

This controversy of reservation came at the time when BJP was busy with preparations for the Uttar Pradesh assembly elections. The BJP strategists were numb because during the Bihar elections, Sarsanghchalak Mohan Bhagwat's statement reviewing the reservation had proven expensive for the party. This time Manmohan Vaidya had reportedly made a similar statement. In these five years, the BJP seemed to be caught in the 'loop' of reservation, which was not easy to recover from. But both the BJP and the Sangh, who had suffered it in the Bihar elections, were very cautious this time and in just two hours, the entire dispute was clarified. But when Manmohan Vaidya's statement about reservation came out in the media, Prime Minister Narendra Modi became very angry in Delhi, after which the activities of top strategists of the government and BJP increased and calls were made to Jaipur where both the Sangh leaders were present. Ashok Parnami, the then Rajasthan BJP president, got the first call from Delhi, who was present at the 'Jaipur Literature Festival' along with Sangh's Saha Sarkaryavah Dattatreya Hosabale, Akhil Bharatiya Prachar pramukh Manmohan Vaidya and the then Chief Minister Vasundhara Raje. After this, the damage control exercise continued till late in the cold of Delhi and in the pink city engulfed in the slight cold. Two-three rounds of talks were held between the BJP's general secretary Ramlal, Sah-Sarkaryavah of the Sangh (now Sarkaryavah) Dattatreya Hosabale and Suresh Soni. Hosbale then told me in a special conversation, "Both the statements were made on the same platform at an interval of three minutes, in which the Sangh's support for caste-based reservation was spoken about. But after about an hour, we came to know that the entire context on reservation has been changed and confusion has spread. There is an atmosphere of elections; so, naturally it was linked to elections. That's why I decided right there that I will clarify it and called the media and reiterated with clarity what was said on the stage." After Hosabale, Vaidya also gave his explanation in this matter. But the BJP was stressed also because the party had suffered a lot due to the statement of Sarsanghchalak Mohan Bhagwat during the Bihar elections.

At the government level, this issue was directly handled by the then Union Finance Minister Arun Jaitley. He directly made a phone call to Vasundhara Raje. But at that time, there was a clear instruction from Raje to the staff that no phone should be given to her. The same thing was conveyed by the staff to Jaitley's staff. But the very next moment in the second call, Raje's staff was asked to give the phone directly to her. The staff panicked and Arun Jaitley's phone was given. In this discussion, Raje was instructed to get a press conference organized by Hosabale and Vaidya because the clarification given to the TV channels alone would not work. The news running in the print media probably could not be stopped because it was night. On the other hand, both the leaders of the Sangh had left for the railway station. After the discussion from Delhi, Hosabale-Vaidya returned and held a formal press conference at 9.30 pm and reiterated the stand of the Sangh supporting SC-ST-OBC reservation. In Delhi, party and senior Ministers of the government were engaged till late at 2 pm to ensure that the news published in the media would give priority to the news of rebuttal by the Sangh. The spokespersons were instructed from the office of BJP President Amit Shah himself to vigorously debate the RSS's statement regarding Muslim reservation and the denial regarding caste-based reservation. When I spoke to Vaidya on this matter, he was so hurt by the twisting of the news that he said that he would not comment and that only those who created unnecessary controversy should be asked. But then a BJP leader said that there was nothing wrong in whatever opinion the Sangh held regarding reservation. But controversy was created by taking out its implications and it was not politically suitable for BJP. The leader said, "Opponents should look into history because religion was mentioned for the first time in reservation in 1916 when there was talk of separate electorate, which sowed the seeds of Indo-Pak partition and that was Vaidya's intention. Sangh is the only organization working with Adivasis and Dalits in the whole of India. Therefore, it would not be reasonable to say that the intention of the Sangh is to abolish reservation."

The BJP and Sangh showed maturity by resolving the reservation dispute in two hours before the Uttar Pradesh elections whereas it had taken an entire day during the Bihar elections. But beyond these arguments was the question which has been the centre of debate in the BJP since the time of LK Advani. Since that time, it has been discussed that the views of the Sangh on purely political matters are not conducive to the BJP. In any case, when the BJP is in power, any such statement by the Sangh in the political field is bound to be deeply probed. The reaction to any idea of the Sangh is also natural. In such a situation, the Sangh had to decide whether it would be balanced in view of the compulsion of its political face BJP or would like to take a missionary direction. The Sangh accepted the role of moral guide so that the opponents did not get a chance to target the Vichar Parivar. The Sangh also understood that for the first time its own government had won a majority on its own. In such a situation, the emphasis should be on pursuing its advantages more than its shortcomings as the Modi government was working on a long-term strategy and the BJP was also imbibing new methods. But in order that the role of the Sangh as an organization did not appear completely political, the Sangh and its affiliated organizations engaged in issue-based symbolic protest, but they did not take it towards confrontation. But the major reason for the conflict over reservation was the non-acceptance of the Sangh among those sections of the society who are entitled to or are taking benefits of reservation. The Sangh had already understood this and after the formation of the Modi government with an absolute majority, it started working on this mission so that it could penetrate all sections of society and try to remove prejudice against the Sangh which was at the root of the frequent controversy.

❑

11

CHAPTER

Harmonious Expansion and Government

With its government in power, how did the Sangh pursue the initiative to break the myth of the upper caste image and expand the social base?

For the first time in the 2014 general elections, the BJP won a majority on its own at the Centre. The Sangh saw this victory as a golden age for its expansion and started implementing the formula of reaching out to every section of the Hindu society by preparing a unique agenda of social expansion. In the first Akhil Bhartiya Pratinidhi Sabha held in Nagpur after the formation of the Modi government, Sangh Chief Mohan Bhagwat did not take the name of the BJP. However, he indicated that it was the most favourable time for the expansion of the organization and it was necessary to run a special public awareness campaign for the next three years. Certainly, the Sangh wanted to take advantage of the BJP government at the centre for its expansion and the BJP also felt the need to break its old image and move forward. In the general elections, the people of the backward classes had expressed their trust in Modi by breaking the barriers of all castes, which was now not only the challenge for the BJP to keep them completely aligned with itself, the Sangh also saw a factual basis for its expansion in it.

The Sangh took a historic decision in Pratinidhi Sabha. For the first time in the history of the Sangh, V Bhagayya, who belonged to the Other Backward Classes (OBC), was made a Sah-Sarkaryavah and was given a place in the top six leaders of the Sangh. An illusion has always been spread about the Sangh that only Brahmins and Banias dominate the top level and this organization has been seen from this perspective. But this was probably the first time that the Sangh had made 65-year-old V Bhagayya, who hails from the Other Backward Classes (OBC), as Saha Sarkaryavah. With this appointment, the Sangh sent out a clear message that its campaign was beyond caste and was a befitting reply to those who alleged casteism. But it is not in the nature of the Sangh to shirk and bow down to the charges. Therefore, the Sangh finalized and started the work of implementing the public awareness campaign of social harmony.

One Temple, One Well, One Crematorium

In the meeting of the Akhil Bhartiya Pratinidhi Sabha, RSS Chief Mohan Bhagwat gave a message that the time was favourable for the expansion of the organization. But in this meeting some facts were also revealed from the feedback received by the Sangh from all over the country, according to which the society rooted in the castes was against it. Surveys conducted in some states like Jharkhand, Andhra Pradesh were also presented in the meeting, in which it was assessed as to how caste was a hindrance in the expansion of the Sangh. The Sangh then put forward a larger agenda, which was put forward by the then International Working President of VHP Praveen Togadia in Mumbai during the opening ceremony of the Golden Jubilee celebrations of Vishwa Hindu Parishad on the instructions of the Sangh. Togadia prepared a presentation titled 'Vision-2025' and placed it before Bhagwat, a copy of which I have with me. In it, mainly all Hindus have been advised to make a Hindu family friend in a caste other than their caste, eat together, celebrate festivals and go on tours together. The presentation stated that a village should have one well for water, a temple for worship and a cremation ground for rituals such as funeral rites for all Hindus. Accepting this Vision-2025, the Pratinidhi Sabha made a long-term plan to expand the organization. Not only this, according to the plan of the Sangh, a special strategy was made to bring Hindus under one umbrella and this responsibility was entrusted to Vishwa Hindu Parishad so that Hindu society could be kept united. On the completion of 50 years of Vishwa Hindu Parishad, the Golden Jubilee celebrations were carried out on 16-17 August 2014 at Sandipani Ashram, Mumbai, where Vision-2025 was laid. However, this vision was formulated in the context of Vishwa Hindu Parishad. The presentation, composed of 20 slides, focused on core issues as well as uniting the community. Many of these goals have been fulfilled and regarding those which were impossible to meet even while in government, better coordination had been established in the family.

This was Vision-2025

Slide-1

Presentation at Golden Jubilee Celebrations of VHP.

Slide 2

Started with a small organization. Then working for the betterment of Hindus since 1964, today VHP has become the focal point of Hindu unity at national and international level.

Slide-3

After 50 years of experience, the time has come to work for the optimistic and in a full fledged manner for Hindus at national, global, micro and micro level.

Slide 4

The Hindu: Harmony, Security, Prosperity and Respect.

Slide-5

Samaras Hindu : Under Hindu Mitra Parivar Abhiyan, we make a person of other caste a family friend and eat food together with him at each other's homes, both the families to celebrate festivals and ceremonies together, the families to go out or on a tour together. Overall, the two should become like extended family to each other. We aim for Hindu families in villages to have one well of water, all to eat together, all to get darshan of God in one temple and all Hindus should have only one crematorium.

Slide 6

Safe Hindu: Complete Security—Country, Life, Property, Family, Living, Religious Place. That is, complete security of Hindus should be ensured in all these things.

Slide-7

Prosperous Hindus: Education, business, jobs, health should be ensured for the prosperity of Hindus.

Slide-8

Hindu Respect: The time has come for Hindus to get full respect like 'Hindu', whether it is related to cultural heritage or contemporary subjects. That is, a grand temple of Lord Ram should be built in Ayodhya, a national law should be made against cow slaughter, Article 370 should be abolished, Uniform Civil Code should be implemented, there should be no reservation on the basis of religion and other topics which will occur contemporarily.

Slide 9

Organized Hindus : Hindus are one and will always be one. As Hindus, we will stand with all the Hindus in the country and the world. Staying united is an essential aspect in the progress of any country and religion.

Slide 10

Hindu Solidarity : Now no Hindu will be alone in the world. 50 years ago, the then Sarsanghchalak Guru Golwalkarji had given inspiration and started the VHP. Now in the year 2012, Mohan Bhagwatji, the current Sarsanghchalak, launched a unique campaign- 'Hindu Ahead', whose goal is-Practicing Hindu, Aware Hindu, Active Hindu.

Slide-11

Swarna Lakshya : Under this, VHP's own expansion and these will be targets for the year 2025. Every village will have VHP. There will be a committee for the population of every 2,000. Religion-expansion activities in every district, weekly aarti-devotees congregation in every temple. Releasing temples, monasteries, Hindu religious places from the control of the government.

The subsequent nine slides mentioned VHP's golden jubilee goal, which included education, women, youth, health, Hindu human rights, environment, cow protection mission and nutrition to expand the social circle. In every field—be it law, science, art, health, media, agriculture or economics—there must be a Hindu expert. About education, with the goal of educating every Hindu, there was a mention of increasing the number of hostels, to ensure free education in tribal areas from 51 thousand to one lakh villages, increasing hostels from 146 to 500, increasing the number of orphanages from 46 to 200, running a special campaign for the education of the girl child, providing new platforms for special category children. There was also a mention of setting up special health check-ups for women, self-help groups, and Sanskar Kendras for young girls. Communicating with 1 crore youth through social media, ensuring employment or business to every Hindu, motivating youth especially so that they join Army, Navy, Airforce with the spirit of service to the country. Creating a directory of 10 lakh Hindu blood donors in the field of health, providing free health check-up facilities to the poor, planting 10 lakh trees in the field of environment, campaign for cleaning Ganga - many such goals were kept under 'Vision 2025'.

The Blueprint of Harmony through 'Symbols'

The Sangh did not delay this harmony campaign as the brainstorming on it had started soon after the government sharing its philosophy had assumed power at the Centre. Therefore, in 2015-16, on the birth centenary year of the third Sarsanghchalak of the Sangh, Balasaheb Deoras, the Sangh announced special programmes of social harmony in 50 thousand locations in the country. But in order that no controversy should arise during this campaign on other issues, the Sangh Chief also cracked down on the statements that provoked religious sentiments by the leaders associated with Sangh and VHP. They were told that instead of making outrageous statements, they should work on the ground by staying within their ambit, that is, the whole focus of the Sangh was to strengthen their reach in all the societies by realizing the campaign of social harmony for the next three years. But here the difficulty of the Sangh was that what kind of symbols should be adopted for different communities so that it could be easy to connect the people with the Sangh, which had been fully prepared by the top leadership of the Sangh.

The preparations of the Sangh can be gauged from the fact that in the meeting of the Pratinidhi Sabha in March, the harmony campaign was launched along with the slogan 'One temple, one well, one crematorium' and on April 14, 2015, the Sangh's mouthpiece 'Panchjanya' ' and 'Organiser' published a special issue which caught the attention of the media of the country. That symbol was – Babasaheb Dr Bhimrao Ambedkar. Usually, when a magazine publishes a special issue, it does not conduct a big function for it. But the mouthpiece of the Sangh not only printed the special issue in Hindi and English, but also launched it in a grand manner at Siri Fort Auditorium in Delhi on 14 April, in which Sarkaryavah Bhaiyyaji Joshi of the Sangh was present as the Chief guest and Social Justice and Empowerment Minister Thaawarchand Gehlot was present on behalf of the Modi government. Apart from them, Narendra Jadhav, an economist and a member of the Planning Commission, was also present.

Who does Ambedkar belong to? And why did the saffron brigade choose him?

In fact, a policy decision was taken in the first Akhil Bhartiya Pratinidhi Sabha meeting held in 2015 after BJP came to power. That decision was—now in the meetings and offices of all the organizations of the Sangh, the picture of Dr. Ambedkar will inevitably be displayed along with the idols of the Sangh. With this thought, on the occasion of 125th birth anniversary of Bharat Ratna Dr. Babasaheb Bhimrao Ambedkar, for the first time more than 3 lakh copies of this collectors' issue of 'Panchjanya' were printed. As part of the strategy to make inroads among the Dalits, the Sangh had made preparations to paint Ambedkar's legacy in its hue. Therefore, in this special issue, Ambedkar's views opposing Hinduism were not included; rather only those ideas were included whereby his views could also be established like that of any Hindu nationalist leader. When I did a thorough investigation while working in 'India Today', Hitesh Shankar, editor of 'Panchjanya', said that Dr Ambedkar was not featured on the cover of the RSS mouthpiece for the first time; he had also been given a place on his 100th birth anniversary. Although Ambedkar was given a place with Hedgewar in the March 17, 1991 issue, in response to the question as to why 'Panchjanya' did not incorporate Babasaheb's anti-Hindu views, Hitesh Shankar said, "Hedgewar and Ambedkar had the same views on untouchability. The pain of two sages of the same period were also similar regarding social issues. Sangh always thinks of uniting rather than breaking. So, in 'Panchjanya' also the same things are printed which are positive." But even about sorting and publishing the anti-Muslim views, Hitesh Shankar argued, "The officials of Pope and Nizam went to Babasaheb. But he said that if he accepted Christianity or Islam, then the country would be in great danger. Therefore, he said, he was choosing the path which was associated with the fundamental philosophy of this country." Even on the occasion of the release of the special issue, Sarkaryavah Bhaiyyaji Joshi raised the question as to why Mother Teresa was given 'Bharat Ratna' before Ambedkar? In fact, the Sangh's strategy was to convey the message that Ambedkar was the leader of all rather than a particular community by presenting Ambedkar's positive ideas and those that matched with the right-wing ideology. The Sangh also considers Ambedkar's adoption of Buddhism as going from one room to another in the house; in the internal discussions, it believes that if you listen to Ambedkar's thoughts by removing his name, then they seem to be the thoughts of a Maharishi and which match with those of a Hindu nationalist leader.

But it was not as if the strategy of 'adopting Ambedkar' was made only at the level of the Sangh. A lot of strategies were made at the level of the government as well. The BJP's strategists believed that apart from the dedicated workers of the party, leaders of other political parties, its ideals were deeply known to a select few people. In such a situation, it is only through the symbols of the communities that the BJP can realize its future political vision. Both the Sangh and BJP had realized that in the Modi wave people from all sections of the society had turned towards BJP because of their disillusionment with their regional leaders. The BJP's Dalit vote doubled in the 2014 elections as compared to the 2009 Lok Sabha elections, and for the first time, the BJP came to power with a huge mandate of 282 seats. In the 2009 elections, where the BJP had won 21 seats in Dalit-dominated areas, the number increased to 73 in 2014. Certainly, people had broken away from other parties and there should be a basis to make them stay with us. It was not possible to connect all of them by giving any direct benefit. Hence, the strategy of conveying the message through symbols was formed. In such a situation, the Sangh Parivar worked on it by making a holistic policy and on the occasion of 125th birth anniversary of Ambedkar, it started an aggressive policy of making Ambedkar, the messiah of Dalits, its symbol by organizing more than 300 programmes across the country.

However, the then BJP MP Dalit leader Udit Raj had said that the BJP had understood Ambedkar's thinking, hence 'When you wake up, it's morning!' He said that the party saw the firepower of the middle class, intellectual and bureaucratic class that emerged from the Dalit society and it is an attempt to increase the mass base because of Ambedkar. Udit Raj attributed the BJP's defeat in 2004 to former Union Minister Arun Shourie's book 'The Worshiping of False God' and said that the party should have taken the same action against Shourie at that time as it had taken against Jaswant Singh for writing the book on Jinnah. Shourie should have been shown the way out of the party at that time. His opinion was also supported by Sanjay Paswan, the national president of BJP's SC Morcha and a Minister in the Vajpayee government. But Paswan said that it is well known on which side Shourie is standing today. Sanjay Paswan had also said on this initiative, "The party's strategy is to stop the votes pulled by Ambedkarites in the elections. If Congress talked about campaigning using Ambedkar's name to regain its lost support base, then why would the BJP lag behind! Our aim is to stop Congress." Union Minister Thaawarchand Gehlot had then said on this initiative, "The thinking of the BJP is positive and we have been giving respect to Ambedkar since the time of Jana Sangh. But I am sad that today people are making it a topic of discussion."

For Ambedkar's legacy, many big projects were started by Modi government, including a grand building on Janpath Road in Lutyens' Zone of Delhi at a cost of Rs 192 crore, which has been completed. Its name is 'Ambedkar International Centre'. In addition, at 26 Alipore Road where Ambedkar died, a grand monument in the shape of the Constitution book was built at a cost of Rs.100 crore. The Maharashtra government, together with the central government, started the process of buying the house in London in which he lived during his studies in 1921-22, which has been completed. Ambedkar Institute, established in Mhow, the birth place of Ambedkar, was given the status of State University in Madhya Pradesh on the occasion of his birth anniversary. So, the government and the Vichar Parivar strategically worked on the symbols of Ambedkar to strengthen their penetration in this section of the society. The Sangh too, breaking the myth of its image, decided to give responsibility in the committees of its initial level units- Mandal, Basti, Mohalla Sangh. Also, the Sangh had started the 'Dalit Ke Dwar Dastak' program under the Samarsata Abhiyan. But the biggest challenge in winning the trust of the Dalit community was its opinion about reservation. However, it is also a fact that the Sangh had accepted the proposal of reservation in 1989 itself. But the Sangh has been in favour of a review of its beneficiaries, which often leads to a dilemma in the ideology family, which has been overcome by better coordination between the BJP and the Sangh. But during the Bihar assembly elections, Sarsanghchalak Mohan Bhagwat's alleged reservation statement created confusion and the BJP had to suffer political losses, which was also mentioned by many MPs and leaders of the party after the Bihar election results by making public statements. But despite this contradiction, the BJP-Sangh Parivar had started work on a long-term plan to serve the Dalit society by making Dr. Ambedkar a medium in the year 2015 itself.

Message of - from 'Baba Saheb' to 'Bala Saheb'

In November 2015, the issue of reservation dominated the results of the Bihar assembly elections, which started during the election campaign with the statements of Sangh Pramukh Mohan Bhagwat. But the Sangh has been keeping pace with the changing times. In such a situation, the momentum of social harmony campaign did not stop. After the meeting of the Pratinidhi Sabha in Nagpur in 2016, the meeting of the Akhil Bhartiya Pratinidhi Sabha was held from March 11 to 13 in the medieval city of Nagaur in Rajasthan, when the Sangh not only made fundamental changes, but also indicated its thinking for the future. The main pavilion of the annual meeting of this Akhil Bhartiya

Pratinidhi Sabha of the Rashtriya Swayamsevak Sangh (RSS) in Nagaur of Rajasthan was completely dedicated to Dr. Bhimrao Ambedkar. There was a big picture of Babasaheb Ambedkar at the entrance itself and as soon as one entered, a small pavilion on the right side had a picture exhibition with the picture of Balasaheb Deoras, the former Sarsanghchalak of the Sangh. In this meeting on March 13, 2016, the Sangh, through a special resolution on social harmony, appealed to all citizens, religious and social organizations to make efforts towards an egalitarian and exploitation-free society. That means the constant initiative of the Sangh in this direction was part of its well-thought-out strategy so that it could increase its penetration among the Dalits and Backward. In the year 1973-74, Balasaheb Deoras had launched a special campaign from Sangh to remove untouchability from the Hindu society. Through these symbols, the Sangh was trying to fit the ideas from 'Baba Saheb' to 'Bala Saheb' in one frame. That is why it considers the reservation of Scheduled Castes and Scheduled Tribes justified. But the Sangh's words on the reservation of backwards again troubled the BJP. The Sangh made it mandatory for all its organizations to have Ambedkar's photo in programmes and offices, from the city to the central level, in order to widen the base and make acceptance easier among all sections of the society.

BJP again uneasy due to Blunt talk on Reservation

Actually, at that time two communities in Haryana and Gujarat had taken to the streets for reservation under backward classes. In such a situation, there was a debate in the society that the community which is considered to be affluent is now demanding reservation! Meanwhile, after the meeting was over in Nagaur, the Sangh's Sarkaryavah Bhaiyyaji Joshi was asked a question on the struggle for reservation by the Jats of Haryana and the Patidars in Gujarat. He sais, "Even when the affluent section of the society demands reservation, we feel that this thinking is not in the right direction. Rich people should actually help the weaker section. But instead of doing so, asking for reservation for yourself is against Ambedkar's thinking." During this event, as a journalist of India Today, when I spoke to Manmohan Vaidya, the RSS's Akhil Bharatiya Prachar pramukh (now Sah-Sarkaryavah), he said, "Jats and Patels have been affluent classes. Instead of asking, they should give facilities to others. If even after 60 years, the weaker sections among Dalits have not got the benefit of reservation, then it should be meditated upon. For this, the people in the society should come forward. The same thing was said by Sarsanghchalak (Mohan Bhagwat) ji at that time (in the reservation statement at the time of Bihar elections)." In fact, Sangh believed that the manner in which the Jats organized a violent agitation demanding reservation in Haryana troubled the ruling BJP at the Centre and in the state. Those agitations naturally increased the concern of the Sangh. A senior leader associated with the Sangh Parivar had then said, "Sangh always thinks as a nation and every person or organization talking of homogeneous society will say what Sarsanghchalakji had said during the Bihar elections or the voice that now came out of the Nagaur meeting." The Sangh believes that due to politics and vote bank, the issue of reservation of backward classes keeps popping up every now and then. His concern was also about the fact that people celebrate the birth anniversary of personalities who have done great work for the society and the country in the name of caste which is a social curse, whereas the Sangh has never held any programme in the name of caste since its inception. It believes that political people have promoted social curse in the name of caste for power and in the present scenario, no plan can be seen as to how it will end and who will initiate it. However, Sangh has clarified about the SC-ST reservation and said that it is the duty of any nation to support people who have been victims of social injustice for centuries, but it is wrong to play party politics under its guise. Though Sangh has been talking about a nationwide debate on reservation and the statement of Sangh that was issued from Nagaur after Bhagwat's was also in the same context the dilemma of the Sangh Parivar was also that BJP, its ideological organization working in the political field could not support the review of reservation at any cost. In such a situation, when a message on OBC reservation came out from Nagaur that was uncomfortable for BJP, a voice was raised in the Parliament on 14 April. On the allegations of BSP leader Mayawati, SP leader Ram Gopal Yadav in the Rajya Sabha, the Leader of the House and the then Finance Minister (Late) Arun Jaitley had said, "The policy of the government is clear that the existing system of reservation will continue, will remain in any condition."

BJP's difficulty had more to do with politics than Vichar Pariwar because a year ago when BJP President Amit Shah first formed an OBC front within the party, he said, "We have been in power for a very short time, but BJP has given the most numbers of OBC Chief Ministers, MPs-MLAs and even today the BJP has the maximum number of MPs and MLAs from this class. We have even given the first OBC Prime Minister to the country. There was also a factual reason behind saying this. In the 2014 Lok Sabha elections, the party got immense support from the OBCs. The BJP got 34 per cent OBC votes, which was 12 per cent more than the 2009 general election. BJP which won 244 out of 282 Lok Sabha seats in the Hindi belt alone got 48 per cent OBC votes from this belt. However, in view of the controversy on this issue, it was argued on behalf of the Sangh that the initiative of reviewing the reservation should be taken only by the enlightened people of the reserved classes so that all the people of this society can get its benefit.

Graphics

BJP received support from reserved category in Lok Sabha elections				
	Vote Share 2014		Gain/Loss since 2009	
Category	**National**	**Hindi Belt**	**National**	**Hindi Belt**
OBC	34	48	+12	+6
SC	24	34	+12	+6
ST	38	55	+14	+7

Source: N.E.S. 2014 and C.S.D.S.

Message of Modernity from the Medieval City of Nagaur

In the Nagaur meeting, the Sangh may have reiterated its stand regarding reservation, but the most different thing was that the RSS gave the message of taking a bold stand in the process of keeping pace with the times. To woo the youth, it changed its uniform and expressed its candid opinion on reservation, which India Today reported in its March 30, 2016 issue as follows—Indeed, its intention is to attract that youth power which considers reservation as unnecessary. It was also clear on the current burning issue of 'nationalism' luring the youth and condemned the alleged anti-national slogans raised in some universities. Moreover, showing progressive thinking, it supported the entry of women in temples. On the subject of gender equality, the RSS meeting in Nagpur made it clear in a conversation with the media that it is in favour of the entry of women in the sanctum sanctorum of Hindu temples. But it said that the process of admission should be decided through intense consultation and cooperation and not through confrontation.

The then BJP general secretary Muralidhar Rao had said, "RSS has always been in favour of progressive interpretation of religious books and the Vedas say that there is nothing like a man or a woman in front of divine power. The new thinking that many experts say is not new to the RSS, but has been a part of its ideology since its inception. However, the decision that really created a sensation in the media was the change in the

RSS uniform. Now khaki shorts were replaced by brown pants. The debate on this issue had been going on in the RSS since 2010. The main reason for the change in uniform was the effort of the 91-year-old organization to attract the youth. But a change in dress may not be enough to attract them. The Sangh leadership knew that the fight to bring youth into the organization would have to be fought on the ideological front as well. For this, the Sangh worked on organising training camps for the youth, after which the branches of the Sangh grew. For this too, in the year 2015, about 15,000 RSS workers took a week's leave from their homes to spread its message, after which the number of shakhas increased rapidly. The far-reaching objective was that there should be one branch each in all the 6 lakh villages of the country. Although the reach of the RSS has grown rapidly over the past six years, the majority of those who have joined it are still students of either higher secondary schools or colleges. A section of it has been attracted by the politics of power as the BJP-RSS came to be seen as the forces of the ruling establishment. Studies show that those who join at the primary school level or at a young age tend to be more ideologically stronger as they grow up, while those who join at an older age are not as ideologically strong. But these days the number of people of the first type is less as most of the parents consider the outfit of khaki shorts to be 'old-fashioned'. They do not like to send their children to the shakha despite being influenced by the nationalist ideology of the organisation. A senior RSS functionary then argued, "The decision to replace shorts with pants has been taken very carefully. The aim is to attract children to Shakhas so that they can be made ideologically strong cadre in future."

The need to provide affordable quality education and affordable healthcare was stated in two other resolutions passed in the Akhil Bhartiya Pratinidhi Sabha of Nagaur. RSS's Akhil Bharatiya Prachar pramukh Manmohan Vaidya had said, "The RSS has been keeping pace with the wave of change since its inception. We are moving forward despite attacks from ideological opponents." The Nagaur assembly witnessed excitement on the last day as the Sangh clarified its stand on most controversial issues, usually used by Left strategists, who blame Hindus for discrimination against a class on the basis of caste and the opinion of the Sangh was in line with the times. So, Pratinidhi Sabha sent out a message that religious texts have never preached discrimination, but have been distorted later. This message was a great success of this meeting. Overall, the medieval city of Nagaur is known for its strong fort and has witnessed many changes in history, where it also witnessed fundamental changes in the largest family of the country, the Sangh Parivar.

That means Sangh not only took the initiative to attract the younger generation by making fundamental changes to widen its social base while keeping pace with modernity but it also worked with BJP behind the scenes and created the blueprint of ideological intellectual fellowship and laid ground for social expansion. But during this period, some anti-Dalit incidents in the society were also putting the Vichar Pariwarin a dilemma, due to which the initiative of social harmony also started facing hurdles. In such a situation, along with penetrating the society, the Sangh also intensified the work of creating a group of intellectuals, who play an important role in creating any kind of positive or negative concept.

❑

PART-6

Intellectual Movement

From its inception till now, the Sangh regretted that despite its presence in every sphere of politics and society, it was pushed on the backfoot in the intellectual arena. Left intellectuals turn every debate in their favour. In such a situation, after the JNU incident, the Sangh made a blueprint to create an intellectual movement after brainstorming and intensified the work on it as per the strategy. Think tanks inspired by the ideas of the Sangh were activated. The Sangh directly took a meeting of Education Ministers on how to take forward the intellectual battle with a long-term thinking and also work on the change in education for that. In this, how Rajasthan became a model and started a programme like Lok-Manthan to gather intellectuals. How the visit of former President and Congress veteran Pranab Mukherjee to the Sangh headquarters proved to be a historic event, which became a factor in the acceptance and expansion of the Sangh?

❑

12

CHAPTER

Our "Intelligentsia"

After the episodes like stalemate in social harmony from the Vemula, Una episode, award-vapsi and JNU scandal, the Sangh lagging behind in the intellectual battle made a new beginning; but in every intellectual initiative, it also took into account the social equation.

The Sangh was giving impetus to its harmony campaign. Suddenly, incidents of atrocities against Dalits on issues like cow protection started coming to the fore. Prime Minister Narendra Modi had also publicly condemned the incidents taking place in the name of cow protection in strong tone. But the Sangh-BJP saw a hindrance in their social harmony campaign due to frequent incidents, while on the other hand the intellectuals with a view against the party and the Sangh were allegedly creating a negative perception of these organizations being anti-Dalit on the basis of these incidents. It was certainly a time of concern for the Sangh Parivar. The reason for this was that the party had got 24 percent Dalit votes in the 2014 Lok Sabha elections, the year of Modi wave. During that, BJP had won 39 out of the total 84 reserved seats in the Lok Sabha, capturing all the 17 reserved Lok Sabha seats in Uttar Pradesh. In the Hindi belt alone, BJP had got 34 percent Dalit votes.

It was in order to connect this vote to itself that along with social harmony, the government gave priority to the heritage related to Babasaheb Ambedkar and also had a comprehensive debate on Constitution Day in Parliament. If we look at the preparation of Narendra Modi since the time of the 2014 elections, after the inclusion of Ram Vilas Paswan's Lok Janshakti Party in the NDA, on March 3, 2014, Modi had said in an election meeting in Muzaffarpur, Bihar, "The BJP, which was called the party of Brahmin and Banias has now become a party of Dalits and Backwards. The coming times belong to the Dalits and Backward." There was also a solid basis behind Modi saying this. During the Lok Sabha elections, except Mayawati, BJP had included all the prominent Dalit leaders in its movement of social equation. In Delhi, Udit Raj, who openly attended *Mahishasur* celebrations and who had converted to Buddhism against Hinduism, was also included. Similarly, it took along Ram Vilas Paswan in Bihar, who had resigned from the Atal Bihari Vajpayee-led NDA government in Gujarat due to the riots in Gujarat when Modi was the Chief Minister. Similarly, in Maharashtra, Ramdas Athawale's RPI(A) and in Tamil Nadu, Vijayakanth's party DMDK were added, which benefited BJP.

How much Dalit vote for whom			
Party	**Votes in Lok Sabha Elections (in percentage)**		
	2004	**2009**	**2014**
BJP	13	12	24
Congress	26	27	19
BSP	22	20	14
Others	39	41	43

Source: C.S.D.S., Election Commission

But after coming to power, it was facing difficulties on Dalit issues. In fact, in the last two-three decades, Dalit politics has become so sharp and reactionary that it could not be matched with the social base of the BJP at that time. Therefore, there seemed to be a contradiction in the strategy at times. Although Sangh's projects such as Seva Bharti, Vanvasi Kalyan Ashram, Ekal Vidyalaya have been working for the Dalit-Adivasis, yet there was a perception about BJP and Sangh that they were confined to the middle and upper-caste sections of the society. Going into the history of this fact, the Sangh gave priority to the politics of symbols to break this image. In 1967, the Dalit organization DS-4 and later the BSP coined many slogans like 'Tilak, Taraju aur Talwar' against the Brahmin and Banias and openly protested. But for the purpose of giving a message to the Dalits, it was the Sangh that had advised the BJP to forge an alliance with

Mayawati's party in Uttar Pradesh thrice. First, it decided not to support Mayawati in 1995 when the party could not form the government in UP in the 1993 elections despite the tide of the Ram Mandir movement. At that time Kalyan Singh was completely against this decision. Then it was repeated in 1997. In 2002, despite the reluctance of veteran BJP leader Rajnath Singh, the BJP again supported Mayawati. The RSS was entirely behind these decisions as the BJP's Dalit strategy has been considered to be completely Sangh-supported. Therefore, when there was an incident of lynching of Dalits in the name of cow protection in Gujarat's Una in July 2016, there was a lot of noise in the Parliament. Debates broke out across the country. BSP supremo Mayawati was vocal against the BJP after this incident. Meanwhile, in Uttar Pradesh, BJP vice-president Dayashankar Singh made an indecent remark against Mayawati in fervour, "Today Mayawatiji has become a character worse than a prostitute. That's why the workers nurtured by Kanshi Ram are leaving her and the BSP is coming to an end. Mayawatiji gives ticket to someone for 1 crore rupees, but if someone gives 2 crores, then she gives him a ticket and if someone is ready to give 3 crores in the evening, she gives him the ticket." There was uproar as soon as this video of Dayashankar's went viral. Parliament was in session and Mayawati was present in the Rajya Sabha, When the opposition raised this issue, the then Finance Minister and Leader of the House, Arun Jaitley, address her as 'Behen Mayawati'; he first condemned Dayashankar's statement and expressed regret. After that he bluntly said that strict action will be taken against Dayashankar. Within hours, Dayashankar was thrown out of the party.

But soon after this incident the BJP-Sangh indicated that language like Dayashankar's would not be tolerated at all on the Dalit issue. How seriously the Sangh leadership had taken this matter could be gauged from the fact that immediately after the episode, Dr Krishna Gopal, Sangh's *Sah-Sarkaryavah* and who was responsible for coordinating with the BJP visited the residence of the then Home Minister Rajnath Singh. He had two rounds of consultations with BJP National President Amit Shah and other senior leaders at 17 Akbar Road. In this further strategy was considered. In the discussion held in this meeting, the Sangh-BJP leaders also felt that whether it is the Rohith Vemula episode or the Una incident, the secular brigade drags the BJP into it as part of the conspiracy because the secular camp has realized that putting BJP in the dock of communalism gives them political advantage. So, now an attempt is being made to defame the BJP on the social agenda.

Then, Raksha Parv which is celebrated by the Sangh on the occasion of Rakshabandhan was on August 18 that year. Under the damage control strategy, this time the Sangh directed the Swayamsevaks to get Rakhis tied by the Dalit sisters and go to their homes and talk so that social goodwill/harmony can be created again. BJP also instructed its workers to participate in this Raksha Parv. Simultaneously, the Sangh started working on a strategy to keep a watch on the cow protectors. The impact of the Una incident was that the then Chief Minister Anandiben Patel's departure in Gujarat was sudden (Anandiben announced her resignation in a Facebook post on August 2, 2016), while her farewell was earlier linked to the BJP's retirement age of 75 years. To compensate for the Dayashankar case, Amit Shah instructed the leaders to keep a check on rhetoric while the then Uttar Pradesh BJP President Keshav Prasad Maurya also repeated this warning by meeting the officials. The BJP directed all its 17 Dalit MPs from Uttar Pradesh to hold a goodwill ceremony and increase travel to Dalit areas. Amit Shah himself went to a Dalit house to have meal. In other states, Dalit leaders were asked to create a new social platform at their level and run a campaign to uphold the faith of Dalits. To thwart anti-Dalit sentiment at the national level, the party devised a four-pronged strategy—first, a systematic response, in which the statistics of Dalit atrocities were compared. Second, to establish direct contact with Dalits at the lower level, especially non-Jatav Dalits. It included talk of setting up new enterprises from the loans given to Dalits under Stand-Up India and the benefits of Mudra Bank scheme. Third, by using the Sangh's network to improve the image among Dalits and to participate in the Raksha Parv of the Sangh. Fourth, the attempt to connect most of the Dalit leaders with the BJP so that the message goes out that the party is with the Dalits.

BJP leader and former Union Minister of State Sanjay Paswan told me at that time, "No political party is able to understand the aspirations of the new generation of Dalit youth. Nothing will change with the gimmicky symbols of eating and bathing with Dalits. This society understands the language of the eyes, not the numbers. Now we have to talk to the new generation of Dalit youth." Paswan had further added, "Congress, Communists and Socialists talk about caste with full conscious mind whereas BJP always does so with subconscious mind. So, we have made mistakes in understanding the recent events and in assessing the circumstances." Whether the party or the Sangh publicly agreed with Paswan or not, but both the organizations realized that whether it was Dalit or other sections of the society, they would have to communicate with the youth to connect them. For that social harmony cannot be established only through symbols and social media, but a group of intellectuals will also have to be created.

Brainstorming for a New Intellectual Movement before Holi

The Sangh-BJP had realized that it was still on back foot in the fight for social perceptions and a new strategy needed to be worked out. The image that it was more concerned about cow than humanity was created by the intellectuals of the so-called opposing ideology, which was a challenge for the Sangh-BJP to break. Earlier, even before the Bihar Assembly Elections held in October-November 2015, intellectuals of opposing ideologies had created an atmosphere by raising the voice of 'intolerance' by taking steps like returning awards. That was followed by the

Jawaharlal Nehru University (JNU) episode in February 2016, where Parliament attack convict Afzal Guru's death anniversary celebrations were held and anti-national slogans were allegedly raised (the confirmation in court is awaited). In the same case, on February 12, 2016, the then president of the JNU Students' Union was arrested in connection with the event where anti-India slogans were raised, after which the atmosphere worsened. Both the BJP and the Sangh got opportunities to issue explanation on the issue of patriotism versus anti-nationalism. The BJP very smartly gave preference to the word 'nationalism' over 'cultural nationalism' so that it could not be labelled as communal. Congress, Left supported those JNU students on whom there were allegations of raising anti-national slogans like 'Bharat tere tukde honge'. The intellectuals opposing the BJP-Sangh had also opened a front against the Modi government. The BJP-Sangh was not able to counter the atmosphere being created by the intellectuals in the required manner.

In February 2016, the JNU episode became the immediate cause. The Sangh and the BJP felt themselves surrounded by issues like the suicide of Rohit Vemula in January 2016 who was a Dalit student at the Central University in Hyderabad, the Dadri incident during the 2015 Bihar Assembly elections and award-return in protest against it and intolerance. The saffron family was shocked by intellectuals with opposing views on these episodes. The way in which a perception on the issue of nationalism was being created in the intellectual world about BJP and Sangh during the JNU incident, it created a deep rift in the mind of the Vichara Parivar. The pain was more about the fact that on all such cases it got the support of its cadre, but the whole group of intellectuals stood against it. In such a situation, a meeting of top leaders of the Sangh-BJP took place. It was probably from March 22-23, 2016. Some prominent policy-makers of the Sangh Parivar gathered at Haryana Bhawan located near Mandi House in Delhi. During the meeting on first day, 14 important faces including Sangh's *Sarkaryavah* Bhaiyyaji Joshi, Saha-*Sarkaryavah* Dattatreya Hosabale, Dr. Krishna Gopal, J. Nandakumar and BJP National President Amit Shah, National General Secretary Ramlal, Ram Madhav were present. The next day, on March 23, the number increased four-fold, which included some intellectuals as well. The bottom line of two days of great churning was -'This is happening due to lack of influence in education, NGOs and English media. We have to intervene at the intellectual level and form our own intellectual group strategically." The restlessness of the Sangh and its organizations actually stemmed from the irony that it has a strong base and influence in the political-social sphere, including among students and farmers-labourers, But the Sangh, which is 91 years old (in 2016 according to the establishment of the Sangh), does not have the same effect in the intellectual field. It was a time of self-reflection for the Sangh because in these 91 years it has spread its 'branches' in every direction, but why could it not establish its 'roots' in the intellectual world?

In the words of a leader who attended the meeting, "In the 2004 and 2009 Lok Sabha elections, the BJP has been taking 20-22 percent votes even when it faced defeat. We have reached the nooks and corners, but are weak in the intellectual world. Now while maintaining our neutrality, we have to try for those who would speak in our favour. If we have a government at the Centre, then there should be a successful effort to expand its scope." After this brainstorming, some activities started immediately while long-term blueprints were made for some, which will be mentioned later. But it was implemented immediately in the Haryana Bhawan meeting itself and the first important decision was taken that the people of this cadre-based organization immediately handed over the responsibility of raising their cadre in the field of intellectuals to J Nandakumar, the then All India *sah-prachar pramukh* of the Sangh. Nandakumar has been working in Kerala which is the stronghold of the Left, and after the Modi government acquired power in Delhi, the Sangh entrusted him with the responsibility as *sah-prachar pramukh* under a strategy. The following year in March 2017, at the meeting of the Akhil Bhartiya *Pratinidhi Sabha* held in Coimbatore, Tamil Nadu. J Nandakumar was appointed by the Sangh as the national convener of its apex ideological body *'Prajna Pravah'* . This organization was started by stalwarts like KS Sudarshan, Dattopant Thengadi and P Parameswaran of Sangh with the aim of firmly fighting the Left ideology. With this appointment of Nandkumar, the Sangh seemed to have expressed the agenda of its secret meeting in Haryana Bhawan. Nandakumar has given a tough challenge to the Left in Kerala and was very active on social media, especially on Twitter. He also played an important role in its inclusion in the Sangh. But there was also a challenge in taking this campaign forward because most of the autonomous organizations with the help of which the Sangh wanted to establish intellectual roots, seemed to be competing for credit by focusing on seminars and aiming at gaining influence in power. In such a situation, before producing its intellectuals, the Vichar Pariwar needed to do research on the Left itself because intellectuals like Bipin Chandra, Romila Thapar among the left remained academic from beginning to end. But such situation is not seen in the right wing, which the Sangh calls 'Nationalism'. Therefore, Sangh made up its mind to itself handle the responsibility of coordination in the organizations.

After the brainstorming in Haryana Bhawan, a temporary office was built in the back of the government residence of the then Union AYUSH Minister Shripad Naik, from where the focus was mainly on teachers related to social science, history, political science. Simultaneously, the team sat here and started the work of selecting teachers who were related to or close to their ideology. On the other hand, the BJP strategically intensified its fight in the name of nationalism. Every fortnight on behalf of the Sangh, under the supervision of Dr Krishna Gopal, about a dozen such meetings were held in Pusa or other places, in which separate sessions of intellectuals of Dalit and backward classes were held. Arjun Ram Meghwal, MP from Bikaner also participated in similar meetings and he spoke effectively. Later, he was also rewarded by being included in the Modi cabinet. So, Sangh considered it necessary to cultivate social balance even while connecting the intellectuals because the hegemony of a particular class could weaken this movement. Also, many times the issues are related to a particular community or caste and if the intellectuals of the same society share their thought about it, then its effect is different.

Intellectual Fellowship Initiative: From *Ujjain Simhastha* to *Vichar Mahakumbh*

An important initiative in this regard was organized on May 12-14, 2016 at Ninaura near Ujjain by organizing the International *Vichar Mahakumbh*, the script of which had already been written. Apart from this event held during Ujjain *Simhastha*, another new thing happened at that time - BJP President Amit Shah's harmony ablution with Dalit saints and monks. Just a day before the *Vichar Mahakumbh*, an ablution programme of Dalit saints with Shah was organized in *Simhastha* which was first called *'Shabri Snan'*, but later it was renamed as 'Social harmony'. But the monks and saints strongly opposed it. So, in the end it was named *'Sant Snan'*. Publicly, (Late) Anil Madhav Dave who was the convener of *Vichar Mahakumbh* and a BJP leader and who later became a Minister in the Modi government called it a product of the media. His argument was, "Everyone is same in the river, then where does the talk of harmony come from?" But be it Sangh or BJP, there was a special purpose hidden in its working style, which Sangh calls socialism and BJP calls politics. Ablution took the agenda ahead. The next day on May 12, the three-day *Vichar Mahakumbh* began completely under the patronage of the Sangh. It was inaugurated by *Sarsanghchalak* Mohan Bhagwat himself and *Sarkaryavah* Bhaiyyaji Joshi who was the second important person in the Sangh was present in the event during all three days. It was named ideological intellectual conference, in which there were also sessions of discussion on various topics like education, health, agriculture, women empowerment, values of life, relationship between science and religion. But the strategy of the Sangh Parivar was to widen its social base by focusing on the lowest strata of the society through all these initiatives. Therefore, the then Shivraj Singh Chouhan government of Madhya Pradesh organized this 'Vichar Mahakumbh' under the direct supervision of the Sangh. Anil Madhav Dave, the convener of this Mahakumbh told me, "Vichar Mahakumbh is like a religious parliament. Its purpose was to contemplate for change, where a new way has begun."

The strategy of this event was started at the time when the Modi government was allegedly being called a government for 'suit-boot' or 'corporates'. After holding discussions in different forums in BJP and Sangh, the blueprint of *'Vichar Mahakumbh'* in *'Simhastha'* was woven. It was a part of the celebrations of the birth centenary year celebrations of Pt Deendayal Upadhyay, the founder of Jana Sangh which was the predecessor of the BJP. A strategy was made to convey the message that emerged from the brainstorming at Vichar Mahakumbh in Ninaura to other states also through different mediums. There was a strategy to spread the message emanating from this gathering, especially in the BJP ruled states. According to a BJP leader, "The controversy over the recent removal of Pandit Jawaharlal Nehru from the curriculum by the BJP government in Rajasthan is part of the same agenda that was weakened by allegations of saffronisation during the Vajpayee government. But now there is no compulsion of alliance. Hence the Sangh is thinking of including Indian sages, gods and goddesses and spirituality in the NCERT syllabus as well." Since such an effort cannot be successful in a day, the Sangh took steps to create an atmosphere through a series of big events like *'Vichar Mahakumbh'* . *Sarsanghchalak* Mohan Bhagwat, during the inauguration of *'Vichar Mahakumbh'* , described the current environment in the country as favourable to their ideas. He said, "Let us create an environment to bring change in the society. Today the environment has been created in the country, but we need to work in that direction." National General Secretary Ram Madhav, who had come directly from the Sangh to BJP, also addressed a special session on 'Ideological Vision and Society' at the *Mahakumbh*. So, the strategy of the family was to widen the ideological-political base by penetrating the lower strata of the society so that the idea of organizing the society which the Sangh has been working on for three generations, can be realized in its own way in the present environment. It meant that the people of the lower strata should be connected with the Sangh-BJP at the ideological and political level, while connecting them with the stream of development.

Media...Medium...Concept: A Professional Initiative

The Sangh had realized that the media also plays a role in creating any kind of perception. Therefore, during the *'Vichar Mahakumbh'* organized at Ninaura during the *Simhastha* of Ujjain, the Sangh had decided that the multilingual news agency 'Hindusthan Samachar' related to its views would be moulded in a professional manner. As to who should be given the command of this agency running in a dormant state, four people were shortlisted at the level of the Sangh. But the Sangh wanted that its command should be handed over to a person who is devoted to the ideology. While working in 'India Today', I investigated it thoroughly and it came to the fore that the blueprint was already ready, like pieces on a chessboard. But the Sangh is working only on when and where to put which pieces, and there was definitely a discussion with the BJP for the work to be done at the government level. The *'Ninaura Vichar Mahakumbh'* was inaugurated by *Sarsanghchalak* Mohan Bhagwat and concluded by Prime Minister Narendra Modi. *Sarkaryavah* Bhaiyyaji Joshi was present in the event on all three days.

Meanwhile, the then Rajya Sabha MP of BJP and industrialist RK Sinha gets a call. Sinha is given a message from the other side – 'Reach Ninaura immediately, the Sangh leadership wants to talk to you.' Bhaiyyaji Joshi and Sinha meet alone. What was formally said in this conversation is not disclosed, but according to those who worked on the full script, Sinha is given a message from the top leadership of the Sangh - 'The Sangh leadership has decided to hand over the *Hindusthan Samachar Samvad Samiti* to you and now you will take care of it.'

Under Sangh's strategy, Sinha executes it immediately and three days later on May 17, 2016, he is made the custodian of the Communication Committee at the meeting of the Board of Directors. In just 12 days, a grand building built by Sinha in Sector-63 of Noida, adjacent to Delhi, is prepared according to the needs of Hindustan News, whose formal inauguration is also done by Bhaiyyaji on 1st June. Then on June 10, Dattatreya Hosabale, *Sah-Sarkaryavah* of the Sangh, reaches this office in Noida and also guides the entire team of the *Samvad Samiti* in this way, "You should give more support to positive, development-oriented news and don't over-promote the news about violence, crime, terrorism."

It is also a coincidence that the day Hosabale reaches the Hindustan News Agency's office, the Union Information and Broadcasting Ministry announces a new advertising policy, which was a long-standing demand in the media. But by adding Hindusthan Samachar in the criteria of this policy, this agency connected to the Vichar Pariwar seemed to be getting the direct benefit. After that, disputes about this policy started to arise. Naturally, it was alleged that because of the Sangh Parivar, Hindusthan Samachar has been added to this policy. To understand the whole matter, one has to look at the advertising policy as well. The Narendra Modi government, with an absolute majority of the BJP, had implemented the new advertising policy, due to which Hindusthan Samachar seemed to be rejuvenated. In the new advertising policy, the government had made a criterion of 100 points for advertisements. Earlier there was no such criterion for advertisements from the government, i.e. DAVP. According to the new policy, the criteria was as: 25 marks for having RNI/ ABC certificate, 20 marks for deducting provident fund of employees, 15 marks for PTI UNI/Hindustan news subscription, 10 marks for having own printing press, 10 marks for paying press council fee and 12 to 20 marks pages wise. Now the policy of giving proportion and prices of advertisements according to the numbers was made. The most advantageous thing for the agency in the new policy was that it was now mandatory for newspapers to take subscription of the agency separately for each edition, only then it could get its benefit in getting advertisements. This policy was bound to benefit Hindusthan Samachar as it is the only agency that is multilingual and has very low monthly rates. Due to this policy, new competition among agencies was natural. Rakesh Manjul, the then CEO and Editor-in-Chief of Hindusthan Samachar said in a conversation with 'India Today', "We are going to tie up with a big Indian IT company of print media that will help us. We want to give big support to small newspapers in the unorganized sector. Very soon many big brands will be joining us." However, MK Razdan, CEO of the then-established news agency Press Trust of India (PTI), expressed his opinion on this new policy, "We are a news agency. If any policy is promoting a news agencies, then why should we object?"

Hindusthan Samachar: A Long-term Thought

Before the strategy of the Sangh, the basic objectives of the establishment of *Hindusthan Samachar Samvad Samiti* have to be seen, because often the brigade who defames any organization by tagging the Sangh also creates trouble. The top leaders of the Sangh were aware of this. The foundation of Hindusthan Samachar was laid after independence by Shivshankar alias Dadasaheb Apte, a senior *pracharak* of the Sangh in 1948. At that time, it was established as a company for 'Indian journalists with national views' and in 1956 it was given the form of a cooperative. It is the only multilingual news agency in the country that gives news in more than a dozen languages like Bangla, Odia, Telugu, Kannada, Malayalam, Gurmukhi, Marathi, apart from Hindi and English. The agency also claims that this had given the first news of China's invasion of India in 1962. Its condition actually worsened during the Emergency, when former Prime Minister Indira Gandhi imposed emergency in the country and also attacked the institutions seen in protest, including the leaders of the opposition parties, after which the Hindustan News never gained full strength. When the NDA government was formed at the centre under the leadership of Atal Bihari

Vajpayee, even then the government could not revive it due to political reasons. Although this agency was kept alive by some Sangh loyalists by changing its locations, but it could not retain its sharpness.

But after the formation of the Modi government at the centre, the policy of DAVP changed and this institution was handed over to the corporate to be run in a professional manner. There were also some reasons behind the policy change at the government level and handing over the Hindustan News Agency to the old *swayamsevak* on the other. Sangh Chief Mohan Bhagwat had said in the *Ninaura Vichar Mahakumbh*, "We should create an environment to bring change in the society and the environment that has been created now, we need to work in that direction." The Sangh actually wanted to build a dedicated commercial media establishment on the ideological foundation. For example, Kashmir is called an issue or dispute in the media, but the Sangh is of the view that the dispute ended on the very day the Parliament passed the resolution. So, now Kashmir can be a problem, but it cannot be an issue or a dispute. Similarly, Sangh does not accept the word '*Dharmanirpekshta*'. It looks at it as '*Panthnirpekshta*'. The Sangh does not accept even a word like 'polarization' on the basis of religion. Sangh thought that its glimpse should be clearly visible in the Hindusthan Samachar. The Sangh has also taken forward the strategy of rejuvenating this Multilingual *Samvad Samiti* so that no news related to ideological point of view gets suppressed. The Sangh wants a news system in line with its nationalist ideology because even today the media has its own credibility which at first glance plays an important role in creating or distorting the impression in one's favour. Therefore, when the Sangh worked out a plan to professionalize this *Samvad Samiti*, it wanted to entrust its responsibility to a person who would not deviate from its ideology. The top leadership of the Sangh decided that a person who had worked in Hindusthan Samachar should be given the responsibility, who should be a corporate person later; first his background should meet the criteria of the ideology family.

For this, the Sangh also understood the sentiments of the four people through messengers. Finally, when *Sarkaryavah* Bhaiyyaji Joshi called RK Sinha to Ninaura and himself informed him, Sinha replied, "In the institution where I have worked for Rs.25, I will be lucky if I am given an opportunity to take its responsibility as a director." Ultimately, the responsibility was handed over to Sinha, the founding chairman of SIS International and the then BJP MP. Sinha was ousted from journalism during the JP movement. During the same period, on advice of JP, the company called SIS that was established as a social enterprise, was recognized in the country and the world over and gave permanent employment to lakhs of people. Sinha is said to have met Guruji and Pandit Deendayal Upadhyay, the then Sangh Chief, for the first time at the age of 15 when he went to the Sangh Shiksha Varg. At that time, there was a lot of discussion about the devaluation of the rupee by the government of Indira

Gandhi. At the same time, seeing Sinha's understanding on this subject, it was suggested to be used in the work of Jana Sangh. As a journalist, he was associated with Hindusthan Samachar and remained with this agency till 1971. Then he joined 'Hindustan Times'. He worked as a war reporter during the Bangladesh war and was ousted due to critical articles during the Emergency. After that, with JP's inspiration, he laid the foundation of a private security agency. Now after being in active politics for the last 15 years, the security agency has been completely handed over to the professionals. By joining politics and social service, he is working towards uniting the society, arranging marriages without dowry etc. It was because of his penchant for corporate as well social concerns that the Sangh leadership was inclined towards him. The Sangh had advised him not to give prominence to the news promoting anti-social elements, anti-national, anti-national and terrorists through this agency, while giving him the freedom to run this institution in a completely professional manner. Through this, people associated with creative work should be encouraged irrespective of their ideology.

Manmohan Vaidya, the then Akhil Bharatiya *Prachar pramukh* of the Sangh and the current Sah *Sarkaryavah*, had clarified it a little more in a conversation with me, "The Sangh never supervises directly. It simply guides. The specialty of Hindusthan Samachar is that it is the only all-India news agency available in many Indian languages, the rest of the agencies provide services only in Hindi-

English. We wish that other important news of national concern, which the media used to ignore, should now come out. To run the institute in a professional manner, it has been handed over to the corporates." Certainly, even within the Sangh, there was an eagerness to change the image regarding Hindusthan Samachar. So, the agency also started working to break the image of being tied to a particular ideology by adopting a professional approach. Apart from the transparent process of recruitment, people like Achyutanand Mishra, Ram Bahadur Rai, Jagdish Upasane and BK Kuthiala were added to the 21 members of the Board of Directors. Apart from this, it was decided to invite people of all views and regions to editorial programmes like 'Guest of the Week'. By keeping political news limited to 50 percent, a policy was made to give news of other sectors of the society. The Sangh fulfilled its responsibility. But the next step was to take forward its initiative in the field of education so as to bring forward the intelligentsia associated with the sense of nationalism, but with the priority of its initiative of social harmony.

Nationalist Writers Meet

The Sangh's strategy regarding the media was not limited to the Hindusthan Samachar Samvad Samiti. The Sangh's strategists were systematically engaged in carrying out every activity which plays some role in creating or distorting some kind of perception in the intellectual world. The two-day Nationalist Writers' Meet was organized on July 30-31, 2016 at the NDMC Convention Centre near

Connaught Place, Delhi, as per the strategy prepared in the Haryana Bhawan meeting with a view to create a new intellectual movement. Organized under the banner of Dr. Shyamaprasad Mookerjee Research Foundation (SPMRF), that was working with BJP, independent bloggers and writers including supporters of *Vichar Parivar* were invited from across the country, who were active through their articles. In this meeting, the leaders of the Sangh and BJP had an open dialogue for two days and an initiative was taken to clear the confusion and misconceptions through question and answer. Regarding questions like differences and U-turn in the Sangh Parivar, Sangh's *Sah-Sarkaryavah* Dr. Krishna Gopal cleared some misunderstandings. He said that there is no such word as '*Sangh Parivar*'. This phrase was coined in 1992 with the aim of banning all the organizations of the Sangh after the fall of the Babri structure. In this event, Dalit thinker Arvind Neelkanthan tried his best to prove that Dr Bhim Rao Ambedkar's thoughts where like that of Hindu nationalist leaders. He described Ambedkar's adoption of Buddhism as going from one room to another in the house so that when such questions arose on the path of the harmony campaign, they could be answered. The BJP-Sangh, which is constantly on the backfoot regarding the Dalit issue, explained to the writers that if we remove Ambedkar's name from many of his quotes, then they will seem like thoughts of a Maharishi. Drawing the attention of freelance writers to some of these points, tips were offered to work with facts. In its conclusion, then

BJP President Amit Shah gave mantras regarding politics and ideology. But the Sangh, influenced by the ideas of these nationalities, asked writers, bloggers, independent thinkers to write keeping in mind various aspects of the society while maintaining their neutrality.

Behind this initiative, the pain of the Sangh was deep. The people of Sangh have been expressing anguish over the fact that during the NDA-I government, they could not even find a face with their views who could be made the President of the Indian Council of Historical Research (ICHR). More or less the same crisis arose during NDA-2 also. Then the intellectual brigade ridiculed the appointment of Gajendra Chauhan in FTII and then appointment cricketer Chetan Chauhan in NIFT which is associated with fashion. A large section of the Vichar Pariwarbelieved that the mainstream media held a grudge against it. The BJP-Sangh leaders used to express their pain like this, "The media makes fun of us if we remove the CM at the age of 75, but keeps silent on the 78-year-old Sheila Dikshit being made the Congress's CM candidate in UP. It also portrays Amit Shah in a wrong way. We have to work to change such interpretations of the media and the intelligentsia." Vinay Sahasrabuddhe, BJP vice-president and director of PPRC, said, "Research on Indian civilization-culture has become a fashion in western countries. But India's intellectual climate and research, which should have remained objective, are dominated by politics. There is never any research on ocean security, Bangladeshi infiltration, there is no research on food donation from our monasteries and temples. If there is any research on historical things or there is talk about them, it is ridiculed. Sahasrabuddhe even said, "There is an atmosphere of ideological untouchability towards the Sangh in the country and the students of the Sangh ideology do not get good guides or are not given good marks. We naturally want to abolish politico-ideological untouchability."

Marathon Exercise to Create Intellectual Pressure Group

The strategy that the Sangh-BJP had made to overpower the Left intellectuals was not limited to being in power only. However, it was certain that the Sangh Parivar, taking advantage of a stable government, wanted to move forward on this strategy rapidly. In such a situation, it created such forums or took new initiatives while retaining the autonomy of the already active organizations so that these organizations could become the carriers of right-wing ideology. The Sangh's strategy was a long-term vision, in which the right-wing organizations, while retaining their autonomy, should act as pressure groups in the same way as the Left did for decades. According to this strategy, the Sangh removed the condition of going to the '*Shakha*' to connect such people who, despite being in their profession, wanted to join the Sangh's thought forums so that such people can be identified as impartial intellectuals. The work of more than a dozen such organizations is mentioned below, which were active in various fields at that time, but later on the activities of equipping them with specific subjects started taking place. Who in the terminology of the Sangh are called 'having thoughts of nationality'; were involved in creating new intellectuals through seminars, publications, social media, etc. to compete with the Left. (See Graphic—On whom the Sangh relied) This was elaborated by India Today in its September 7, 2016 issue.

In fact, the BJP's 2014 Lok Sabha election victory played a key role in the Sangh Parivar's strategy of building a network of its intellectuals. Under this, the BJP-Sangh organized a three-day *'Vichar Mahakumbh'* at Ninaura at the time of Ujjain *Simhastha*. It was decided to hand over the Hindustan News Agency to a corporate with ideological commitment. On the other hand, BJP President Amit Shah had already handed over the responsibility of the party's magazine 'Kamal Sandesh' and the publication department to Dr. Shivshakti Bakshi, the leader of ABVP in JNU. On the lines of Rajiv Gandhi Foundation, Dr. Shyamaprasad Mookerjee Foundation started working as a think tank for BJP, which was being supervised by Amit Shah himself. Its office also shifted to 9 Ashok Road, next to the then BJP headquarters 11 Ashok Road (now shifted to Deendayal Upadhyay Road), which used to be the official residence of senior party leader Arun Jaitley while in opposition. The director of this foundation, Anirban Ganguly, started the work of giving online platform to the those whose thinking was favourable to ideology through the nationalist website and on the other hand, his team was involved in carrying out the work from book publication to the volume of biography of Shyamaprasad Mookerjee and articles on the policies of the Modi government.

Amit Malviya, the head of the IT and Social Media Department at the BJP headquarters, along with two dozen professionals, was engaged in an aggressive defense of the party in the social media war after doing instant research from the headquarters day and night. Inspired by the thoughts of the Sangh, the organization 'India Policy Foundation' (IPF) used to provide research material to the top officials of the Sangh. Its head Rakesh Sinha had published 40 books in the last seven years, i.e. from 2009 to 2016. This is what he said in a conversation with me on the intellectual initiative of the Sangh, "The way in which the Sangh and its ideology were systematically marginalized in the intellectual discourse of India, defeating it with facts and logic is an important dimension of today's discourse." The Sangh may not be formally associated with this organization, but it states that the Sangh's Saha *Sarkaryavah* Dattatreya Hosabale, Suresh Soni and the then *Akhil Bharatiya Prachar pramukh* (now he is also a *Sah-Sarkaryavah*) Manmohan Vaidya are also informally associated with the Foundation. This was the time when Sangh, for the first time, also assumed the responsibility of coordination among the organizations inspired by its ideas.

Questions were also Raised on the Strategy of the Sangh

I also interacted with leftist and socialist thinkers at that time about this intellectual campaign of the Sangh. The

Sangh was accused of lagging behind the times and working with one-sided thinking. Political analyst Yogendra Yadav argued, "The BJP-Sangh today is in a world which is 25-30 years behind when the academics were dominated by the Left. The second truth is that because of the narrow and negative thinking of the Sangh, the best intellectuals of the country want to remain free from saffron stains. Despite being in power and having many incentives to distribute, only third-rate intellectuals are joining them. Whereas Prof Anand Kumar at JNU added another to his assessment, "The Sangh and BJP's approach towards Indian civilization and society lacks historical authenticity. Its attitude towards history is flat. They present Hindu vs Muslim according to their convenience. Their grasp on economics is also incomplete, which is supportive of simple capitalism and the economics of nationalism is irrelevant in today's world." But Anand Kumar welcomed the Sangh Parivar's initiative to develop its intellectual base. But he had also warned the Sangh that if instead of absolute truth, they resorted to small and incomplete facts, then their act of intellectualism would prove to be short-lived.

But when we look at the comments of these two contrasting ideologues and look at the best coordinated strategy of the Sangh-BJP after the year 2014, it becomes clear that the Sangh Parivar did not take temporary action which would only be limited till the BJP came to power. Rather, it was engaged in carrying out its intellectual movement with a long-term thinking and only after preparing the complete script. The purpose of the Sangh-BJP is also mentioned above. But it is necessary to reiterate here that even when there is no saffron-minded government in the country, this organization should work as a pressure group, the job which till now intellectual group of the left has been doing. It is also pertinent to note the views of the people associated with the Sangh and BJP regarding this initiative, with whom I spoke at length. Mahesh Sharma, editor of 'Deendayal Vangmaya' and 'Ekatma Manav Darshan Research and Development Foundation', said, "The pride of being Indian is not inherent in the education system of the country. Sangh is working for this pride only because at present we are studying western. Whereas Dr Shivshakti Bakshi, Head of BJP Publications Division argued, "Future India has to move beyond the Marxist rhetoric of the '70s. Intellectual movement is the need of the hour."

"Our aim is to establish cultural nationalism by minimizing Marxist dominance in intellectual discourse," said Rajya Sabha MP Dr Rakesh Sinha. According to KN Govindacharya, a Sangh *pracharak* and BJP leader, "Sangh's ideology was considered hostile by the Left. Even after coming to power, BJP's lack of experience is evident." BJP IT department Chief Amit Malviya, who was involved in the 'Nationalist Writers' Meet', said, "We want to make the BJP a brand that is capable of engaging more people based on ideology and good governance."

That is, the strategy of the Sangh had been actualized to a large extent and the people associated with it were also beginning to express it, the aim of which was to create an environment in which such intellectuals, who play a neutral role, would be inclined towards Sangh. Not only this, emphasis was also laid on calling representatives of opposing ideologies in seminars or other events so that the views would not remain one-sided. For this purpose, the details of the work of the organizations on which this responsibility rested, were as follows:

Attempts to deepen the dominance of nationalism / right-wing thinking, on whom rested Sangh's responsibility

Vivekananda International Foundation

What it does: Works as a think tank on national security, diplomacy, especially advising the government on the issue of Pak-China. Interaction with delegations visiting from abroad.

Activities: Monthly talk series titled 'Vichar'. Apart from security, the problem of rivers also discussed. Discussion on security and foreign policy with about 100 people in a one-day conference. Discussion on India-EU relations was held in Delhi on 1 August 2016. Round table conference on topics related to diplomacy. Round table discussion with leaders of various parties on the need of Rajya Sabha in July. Since Modi government assumed power, about 150 such events had taken place in just two years till the year 2016.

Publication: Vivek (e-Journal).

Who is the Chief: General NC Vij (Retd.) became the director after Ajit Doval became the National Security Advisor, then former Ambassador Satish Chandra, former RAW Chief CD Sahai and RK Sahni retired from Military Intelligence joined.

India Foundation

What it does: Active on national security, foreign policy and cultural issues.

Activities: Organizing 'Idea Conclave' every year, in which the top functionaries of the Sangh and Ministers of the Modi government have also been involved. Organized in Goa in the year 2015. A conclave was held in Jaipur on the issue of counter terrorism. Held bilateral dialogue in June-July 2016 on India-Myanmar relations. In March 2016, the 'Young Thinkers Meet' took place in Panchmarhi, where Dattatreya Hosabale and Krishna Gopal from the Sangh participated.

Publication: India Foundation Journal

Who's heading: Ram Madhav (BJP General Secretary) and Shaurya Doval directly responsible; many Ministers from the Modi government are on board of directors.

India Policy Foundation (IPF)

What it does: Acts as a think tank to provide ideological material by researching the Sangh's own issues. Finding solutions by discussing contemporary problems intellectually.

Activities: National Seminar on NITI Aayog - the new avatar of Planning Commission, Organized Seminars on topics like Integral Humanism, Moral Crisis, Effects of Neo-liberalism, Equal Opportunity Commission, Communal Violence Bill, Pakistan. Regular dialogue with the top leaders of the Sangh and discussions on contemporary matters. On August 8-9, 2016, Sangh's Saha *Sarkaryavah* Dattatreya Hosabale held frequent meetings at the IPF office. Such meetings keep taking place.

Publication: Daily translation and fortnightly publication of 25 Urdu newspapers. Quarterly magazine named 'Pakistan Watch'.

Who's heading: Before being nominated as a Rajya Sabha MP, Dr. Rakesh Sinha, who was the ideologue of the Sangh, was looking after it as the director, while Bajrang Lal was its chairman. Now Dr. Kuldeep Ratnu is the Director and Prof. Kapil Kapoor is the Chairman. Apart from these, more than a dozen professors, academicians are associated with this think tank.

Dr. Shyama Prasad Mookerjee Research Foundation

What it does: Researching ideology, promoting nationalist ideas, and creating a suitable platform and environment for government policies, directly under the supervision of the BJP, just like the Rajiv Gandhi Foundation of the Congress.

Activities: A two-day Nationalist Writers' Meet in Delhi for independent bloggers-writers from across the country on 30-31 July, 2016 in which Sangh's *Sah-Sarkaryavah* Krishan Gopal and BJP's Sah-*sangathan mantri* BL Santosh were present. Amit Shah also joined. Nationalist online website for like-minded writers, 'Modi Doctrine' – a book on Modi's foreign policy was released on August 13, 2016.

Publications: Values on Syama Prasad Mookerjee, e-Journal, website.

Who's heading it: Director Anirban Ganguly

Research and Development Foundation for Integral Humanism

What it does: To conduct research on the philosophy of Pt Deendayal

Upadhyay, the ideal of BJP-Sangh, to organize discussions on various dimensions of Integral Humanism.

Activities: Organizing Deendayal Memorial Lecture every year. On November 29, 2015, it was on the relevance of Integral Humanism, in 2016, Dr. Krishan Gopal, *Sah-Sarkaryavah* of the Sangh gave an address on 'Importance of Pt Deendayal's Literature'. Organizing Swadhyaya Mandal every month, in which discussion on good governance and Integral Humanism. Swadhyaya Mandal recently took place on how Muslim nations worship their country as their motherland.

Publication: Editing of 'Deendayal Sampurna Vangmay'

Who is heading: BJP Leader Mahesh Chandra Sharma

Deendayal Research Institute

What it does: The work of putting the philosophy of Pt. Deendayal Upadhyaya into practice. Trying to actualize the philosophy of Integral Humanism by making it a model of rural development in Chitrakoot, Beed and Gonda.

Activities: Cultural activities to develop thinking of country, nature and self-reliance on the points of education, health, self-reliance and virtue. Discussion on topics like malnutrition and skill development by conducting seminars for intellectuals every month.

Publication: Yuganukul Nav-Rachana (quarterly).

Who is the Chief: Principal Secretary Atul Jain is in the role of Chief Executive and Abhay Mahajan is the Chief in the role of National Organization Secretary.

Bhartiya Vichar Kendram

What it does: Founded in 1982 by the *Pracharak* of the Sangh in Kerala, which serves as a forum for intellectuals. The state continued to be considered a bastion of leftist ideas. Therefore, this organization united like-minded organizations and people by starting the work of promoting Indian civilization and cultural values.

Activities: Monthly seminars on topics such as history, philosophy, economics, politics, social life, education. College based education on important subjects, special courses for youth. Organizing lecture series by people from different fields.

Publications: Philosophy and Concept of Deendayal Upadhyay, Progress of Science.

Who is the Chief: P Parameswaran, who was the *pracharak* of the Sangh and the vice-president of Jana Sangh, who was also the director of the Deendayal Research Institute. He passed away recently.

Public Policy Research Centre (PPRC), Rambhau Mhalgi Prabodhini

What it does: Providing material by researching policies to other leaders-MPs including BJP National President Amit Shah. Preparation of research reports on social, economic and political subjects, while Prabodhini's job is to give training to the people of Sangh-BJP from time to time. Such activities keep taking place.

Activities: Did a survey of the villages in Jharkhand-Maharashtra on how the village returns to its old pattern after being free from open defecation and submitted the research report to the Prime Minister. Prepared a report on government's performance for two years. Research on the socio-cultural change brought about with electricity supply to every village.

Publications: Writing on various topics, 'Netrutva Sadhana' camp for technocrat youth and research report on various schemes. Organized a 'Netrutva Sadhana' camp also in Srinagar during the first term of the Modi government.

Headed by: BJP National Vice President and MP Vinay Sahasrabuddhe and Nalin Kohli. Sahasrabuddhe is the Vice Chairman of Rambhau Mhalgi. Ravindra Sathe is the Director General of Rambhau Mhalgi, while many leaders of the Sangh like Anirudh Deshpande, V Satish are associated with its management team.

Hindusthan Samachar

What it does: Multilingual news agency that draws inspiration from the thoughts of the Sangh and BJP. But after the formation of the Modi government, preparations were made to pursue it in a professional manner. Responsibility of removing the alleged ill-will towards the Sangh-BJP in the media.

Activities: In order to promote the news agency as a professional, the impetus was given and changes were made after Modi government came to power. The Modi government has also given this agency a place in the category of PTI and UNI through a new advertising policy. The grand office was inaugurated by the Sangh's *Sarkaryavah* Bhaiyyaji Joshi and Saha-*Sarkaryavah* Dattatreya Hosabale guided. The top officials of the Sangh are in direct contact.

Publications: Three magazines weekly, fortnightly and monthly.

Who is the Chief: RSS volunteer and BJP Rajya Sabha MP RK Sinha is its patron, while Ram Bahadur Rai is looking after it as the group editor.

Other Institutions

– Centre for Economic and Policy Research

– Policy Review Centre

–'Think India' under the banner of ABVP

– Indian History Compilation Committee

– Jammu and Kashmir Studies Centre

I spoke to eminent media analyst Sudhish Pachauri on the initiative of the Sangh-BJP intellectual movement and it is necessary to quote a part of what he said. He said that leftist or rightist, both have to understand that intellectuals are not made by using sticks but by sensitivity. In fact, as part of its strategy, the Sangh was engaged in creating such an environment in the society and the intellectual world by which the intellectuals would realize how history was viewed with lop-sided thinking for a long time and every initiative of the Sangh was seen in a particular colour. That is why in every meeting when Sangh BJP leaders and neutral intellectuals met, it was mentioned with examples how the Left intellectuals distorted the facts according to their own will. Pachauri said, "Intellectuals are not made to order. Though the Rashtriya Swayamsevak Sangh is in power through the BJP they are still anguished. They have a remorse that they do not have their own media or a queue of famous intellectuals and artists! Their movement of 'nationalism' too often gets caught in the wrath of the oppression of minorities and Dalits nowadays. For now, they have a shield of power. But what happens when there is no power? What about the potential 'backlash'? Perhaps that is why by holding a meeting of academicians, intellectuals and writers who are with them they have decided that such arrangements should be made that in the coming days, along with their media, such think tanks, writers and artists should be gathered who also gain 'acceptance'! The Sangh has every right to think so. But is it possible the way it is being desired? That is, can they, too, have right-wing intellectuals to compete with left-wing and liberal intellectuals as they do in the West? At the heart of the Sangh's ideology is a past melody derived from orientalism and a sense of uncritical pride in it, which goes on like this – we were 'Jagadguru' 5,000 years ago. Our country was called the golden bird. Milk and curd flowed like river. We had '*Pushpak Viman*'. There was also the atom bomb and there was also plastic surgery. The western invaders stole everything and made us slaves. Western education and values taught us to hate ourselves. Left liberal intellectuals are the carriers of this. We have to become Vishwa Guru again. Whatever heretical and western cultural obstacles are in this path have to be corrected. The Sangh also runs '*Bauddhik*' for its workers, where intellectual education is given. But there is no room for questioning, argument, controversy, disagreement in them. A person initiated into such a '*Bauddhik*' stays away from the intellectual development and depth of thought that is found in many left-wing and liberal intellectuals. If Communists are in power, they suppress opposite intellectuals with sticks, as it was once seen in the Soviet Union or is still seen in China and as Hitler used to suppress people in Germany. Similarly, the *Hindutvavadis* also seem to believe in '*Lathi-Lathi Jayate Tattvabodhaha*' instead of '*Vade-Vade Jayate Tattvabodhaha*'. The concept of nation formed in the freedom struggle was 'inclusive', in which everyone had a place. But the concept of 'Hinduist nationalism' believes in 'exclusion', in which there is no room for dissent. Why such widely acceptable intellectuals have not yet been seen in the Sangh's long history? By ordering, 'thought police' can be created, but such intellectuals or artists cannot be made who can make *'sursari sam sab kahen hit hoi'*(welfare of all) possible like Tulsi!

Certainly, Sudheesh Pachauri highlighted the flaws of both left or right intellectuals. But Sangh had learned from the past and had a discomfort. The Sangh does not hesitate to assimilate the modern thoughts. In the words of Manmohan Vaidya, the then Akhil Bharatiya *Prachar pramukh* (current *Sarkaryavah*) of the Sangh, himself, "The RSS has been keeping pace with the wave of change since its inception. We are moving forward despite attacks from ideological opponents." Due to the need of the hour to integrate tradition with modernity, the Sangh officially joined the social media platform, which it earlier avoided. It changed the uniform. The message of welcoming many such changes with an open mind had gone out from the Sangh, which naturally had an impact in the intellectual world. The Sangh worked for this in a sequential manner. Some kind of thought was formulated through group meetings and then instead of implementing it directly, it was designed by forming a group of intellectuals. In such a situation, the Sangh-BJP took a special initiative in the field of education with coordination and Rajasthan became its laboratory. Through the field of education, the Sangh organized such events, which were necessary to strengthen its intellectual roots and for the BJP, the ground for 2019 election was being laid.

❑

13

CHAPTER

Gyan Sangam

After preparing the script of the intellectual movement, the Sangh carried out a campaign of change in education to nurture its roots and brainstormed ideas to create an atmosphere.

The Sangh Parivar had started the intellectual movement, but its roots could not be established only by increasing the activities of the think tank. For this, it was necessary to sow the seeds from where the thinking develops. The education received by a person plays an important role in his thinking. Hence the Sangh devised a strategy to nurture the 'roots' through BJP governments (state and centre). In the year 2016 itself, in the three-day meeting of the Akhil Bhartiya *Pratinidhi Sabha* of the Sangh, which was held in Nagaur, Rajasthan, a resolution regarding education was passed, through which the Sangh had indicated the future outline with the work that was already going on. Education is an aspect touching every section of the society. But due to the commercialization of education, the rich class educates their children in big schools, but the poor class has to depend on government schools. In such a situation, the Sangh, in its important proposal on education, emphasized on making quality and affordable education accessible to all.

The proposal of the Sangh was – “Education is an essential tool in the all-round development of any nation and society; the responsibility for its maintenance, promotion and protection lies with both society and the government. Education is a means of holistic development of the personality of the student by nurturing the qualities and possibilities which are inside of him in the seed form. In a public-welfare state, it is the fundamental responsibility of the government to ensure the availability of food, clothes, house and employment as well as education and medicine to every citizen. India is the country of the largest number of youths. It is the responsibility of the society and government to make this youth a participant in the scientific, technical, economic and social development of the country by providing him uninterrupted opportunities for proper education according to his aptitude, ability and capability. Today, all parents want to provide good education to their children. Whereas there has been a significant increase in the number of students getting education, it has become rare for all of them to get affordable and quality education. In the past years, due to inadequate allocation in education by the government and lack of priority to education in the policies, institutions working for profit motive have got open space. Today poor students are being deprived of proper and quality education. As a result, the increasing economic inequality in the society is a matter of concern for the entire nation. In the present educational scenario, the government should come forward for its responsibility of providing adequate resources and formulating appropriate policies. The increasing commercialization of education should be stopped so that students are not forced to get expensive education. The government should strengthen the autonomous and self-regulatory system of determining the level of educational institutions, infrastructure, service conditions, fees and norms, etc., so that the policies can be implemented transparently. It is the belief of the Akhil Bharatiya *Pratinidhi Sabha* that every boy and girl should get value-based, nationalistic, employment-oriented and skill-based education in an environment of equal opportunity. To improve the level of teachers of government and private schools, proper training, proper salary and strengthening of their dutifulness is also very necessary.

Traditionally, society has played an important role in providing affordable and quality education to the common man in our country. Even in the present context, all religious-social organizations, industry groups, academicians and prominent persons should consider their responsibility and come forward in this direction."

The last two lines of this resolution were important – "*Akhil Bhartiya Pratinidhi Sabha* urges the Central and State Governments and local bodies to ensure proper resources and suitable legal provisions to make affordable and quality education available to all. Akhil Bhartiya *Pratinidhi Sabha* also calls upon all the countrymen including *swayamsevaks* to come forward for the sacred task of imparting education-especially in rural, tribal and underdeveloped areas-so that a capable, able and knowledge-based society can be created, which will play an important role in its upliftment and development." In a separate resolution on education passed in the meeting of the *Pratinidhi Sabha*, these last two lines left a look of comfort and a smile on the face of a 68-year-old RSS swayamsvak named Vasudev Devnani, who was then the education Minister in the Rajasthan government; this meeting was taking place in one of its cities. Devnani was not a part of that government when Vasundhara Raje became the Chief Minister after a historic victory in Rajasthan in December 2013. But in October 2014, he was inducted into the cabinet and the Department of School Education (Primary-Secondary) from Cabinet Minister Kalicharan Sarraf was handed over to Devnani as independent charge. As soon as Devnani took over, the script was written to change the curriculum of Rajasthan as per the planned strategy.

In the initial weeks after Devnani became the Minister, he discussed the agenda of change in detail by meeting with all the organizations related to the education sector of the Sangh. Representatives of Vidya Bharti, Shikshan Mandal, Shiksha Bachao, Teachers' Union and Akhil Bharatiya Vidyarthi Parishad were present in these meetings. Three points emerged from these meetings- 1. To include the brave heroes of Rajasthan and the country in the curriculum, 2. The course material should be such that there is a feeling of pride in Indian culture, 3. Students should become patriots and best citizens. The work on this was done for about a year and a half. But since effecting a change in the middle of the teaching-session was not possible, the lessons of great men like Maharana Pratap, Guru Gobind Singh and Subhas Chandra Bose were added in the middle through supplementary courses. After that the Vasundhara government decided about the educational curriculum as a policy, according to which, from class I to V, 75 percent part will be about Rajasthan, 25 percent about India, and from class VI to VIII it will be 50-50 percent. From ninth grade onwards, the things about the world will be taught. Devnani took a step towards complete change and started the work of rewriting the syllabus by forming different committees. From the year 2016, it was decided to change all the courses. As such, allegations were bound to be made. The matter was not confined to Rajasthan only, some cases even reached the Parliament. But Devnani, the real swayamsevak of the Sangh, cared neither for any criticism nor for the objections of his close ones. He went ahead like a disciplined swayamsevak. The opposition even termed it as 'saffronisation of education'. But Vasudev Devnani, the Education Minister of the then Vasundhara

Raje government of Rajasthan, was not at all distracted by these allegations. He said, "Saffron is also in our Tricolour. Saffron is a symbol of sacrifice and dedication. If the new curriculum creates a sense of spirituality along with nationalism, whether one calls it saffronisation or anything else, we do not care."

This is how the Curriculum was Changed

The way in which the first experiment to change the courses took place in Rajasthan, there was a lot of controversy. Most of the controversy was due to the addition of the study of some new great personalities and the removal or reduction of the already included ones. Most of the controversy took place over the removal of parts related to the country's first Prime Minister Pandit Jawaharlal Nehru. The text on the unification of the states earlier had the picture of Pandit Nehru; but in the new textbook, Sardar Vallabhbhai Patel was put. The matter was vigorously raised in the Monsoon Session of Parliament which was rejected by the Government because Nehru had not been removed from the curriculum, rather the inclusion of others was argued about. Then Vasudev Devnani said that earlier history was confined to a particular family, but now Subhash Chandra Bose, Bal Gangadhar Tilak, Sardar Patel, Babasaheb Dr. Bhimrao Ambedkar etc. have also been given proper place.

Apart from Congress-Left organizations, intellectuals were also becoming vocal against the BJP government regarding the change in education. But the BJP was fully armed with facts. Devnani said, “The Congress had removed the text of nationalist leaders during its rule. The pages of the text of Mookerjee, Upadhyay, Savarkar were torn from the books in the middle of the session. Even the Ram-Laxman dialogue and Kumbh Mela were removed. But the BJP government has not removed any great men, but has added more. As for Nehru, he is mentioned at fifteen places in the curriculum. But when other great men are given their due place, of course, the share of the already existing ones will be less.”

In a conversation with me as a journalist for India Today, former Rajasthan Chief Minister Ashok Gehlot had said that names were removed for social harmony during his government. That is, the removal of Shyamaprasad Mookerjee, Deendayal Upadhyay, Veer Savarkar, Ram-Laxman dialogue, Kumbh Mela etc. was associated with social harmony. He said, “We did not make changes to spread communalism, but for the sake of harmony. But the whole country is worried about what the BJP is doing. BJP changed the name of ‘Rajiv Seva Kendra’ to ‘Atal Seva Kendra’. But if we form the government, we will not remove Atal’s name, but will change the name to ‘Rajiv Gandhi Atal Seva Kendra’. There is a big difference between their thinking and ours.”

But the important aspect was that the BJP government of Rajasthan included in the curriculum Jan Sangh founder Shyama Prasad Mookerjee’s Kashmir movement for ‘One Nishan, One Vidhan, One Pradhan’, Pt Deendayal Upadhyay’s Ekatm Manav Darshan, former

Sarsanghchalak KS Sudarshan's poem on Environment along with the names that were directly associated with the Sangh-BJP such as BJP leader Maneka Gandhi, Nanaji Deshmukh, Veer Savarkar. In addition, many names of those whom the Sangh considers its role model were also added to the curriculum. Among these, Bhaskaracharya, Aryabhatta are part of Sangh's early morning recital, while Panna Dhaya was added with special importance on the request of Vidya Bharati and Shikshan Mandal. However, the poem on Rani Lakshmibai, taught in Class VII, was also removed first and added latter, after the controversy. In this poem, there are lines like 'Leaving the capital', describing Scindia as a friend of the British and it was said that for this reason the poem was removed. Not only this, the thinking of the Sangh also reflected in the course on history. Now Akbar was not prefixed as 'Great' but only a Mughal ruler and, in his place, Maharana Pratap was described as 'Great'. All the Prime Ministers of the country were covered in the course, however, BJP leader and former Prime Minister Atal Bihari Vajpayee and the current Prime Minister Narendra Modi (both had a total tenure of only 8 years then) were given only nine paragraphs, while Manmohan Singh, who was PM for 10 years, was reduced to just one paragraph.

Not only this, all the model schools in Rajasthan were named after Swami Vivekananda. The curriculum includes Bhagavad Gita, Yoga, Vande Mataram, Suryanamaskar, Saraswati-worship on Vasant Panchami and awards for topper students were named after Eklavya and Meera who were idols of the Sangh. An interesting aspect was also that Amavasya was fixed for the meeting of the School Development Committee (SDC) constituted at the local level. When the Sangh started two new projects on social harmony and environment, Devnani also carried forward this agenda in Rajasthan. To woo the Gurjar community, Lord Devnarayan, Maharaja Surajmal from Jat society, Maharana Pratap, Veer Durga Das Rathod and Prithviraj Chauhan from Rajput society, Mahavir Swami, Acharya Tulsi from Jain society, Bhambhoji Maharaj and Guru Jambheshwar from Vishnoi society, tribal community Govind Guru from the Brahmin community, Chanakya from the Brahmin community, Hemu Kalani from the Sindhi society and Maharaja Daharsen, Jyotiba Phule from the Mali community were added to the curriculum. With the change in the curriculum, Devnani also indicated to be progressive while plugging the loopholes in the system.

Rajasthan became the Sangh's laboratory for change in education, but instead of looking at it as an agenda, it should be seen as a change according to the times, for which there was a need to create an atmosphere in the intellectual world and to spark a wide debate with the thought of 'Rashtra Sarvopari' (Nation is paramount). The responsibility of this work was given to Sangh's ideological body 'Prajna Pravah', which started a series of intellectual conferences taking forward the Sangh's thinking. In Bhopal, together with the Culture Department of the then Shivraj Singh Chouhan government, *'Lok-Manthan'* from November 12 to 14 was organized. But even before that the activities continued. On the lines of the 'Nationalist Writers' Meet' held in Delhi, the Sangh's Publicity Department organized a 'Writer's Camp' in Lucknow in September 2016 Like every year, the India Foundation's 'Idea Conclave' was organized in Goa in November, which had been supervised by the National General Secretary Ram Madhav, who had come directly to the BJP from the Sangh.

Lok-Manthan of 'Rashtra Sarvopari' (Nation is paramount) to challenge colonial mindset

A three-day *Lok-Manthan* programme was organized in Mansarovar Auditorium of Madhya Pradesh Legislative Assembly. Madhya Pradesh-Gujarat Governor Om Prakash Kohli, Saint of *Juna Akhara* Shri Mahamandaleshwar Swami Avdheshanand Giri, Madhya Pradesh Chief Minister Shivraj Singh Chouhan, Rashtriya Swayamsevak Sangh *Sah-Sarkaryavah* Suresh Soni, BJP's National Vice President and Rajya Sabha MP Vinay Sahasrabuddhe, the then Culture Minister Surendra Patwa and then State Culture Secretary Manoj Srivastava were present. A closer look at the agenda of this three-day event reveals the Sangh's thinking, according to which the country is still a slave to the colonial mindset, whose shackles need to be broken. On the agenda of the first day, there were topics like Impact of Colonial Mindset on Literature, Impact of Colonial Trends in Sociology, Colonialism in Political Discourse, Colonial Mindset in the field of Art-Culture, Impact of Colonialism on Science and Technology, Colonial Mindset in Social

Life, brainstorming on health and overall lifestyle. On the agenda of the second day, there were topics like nationalism does not mean opposition to modernity, the concept of modernity and lifestyle, geo-politics of India and the current global scenario, *Swadeshi* economy, industrialization and Sustainable Development, Culture in Nationality, Status of Folk Tradition and Rituals, Appropriation of National Identity and Other Identities, Women Power: in the Context of India and the West, Changes in Dalit and Deprived Narrative, Northeast: Present Scenario and Prospects, Present scenario of Jammu-Kashmir-Ladakh. On the agenda of the third and last day, there was discussion on 'Role of Art, Culture, History and Media in Nation Building', apart from the speeches of selected people and organizers on issues like nationality.

It is clear from the agenda of *'Lok-Manthan '* that the main theme of this event was freedom from colonial mentality and giving importance to the ideas full of nationalism. The Sangh also had a long-term vision behind this event because around 150 scholars from all over the country and the world participated in it. The age of more than 800 delegates who were selected to attend the event was kept at 40 years or below, which meant that the Sangh has been eyeing the young and the new generation for the ideological battle since then.

Regarding the organization of *'Lok-Manthan'*, J Nandakumar, national convener of *'Prajna Pravah'*, said that it is necessary to remove the pro-Western concept regarding nation-building, for which our goal is to establish the concept of nationality by taking India's history, art, science, culture, geography and psychology out of European theism. Even in this event, the pain of the Sangh-BJP was evident, which it had seen in the form of Dadri incident and then award-return episodes during the Bihar elections, when the intellectuals with opposing ideologies opened a front and tried to create an atmosphere against the Sangh Parivar. During *'Lok-Manthan '*, Dattatreya Hosabale, the *Sah-Sarkaryavah* of the Sangh had also said, which was mentioned by the magazine *'Yathavat'* published under the Hindusthan Samachar Samvad Samiti in its issue. Hosbale had said, "In the recent past, people of a particular ideology have tried to raise questions on nation and nationality in a systematic manner. In this sequence, they have not only neglected the idea of nationalism but have also ridiculed it, whereas in this country, the national spirit is manifested in the lives of farmers standing in the fields, workers working in factories, thinkers engaged in literary creation, artists and even common citizens. Along with this, it also appears that even after 70 years of independence, mental colonialism has kept the country occupied. That bond must be broken. *Lok-Manthan* will prove to be a means to remove this mental slavery."

Such words were spoken in Bhopal *Lok-Manthan*

'Rashtriyata' - This is commonly called *'Rashtrawad'*. But the Sangh does not accept the term *'Rashtrawad'* as

appropriate. It sees it only in the form of *'Rashtriyata'*. Speaking on the concept of nationality in the inaugural session of the *Lok-Manthan*, Suresh Soni, the *Sah-Sarkaryavah* of Sangh, had said that in front of India, on the one hand, there are life-values and social, economic, cultural creations based on the experiences of thousands of years and on the other hand, due to the invasion of new ideology, efforts have been made to adapt the compositions of the society according to them. Due to this, a situation of conflict has arisen between the two. To establish the real identity of India, we have to make the country stand on the basis of our identity. The Chief guest of the opening ceremony, *Juna Akhara* Peethadheeshwar Mahamandaleshwar Swami Avdheshanand Giri said that science has taken away sleep and mental consciousness has become blunt whereas in the scriptures it is said that one should worry about the mind. Indian sages cared about the mind, not matter. The world is a market for the West while Indian philosophy and religious traditions regard the world as a family. He said that the tendencies of indulgence are increasing. The tendency of storage and accumulation is not proper. In the context of the decision taken at that time in the economic field (referring to demonetisation), he said that this would stop the trend of collection. He said that this decision is going to bring a big change in India. There will be a big transformation of the country. He also said that as citizens of the nation, it also needs to be remembered that we also have a debt to the society, it has to be repaid. Swami Avdheshanand Giri said in his address that in the present time there has been awareness about rights, but indifference towards duties has also increased. But we have to take a pledge to keep the public mind pure. There has always been a concern about equality, impartiality and common sense, rights of animals and birds in Indian life-values. Earlier in the welcome address, the then Chief Minister Shivraj Singh Chouhan said that we have recently transported the 51 nectar-points *(amrit-bindu)* of *'Vichar Mahakumbh'* in Ujjain all over the world and now we will also spread the nectar that comes out of *'Lok-Manthan '*. Chouhan also said that in the series of the traditions of nationalist thoughts, six major events have been successfully completed in the state. In his address, he said that India is a great nation and when people in developed countries used to cover their bodies with the bark of trees, silk and muslin were made in India and there were universities like Nalanda and Taxila. When many developed countries did not exist, then the Vedas were composed in India. The history of India goes back to 5,000 years.

BJP's MP Dr. Vinay Sahasrabuddhe threw some light on the concept of *'Lok-Manthan '*. He said that it is a collective thought, which is inspired by the spirit of making Swadeshi present era-friendly and to make one that is from foreign Swadeshi-friendly. International writer Rajiv Malhotra, while addressing a session on the topic of 'Liberation of Indian People's Mind from Colonialism', said that China, Russia, Japan are very aware of their identity, but this kind of tendency or desire is not visible in India. In the session on the topic 'National identity and adjustment of other identities', noted author

Tariq Fateh said that we should recognize our friends and enemies. America is not our greatest enemy and neither is Bangladesh as much as Pakistan is. He said that everyone should understand that as long as Pakistan is present, there will be no peace in India.

The same session was also addressed by 'Dalit Indian Chamber of Commerce and Industry' Chief Milind Kamble and political scientist Prof. Ashok Modak. Former Union Minister Dr. Murli Manohar Joshi while discussing the topic 'Nationalism in Neo-liberalization and Globalization' said that globalization is the result of fragmented vision. Globalization is not for poor countries. At its core is the same western thought that the conscious can exploit the unconscious, whereas in Indian culture the basis of economic-contemplation *(arth-chintan)* is ***arthayam***, that is, balance.

Dr Vivek Devrai, former professor at 'London School of Economics' said that in the name of globalization, our culture which is thousands of years old is under threat. If we are not proud of India, it means that I am not proud of myself either. On the topic 'Role of Art, Culture, History and Media in Nation-building', Dr. Sonal Mansingh said that there is a dearth of news in TV channels and newspapers about teachings inspired by religion, art and culture. Film actor Anupam Kher spoke on patriotism. He said that today when it comes to patriotism, some people start feeling troubled. They say that don't teach us patriotism. It is true that no one can teach patriotism to anyone because it is the voice that comes from within you.

But I don't understand why some people feel pain when we talk about patriotism. Somdong Rinpoche, former Prime Minister of Tibet's government-in-exile, said that everyone discusses the challenges, but no one has the solution. The extreme escalation of violence is visible in the form of war and terrorism. Greed and business are behind the violence that is taking place.

Dr. Chandraprakash Dwivedi, who was the Chief Executive of the *'Lok-Manthan '* organizing committee, said that we have tried to remove the veils from the mind in *Lok-Manthan* . His was the last address in the concluding programme of *'Lok-Manthan '* . His full address is available on YouTube, which was later written by the news website 'pravakta.com'. In that address, the future strategy of the Sangh-BJP was announced and the script of the intellectual movement was also contained in it. As such, it would be more appropriate to present that address in his own words. Film director, Dwivedi, who played the role of Chanakya in the serial 'Chanakya' and also directed it, brought out the importance of *'Lok-Manthan '* through quotes from history. In his address that stirred up thoughts, he said that the scriptures say, there is no other. Kabir also said that *'Prem gali ati sankri, ja mein duin na samaaye.'* Therefore, there is no one else in the auditorium here. So dear *Atman,* first of all let us consider what is slavery? Also, has there ever been a desire for freedom from foreign slavery? Dwivedi shared a story, "One day one of his soldiers named Koyanas came to Alexander; he stood in front of Alexander for his army.

One can say that his was the first revolt. He said, 'We want to return to our homeland.' His pain was that the clothes he was wearing belonged to the conquered territories, not to his homeland. He did not even accept the clothes of the conquered territories. Now look into your conscience and see the difference!" Through another example, he said, "Dandayana Rishi lived in the forests. Alexander's general approached him and asked the reason for his stay in the forest. The sage replied, 'This house needs the least repair'. Similarly, another soldier of Alexander's approached a sage named Seletus. The sage was lying naked on a rock. Rishi asked him what he wanted. The soldier said, 'I want to have discussion about knowledge with you.' The sage asked him to take off his clothes and lie down on the rock near him and said if he was not ready to take off his clothes, them how he would take off the veils from his mind?"

Chandraprakash Dwivedi said that in the last three days they had tried to remove the veils from the mind in this *'Lok-Manthan '*. The question is, what is its usefulness? Will society get something out of this? There a story of Buddha – a disciple of Buddha felt that he had attained enlightenment. He started preaching in the streets and squares. He would stop the passing passengers and preached knowledge. The matter reached the Buddha. He called the disciple and said, 'Will you get milk by counting the cows?' The disciple said, 'No, you have to serve the cows, feed them fodder, then you will get milk.' Will society get nectar only through intellectual discourse? This discourse has to be taken forward; this discussion has to continue in the family, in the society, everywhere. Thought is a seed. If the environment is favourable, the seed can germinate and become a tree. This thought has to be put into action. We have to be diligent. It has to start from oneself, only then will it reach the society. Most of the speakers of *'Lok-Manthan '* pointed towards spirituality. This is the same ancient tree which was watered by Madhvacharya, Adi Shankaracharya, Yajnavalkya, Madhusudan Shastri and even Dara Shikoh; Vivekanandji had proclaimed it in Chicago. There are two reasons for giving up on the goal—the fear of failure or death. What will people say, they will insult us etc. If you take the responsibility, what is there that cannot be accomplished. Every great man in history has been insulted. Chanakya was thrown from the gathering of Ghanananda. A destitute teacher took a vow – this country has to be united and I will do that. Mahatma Gandhi was also thrown from the train; everyone knows the result. Chanakya said that there is no dearth of followers; there is a shortage of connectors, guides. Some people say that there are no means, how will I get that? Tulsidas was abandoned by his parents at birth considering him to be unlucky. He grew up begging in his childhood. When he found the purpose of life, he changed the history of India. Valmiki's 'Ramayana' is India's first and Tulsi's 'Ramcharitmanas' is the last epic of India. Even in Vivekananda's visit to Chicago, determination was the main thing. Give up hope of reverence. It is said in the Rigveda that the wise should consider reverence as poison and run away from it because insult will strengthen the man. In the Yama-Nachiketa dialogue, Nachiketa says – I do not want money because the thirst for money will never be quenched. Tell me the truth.

Whenever we look within ourselves and search for truth, that too is called churning. The churning can happen in the house also, it can happen in the family also. The churning does not require many people, there is no churning in the crowd. The nectar of 'Gita' was achieved from the dialogue between Krishna and Arjuna. The question is why did Krishna choose Arjuna for this and why not Yudhishthira? Because he knew that only Arjuna had the power to change the outcome of the war. So, the best speaker in the world chose the best listener. It is said in **'Katha Upanishad'** - 'Arise, awake and do not stop till you achieve your goal.' Pt. Madan Mohan Malviya said that I am worried about the world; that's why I worry about India because all the questions of the world will be answered by India. At the same time, Guru Golwalkarji has said that the activity of the wicked has not caused as much harm as the inaction of the good has. What more than a hundred scholars said in this event was indeed a wonderful ideological *yajna*. Heartfelt gratitude to all the workers and guests who made this event a success including *'Prajna Pravah'* and the Government of Madhya Pradesh for this grand and divine event."

Confidential Meeting of Education Ministers and Uniformity in Change

Consistently successful events had given strength to the Sangh Parivar and Chandraprakash Dwivedi's concluding address in *Lok-Manthan* was a sign of strategic communication. In such a situation, for uniformity in the changes taking place in education, the Sangh convened a special meeting, in which only the education Ministers of BJP-ruled states, top leaders of the Sangh and representatives of allied organizations related to the education sector of the Sangh attended. A very secretive meeting was held on 4-5 February, 2017, which was not covered by cameras and the media. Organized under the guidance of the Sangh, this meeting was held at Rambhau Mhalgi Prabodhini Sabha in Mumbai. The meeting was held under the banner of 'Good Governance Cell' under the leadership of BJP's National Vice President Dr Vinay Sahasrabuddhe. In this, apart from the education Ministers of the then BJP-ruled states-Jammu and Kashmir, Rajasthan, Madhya Pradesh, Chhattisgarh, Haryana, Jharkhand, Maharashtra, Gujarat and Assam, the then Union Human Resource Development Minister Prakash Javadekar, along with him, Minister of State Mahendra Nath Pandey and Sangh's *Sarkaryavah* Dattatreya Hosabale, along with *Sarkaryavah* Bhaiyyaji Joshi, Dr. Krishna Gopal participated. In the meeting, since the matter was related to education, *sangathan mantri* Sunil Ambekar (now All India *sah-prachar pramukh* in Sangh) from the affiliated organization Akhil Bharatiya Vidyarthi Parishad (ABVP), Atul Kothari of

'Save Education', Shikshan Mandal, Representatives of Sanskrit Bharati, Vidya Bharati and various ideological organizations associated with the field of education were called.

In fact, in view of the delay in the new education policy after the removal of Smriti Irani from the Ministry of Human Resource Development, the Sangh Parivar not only brainstormed to take it in a decisive direction, but the agenda of this two-day meeting was completely ideology-focused, where the education Ministers of all the party-ruled states gave detailed presentations under the theme of quality of education from an ideological point of view. Javadekar also spoke about the new education policy. However, describing this meeting as completely informal and regular, Vinay Sahasrabuddhe told me, "This type of event is organized every year to assess the changes taking place in education in the states and to sit together and assess the plans, in which usually the Chief Minister, Education Minister and like-minded people take part." However, Sahasrabuddhe maintained that such meetings are part of organizational activity. But in the meeting, Bhaiyyaji Joshi, the *Sarkaryavah* of the Sangh, gave a clear message, "We should do the work of taking forward the Indian values and old heritage so that it can be carried forward together." That is, his message was clear that there should be uniformity in the steps taken by the BJP-ruled states in education, giving prominence to ideology. For this uniformity, the Sangh put forward the Rajasthan model.

In this meeting, the Sangh had advised that instead of breaking up the fundamental changes that were taking place in education on the basis of ideology in BJP-ruled states, if the plan of any state is good, then the rest of the states should also implement it so that the ideological changes may it be strengthened. In this series, the then Raghuvar Das government of Jharkhand presented a scheme that emphasized on girls' education - 'first study, later marriage' and on behalf of the Maharashtra government, the then Education Minister Vinod Tawde presented his initiative that the 10th failed students' examination be conducted in July itself instead of October. On behalf of Rajasthan, the then Higher Education Minister Kiran Maheshwari and School Education Minister Vasudev Devnani attended the meeting. In the meeting, Devnani discussed the inclusion of 200 personalities in the new curriculum in the name of national pride and it was agreed that those great personalities associated with the state and the country should be included in school education. The thinking of the Sangh behind this was that it would increase the inclination towards the motherland. The Rajasthan government, instead of calling Akbar great, added a text describing Maharana Pratap as great and on mentioning this, the state was praised in this meeting; Devnani even decided to change the name of Akbar Fort in Ajmer to 'Ajmer Fort'. Along with many modern initiatives, PTM (Teacher-Parent Meeting) was introduced for the first time in the government schools of the state on *Amavasya*. Devnani had also had the cycles given to the girl students of class IX painted in orange colour which was close to saffron colour. In Rajasthan schools, the colour of the dress was changed after 25 years and from the year 2016, brown pants and light brown shirts were kept, whereas earlier there were khaki pants and blue shirts. That means the colour of the pants was somewhat similar to the new uniform of the Sangh, which was approved in the Sangh meeting of Nagaur.

Devnani kept the Sangh and its ideas in his mind while undertaking such initiatives. Despite these allegations of saffronisation from the opposition parties, the central government was moving forward on the agenda of the Sangh. Of the steps taken in Rajasthan, more than half a dozen points had become part of the draft new education policy of the Centre and it was only after the union leaders' meeting in Mumbai that the HRD Ministry decided to make changes to the draft for the third time. However, it is necessary to mention here that due to controversies, the new education policy could not be made public before the 2019 general elections and now after the formation of the Modi government again, the draft has been made public. The Sangh was giving impetus to its initiative and after the atmosphere created by frequent events, a time came when it publicly declared its initiative by organizing a conference of intellectuals under its banner.

The Confluence of Knowledge became the *'Bauddhik Mahakumbh'*

March 25-26, 2017 - exactly a year had passed since the Sangh-BJP contemplation for the intellectual movement after the JNU incident. By organizing the *Kumbh* of the education world in the capital of the country, the Sangh Parivar openly expressed its thought process. Maharaja Agrasen Institute of Technology and Management witnessed a gathering of 721 academicians, including professors, assistant professors, associate professors and 51 vice-chancellors (from 20 central universities and 31 state universities). Located in Delhi's Rohini, the institute is owned by BJP leader Nand Kishore Garg, where representatives of the education world from 29 states had gathered.

Organized under the banner of *Prajna Pravah*, the intellectual wing of the Sangh, this programme was named *'Gyan Sangam'*. But the design of the event was no less than a *Mahakumbh*. This was perhaps the first time that such a large number of academicians and Vice-Chancellors had attended a federally sponsored meeting. At the very beginning of this *'Gyan Sangam'*, *Sarsanghchalak* Mohan Bhagwat drew a clear line - "India's knowledge tradition and education system have been contemplated upon, but there came a period when the environment during the reign of Mughals and British was not favourable and because of that, this contemplation had stopped. But after 500 years, now that there is open discussion, the society will have to come forward because only Indian society can bring about a change." If one had to interpret his message, his message was clear that in this era of political domination of the BJP, the saffron ideology of nationalism should also be promoted at the same speed. In fact, the Sangh wanted to inculcate it in its ideas of nationalism by radically changing the education system. For this, the initiative was being taken with a well-organized strategy. When I spoke to Manmohan Vaidya, the then *Akhil Bharatiya Prachar Pramukh* of the Sangh at that time about the purpose of the meeting, he said, "There is a need to free Indian intelligence from the colonial mentality and it should start with education. There should be Indianness in the aim, content and system of education. The Sangh believes that permanent change in society is more effectively brought about not by power, but by society."

The Sangh believed that the Indian education system was dominated by British influence and the Left ideology. Therefore, initiative should be taken to bring about change by taking advantage of the favourable environment created by BJP coming to power. The concept of the Sangh behind such events was that the Mughals and Turks attacked the temples and Indian educational centres and the British developed an education system which destroyed the faith, while the colonial thinking still proves to be a hindrance to the Indians in doing something new. Therefore, there is a need to revive the Indian civilization and the centres of knowledge so that the thinking of the masses is Indianized and the winds of change blow, for which the Sangh took the initiative of cultivating education through Saraswati Shishu Mandir and Vidya Bharati for primary and in some locations, secondary education in the 1950s only. However, it did not have much penetration in higher education.

In the first NDA government formed under the leadership of Atal Bihari Vajpayee at the centre, when the then Human Resource Development Minister Murli Manohar Joshi took some initiative in this direction, there was an allegation of saffronisation and due to the compulsions of the coalition, the Vajpayee government couldn't be more vocal and advance the Sangh's agenda. But now for the first time the BJP had a strong government at the centre on its own with a majority and its leadership was also in the hands of a powerful person like Narendra Modi, who had basically been a *pracharak* of the Sangh. As such, the Sangh realized that this was the most favourable time for change. Therefore, the seriousness of the Sangh regarding *'Gyan Sangam'* can also be gauged from the fact that *Sarsanghchalak* Mohan Bhagwat himself was present in the meeting on both the days and had open dialogue with the people of the intellectual world. Prominent leaders of all the organizations related to the education sector of the Sangh also participated in it. Along with Bhagwat, *Sah-Sarkaryavah* Suresh Soni, Dr Krishna Gopal were present. Also were present the then Sangh office bearers - All India *Sampark Pramukh* Anirudh Deshpande, *Akhil Bharatiya Prachar Pramukh* Manmohan Vaidya, Akhil Bhartiya *Bauddhik Pramukh* Swant Ranjan, Akhil Bhartiya *Sah-Bauddhik Pramukh* Mukund C.R. and *Prajna Pravah* National Convenor J. Nandakumar.

Sangh's *Sah-Sarkaryavah* Suresh Soni tried to introduce Indianism in his statement in the meeting. Soni presented the Sangh's ideology of Indianness, "India's education system has been completely spirituality-based. Financial earning is necessary, but that is only for living. The nation can progress only on the basis of spirituality. Other countries of the world are also promoting their culture." After that, S. Gurumurthy presented his thoughts on the Indian vision of Indian economics and then Prof. Ved P Nanda and Manohar Shinde from America presented ideas in a session.

... Bhagwat said - will have to play for India

In *'Gyan Sangam'*, *Sarsanghchalak* Mohan Bhagwat interacted directly with the participants from his level and which showed a very interesting style. To further the process of exchange of ideas, participants were divided into groups according to almost a dozen subjects, that is, more than twelve groups were formed on each topic. After that, after dividing the groups into two parts, there was a programme of discussion directly with Mohan Bhagwat. In this discussion, Bhagwat was asked an interesting question by a participant, which would be appropriate to mention here. The question was- "There is power and time is also favourable. In such a situation, why is the country not able to stand with self-respect?" The meaning of this question was clear that even when the BJP is in power, why is the country not standing with self-respect according to the agenda of the Sangh? Bhagwat also answered this with a smile giving a very interesting example. He shared an anecdote with everyone about how he was listening to the commentary of the India-England cricket match once during his stay in Mumbai. The people listening to the commentary were talking about England's victory first. But India won and on the commentator's question, Navjot Singh Sidhu had said that every player of ours was playing for victory. Government cannot change the society, but society can change the government if it wants. This work has to be done by the society itself.

A Line of Words was Drawn

The Sangh's vision is to create a pressure group of a right-wing ideology (which is called *Rashtriyata* by Sangh and '*Rashtrawadi*' in common parlance) in opposition to the leftist ideology through changes in education, which, in absence of a saffron-minded government will work as a pressure group. Dr. Krishna Gopal, who is the *Sah-Sarkaryavah* of the Sangh and looks after the coordination between the BJP and government, also had a separate meeting with the vice chancellors of 20 central universities and 31 state universities in the '*Gyan Sangam*'. Former HRD Minister Murli Manohar Joshi and ABVP's Sunil Ambekar were also present in it. Krishna Gopal himself was overseeing this intellectual campaign at the top level on behalf of the Sangh and it was his most thought-provoking address in '*Gyan Sangam*'. Krishna Gopal had said in the address, "There was a time when foreigners like Hiuen Tsang wrote about

India in glowing terms that people here are prosperous, but people like Rudyard Kipling had to write that Indians are uncivilized." He indicated that all this was done under the design of the Christian missionaries and church. So, now there is a need to explore history because Indian history is written by hunters and not by lions themselves. He also gave specific mantras for intellectual campaign—identify your people in each subject, form subject wise groups, make a bibliography of Indian thought while writing books and articles, have your book included in the university where there is a favourable atmosphere. He said that education in India should be promoted only from the Indian context. Not only this, apart from mobilizing like-minded teachers, the Sangh's strategy was to take initiatives in other areas of writing and art. The authors were asked that while writing books and articles on a dozen subjects, they must mention the books with similar thoughts in the reference list. A group called 'Udaan' was also formed in the theatre. There was also a strategy to answer the challenge posed to the Modi government by the left intellectuals through its intellectuals. Apart from this, the Sangh's strategy was to get maximum number of books related to its ideology included in universities-schools with a conducive atmosphere.

After the *'Gyan Sangam'* meeting, on 1st April, the next week, Dattatreya Hosabale, *Sah-Sarkaryavah* of the Sangh, held a meeting with selected Vice Chancellors associated with major universities. This was followed by a similar meeting on 21st April, in which Dattatreya

Hosabale and another *Sah-Sarkaryavah*, Dr. Krishna Gopal, looking after the work of intellectual coordination, were also present. It was organized by Sunil Ambekar, the then *Sangathan mantri* of ABVP, in which there was brainstorming on connecting yoga with curriculum and other topics. Enthused by *'Gyan Sangam'*, the Sangh devised a strategy to organize similar events in other parts of the country. The spurt in this initiative of the Sangh was not only caused by the shocks of the Rohit Vemula episode, the Kanhaiya episode in JNU, the Jadavpur University incident in West Bengal and the award-return of intellectuals against intolerance just before the Bihar elections; rather, the Sangh believed that after Modi government had come to power, the Left, as a strategy, selected universities as the weak link, where they still dominated and NGOs seem to be standing with them. The presence of 721 professors and 51 vice-chancellors in such an environment forced the Sangh to build a group of intellectuals with a precise strategy and to accelerate the campaign for Indianisation of education. This event of the ancillary organization *'Prajna Pravah'* made the Sangh feel happy.

To add intellectuals of another ideology...the concept of all are ours and we are for all

The Sangh Parivar had accelerated the intellectual movement, but the spirit of untouchability was becoming a hindrance. That is, intellectuals of other ideology wanted to join, but they were not being trusted. In such a situation, hard principles could weaken the campaign to build their intellectuals. So, on the basis of the experiences of the past, once again an important meeting was held in Delhi's Gandhi Darshan Samiti on 26-27 August 2017 under the leadership of RSS Chief Mohan Bhagwat. The selection of the place was to give a symbolic message and the direction of giving up dogma in the intellectual movement was given by the Sangh Chief. Out of 72 invitees, 68 thinkers attended the meeting organized by Pragya Pravah. Then on August 28, a meeting was held at the residence of Human Resource Development Minister Javadekar to implement the conclusion of the meeting. Concluding the two-day meeting at Gandhi Darshan Samiti at Rajghat in the capital Delhi, Sangh Chief Mohan Bhagwat gave the mantra that while connecting people associated with the intellectual world, those people should be welcomed who want to leave the old ideology and join the Sangh. When I spoke to a senior leader who attended the meeting, he pointed out the presence of Mohan Bhagwat throughout the meeting on both the days where Bhagwat had bluntly said, "We have to move forward with an inclusive mindset and keep in mind that all are ours and we are for all. Dr. Hedgewar had also held this belief before independence. According to the same concept, we should carry forward the ideology of the Sangh by doing studies and research.

In this meeting, especially there was discussion regarding the new national education policy. In addition to the top office bearers of the Sangh, former Union Human Resource Development Minister Murli Manohar

Joshi, BJP General Secretary Ram Madhav, BJP National Vice President-MP Vinay Sahasrabuddhe, Atul Kothari of 'Save Education', then DG of IIMC KG Suresh, many professors associated with JNU and Delhi University, RSS ideologue Rakesh Sinha were present. On the next day of this meeting i.e. on August 28, a meeting was held with Union Human Resource Development Minister Prakash Javadekar in the afternoon at his official residence. It was attended by RSS *Sah-Sarkaryavah* Dattatreya Hosabale, ABVP's *Sangathan Mahamantri* Sunil Ambekar, BJP national vice president Vinay Sahasrabuddhe and the then chairman of Prasar Bharati A Suryaprakash. They had a long meeting and brainstormed on the education policy.

Not Leftist, eyeing Socialist, Lohiaist, Gandhian

The Sangh Parivar was constantly working at a very fast pace to create an ideological group of intellectuals and change the education system. According to the thinkers involved in this meeting, the message of the Sangh Chief was clear that whenever it comes to the Sangh, it is seen from the point of view of Hindu-Muslim and since its inception in 1925 till now it is seen from the point of view of fundamentalism. Whereas basically the Sangh neither thinks nor does so. No such thinking is followed while working in different organisations of the Sangh like Vanvasi Kalyan Ashram, Seva Bharati, Shishu Mandir etc. Despite that, the perception about the Sangh becomes a hindrance in its intellectual expansion. Hence the message of the Sangh Chief was that the background of the intellectuals should be kept in mind while adding them. The Sangh, which is engaged in intellectual expansion, realizes that the base will not become strong if it insisted on growing of new intellectuals. Therefore, old ones who come with a changed thinking should also be welcomed. However, a leader attending the meeting points out that the Sangh Chief did not mean at all that we would include people with left-wing ideologies. According to him, when the Sangh Chief talked about welcoming the people of other ideologies when they change their thinking was not meant for leftists, but it was only for people of socialist, Lohiaist and Gandhian ideology. A senior leader of the Sangh said that the founder of the Sangh, Dr Hedgewar himself came from the Congress. Dattopant Thengadi first worked in 'INTUC' and after that Bharatiya Mazdoor Sangh was formed. In this category, he also named people like Arun Shourie and Girilal Jain. Jain was a columnist, who was later associated with '*Panchjanya*'.

Mohan Bhagwat also stressed on strengthening the Sangh's ideological prestige *'Prajna Pravah'* as an autonomous body. For this, he said that the organizational structure of *'Prajna Pravah'*, which is presently at the provincial level, should be extended to the district and there should be a team of at least five people who have come out of their ideology organization. The Sangh wanted to keep this team as a 'Quick Response Team', which can give immediate factual answers to the opponents on any occasion. In the meeting, the participation of women in different sessions, social harmony by connecting all castes, economic issues and socio-economic caste census were also discussed. There was also a special discussion on the Economic Caste Census. The significance of this meeting was also in the context that the BJP had registered a historic election victory in Uttar Pradesh after completing fourteen years of exile, in which the BJP along with the Sangh had carried out social engineering in a strategic manner. This decision was an absolute seal on the decision of demonetisation.

Doubt and Dialogue on Demonetisation

On November 8, 2016, when Prime Minister Narendra Modi announced demonetisation in the country, everyone was astonished because not everyone was aware of it even in the government till the last moment. The decision was taken directly at the level of Prime Minister. In such a situation, no question could be raised from the party's side though in the beginning the Sangh was also sceptical. At that time, a senior RSS leader told me, "The Indian economy cannot be made like that of America. In the US in 2008, when a bank went bankrupt, the whole economy was seen to be in shambles. But if this happens in India, then the whole economy is not affected because the basis of our economy is savings. So many foreign invaders from the Mughals to others came, but there was no significant effect on the health of the people of India because our basis is savings." He said that due to this decision, if the economy slips from the bottom, it will increase the difficulty and in the long run the government may also have to suffer political losses.

At the time of demonetisation, when the Modi government was being targeted by the opposition in the country, no statement in support from the Sangh was also a matter of discussion in the BJP. One of the reasons for the Sangh's unease was the custom of traditional Gurudakshina, which is completely secret and in cash. Others do not know about how much one donates. The concept of Sangh behind this has been to create an egalitarian society. But weakening of the system of cash transactions and making transactions by check could break this tradition. The Sangh kept silent on demonetisation for some time and then it also started assessing the political impact of this decision. After about a fortnight, the Sangh gave a very precise statement and in an official statement released on November 22, 2016, termed Modi government's move as an honest step in the national interest. In a statement issued by Manmohan Vaidya, the then *Akhil Bhartiya Prachar Pramukh* , it was written – "It is a sincere initiative aimed at promoting clean and transparent financial transaction practices, which is being felt everywhere. Anti-national, extremist activities have come to an end with this decision. Normalcy seems to be restoring in Kashmir too after a long time. It is causing some problems, but it is an important step towards making the economy strong and secure." The Sangh appealed to the people that even with some temporary and unavoidable troubles, people should support the government's 'good effort'. The Sangh expressed confidence that the patriotic people of India would certainly extend their support to the government for a bright future and a better tomorrow for India.

On the other hand, Prime Minister Modi also associated the decision of demonetisation with his prestige as he had taken such a risk that his own people as well as his opponents were also upset. In such a situation, the success of Modi would have given him a place in history and if not, he would have to go through the biggest tempests of history. As such, its first advantage was seen in the Panchayat elections in Odisha, where the BJP overtook the Congress and carved a significant place in the state after the Biju Janata Dal. In many places, it had also given a blow to the ruling Biju Janata Dal. The assembly elections of Uttar Pradesh that followed was the biggest test of demonetisation, where Narendra Modi had put his stakes and had declared that if it failed, he would go away like a *fakir*. On the other hand, the Sangh was also focussing on the Uttar Pradesh assembly elections. The centre of Sangh's *Sah-Sarkaryavah* Dattatreya Hosabale was now Lucknow instead of Patna and he was objectively looking at the functioning of the BJP. On the other hand, Saha-*Sarkaryavah* Dr. Krishna Gopal, who was in the role of coordinator with the BJP and originally belonged to this state, was keeping a direct eye on the election.

In the end, the party won an unprecedented victory in Uttar Pradesh. The Sangh held a coordination meeting in Mathura, after which it had openly said that the country would benefit in the long run from the Modi government's decision of demonetisation. Modi's decision of demonetisation had definitely got a political stamp and the Sangh Parivar also stood together with it despite the hesitation on this historic economic decision because the opposition on it would not only give opportunity to the opposition it would also create confusion in the public mind. Once again, *Vichar Parivar* gave a message of solidarity on demonetisation by better coordination through communication.

Chief Minister's Command to Yogi and Sangh-BJP Coordination in Mathura

While expanding the activities of social harmony and intellectual movement, the Sangh was constantly trying to coordinate with its like-minded political organization BJP. At the end of August, the *Sarsanghchalak* brainstormed with the intellectuals at Delhi's Raj Ghat, then four days later the entire Vichar Pariwargathered at Krishna Janmabhoomi, Mathura, where an important coordination meeting of forty-nine Sangh organizations including the BJP lasted from September 1 to 3, 2017. The purpose of organizing an All-India Coordination Meeting in Mathura, the birthplace of Lord Krishna from September 1 to September 3, was to have a formal exchange of ideas, amid a huge victory in Uttar Pradesh and Prime Minister Narendra Modi's call to make new India so that there would be no hindrance in the ongoing projects for expansion.

Such a meeting in Uttar Pradesh was also important because after the record victory in the assembly elections, there was a tussle between the Sangh-BJP over who should be made the Chief Minister of this state. The picture about Manoj Sinha was almost clear. Protocol had also reached Sinha. But the Sangh's argument was different with respect to Uttar Pradesh. It argued that the party had come to power after fourteen years of exile. In such a situation, to stay in power for a long time, it was necessary to facilitate the construction of Ram temple in Ayodhya. The Sangh believed that the saffron-clad Yogi Adityanath would be suitable for this. The Sangh's thinking was to improve the administration as well. It believed that social pressure would be important in the construction of Ram temple and if someone could handle the unbridled bureaucracy of UP firmly, then Yogi was the better face. BJP President Amit Shah was also in favour of Yogi and Yogi was the most suitable face in terms of the Sangh-BJP ideological equation. But Manoj Sinha was at the top as Prime Minister Modi's choice. But after dialogue and coordination, Modi gave full consent and finally Yogi became the Chief Minister. There could not have been more suitable face than Yogi's for Hindutva and polarization and in the end, when there was a consensus in the ideology family, Yogi also assured to take the organization along and not allow his *Hindu Yuva Vahini* to dominate the government, which was BJP's concern.

In such a situation, this Mathura coordination meeting of the Sangh was very important. In this meeting, along with *Sarsanghchalak* Mohan Bhagwat, all the top officials of the Sangh and prominent leaders of all the organizations participated. On behalf of the BJP, the then National President Amit Shah, Organization General Secretary *(Sangathan Mahasachiv)* Ramlal, the then National Organization Minister Sunil Ambekar from Akhil Bharatiya Vidyarthi Parishad, Atul Kothari, the representative of the education sector, etc. were present in this meeting. In the coordination meeting, the achievements of BJP led Modi government at the centre and organizational progress were discussed. Regarding this meeting, Manmohan Vaidya, the All India *Prachar pramukh* of the Sangh, had then said, "The Sangh works through many organizations in different areas of the society. The meeting of the *swayamsevaks* working in such organizations is held every year in January and September. No decision is taken at this meeting; rather all the organizations share their achievements and experience as well as give their comments." The importance of such coordination meetings increases for the Sangh when there is a BJP government at the Centre. The Sangh Parivar establishes such mutual dialogue within itself so that there is no conflict between the government and its like-minded organizations on any issue.

BHU Vice Chancellor Controversy: Sangh-Government Coordination

The coordination meeting took place in early September and it was only in late September that a matter which could have created immediate differences between the Sangh-BJP came to the fore. But the coordination between the Sangh-BJP and like-minded organizations during the Modi government has become an example, the example of which was also reflected in the case of the then Vice-Chancellor of Banaras Hindu University (BHU), Girishchandra Tripathi. Tripathi was made the vice-chancellor of BHU as per the choice of the Sangh. But on September 21, 2017, some girls sat on a dharna over complaints of molestation and other problems and were adamant on meeting the Vice-Chancellor Tripathi. A fine arts student was molested by three boys. But two days later, on 23 September, the girls got up from the protest site and moved towards the Vice-Chancellor's residence, when the administration chased them away with the help of the police, in which many students were injured. After this, the atmosphere turned violent and a holiday had to be declared in the university. As it was the issue in Varanasi which is the parliamentary constituency of Prime Minister Narendra Modi the matter got publicity at the national level. Questions were raised on Tripathi's working style and administrative ability. Incidentally, the Prime Minister's visit was also to take place around the same time. Prime Minister Narendra Modi himself had decided to take strict action against Vice Chancellor Tripathi. But Girishchandra Tripathi was in no mood to withdraw. On September 27, Prime Minister Narendra Modi, taking a tough stand on the BHU issue, directed then HRD Minister Prakash Javadekar to remove Tripathi before the end of the university holidays. But Tripathi flatly refused to resign, following which Javadekar held talks with Sangh Sah-sarkaryawah Dattatreya Hosabale, Dr Krishna Gopal and ABVP national organization matri Sunil Ambekar on 29 September. Initially, the Sangh functionaries were also against Tripathi's removal from the post. Sangh leaders believed that the entire issue of BHU is sponsored by the Left and Tripathi is about to retire after one and a half months on November 27. In such a situation, removing him from the post earlier than that will boost the spirits of the Left. But then Javadekar directly cited the instructions of the Prime Minister and asked the leaders of the Sangh to find a way out as the matter was gaining political momentum. After this, Hosabale and Krishna Gopal spoke to Tripathi on 29 September, where Ambekar was also present. But Tripathi refused to accept both the proposals like resigning or going on long leave. Taking into account Tripathi's insistence and the questions being raised on the Modi government at the Centre and the Yogi government in the state, Saha-*Sarkaryavah* Dattatreya Hosabale canceled his tour out of Delhi. He was to leave Delhi on the night of 29 September. But he stayed in Delhi and sent a message to Tripathi that the next day, i.e. on 30th September, he should reach Delhi and meet him. On September 30, after meeting with the leaders of the Sangh and the assurance about the future, Tripathi accepted the proposal of the Sangh to go on a long leave instead of resigning.

The Sangh busy in accelerating the change in education and creating a group of intellectuals, did not want a message to go outside that there was a difference of opinion in the family regarding any issue in the Modi government. The leaders of the Sangh believed that there are some misconceptions about the Sangh in the society and in their removal such small issues are important and it has some effect on the socio-politics Such incidents could hinder the path of his educational agenda and intellectual movement with social harmony. So, the Sangh took quick steps on every small or big issue that arose. The Sangh wanted the future activities to be increased in such a way that the assumptions made about the organization could be broken.

❑

14

CHAPTER

'Congress General' in Nagpur

By inviting Pranab Mukherjee for an address at the Sangh headquarters, the tag of being 'untouchable' was removed and the Modi government showed generosity by giving 'Bharat Ratna' to Pranab Da, who belonged to the opposition party.

The Sangh and BJP started the year 2018 with a bang. In Tripura, the BJP had achieved an ideological victory by going from zero to gaining power. After West Bengal, another ideological foundation of the Left ideology had collapsed. But the demolition of the Left's fortress in Tripura was more important because the work of demolition was done by the opposition right wing ideology. Sangh was more involved in preparing the script for this victory than BJP.

On June 17, 2017, a huge Hindu convention was held in Agartala, the capital of Tripura. When the Sangh organized this conference, Tripura was an important bastion of the Left. But the Sangh's seriousness towards Tripura became apparent when Dr. Krishna Gopal, the Sangh's *Sah-Sarkaryavah*, who was looking after the Sangh's coordination with the BJP, proposed to then BJP national president Amit Shah that Biplab Dev should be handed over the command of Tripura State BJP. Shah also accepted this proposal as the Sangh had been working there for a long time at the grassroots level. When the Sangh organized the Hindu convention about eight months before the assembly elections, it had a special purpose. Prior preparations for this programme of June 2017 were made according to the strategy. Efforts were made to reach all the Gram Panchayats and ensure representation of maximum villages. Contact with all the tribal groups was planned. Programmes for *Guru-Poojan*, *Raksha Bandhan* and *Vijayadashami* were arranged. Through about 3,346 house-to-house meetings 15 thousand people were mobilized, efforts were made to reach new places and new families through Sangh Introduction sessions etc. The invitation of the programme was sent through contact without using the popular means of publicity. In the series of the programme, there was a programme to install saffron flag at home. Success in reaching more than one lakh homes in two days was achieved. When this huge conference took place, *Sarsanghchalak* Mohan

Bhagwat himself was present in it. A total of 26 thousand people participated in this and more than 800 workers were active for this.

When the Sangh *Pratinidhi Sabha* met in Nagpur on March 9, 2018, *Sarkaryavah* Bhaiyyaji Joshi made a special mention of it in his report as, "The huge Hindu convention held in the Tripura state of the Northeast has been fruitful in all respects." Just six days before this meeting, the results of the Tripura assembly elections were out, in which the BJP had won power, but the Sangh Parivar had won an ideological victory in the Left bastion.

But now after this ideological victory of the Sangh, the need was to remove the feeling of intellectual untouchability, for which work was started and some programmes were designed at short intervals so that favourable atmosphere was created. The first thing that the Sangh did is that the summer training class and finally the third year of the Sangh education session ends in Nagpur, in which the Sangh has a tradition of inviting dignitaries. But this time strategically, the Sangh took the initiative to invite Pranab Mukherjee, a veteran Congress leader for 43 years and considered a trouble-shooter. He completed his presidency on July 25, 2017. His relationship with Prime Minister Narendra Modi was so good that Modi even called him as his father figure. Even as President, the rapport between Pranab Mukherjee and Prime Minister Modi was very cordial. The cordiality of the relationship between the two can also be gauged from the fact that in an interview in October 2017 after retiring from the post of President, Pranab Mukherjee praised Modi openly, in which he called Modi a hardworking person determined to achieve his goal and a personality with will-power and clear vision. Pranab Da also said that despite having little experience in Parliament, he has understood and worked well on administration and foreign policy. Not only Modi, his relationship with *Sarsanghchalak* Mohan Bhagwat was so cordial that he even broke protocol to receive Bhagwat once as President. Pranab Da and Bhagwat met in December 2015 and June 2017 when he was President. Even after leaving the post, there were meetings between the two. So, the atmosphere was suitable, all that was needed was a formal invitation.

As soon as the information that Pranab Mukherjee would be the Chief guest in the third-year program of *Sangh Shiksha Varg* became public on 30th May, 2018, there was a political earthquake. Congress was almost paralyzed. Many big leaders of Congress appealed to him not to go to the Sangh headquarters, while some started speaking bitterly. Even Pranab Mukherjee's daughter and Congress leader Sharmistha Mukherjee asked him to refrain from going to the RSS headquarters in Nagpur. As the controversy escalated, the Sangh formally issued a statement. In this statement, the Sangh said, "It is not surprising or new to anyone who knows or understands the Sangh. This is normal for them as the RSS keeps inviting famous people and people associated with social service. This time, the RSS has extended an invitation to

Dr. Pranab Mukherjee and it is his magnanimity that he has accepted the invitation. The 25-day 'Third Year Varg' is celebrated every year in Nagpur, in which members from all over the country participate for training. This year it started on 14th May and will end on 7th June with 709 *swayamsevaks* from different parts of the country registering their presence. People have been visiting Sangh's training sessions; Even Mahatma Gandhi visited the camp in Wardha and later said that he was impressed by the organization's strict discipline, simplicity and absence of discrimination. Other celebrities including former President Zakir Hussain, socialist leader Jayaprakash Narayan, Field Marshal KM Cariappa have also participated in the RSS functions. India's first Prime Minister Jawaharlal Nehru also invited it to participate in the Republic Day celebrations in 1963, seeing the role of the RSS during the 1962 war with China. The then Prime Minister Lal Bahadur Shastri had also invited the RSS to an all-party meeting in 1965 during the war with Pakistan. Sangh has been working for the last 92 years to make an egalitarian society and getting success in it. Whoever agrees with its idea and work participates in the functions of the Sangh and cooperate.

Before his special address at the Sangh Headquarters, Pranab Mukherjee laid a wreath at the memorial built at the birthplace of Dr. Keshav Baliram Hedgewar and in the visitor's book kept there, Mukherjee wrote - 'Today I have come here to pay respect to the great son of Mother India.' Pranab Mukherjee said from the stage, "I have come here to explain the nation, nationalism and patriotism. India is the first nation in the world and faith in its constitution is the real patriotism. Diversity is our greatest strength. We see unity in diversity. We all have the same identity 'Indianness'. It is to be noted that even the Sangh always talks about Indianness. Pranavada also said in his address that dialogue is very important for equality of views. Solution to every problem is possible through dialogue because tolerance is the basis of our society. He said that every topic should be discussed, whether we agree with any view or not. He said that everyone has accepted the fact that Hinduism is a liberal religion. Hiuen Tsang and Fa Hien have also talked about Hinduism. Nationalism is the identity of any country. Patriotism means faith in the progress of the country. He said that nationalism is derived from the universal philosophy *'Vasudhaiva Kutumbakam', 'Sarve Bhavantu Sukhinah Sarve Santu Niramayah'*. On this occasion, RSS Chief Mohan Bhagwat said that there is no restriction on the entry of anyone in the Sangh. You can come here and find out about the Sangh. Well, we know the Sangh and you should also know and make up your own mind. Bhagwat reiterated that the Sangh is not just an organization of Hindus. We want to take people of all views along. But for this everyone should have the same goal. He said that it is very important to have character with power and this is what the Sangh is doing. Regarding the criticisms also, he said that the Sangh has been progressing despite the blows. Bhagwat said that uncontrollable power is destructive. We have to bring common people on par. Hindus are responsible for deciding the fate of India. Today the Sangh has become a huge organization He said that we do not lack good thoughts, but we were poor in implementation, which has changed a little now. On the controversy surrounding Pranab Mukherjee, Mohan Bhagwat said that we invite known personalities every year; those who want to come accept our invitation and come here.

Although the Congress had termed Pranab Da's address as an advice to the Sangh late at night itself it was just an attempt to allay the annoyance as the Sangh had succeeded in conveying the message that it was trying to through the event, which was reflected within a fortnight of the event through a news that appeared in the media. The interest of people, especially from West Bengal, for membership of the Sangh had increased after former President Pranab Mukherjee joined the Nagpur RSS programme. Senior Rashtriya Swayamsevak Sangh (RSS) leader Biplav Roy was quoted as saying that after Pranab Da speech at the Sangh headquarters in Nagpur, the maximum number of applications for membership of the RSS are being received from West Bengal. Biplav Roy told reporters that between June 1 and June 6, on an average, they received 378 requests daily on their website 'Join RSS'. But after Pranab Da's speech, they received applications from 1,779 people. After June 7, they were getting 1,200-1,300 applications daily. He said that out of this 40 percent applications had come from West Bengal.

Certainly, there is a strategic thinking behind such events. Just as a huge Hindu convention was held just eight months before the Tripura elections, making deep inroads into the society, Similarly, by inviting former President Pranab Mukherjee, who served as the Congress general and trouble shooter for more than four decades, to the Sangh headquarters in Nagpur about nine months before the Lok Sabha elections, the Sangh sent a strong message to the intellectuals of West Bengal as well as the country. West Bengal is Pranawada's home state and he has been a tall leader in the country's politics. In view of his merit and contribution to politics, he was awarded the country's highest honour 'Bharat Ratna' on the eve of Republic Day of January 2019, which was also criticized by the opposition. Even though the Sangh-BJP may have had a strategy behind it no party could underestimate the ability of Pranab Mukherjee and his contribution towards the country. If it is a matter of strategy, then there is no doubt that such things also affect the Indian public mind. Whether it is the BJP-Sangh's thinking of capitalizing on the feeling of Bengali pride in its favour or to give respect to it, showing such a large heartedness in politics will also be remembered as a great action. Former Prime Minister Atal Bihari Vajpayee, a veteran BJP leader, was not given the 'Bharat Ratna' during the ten years of Manmohan Singh's Prime Ministership. Later, he got 'Bharat Ratna' when Modi government was formed. But by giving 'Bharat Ratna' to Congress leader Pranab Mukherjee, the BJP government gave a message of generosity. BJP and Sangh leaders would not have found their generosity going in vain when the results of the Lok Sabha elections came out as West Bengal played a key role in making the BJP's 2019 election victory bigger than the 2014 election victory.

The Sangh not only broke the illusion of considering Nagpur Sangh headquarters as 'untouchable' by inviting Pranab Da but it also infused a positive spirit in the minds of the youth full of aspirations. Despite this, to break the illusions that were visible in the enlightened world, the Sangh Chief organized an event that probably never happened in the history of the Sangh.

❑

PART-7

Sangh and the Initiative to Remove Confusion

The acceptance of the Sangh was increasing due to the favourable government and ideological environment. But there were still some issues on which the opponents were spreading confusion. Instead of denying everything, the Sangh continued with the principle of working amidst the society. But considering the growth with time and the eagerness of the newly joined people to learn, for the first time, the Sangh organized a three-day intellectual programme at Vigyan Bhawan to clear the misconceptions and give an opportunity to look at the Sangh through the eyes of the Sangh. After this, the Sangh organized an intellectual fair in Ranchi through Lok-Manthan .

❑

15

CHAPTER

'Sanjay Uvacha' (Sanjay said) of Sangh

How did the Sarsanghchalak speak like 'Sanjay' six months before the 2019 election Mahabharat and said- what is Sangh? Efforts to strengthen and rationalize the efforts by clearing misconceptions.

The BJP was busy as usual in the preparations for the Lok Sabha elections. The ideological victory in Tripura had raised the spirits of the Sangh Parivar. But only 17 days after this victory on March 3, 2018, the Supreme Court's decision on the SC-ST Act on March 20 had put not only the BJP but also the Sangh Parivar in a tizzy. With this decision, the provisions of protection being given to Dalits in the Act seemed to be weakening. There were apprehensions of possible loss of Dalit votes in the election. Then the Modi government reversed the decision of the Supreme Court from the Parliament, but by then the fight had gone to the streets. When an attempt was made to stop the anger of the Dalits, the upper caste society got angry. At that time, the atmosphere in the country became such that the BJP and the Sangh Parivar could see their campaign in trouble. The opposition was constantly trying to prove BJP and Sangh Parivar as anti-Dalit. But by inviting Pranab Mukherjee to the Sangh headquarters, the Sangh Parivar had given an answer to the enlightened world creating a hostile atmosphere. On the other hand, before the Lok Sabha elections, the election movement had started in the three states-Madhya Pradesh, Chhattisgarh, Rajasthan, which were seen as semi-finals. But due to sudden conflict-like atmosphere in the society, the dilemma of the Sangh Parivar was natural because it was working to unite the Hindu society through campaigns like social harmony. But these circumstances had increased the troubles of the ideology family. BJP planned a strategy for night travel in 20 thousand Dalit dominated villages for damage control. Then from April 14, 2018 which was Ambedkar Jayanti, it started 'Gram Swaraj Abhiyan' which continued till May 5, 2018. National President Amit Shah started it with a meal at Dalit's house in Odisha. The Sangh also shared the feedback received from the *swayamsevaks* regarding the displeasure of the Dalits, after which the BJP worked on four important strategies. These included efforts like activating the SC-ST front of the BJP, sending office bearers to the Dalit area, making it mandatory for the presence of effective leaders-Ministers of the party from this society at the district level and ensuring Dalit representation at the level of organization and government and trying to connect other Dalit leaders with the party.

In the midst of the Sangh's ongoing harmony campaign, once again the intellectuals of the Left ideology mobilized to create an atmosphere, while the government and the *Vichar Parivar* were nurturing their strategy with symbols through the heritage and dates associated with Ambedkar. The intellectual movement was also in full swing. Not only this, keeping in mind the future politics, apart from coordination with women, spiritual figures, a special survey was also being done by the Sangh-BJP, which will be mentioned in the next chapters. The Sangh was being targeted because of some incidents in society and politics, for which the opponents were using the earlier assumptions about the Sangh as a basis. Whether it was a matter of nationalism or social harmony or an attempt to connect intellectuals and women, the alleged role of the Sangh in the freedom struggle, Tricolour versus saffron flag, upper caste versus backward-Dalit, it was being targeted through comparative pictures. On August 24, 2018, Congress leader Rahul Gandhi had criticized the Sangh even on foreign soil, where he likened the Sangh to the 'Muslim Brotherhood' and termed it as a bigotry-hatred organisation. Rahul also often called it an anti-SC-ST organization. That is, on the whole, the long-standing perception about the Sangh as made by the people of the Left and opposition ideologies was not getting broken. The reason for this was also that the Sangh did not deny these things in any way because it has always believed in continuing to run a campaign of public awareness in the society, regardless of what is said about it in the media or elsewhere.

But after the formation of the Modi government, the Vichar Pariwar started working on a long-term script based on coordination. In such a situation, the Sangh felt the need to officially clarify the position on the assumed idea about the Sangh, so that it can express its views on what the Sangh is and what it thinks on the subjects of various national importance. That is, people should understand about the Sangh from the Sangh itself and not from any third party that interprets it according to their thinking. A blueprint was made for this and the Sangh organized a three-day programme on 17-19 September, 2018 in the most exclusive place for government events in the capital Delhi - 'Vigyan Bhawan', which probably had not happened ever in the 93-year history of the Sangh. The name of the event was 'Future India: Sangh's Vision', which clearly indicated that the Sangh had come out for public dialogue with a far-reaching vision. Its specialty was that this dialogue was conducted by the *Sarsanghchalak* Mohan Bhagwat himself for all three days so that there would not be a trace of confusion left.

But just six months prior to Lok Sabha elections, before any question could arise on the crux of the Sangh's event in 'Vigyan Bhawan', the opposition started raising questions about the purpose and the permission given by the government to organize the event in 'Vigyan Bhawan'.

But regardless of this, the Sangh made it clear what its thinking was behind this event! Sangh's Akhil Bharatiya *Prachar pramukh* Arun Kumar had then said, "India today is on the way to attain its special place in the world. In such a situation, it was felt that a large enlightened section of the society is eager to know the proper perspective of the Rashtriya Swayamsevak Sangh on the subjects of national importance and this programme has been organized with this thought. Alok Kumar, working president of Vishwa Hindu Parishad, clarified on this a little more, "The Sangh does not believe in ideological untouchability. But it is unfortunate that dialogue has stopped between people of different ideologies. The Sangh wants to restart this dialogue. That's why we have invited prominent and enlightened people from all walks of life in this event. Our expectation is that people understand the Sangh from the Sangh itself and not from any third party." The point to note is that the Sangh did not take the name of BJP anywhere regarding this programme but as Arun Kumar said, "India today is on the way to attain its special place in the world. In such a situation, the thinking of the Sangh..." He did not take the name of Prime Minister Narendra Modi, but pointed to the weightage of Modi and the changed environment in the world. The coordination was not one-sided. In the whole arrangement of organizing this grand event, the entire team of the Sangh in Delhi region was naturally involved. But behind the scenes, the then National General Secretary of BJP Bhupendra Yadav from the ruling party was supervising the management, who was in touch with the top leaders of the Sangh on the instructions of BJP President Amit Shah. That is, the coordination between the Sangh and the BJP in the background continued in a manner that provided a positive environment for the expansion of the Sangh and these efforts were helping the BJP to increase its political base. But the way the Sangh was being targeted by the opposition along with the BJP through the events in politico-social field, there were many issues like Hindutva, mob lynching, cow protection, caste, reservation, on which the Sangh gave an open invitation to a public event—Come on, Learn About the Sangh!

India of the Future: Sangh's Vision

(September 17, 2018: Day 1)

In 'Mahabharata', Sanjay - the charioteer of King Dhritarashtra of Hastinapur, told him the whole story of Kurukshetra live without being present there. But before the election Mahabharata of 2019, when Narendra Modi was at the centre of power, the nucleus of the ideology was the Sangh. To break the misconceptions and assumptions about it, the sixth *Sarsanghchalak* of the Sangh, like Sanjay, gave a bird's eye view of the life journey of Dr. Keshav Baliram Hedgewar, the founder of the Sangh, which is considered to be the world's largest voluntary organization, from his role in the freedom movement to the Sangh's journey till now and on all the burning issues related to the country and society. His entire speech and question-and-answer are available on the Sangh's website. But in this whole context, it is necessary to present here the Bhagwat's speech that emanated for the Sangh, by the Sangh and from the platform of the Sangh. In this event, Mohan Bhagwat told the new generation what the Sangh is, why it was formed, what it does and what is its purpose. Since the injury was being inflicted more on the foundation of the Sangh, Bhagwat started talking about the foundation itself. Some excerpts from the speech given by Bhagwat are quoted in his own words, but with slight editing for understanding-

Mohan Bhagwat said in the very beginning that this programme has been organized to understand the Sangh because now it is present in the country as a force and it is discussed in the world. The discussion about the Sangh is natural. But in order to discuss it one must know the reality about it. The Sangh's work is unique, and no comparison is visible. Therefore, it cannot be known by the method of known to unknown. If you try to know, then there are more chances of having misunderstandings. Sangh's method being unique, the workers keep doing their work and do not run after publicity and fame. As the power of the Sangh increases, its promotion happens automatically.

Everyone tries to know what a Sangh is. As the work of an organization increases, it becomes a force. But some people are also afraid of that power. In such a situation, there is also misinformation about it. There is nothing unusual in this. What is the truth about the Sangh? This time has been chosen for official statement and question-and-answer. I am going to place facts before you, the purpose of which is not to force you to believe because it is your right to believe or not. But I will tell you the facts and I will also answer your questions on the basis of my knowledge, in which it is up to you to research further and to amend. But whatever discussion will take place from your side after that, it will be based on the official knowledge of the Sangh, which is enough for us. So, Bhagwat bluntly gave the message that by creating an atmosphere of fear about the Sangh, confusion is being spread, which is a sign of its increasing power and influence. But before explaining the Sangh, he narrated the life journey of Dr. Hedgewar so that it would be easy to understand this organization.

Such was the life of Dr. Hedgewar

(He threw away the sweets of slavery rule in childhood and started the movement of '*Vande Mataram*')

If you want to understand the Sangh, you have to start with Dr. Hedgewar. It is difficult to understand the Sangh without knowing Dr Hedgewar. Born in a lower-middle-class family, Dr. Hedgewar's childhood was spent in the midst of discussions of the freedom movement. We used to call him a born patriot because he was in primary school then. Once the programme of the coronation ceremony of Queen Victoria took place in all the schools of India. Hedgewar was in the third grade at that time. Sweets were distributed in that programme. But he threw the sweets in the garbage. When the teacher asked him if he did not like sweets as he threw them in the dustbin. Hedgewar replied, "How can the sweets of the coronation ceremony of those who snatched our own kingdom be sweet to us? How can this day be a day of celebration for us? It is a day of mourning." He was only 11 years old when his parents, who were engaged in the service of the people suffering from the plague that had spread in Nagpur, also died of plague on the same day.

Later on, *'Vande Mataram Movement'* started. Dr. Hedgewar was in the leading group that worked to organize that *'Vande Mataram Movement'* in the schools of Nagpur. When the inspectors used to come for inspection in the school, they were welcomed in every class with the slogans of *'Vande Mataram'*, which upset the government of that time. It closed all the schools in Nagpur and started searching for the person who raised the slogans. But Dr. Hedgewar had created such a wonderful organization that but no one's name was found even after 4 months. Finally, the parents of the students, the government officials—all together worked out a formula to open the school and when the child enters the school, the headmaster will stand at the gate and ask each one—Isn't it a mistake? So, he had to shake the head and say 'yes'. Admission was to be granted with this modest apology. But two students in Nagpur refused to do so. One of them was Keshav Hedgewar, who was expelled from the school.

For the students who dropped out due to the movement, the leaders of that time ran national schools, from where they completed the remaining study of matriculation. Seeing his activism and spark, the leader of Nagpur of that time raised donations and sent him to study at the National Medical College in Calcutta. On the pretext of studies, he had to coordinate among the revolutionaries from all over the country there because this committee was in Calcutta only. He also passed the final examination after four years in first class and after a difficult examination in these four years, he was admitted to the core committee of the Revolutionary Committee. His code name was 'Cocaine' at that time. Later on, this movement also failed. He rejected the job for the sake of the country and the society. When marriage proposals came, I wrote a letter to his guardian uncle - 'I have pledged to surrender my life to the country by living the life of a lifelong celibate in this life. I don't want to get married etc.' So, then the proposals stopped coming and then agitation was the only way at that time.

When Hedgewar became a Congress worker

(The British sent him to jail for a year in a case of sedition. But in defense, he made such a stand that the judge had to say—this speech is more provocative than the allegation)

Bhagwat recounted such quotes which could make the parties like Congress who had accused the Sangh uncomfortable. A leader like Rahul Gandhi always put the Sangh in the dock that it had no role in the freedom movement. But Bhagwat conveyed the message from the event that Hedgewar was earlier in the Congress and had been welcomed after his release from prison under Motilal Nehru's presidency. This quote was summed up by Bhagwat like this- Hedgewar became a worker of the Indian National Congress which was founded by the people of the country together. When the non-cooperation movement started, he started making people aware, but got arrested because of his speeches. He was accused of sedition and prosecuted in a court in Nagpur. He gave his defense in the prosecution, whereas the people did not give defense in the movement and accepted the punishment which was given. But he said that I will accept the punishment, but I will speak in defence. Since journalists and public also used to come to the court at that time, he got an opportunity to publicize what he wanted to say by giving a speech. He started that speech thus - 'Under which law does the British get the right to rule India? If there is that law, tell me. I do not believe in this right of yours, I do not believe in your law, I do not believe in your justice. I haven't told my people anything wrong. I have made the people of my society aware. Freedom is a human right. I have spoken in speeches about how to become free, how to be free and how to run their life with their freedom. If the British government wants to take it as treason and arrest me and people like me and put them in jail, then the British government should also understand that the time has come for them to leave this country forever." The judge, while awarding him one year's rigorous imprisonment, said that his defense speech was more provocative than the speech of which he was accused. He went to jail for a year. After his release from jail, he was felicitated in a meeting, which was presided over by Motilal Nehru. In that too he gave a speech and said the same thing. He said that only going to jail is not patriotism. We will go to jail if we have to, but to create awareness about the meaning of freedom in the minds of the people, the efforts to achieve freedom while staying outside—this is also patriotism. When I was in prison for a year, I gained weight. There was no side effect on me. But I am sure this work would have been done in the absence of people like us. And again, he started his work of awareness.

Hedgewar's dialogue with Communist Ruikar

(I'm a poor capitalist and you are rich labourer)

The Sangh has always been accused of fighting the Left ideology. But the Sangh Chief clarified that the RSS works with the goal of 'nation first'. But if someone's policies are a hindrance in that path, then there is a difference of opinion. Bhagwat also shared Hedgewar's views on this. According to him, in public life, Dr. Hedgewar met everyone. His nature was such that even if someone's ideology was different or even opposing, as long as the person was authentic and working in the interest of the country, then he did not have any opposition to him. People of all ideologies were his good friends. At that time, there used to be a communist leader in Nagpur named Barrister Ruikar. He was a good barrister and was wealthy. He was known as the leader of the workers in Nagpur. Dr. Hedgewar who hailed from a poor family was a very good friend of his. Dr. Hedgewar used to tell him,

"I am a poor capitalist and you are a rich labourer." That's how their fights went on. Once he asked Ruikar, "What will you do if I come to your house tomorrow morning to report that the British rule is gone and Shivaji Maharaj is back?" Barrister Ruiker said, "Is that even a question! I will distribute sweets!" So, Dr. Hedgewar said that "It means your destination is same as ours. So why fight with each other? Why don't we walk together? Why create so much controversy over petty things?" That was his way of thinking. Due to this, he used to have discussions and talks with all kinds of people.

This is how Hedgewar founded the Sangh

(The society needs to be given some training and no one has the time to give training. Everyone has chosen their own work. I think, I will have to do this work.)

When the revolutionary Rajguru went underground, Dr. Hedgewar had arranged for his stay in Nagpur. He used to have discussions about the country and society. Bhagwat not only cited examples of Hedgewar's patriotism, but also his sacrificing attitude towards society, which laid the foundation of the Sangh. He told that in 1989, when it was decided to celebrate the birth centenary of Dr. Hedgewar, the people of the Sangh invited Triloknath Chakraborty, a revolutionary in Calcutta who had worked with Dr. Hedgewar, to join the centenary committee, which he accepted. Triloknath recalled that once in 1911, Dr. Hedgewar had come to his house. He had said, "Dada, it seems that this society needs some training and no one has the time to train. Everyone has chosen their job. I guess I will have to do this work." Since then, there was a thought in his mind that the society is not fit to be called a free country. Work has to be done to make it eligible. And so, he did experiments for seven or eight years to see what kind of programmes-training could happen! Many organizations were running in the society, whose work he saw. He picked from some of them and some he thought out on his own. He ran some clubs. Thus, a *Rashtriya Swayamsevak Mandal* was also started in Wardha to impart training. He had used the name Sangh only three-four years before the establishment of the Sangh. In this way, he developed a method to build his society by doing all the experiments. On Vijayadashami in the year 1925 in Nagpur on Friday, 27th September he announced that this work is starting from today. He started work with as many colleagues as he could get. Then he only said that this work is just beginning; he didn't say anything else.

What is Sangh, what it does, how are *Swayamsevaks* Made?

Bhagwat also explained the entire process of Sangh and the concept behind volunteer-building. He himself raised questions and answered in the conference of enlightened people. What is Rashtriya Swayamsevak Sangh? This is methodology and nothing else. What does it do? It does the work of personality-building because we want many changes in the behaviour of the society even today. We want a society free from discrimination, we want an equal society, we want a society free from exploitation. Selfishness should also be eliminated, but it will not happen just by thinking. The conduct of society changes in the presence of examples and ideals are here with us. There is no shortage of great men. From time immemorial till this very moment, there have been many people on this land of ours who have sacrificed their lives for the country. But what is the tendency of our society in general? It celebrates their birth anniversary and death anniversary. It will definitely worship them. But it will not become like them even by mistake. Chhatrapati Shivaji Maharaj must be born again; but he should not be born in my house - it will worry about it. He must be born in someone else's house. If in every village, street, locality of the country, people who behave like that of a citizen of the time of independent India, who stick to it in every circumstance, are character-rich, people who have intimate contact with the whole society, then the behaviour of the society will change in that environment. It is the plan of the Sangh to nurture good *swayamsevaks* in every village and district. Good Swayamsevak means one whose character is trustworthy, pure; who works by considering the whole society, the country as his own; he does not look at anyone with discrimination or enmity. Because of this, who has earned the affection and trust of the society, a group of people who behave like this should be created in every village, in every locality. This scheme started in the form of Sangh in the year 1925. Sangh is just that, not more than that. Dr. Hedgewar was asked what will you do? When Sangh's *path-sanchalan* was held for the first time in 1928 in Nagpur, there were hardly 21-22 people. But in our society at that time even 21-22 people walking in one direction - that sight was very rare. So, people were impressed and went to Dr. Hedgewar because they knew that he was a man of revolutionary nature. He has dedicated his live for the country. So, they felt that they must have some distant vision and playing or long term. Taking people into confidence, they said that Doctor, now you have 50 people. Now what will you do next? So, the doctor said that after 50, we will go for 500 and then 5,000 and so on ..." Someone said, "But you haven't reached there!" So, he said suppose it is done. Then he was asked what will you do? He said we will go for 50,000. Thus, it reached 5 crores. Then he got up and asked, "What will you do with them?" So, he said that he will not do anything, he will do only this much. Doctor Saheb said that we have to unite the entire Hindu society. There is no need to create a separate organization in it. Everyone has to be united. We do not have to do any other work except this because after the establishment of such a society, whatever should happen, it will happen automatically. Nothing else has to be done for that. The Rashtriya Swayamsevak Sangh was established at that time to organize the entire Hindu society.

Hindutva: A Value and Idea

The Sangh-BJP have always been cornered on Hindutva. It is wrapped in the syrup of communalism, due to which the enlightened people of the society refrain from associating with a particular identity. The Sangh has been grappling with this for a long time. In such a situation, Bhagwat reiterated from Vigyan Bhavan as to what is Hindutva? According to him, when the Sangh now talks about a value-based society, it means Hindu. Even the people of the world would say that Hindu is a thought. This matter of value-based conduct, culture, our Hindunessis because of that culture. That's why Hindutva unites all of us, that was Dr. Hedgewar's thought. And he said that we will unite the entire Hindu society because in Indian society there are such people who say that we are not Hindus. So, what is the word that unites all? Maybe there is no other word. That's why he categorically declared, "This Hindustan is a Hindu Rashtra. We will unite a Hindu Rashtra." He did not make this announcement because he wanted to oppose anyone. His experience said that you have to fix the society first, connect the society. A society free from discrimination, self-interest is the culmination of national independence. Ideology has its place, policies have their place, governments-leaders have their place; But all these aspirations are fulfilled when these people are in such a society. Hedgewar used to say that the biggest problem is the Hindu here. When we started to live forgetting our values, our downfall started. I do not want to go into detail, but if you study, then you will know that the downfall of our country has started with our downfall. And the solution is that we have to go back to our origins.

Sangh's Discipline: First Consent, then Speak One Language

The question is raised about the top leaders in the Sangh that they make decisions sitting at the top. But Bhagwat said that in Sangh once we agree upon something, there remains no need for everyone to speak again. If everyone starts talking, they will say the same thing, then everyone's point will be different. Therefore, the task of speaking belongs to only one person. When we speak in one voice, only one message is conveyed, and therefore, from on the basis of discipline from the point of view of agreeing, it appears that everything happens as per one person's decision. But that's not how it happens. Now there are millions of *swayamsevaks*. I do not listen to them alone; but there is such a system at the *shakha* level. As ideas come, there is a consensus at the top. Once the consensus is formed, everyone presents their own point of view. If you want to see the most democratic thing, then come to the Sangh. There is no restriction on *swayamsevaks* here. He is only driven by the teachings and wisdom that we have given him. Within its scope, he can do whatever he wants; this is an important part of the discipline and democratic system of the Sangh.

Tricolour vs Saffron Flag

The finger has always been pointed at the Sangh regarding the flag. Opposition said that the Sangh gives more importance to the saffron flag than the Tricolour. In such a situation, when Sangh Chief Bhagwat officially put forth his view on the flag in front of enlightened people, it was natural that headlines were made. Bhagwat tried to answer the opponents by putting forward an anecdote from the time of Pt. Jawaharlal Nehru regarding the donations needed to run the Sangh and the Tricolor. First of all, Bhagwat said that the Sangh is a self-supporting organization, which raises its own money, which comes from the Gurudakshina of the *swayamsevaks*. Regarding the saffron flag as a guru, they offer dakshina as a part of its worship once a year.

But the question is why the saffron flag guru? Because it is a symbol of Indian tradition from the beginning till date. Whenever there is a talk of our history, the saffron flag always exists somewhere or the other. Even in the report given by the Flag Committee on what should be the flag of independent India, it also said that it should be a flag that is well-known everywhere. But later there was a change in it. The Tricolour was introduced, which we have full respect for. The question is also raised that the saffron flag is displayed in the *shakha*, what about the Tricolour flag? RSS Swayamsevak is associated since the birth of and with honour of the Tricolour flag. Bhagwat described how there was a spinning wheel instead of a wheel when the 80 feet flag was hoisted for the first time in the Congress session. Nehru was its president. But the flag got stuck in the middle. No one dared to climb such a height. Just then a young man from the crowd ran and climbed the pole and untied the ropes of the flag.

Naturally people lifted him on the shoulders and took him to Nehruji. Nehru patted him on the back and told him to come in the evening and that they will felicitate him in the open session. But some leaders went to him and told him not to call him saying that he went to the Sangh *shakha*. Mr. Kishan Singh Rajput, who lived in high school in Jalgaon, was that *swayamsevak*.

When Dr. Hedgewar came to know about it, he travelled to meet him. He congratulated him by presenting him a small pot of silver as a prize. So, since the time Tricolour was hoisted for the first time, a swayamsevak of the Sangh has been associated with its honour. Rashtriya Swayamsevak Sangh works for the purpose that the whole society should become one. I don't know what other interest anyone has in it. The Sangh does its work. Many people stick their views on the objectives of the Sangh, which is not quite right.

There is no Remote Control, all Organizations are Self-reliant

The term 'remote control' about the Sangh comes up a lot, especially when the BJP is in power. Be it Vajpayee's rule or Modi's rule, it is run by the RSS by remote control from the headquarters of Nagpur- such allegations are made by the opposition parties. But Mohan Bhagwat gave clarification from his side to people with such thinking in this way. He said that now two things remain – one is the control and the other is the remote control. What should a Sangh Swayamsevak do for the rest of his life, which social work he does - he thinks for himself and chooses his field of work. Today the *swayamsevaks* of the Sangh are working in many fields. But all these organizations, in which swayansevaks are in-charge, are autonomous from the point of view of decision-making policy. Since they are *swayamsevaks* from the point of view of the Sangh, Sangh is concerned that they don't make any mistake. Now that they are old, they have their expertise and no one even needs to advise them. We are not embarrassed about our ideology. We are not embarrassed about what anyone thinks about the Sangh. Coordination meeting is not held because any policy is fixed in it. But these organizations work in an adverse environment because they stem from the ideas of the Sangh. That is why a coordination meeting takes place so that your sanskars are recollected. Discussions take place and exchange of ideas takes place; a decision is not taken.

Women's Participation in the Sangh

Intellectuals used to target in the name of protest against the ban on entry of women in the Sangh. But Bhagwat made it clear, too. He reminded that Dr. Hedgewar was asked by a woman in 1931 that you talk about Hindus, but you have left out 50 percent women. On this, Dr Hedgewar had said that today the environment is not such that men can work among women. That may give rise to many types of misunderstandings. But if a woman wants to work, we will help her fully. That woman ran a similar organization named 'Rashtra Sevika Samiti'. Today that too has become a pan India organization. The working method based on Sangh's teachings in Rashtriya Swayamsevak Sangh for men and Rashtra Sevika Samiti for women—these will run parallelly. These two will not work in each other's field, they will always help each other. If there is a feeling on both sides that there should be a change in it, then it will happen, otherwise it will go on like this. The Sangh is not an organization of sannyasins. Most of the *swayamsevaks* are householders and everybody visits each other's homes. Women are equally active in various activities of the Sangh. After all, if there has to be opposition, then it should be on the basis of the acts. But the main question is why it is only for Hindus?

Day 2 and 3 of the Event (September 18-19, 2018)

When Mohan Bhagwat started his speech on the second day, he responded to the allegations about the Sangh's relationship with politics. He said that from the very birth, the Sangh has ensured that our organization will stay away from politics. It will not do politics of competition, it will not contest elections, no office bearer of Sangh can become office bearer in any political party and Sangh has to stay away from this politics of elections or votes. But the work of the Sangh is to unite the entire society. So, since its birth, the Sangh has decided that it will not go into everyday politics. As the ideology of the Sangh, it has its opinion on the issues and policies related to the nation.

In such a situation, there is infiltration or some issues in which politics has a role. Bhagwat also replied that why are there volunteers or so many office bearers in a party, saying that being familiar with each other, they ask about their well-being and if they need advice, they ask or it. We advise when possible, but Sangh has no influence on the policies. As far as presence of more swayamsevaks in a single party is concerned, it is their own decision. We do not ask any swayamsevak to work for any particular political party. But we say that it is necessary to stand behind those who work with an idea for the nation, with a vision of a policy. That policy can be anyone's. The workers responsible for the work of the Sangh do not get involved in politics at all.

On the second day, Bhagwat gave a slightly more elaborate speech on Hindutva, in which he cited historical and spiritual quotes, saying that the Sangh's idea of Hindutva was not his invention, but it has been carried on by tradition. But how later it became narrow and evils, sins like untouchability entered the Hindu society! Now the Sangh wants that sin should be cleared and according to the country, time and circumstance, there should be a revival of that eternal human religion in India in a new form. Here also, quoting Ambedkar, Bhagwat said that in the Constituent Assembly, Ambedkar had said that because of our fight amongst ourselves, foreigners won and made us slaves. The work of the Sangh is for this brotherhood and there is only one basis for this brotherhood – unity in diversity, the same idea that the world calls 'Hinduism'. But when we say that we are a Hindu nation, it does not mean that we do not want Muslims in it. The day it is said that yes, Muslims are not wanted, that day it will no longer be Hindutva. The day we say that only Vedas will work, Buddhism will not work, if he does not believe in Buddhists, then he will no longer be a Hindu. Bhagwat elaborated the Sangh's thinking about the nation. At last, he reiterated the thinking with which the ceremony was organized. Bhagwat said, "We thought that by calling prominent people, it should be clearly stated in front of you what Sangh wants to do? Why it wants to do it? Why does the Sangh talk of Hindutva? And what is India's vision before the Sangh? I have put those four things in front of you. After hearing all this, if there is any curiosity in your mind and you want clarification about something or to understand something else, then I want you put it in the question box.

On the third, that is, on the last day, the Sangh Chief answered 23 important questions in detail, those that have been raised on the Sangh. The most important among them was the clarification given on reservation. He reiterated his point of view on Hindutva and supported inter-caste marriage in response to the question of the caste system. Bhagwat recalled that the first inter-caste marriage took place in Maharashtra in 1942. During that, messages from Dr Ambedkar and Guruji who was the then *Sarsanghchalak* of the Sangh were received. Describing it as part of the message of social harmony, Bhagwat said that the Sangh's thinking about the caste-system, Indian values in education-higher education, respect for the mother tongue is necessary for the language and said that language is the carrier of emotion. Questions like Sangh's attitude towards women, why resentment regarding Hindutva, cow protection-mob lynching, religious conversion came naturally. On the question of population control law in the present era, the Sangh emphasized on the awareness of the society more than the law.

Straight Talk on Reservation Now

The controversy over reservation was the hot topic of the time. Therefore, when the question arose, the Sangh was also at ease. Bhagwat said, "Some meanings are extracted from the statements that are made periodically. But keep in mind that the reservation given in the constitution to remove social disparity has and will remain with the full support of the Sangh. But for how long this reservation will last will be decided by those for whom reservation has been given; when they feel that it is not needed now, then they will see. But till then it should be continued, such is the very well thought out view of the Sangh and its opinion ever since this question has come up. There has been no change in that. So, whether it was a dispute about Bhagwat's reservation statement at the time of Bihar assembly elections or a message from Nagaur Pratinidhi Sabha or BJP's uneasiness after the Dalits' agitation like 'Bharat Bandh' on April 2 over the dilution of some provisions of the SC-ST Act by the Supreme Court on March 20, 2018, amidst all this, this explanation by the Sangh Parivar was a relief. Earlier, the Sangh's statements were interpreted in such a way that confusion used to spread.

The next question was also about Supreme Court's decision regarding SC-ST Act and the government's initiative to reverse the decision in Parliament. Bhagwat spoke with caution here as well. He said, "I will not speak about what the Supreme Court said and what the government did. The desire of the Sangh is that the law should be protected, but it should not be misused and this problem should be rectified by increasing mutual harmony in the society. Bhagwat also said that untouchability did not come from the law, but from the customs of the society, because of our ill-will. The work of increasing that goodwill has been carried out by the volunteers in the form of 'Samarsata Manch' so that efforts are made to correct it.

Even though Sangh's attitude towards minorities was considered negative Bhagwat said that earlier all belonged to the same society. But Dr. Hedgewar has said something, so now it does not mean that the Sangh will base itself on the same statements. Times change, the state of the organization changes. Our thinking also changes and we have been getting permission to change from Dr. Hedgewar. If you consider the Sangh as a closed organization, then doubts arise in your mind. I ask you to experience first-hand te work Sangh *swayamsevaks* are doing today, experience what they think, how they think. All your doubts will be cleared.

No to NOTA, 100 percent Good People cannot be Found in Politics

Bhagwat also gave an unambiguous opinion about who should be elected in politics and who should not. He said the expectation that only 100 percent good people should be found in democratic politics is like wishing for *Akash pushp* (a sky flower). Even in the Mahabharata period, when there was talk of Yaduvanshis supporting either the Kauravas or the Pandavas, then in this discussion there was talk of the immorality of the Kauravas and the mistakes of the Pandavas.. Then Shri Krishna had said that politics is such a thing that it is difficult to find 100% good people here. But Bhagwat added here that it is a good thing to find someone like Deendayalji. In such a situation, people have only one option-choose the best amongst what is available. Therefore, there is no justification for the provision of NOTA.

Sangh-BJP Relations

Questions on the relationship between the Sangh and BJP were expected. The question arose- if the Sangh is not concerned with politics, then why does it give *sangathan mantri* to the BJP and has it ever supported other parties as well? On this, Bhagwat also pointed out that whoever asks for an organization Minister from the RSS or advice on any issue, RSS gives it; to accept or not depends on the person in front. But he also gave a clear indication that whatever political party supports its issue related to the nation and society, it will get the benefit of the

Sangh. Bhagwat clearly said that RSS gives *sangathan mantri* to anyone who asks for one. Till now no one has asked except BJP. If others ask for it and their work is good, we will definitely give. We have not supported any party. In 93 years, we have definitely supported a policy. Emergency was opposed, and so, the people who fought against it got the benefit. Not only did Jana Sangh get its benefit, but also Babu Jagjivan Ram, SM Joshi, Gopalan of Left got its benefit. It happened only once that we were supporting the policy of Ram Mandir and only BJP was in favour of it, which benefited the BJP. After the year 2014, that is, during the Modi reign, did the work happen according to the Sangh or not? On this question, Bhagwat skillfully said that ask from the year 1947 and not just from 2014. However, he also said that the conditions have changed in the society and today most of the people of our country understand that we will make products in our country. Today the companies of our country are going ahead and competing. Saints like Baba Ramdev are also moving ahead. Entrepreneurship has increased, skill training has increased. People are going abroad after taking education and coming back to work. They are working in agriculture sector, working on skill training; so, there is some hope. The country has to stand on its own feet, that is why it has happened and hope has been created. It would not be appropriate to say 100 percent because when this happens then it will be a golden day, but in today's date it can be said that yes, our country has taken steps in this direction. So, Bhagwat not only expressed his satisfaction over the functioning of the Modi government, but also mentioned about the changed environment in the society.

If the Sangh is democratic, why not elect the *Sarsanghchalak*?

Now about why there is no election of *Sarsanghchalak*. Because Dr Hedgewar has been *Sarsanghchalak* and then Guruji; such people have been there. Therefore, it is a place of faith. Who will be the *Sarsanghchalak* after me? It will be based on my wish and for how long I will be the *Sarsanghchalak* will also be as per my wish. But why is it so? Bhagwat also answered this. He said that the role of *Sarsanghchalak* in the Sangh is only that of friend, philosopher and guide. He has no right to do anything. The one who has authority is the Chief Executive, that is the *Sarkaryavah*. If *Sarkaryavah* says stop it and go to Nagpur immediately, then I will have to do it. But election or this post is held every three years ceaselessly. Ever since the Sangh has given its written constitution to the government, not a single election has been postponed even by a day. The *shakhas* select regional representatives and Sangh leaders at other levels are elected in the district, region and province. *Akhil Bhartiya Pratinidhi* (All India Representatives) are elected who elect *Sarkaryavah* every three years. We are very regular in this matter. I am giving this speech for two days. You must be feeling that I am speaking with my own will. But it's not like that. It was discussed with all the key officials as what to present and what not to present. What I am speaking is the consent of the Sangh. Now no one in the Sangh will object to my words. Everything is decided by consensus. If anyone thinks that only quarreling among themselves is democracy, then it is wrong. The essence of democracy is consensus.

After question and answer, Bhagwat finally concluded the conference for the learned in this way, "Don't believe what anyone says about the Sangh. Don't even believe what I said. Have a look at the Sangh from inside and then form your opinion about the Sangh. Now after this, if any of you wish to be directly involved in the work of the Sangh, then go to the *shakha.* If you do not want to go to the *shakha*, then the *swayamsevaks* of the Sangh undertake a lot of good work, join them." Bhagwat also gave an unambiguous opinion on society, nation, women, reservation to the working style of the Sangh and its relationship with the BJP. He also invited to get closer to the organization to know the Sangh closely. His aim was clear that the misconceptions about the Sangh should be ended and its ideological roots from social harmony to intellectual movement should be strengthened. After this, the Sangh Chief organized an informal programme of dialogue in the group with the representatives of Indian and foreign media so that even in the discussions about the Sangh in the media, the conversation about the Sangh should be according to the reality of the Sangh. So, the strategy of the Sangh was to remove the confusion and to create a new intellectual environment. In this chain, the Sangh's ideological body *'Prajna Pravah'* once again organized *'Lok-Manthan '* and chose Jharkhand, which is considered a backward state, for it.✈

16

CHAPTER

'Intellectual Fair' of 'Indianness'

How did the Sangh give impetus to the efforts to revive the thinking of nationalism by organizing the second big intellectual fair in Ranchi on the tenth day of the message from Vigyan Bhavan?

What was India before and what is it now? The *Mahamanthan* (brainstorming) on this subject was the second attempt to carry forward the link of the Sangh's Vigyan Bhawan message. A *Lok-Manthan* was organized from September 28-30, 2018 in Ranchi, the capital of Jharkhand, by *'Prajna Pravah'* which was established as the intellectual body of the Sangh. The event was being held just a week after Sangh Pramukh Mohan Bhagwat's efforts at Vigyan Bhawan to clear the confusion spread by alleged propaganda about the Rashtriya Swayamsevak Sangh. Certainly, all the activities were part of the strategic link. Earlier, the Sangh had organized the first *'Lok-Manthan'* in Bhopal, the capital of Madhya Pradesh in November 2016, according to the script prepared after the JNU incident, with the theme - Strengthening the idea of nationalism by coming out of the slavery of colonial thinking. Expanding on it, the theme of Ranchi *'Lok-Manthan '* was - *'Bharat Bodh: Jan, Gana, Mana'*. So, it was a part of the Sangh's intellectual movement, which was planned to be accelerated while the Modi government was at the Centre in March 2016 by the Sangh-BJP and all the supported intellectuals in the Haryana Bhawan meeting.

The Sangh and the *'Prajna Pravah'* also reiterated their thinking through the *'Lok-Manthan '* held in Ranchi. But was *'Lok-Manthan '* really just organizing the conference or was it some special idea, which was being worked on? This was also answered in detail at the same time by J Nandakumar, the national convener of *'Prajna Pravah'* through an exclusive interview in Sangh's mouthpiece '*Panchjanya*' and 'Organiser' (published in the issue of August 19, 2018), which should be quoted below. It is necessary so that the entire strategy of the Sangh Parivar can be clearly understood. Nandakumar made it clear that the *Lok-Manthan* was an attempt to revive the national thinking as there was an opportunity to revive the national supremacy after independence. But due to colonial influence, this work was not done wholeheartedly. In such a situation, today there is a need to revive the process of national thought in a comprehensive manner, for which *'Prajna Pravah'* is emerging as a platform for coordination. The basic objective of *Lok-Manthan* is to give a common platform to the thinkers and action-oriented people who consider the nation as paramount. In our tradition, not only the intellectuals, but every person, whether he works as a loader or does painting, governmental or anything else, he is the bearer of the basic concept of the nation. That is why we thought that why not such thinkers and nationalists should sit together and discuss important issues for the country! Seminars and discussions are generally considered to be the exclusive domain of professional intellectuals, but most of them are not aware of the ground realities of India.

But is the Sangh's *'Prajna Pravah'* limited only to the event? Nandkumar points out that the success of the *Lok-Manthan* held in Bhopal in the year 2016 is that it took the discourse of freeing the masses from colonial clutches to a very large section of academicians, intellectuals and action-oriented people. It was also made the subject of contemplation of the common people. After the brainstorming, we did such programmes at many levels, in which people sensitive to the progress and development of the nation also participated in large numbers. Through *Lok-Manthan* in the last two years, we have tried to revive the tradition of dialogue and take it to different levels of the society. I would like to point out that this practice is still alive in our villages and family systems. Our effort is that it should be given some recognition in the intellectual class as well. But how important is it to take it to the masses? Nandakumar bluntly said, "It is not just an intellectual endeavour. I will call it an intellectual fair because fairs have had a different social and cultural place since ancient times. Nandkumar also spoke about what kind of strategy has been made regarding the event. He said that even before organizing the *Lok-Manthan*, we had decided that only one programme at the national level would not make a difference. Therefore, many such initiatives were taken at the state level as well.

In two years, a big national event, which was being held in Ranchi, was taking its theme towards the same nationalism, which had become an important base for the BJP in the year 2019 elections. The theme was- *'Bharat Bodh: Jana, Gana, Mana.'* In the words of Nandakumar, "What is the meaning of India? What is our concept about nation and society? What is the mind of India? Or what was it before and what is it now? In which direction should it move? All these topics will be discussed. We should know what has been the meaning of nation in our tradition? How our society developed various self-supporting systems? Today everything has become government and politics-centric due to its colonial thinking. Our system was never like this, society used to prepare its own system and put it into practice with its own moral norms and reform system. The purpose of our brainstorming is to know how relevant the systems of that time are in today's perspective and what changes should be made in applying them today. He also pointed out that the purpose of this event is not to give direction to political discourse. It is an attempt to determine through collective discussion what should be the direction of our national reconstruction. From this, politics and administration can benefit from the process of discourse. But our aim is not to give any direction to any particular section.

In the last two years i.e. from 2016 onwards, *'Prajna Pravah'* organized *'Gyan Sangam'* for various academic disciplines. In addition to the interdisciplinary *'Gyan Sangam'*, five regional level programmes were organized for academicians at the national level. In these events, not only academic issues, but also related aspects like policy making to material preparation were discussed. The *'Prajna Pravah'* had started *'Gyan Sangam'* and in the same chain, it did a two-day *'Gyan Sangam'* at Indira Gandhi National Open University (IGNOU) and it also decided to organize *'Gyan Sangam'* in the coming times in Kochi on Economics, in Delhi on Philosophy, History in Hyderabad and in Anand on Linguistics.

What kind of education and knowledge system the Sangh wanted was clear and initiatives were being taken to create the necessary environment for it. J Nandakumar again said in an interview to '*Panchjanya*' before the Ranchi *Lok-Manthan* that India has been recognized as a country interested in knowledge, which has been preserving and spreading it. The world studied it and also recognized it. But it is a matter of misfortune that we have not been aware of our treasure. So, presenting the report of the first Education Commission of India, Dr S. Radhakrishnan had said in very clear words that the biggest drawback of the so-called modern education is that there is no tradition of Indian knowledge in it. Later, it was also specifically mentioned in the Dr. Kothari

Commission report that the axis of education system has shifted from India to Europe. To give right direction to India, we have to look towards Indian knowledge system. Nandakumar said that this does not mean at all that throwing away everything in the present and going to the bullock cart era! We only want that we should leave the system of blindly copying others and reintroduce the Indian system based on the acquisition of knowledge.

Regarding this three-day meeting held at Khelgaon, Ranchi from September 28 to 30, Dattatreya Hosabale, *Sah-Sarkaryavah* of the Sangh, also said that the purpose of this event is to strengthen the ideological and cultural aspect of the people, more than 1,000 litterateurs, historians, people from art-culture and ideological backgrounds from across the country participated in this event. So, the continuous events gave momentum to the Sangh in the true sense and Sangh also took the initiative to establish its penetration in that half of the population, which it has been criticized for not connecting with the Sangh. However, Sangh Chief Bhagwat had spoken bluntly about this in the event at Vigyan Bhavan itself. But apart from talking, there was a need to work on the ground as well and work began to make it a reality.

❑

PART-8

Sangh and Expansion of BJP

After establishing roots in the social and intellectual world, the shakhas of the Sangh also started spreading in a massive way. The Sangh also planned to add half the population. The adaptation of power gave effortlessness to Sangh in its expansion; so, time to pay back also came closer. In the election of the year 2019, even though Sangh did not ask for votes for any party as per its principles. But it's swayamsevaks became part of the campaign and launched a voter awareness programme by raising the issues related to the nation, which were on Modi government's agenda. In the name of nationality, the Sangh created the sponge-like land with coordination in the Vichar Parivar, on which Balakot fell like water after Pulwama and helped in winning power by fertilizing the prepared land.

❑

17

CHAPTER

Establishing Roots, Spreading 'Branches'

With the best coordination of ideology with the government, the Sangh increased its influence in the society and the intellectual world. How did the shakhas grow and then what was the strategy for women?

After Modi government came to power in the year 2014, due to the unravelling thread of coordination, Sangh was not only confident but it was fully convinced that the government would not back down from the basic agenda of ideology and development. Sooner or later, the Modi government will remember the sacrifice and devotion of the three generations of the Sangh. So, the entire focus of the Sangh was on the expansion of the organization, for which the family not only paid attention to all the projects in the society, but also made a long-term strategy for them. Leaving core ideological issues aside for the time being, it started creating an environment of social harmony, intellectual initiative, reforms in education so that people would connect with the BJP and Sangh in a positive spirit and not because of being in power. The effect of these activities of the Sangh was that roots were beginning to get established in the society and intellectual world. When the roots of a tree are firmly placed in the ground, then naturally the branches of the tree also grow; it was seen that the strong base of the Sangh, which had been working for more than nine decades in the society, was further strengthened during the Modi regime. The *shakhas* of Sangh expanded very rapidly during this reign, which was also a sign of the increasing influence of its ideological intervention. If one is to understand the growth in the Sangh's *shakhas*, then before the Modi regime, the situation in the BJP at the time of its second consecutive major defeat in the 2009 general elections has to be understood. There was turmoil in the BJP after its defeat in 2004 and again in 2009. Many prominent leaders had opened the front. The confrontation was at a tremendous level. The entire Sangh Parivar, including the BJP, was feeling the pain of the defeat of two consecutive Lok Sabha elections. This was a time when the family was also worried about the decline in the Sangh's *shakhas*.

But during the transition period from 2004 to 2009, the Sangh Parivar had learned that it is difficult to increase the base of the institutions due to the conflict between the organizations. According to Sangh's own report for the year 2009, the number of Sangh's *shakhas* was 43,905, which had come down to 39,823 in 2010, i.e., the number was reduced by 4,082 *shakhas*. This was a period of great concern for the Sangh and it was also discussed in the meeting of the *Pratinidhi Sabha*. *Sarkaryavah* Bhaiyyaji Joshi had placed the report in the *Akhil Bhartiya Pratinidhi Sabha* on March 11, 2011, in which he had said, "For the last three-four years, we are experiencing that the number of *shakhas* keeps on decreasing or increasing. We experience a little stability. There is need to pay more attention to the quality. The workers are paying more attention towards things like branch team *(shakha-toli)*, entrepreneurship etc. The programmes completed in the last year are definitely indicating that we are gradually moving towards consolidation and quality. There is a need to focus on increasing the number as well as the representation of more locations and more branches in our various training classes." After this *Pratinidhi Sabha*, a slight increase in the number of *shakhas* of the Sangh started from the year 2011. From 2009 to 2014, the Sangh's *shakhas* had grown close to 5,000. But when the Modi government came to power in 2014, the number of *shakhas* increased by 6,350 in just one year (see the comparative figures in the box below). So, 5,014 branches grew between the year 2009 to 2014. Then during the last year of Modi rule, that is, just before the notification of the Lok Sabha elections, on March 8, 2019, if we look at the report of the Sangh till the *Pratinidhi Sabha* of Gwalior, then we can see that in about four years and a quarter only, the number had grown to 14,284 *shakhas*, which was almost three times more than in 2009-14.

There is no doubt that the suitable atmosphere in politics had a direct effect on the expansion of the Sangh. During the first year of Narendra Modi's rule, the Sangh's *shakhas* grew by 217 percent and in the subsequent years, though the growth rate was not the same as before the number of *shakhas* was increasing. Whether the Sangh wants it or not, the BJP is considered as the political reflection of Sangh in the political circles. So, why wouldn't Sangh also intensify its efforts to expand its base in a suitable environment? The Sangh had already made headlines by inviting former President Pranab Mukherjee to the Sangh headquarters.

Account of Sangh's branches before and after Modi government			
Year	**Locations**	**Branches**	**increase/decrease in Branches**
2019	37,011	59,266	299 ↑
2018	37,190	58,967	1,734 ↑
2017	36,729	57,233	664 ↑
2016	36,867	56,569	5,237 ↑
2015	33,223	51,332	6,350 ↑
2014	29,624	44,982	2,001 ↑
2013	28,788	42,981	2,000 ↑
2012	27,978	40,891	983 ↑
2011	27,078	39,908	85 ↑, 11 ↓
2010	27,089	39,823	4,082 ↓
2009	30,015	43,905	---

(**Note:** Mohan Bhagwat took over as *Sarsanghchalak* in March 2009 and all the figures are taken from the reports of the Sangh, which are kept by the *Sarkaryavah* in the Akhil Bharatiya *Pratinidhi Sabha* every year in March. These do not include weekly Milan and Sangh Mandali, only branch statistics.)

In the view of 2019 Lok Sabha elections, the activism of the Sangh was going to be important as Congress President Rahul Gandhi from the opposition camp used to attack the Sangh more than the government. A senior Sangh leader told me, "Whenever negative or positive headlines are made about the Sangh, its visibility increases further." To corroborate this claim, that Sangh official said that when Pranab Mukherjee went to the Sangh headquarters, the speed of online membership had increased two and a half times two days before and a day after. Under the Modi regime, where about 350 people were joining the online association daily, during Mukherjee's visit this number had increased to about 850, that is, under the Modi regime, the Sangh's *shakhas* increased three times, and in the era of Digital India, online membership had increased up to ten times. See how the Sangh's activity grew through online membership.

When RSS launched the website in July 2012, keeping in mind the change in lifestyle and education system, a link of 'Join RSS' was put on the website. In this, as soon as a small form is filled, the information reaches the province, district and *shakha* and the people living in the area are connected to the *shakha*. When the Sangh launched its website in July 2012, only 1,000 people were joining in a month, not day, whereas by the end of the year 2018, this number had crossed 10,000 a month, most of the people who were joining were professional youth in the age group of 18 to 40 years. According to the available data till the three-day intellectual event held at Vigyan Bhawan in

October 2018 under Mohan Bhagwat, the number of online members of the Sangh had reached 5,80,482. If we look at the statistics related to *shakhas*, after the formation of the Modi government, the number of *shakhas* increased by 6,350 in the first year itself, then in the second year it increased by 5,237, in the third year by 664 and in the fourth year by 1,734. In Modi's first year, the *shakhas* of young students grew by 6,077. With the aim of connecting the youth, the Sangh started organizing monthly meeting programmes of IT Professionals, Doctors, Lawyers, MBAs etc. every month at the regional centres. Apart from this, for those who are not able to attend *shakha* daily, there are monthly and weekly meeting programmes. In order to attract the youth, the Sangh made a major change especially in the uniform.

The number of *shakhas* of the Sangh had increased by only 5,000 in the five years before Modi's rule. Then in the first year after the Modi government came to power, more than 6,000 new *shakhas* were added. Certainly, in the 2014 Lok Sabha elections, a large section of people who were young and aspirational had turned to the BJP. The inclination of these youths was to be naturally towards the Sangh. As such, the Sangh also took a flexible approach. The Sangh took a decision on the demand that was being raised for a long time regarding the change in uniform. On March 11-13, 2016, in the *Akhil Bhartiya Pratinidhi Sabha* held in Nagaur, Rajasthan, the Sangh approved the decision to change the uniform. Now khaki shorts were replaced by the brown pants. The issue was being debated in the RSS since 2010. The main reason for the change in uniform was the effort of the 91-year-old organization to attract the youth. But a change in dress may not be enough to attract them. The Sangh leadership knew that the fight to bring youth into the organization would have to be fought on the ideological front as well. Therefore, the Sangh also gave impetus to the work of setting up training camps for the youth. In order to increase the number of *shakhas*, Sangh sent about 15 thousand workers door to door with a special message for a week immediately after the Modi government came to power. As a result, the number of *shakhas* increased rapidly. The Sangh decided in the same year that there should be one *shakha* of the Sangh in all the 6 lakh villages of the country.

The Sangh took the Initiative to Widen the Base with New Projects

Samarsata Abhiyan: Efforts to increase penetration among Dalits by giving the slogan 'One temple, one well, one cremation ground'.

Intellectual Introductory Class: Contacted over 40,000 professionals including more than 10 thousand journalists in the year 2018, 540 journalist meetings in 7 provinces, honoured more than 1,300 journalists.

Linguistic Conference: In Delhi, the Sangh started a new experiment - an initiative for connecting the linguistic people of different states with the Sangh by organizing a conference.

Financial base increased: Gurudakshina has increased more than ever before and the Sangh is working towards becoming financially empowered.

Social Media: Earlier the Sangh had kept its distance from it, but now it has verified Facebook and Twitter and is continuously active on it.

IT *Milan*: IT *Milan* programmes at *shakhas* every month. Under the banner of 'Vigyan Bharti', 4 science festivals were organized till the year 2018.

With the policies of the government: Learning lessons from the experience of the Vajpayee government, better coordination during the Modi regime. No direct confrontation and indirectly did the work of taking the policies of the government to the people. A special campaign was launched to improve the atmosphere among the people on the SC-ST Act.

Increasing influence in diverse fields: In diverse fields like film, art, theatre, culture, publishing industry, the Sangh activated its own as well as neutral people by giving its platform and increased its penetration.

However, after the year 2010, when the anti-corruption environment was being created in the country and the then Manmohan government was facing many big allegations, Anna Hazare's movement for the Lokpal Bill had started. Swami Ramdev's movement also started on the issue of black money. In this way, when the atmosphere was created in the country, the Sangh also gave its support on this occasion, due to which the youth started moving towards the Sangh. But the majority of those who attended were still students from either higher secondary schools or colleges.

A section of it was attracted by the politics of power as the BJP and the RSS are seen as the forces of the ruling establishment. Some studies suggest that people who join the Sangh at the primary school level or at a young age are more ideologically stronger as they grow up, while those who join at an older age are not as ideologically strong. It was also emerging from the study that most parents consider the organization 'old-fashioned' because of the khaki shorts. They do not like to send their children to the *shakha* despite being influenced by the nationalist thinking of the organisation. Then a senior RSS functionary told me something like this, "The decision to replace shorts with pants has been taken very carefully. The aim is to attract children to *shakhas* so that they can be turned into ideologically strong cadre in future." In November 2018, '*Bal-Sangam*' programmes of 29 districts were held in Delhi province, in which 5,404 child and 104 adolescent *swyamsevaks* from classes 5 to 10 attended. Out of 11,500 *swyamsevaks*, 5,404 *swyamsevaks* were selected and 2,746 *swyamsevaks* were shortlisted for the primary education category for follow-up. A plan to connect the parents of *swyamsevaks* with voluntary work was made in '*Bal-Sangam*'. That is, when the Sangh took steps, this change also connected the youth, professionals, youth involved in the IT sector with the Sangh and for this instead of daily *shakhas*, they started organizing many events like evening *shakha*, IT *shakha*, due to which the participation of children and college *swyamsevaks* in *shakhas* reached 62 percent. The Sangh trained one lakh youth in the age group of 14 to 40 years annually during this period. In just one year, that is, in the year 2018, more than one lakh youths in the age group of 20 to 35 years joined the Sangh, which definitely reinforced the idea of expansion.

After the change in the uniform in the meeting of the *Akhil Bhartiya Pratinidhi Sabha* in Nagaur, a group of RSS functionaries said that there is a need for a significant change regarding married *pracharaks*. The basic rule is that the *pracharak* must be unmarried and if at any point of time he wants to get married, he will have to resign from his office. Not only this, the *pracharaks* of Sangh are also prohibited from marrying any woman from the women's cadre '*Rashtra Sevika Samiti*'. However, after this change it was also discussed that the Sangh can bring changes in the *pracharak* system also. One reason for this was that there are very few parents who allow their sons to become *pracharaks*. Nowadays having a small family is one of the important reasons for this, whereas in earlier times having a large family and many sons allowed one to become a *pracharak*. A senior RSS worker said, "Sooner or later the RSS will have to make a big change in this matter and it is possible that married *pracharaks* may take responsibility in place of unmarried *pracharaks*."

Although the Sangh considers it necessary to keep pace with the thought of modernity. Till now no decision has been taken by the Sangh regarding the *pracharaks*. But the change in uniform was very important at that time, which gave momentum to the *shakhas* of the Sangh. When the *shakhas* spread, the Sangh took an initiative with a holistic thinking about half the population, i.e., women, because Nitish Kumar had got the political benefit of the announcement of prohibition in Bihar and after the Supreme Court's decision on triple talaq, the initiative of the Modi government had got it the support of progressive women in the assembly elections of Uttar Pradesh. Therefore, the Sangh wished that a separate database should be prepared on the women of the country so that their welfare schemes could be planned with facts.

Mission Half Population

However, this mission cannot be formally called the mission of the Sangh because instead of directly connecting with it, the Sangh was executing it through a non-governmental organization (NGO). But the people of the Sangh and its affiliated organizations were also involved in this campaign of nationwide survey on the status of women from blueprint to implementation. The Sangh wanted the NGO to conduct the study independently so that the report was fair. But the NGO can take the help of its *swayamsevaks* working in different fields for the manpower required for this survey. So, as per the plan, the responsibility of survey on the status of women was entrusted to the Pune based NGO *Drishti Stree Adhyayan evam Prabodhan Kendra* (DSAPK) for women, which is managed by Geeta Tai Goonde. All the work of coordination in the women's field of Sangh is their responsibility. In this work, women *pracharaks* associated with other organizations of the Sangh were also informally associated with it. For example, the responsibility of survey on the condition of girl students is given to organizations like ABVP working among students, for sannyasin women Vishwa Hindu Parishad and Durga Vahini in the spiritual field, Bharatiya Mazdoor Sangh for women labourers, Vanvasi Kalyan Ashram for forest dwellers. The task of survey of the status of women of the border states was also entrusted to the NGO. The purpose of this entire exercise was to prepare a database from this survey on women. At the same time, the State Governments and the Central Government had to be given suggestions to improve the current situation of women. The demands of reforms along with facts on policy issues from the concerned ministries including education, women were also to be made on behalf of the organizations of the Sangh. The strategy of the Sangh was to collect information about the status of women in the country, freedom of women living in villages and cities, standard of living etc through this survey. In this survey that was being carried out to bring the real status of women in front of the country, women of all religions-Hindu, Muslim, Sikh, Jain etc., women living in border areas, village-city, working women, widows, housewives, tribals, forest dwellers, workers and even women living as a sannyasin were also surveyed separately.

The survey was divided into two parts. In the first part, basic information like name, address, age of the women in the concerned field was asked, while the second part included points like work, social status, economic standard of living. The thought of the Sangh behind this survey was that without taking the support of women, there can be no welfare not only in politics but also in any field of the country and society. The Sangh believed that the way the country has moved towards change, this is the most appropriate time when initiatives can be taken to improve the conditions of women in a big way. But for this initiative, there should be data about women's ground reality and factual reports. On the basis of this report, the *Sangh Parivar* organizations had made a strategy to run a public awareness campaign through seminars, gatherings and other programmes across the country. It was also planned to include successful professional women like doctors, engineers, professors, social workers, entrepreneurs associated with the ideology of the Sangh.

This was an activity of the Modi regime that was targeted to be completed before the 2019 Lok Sabha elections began. But due to some incidents, it could not be completed. But the task of reaching most of the houses was completed by NGOs and allied organizations. This report was made public after the historic victory of the Modi government in 2019. RSS Chief Mohan Bhagwat released the report on September 24, 2019. Bhagwat and Union Finance Minister Nirmala Sitharaman were also present at the function. Bhagwat emphatically said that this is an important survey of the NGO 'Drishti Stree Adhyayn evam Prabodhan Kendra'. All the things for this survey were prepared by the organization itself and the work done by the women associated with it is very important in itself. Bhagwat made an important comment on this occasion that the path of development of women cannot be decided by men. In this campaign, 1,081 teams were formed and more than 7,000 women volunteers were engaged, who contacted more than 74,000 women across 29 states and union territories. The survey team was able to reach out to 456 districts of the country. In this, the survey team spoke to about 2,196 unmarried women and all the other married ones. The list of questions was such that it took almost two hours to talk to each and every woman. So, it was not an easy task. A glimpse of what the questions were like is given below.

Following questions were asked in the survey

- Name, age, marital status (unmarried, married, separated, divorced, widowed, others).
- Caste (Scheduled Castes, Tribes, Special Backward Class, Denotified caste-tribe, General, Other Backward Classes).
- Religion (Hindu, Muslim, Buddhist, Jain, Sikh, Christian, others).
- Educational level (Uneducated, non-formal education, 1-4 grade, 5-7 grade, 8-10 grade, 11-12 grade, undergraduate, postgraduate, diploma, others).
- Profession (Student, Housewife, Private Service, Administrative Service, Own Business, Casual Labour-Seasonal/Daily Wages, Others)

- Monthly income, whether the family is joint or nuclear or extended, total family income, interest etc.
- How much time do you spend daily, weekly, fortnightly, monthly with interest in reading, writing, singing, painting, traveling and other activities and how do you spend your free time?
- What problems did you face during education? Options-financial or lack of education near home, lack of infrastructure, lack of family support, sudden family responsibility etc.
- Reasons for leaving education incomplete? Options-marriage, family responsibility, financial compulsion, lack of transport, family culture-traditions etc.
- At what level of education did you drop out?

(Options—no formal education, primary level, secondary, high school, senior secondary level, during graduation, at undergraduate level, post graduate level, still studying)

Some interesting questions, in which ranking from 1 to 5 was to be given-

(Strongly agree, agree, indifferent, disagree, strongly disagree)

- I am not happy with myself.
- I am generally not optimistic about the future.

- There is usually a difference between what I do and what I want to do.
- I am not happy with others.
- I think it is not easy for me to make decisions.
- I think that my life has no purpose and meaning.
- I think I'm not healthy.
- I don't have any memorable happy moments.

The questions asked to the sannyasin women were as follows-

- Name of the cult-sect-Akhara, number of saints, education, at what age they joined, who brought them, reason, what was the challenge, where did they get the inspiration to enter the path of spirituality?
- What transformation occurred in life due to entering the field of spirituality?
- How does your spiritual practice affect culture and society?
- How are your personal expenses and monastery managed? (Options - by donation, by Guru, by self-proclaimed devotees, by disciples, by social organization, by alms, by foreign exchange.)
- Where did you get the inspiration to enter the field of spirituality? (family, guru, particular event, by birth)
- What problems/challenges did you personally face while carrying out this activity?

- Do you get an opportunity to exchange ideas with women saints of other cults/sects? (Yes or No, with reasons)

- What kind of impact does your spiritual practice have in protecting the culture?

(Answer options-increased investment by upper class of society in religious programmes, involvement of society with enthusiasm in religious events, awakening of religious sentiments, rise in fundamentalism, increasing sensitivity of society, rise in religious hysteria.)

- Which texts are studied and taught in the ashram?

(This option—Ramayana, Shrimad Bhagwat, Bhagavad Gita, Upanishads, Quran, Bible, Guru Granth Sahib, others.)

- What do you do to build national spirit in the society? (Options - motivate youth for self-study, organizing national programmes in ashram-monasteries, discussion of national problems through story-discourse and awakening for solutions.)

- What kind of social service work are you doing? (*Gau-seva* (Cow service), education of poor children, donating food, donating clothes, running a hospital, school, distribution of medicines, running an old age home.)

- What challenges did you face as a woman after joining the saint-tradition?

- Is there a system of training for women saints in your sect? (Yes or No. If 'yes' then only for women independently or with everybody)
- What are your views on the arrangement of the residences for women saints (Five options—Not applicable, No response, Satisfactory, Neglected, Needs improvement.)
- What is the condition of *Fakkad* women saints?
- What is the status of *Sevadhari* women?
- Are you in favour of recognition for the *Shahi Snan* in the Kumbh-Snan?
- What obstacles women face in achieving the highest position in the spiritual realm? (Options—traditional ideology, women not exposed, socio-religious beliefs.)
- What is the status of women working in the spiritual realm?

The blueprint of the survey was designed in such a way that not only the socio-economic status of women but also the mental made up as a whole should come before the society and the government so that it can help the government in formulating a scheme related to women. Though inspired by the thoughts of the Sangh the NGO '*Drishti Stree Adhyayan Evam Prabodhan Kendra*' independently prepared a comprehensive survey report, in which the factual status of women in the society was presented. But it is evident from Sangh's interest from the beginning to the end of this entire campaign that its aim is to strengthen its social base among women. During the entire campaign of the survey between the year 2017-18, the BJP was also engaged in strengthening its political base through government schemes and organizational campaigns for women.

Certainly, through social-intellectual expansion in India with dialogue and coordination, the Sangh-BJP not only expanded its old base, but also strengthened it. But as a strategy, the Sangh-BJP did not limit its expansion. The way Narendra Modi's leadership emerged in India and his credibility on the world stage increased, the Sangh also started intensifying its ideological expansion, for which even before independence, the Sangh has been working to connect the Hindus settled all over the world through 'Vasudhaiv Kutumbakam', expanding its base in many countries of the world under the name 'Hindu Swayamsevak Sangh'. The global base of the Sangh and its activities are described in detail in the next chapter.

❑

18

CHAPTER

'Vishwa Dharma' of the Sangh

First, through the Vajpayee government and then the Modi government, the Sangh strengthened the ideological expansion going on before independence in the world. Modi also dominated the world stage. Then how Modi's victory in the year 2014 also increased the acceptance of the Sangh and BJP also got political benefits.

Whether it was the government of Atal Bihari Vajpayee or now the government of Narendra Modi, the Sangh did not have many complaints on global issues. However, during the Vajpayee government, the Sangh was very vocal about the issue of atrocities on Hindus in Bangladesh. Sangh Chief KS Sudarshan had talked to Vajpayee several times about this and also asked LK Advani to take up this issue vigorously. Sudarshan himself has disclosed this in one of his interviews in April 2005. The outrage was such that he had described Indira Gandhi, Narasimha Rao and LK Advani in that interview as strong leaders who took a stand. But he had refused to place Vajpayee among the top leaders because he did not take a firm stand as a government especially in the case of atrocities on Hindus in Bangladesh. But setting this issue aside, in order to understand how the Sangh worked in the world in terms of ideology and the BJP has got its direct benefit, it is necessary to first know the global size and shape of the Sangh.

The Sangh abroad was started on the occasion of Makar Sankranti in 1947 in Nairobi, Kenya. Earlier it was named 'Bharatiya Swayamsevak Sangh', which was later changed to 'Hindu Swayamsevak Sangh' and 'Vishva Swayamsevak Sangh' with expansion in other countries of the world. It was established with the inspiration of the Rashtriya Swayamsevak Sangh. But since it was not appropriate to use the word 'national' on foreign soil, the Sangh laid the foundation of a new organization named 'Vishwa Swayamsevak Sangh' for its ideological expansion in the world. The Sangh does not expand merely by setting up a *shakha*. Rather Sangh makes its social activities its main basis whether it is India or other countries of the world. In Nairobi also, it started service activities through socio-cultural organization. But an important role in the expansion of the Sangh in the world was played by Laxmanrao Bhide, who had become a full-time *pracharak* of the Sangh in 1942 itself. First of all, he was given the work of Sangh in Faizabad, the area of

Ram Janmabhoomi. But in 1959, the task of expanding the Sangh overseas, that is, abroad, was given. Bhide is said to have been of slender stature, who travelled continuously to more than 80 countries and the routine of different countries took a toll on his health. But he played the most important role in spreading the message of the Sangh on the global Scale. In the interest of Hindu and India abroad, he formed many organizations, in which the 'Friends of India Society International' founded in 1978 is prominent. But in 1990, when the Indian embassy itself was tarnishing the image of the BJP abroad, then on his advice, the BJP had also drawn a blueprint to thwart the Congress conspiracy by forming 'Overseas Friends of BJP'. Similarly, once when there were some atrocities on Hindus due to factionalism in Mauritius elections, he arranged for a settlement by making all the parties sit down and the Hindu party won the elections. So, in the matter of spreading the Sangh abroad, Laxmanrao Bhide had made a strong base.

Baleshwar Agarwal, who had started looking after the work of '*Vishva Swayamsevak Sangh*', attempted to give shape to it and turn it into a form dedicated to the ideology of the Sangh-BJP. When the BJP came to power at the Centre in 1998, Baleshwar Agarwal's relations with the then Prime Minister Atal Bihari Vajpayee were friendly. As *pracharaks*, the two knew each other for a long time. In such a situation, he started a big initiative so that not only would India have a different reputation at the global level, its ideological government, which had come to power for the first time at the centre could be used to empower the *shakhas* of the Sangh in the world, for which trust needed to be established. So, Baleshwar Agarwal along with Dr. Laxmimal Singhvi laid the foundation of '*Pravasi Bhartiya Divas*'. He suggested so to the Vajpayee government and for the first time '*Pravasi Bhartiya Divas*' was started to be celebrated so that Indians settled abroad would feel a sense of belonging.

In 1998, he organized for Indian-origin MPs settled abroad and in 2000 he organized '*Pravasi Bharatiya Sammelan*'. The idea of having '*Pravasi Diwas*' on 9th January every year was his. For the convenience of the migrants, '*Pravasi Bhawan*' was also built in Delhi on his advice. It was Agarwal who started honouring those active in the unification and welfare of Indians settled abroad. Things like voting rights for NRIs were also proposed. But such engagement with the diaspora also increased business opportunities. It happened for the first time that the Vajpayee government also appointed Bhishma Agnihotri as 'Ambassador at Large' (Global Ambassador). This special appointment was made to provide comfortable facilities to all the Indian diaspora settled in the world, where citizens of Indian origin needed help and cooperation but faced difficulties in embassies; there was a lot of controversy, too about this.

The effect of all these steps was that in countries where there is a majority of people of Indian origin, he got more respect than the Indian ambassador. In many places people considered him to be member of the family. According to the articles on 'The Centre for World Dialogue', he was honoured by many institutions in the country and abroad. After spending most of his life in migration, in old age, he remained engaged in the interest of Indians settled abroad while living in '*Pravasi Bhavan*'. Not only was Baleshwar Agarwal active during the Vajpayee government, the BJP's 'Overseas Friends of BJP' had also started working in a strategic way. The Vishwa Hindu Parishad also played a role in this, in which especially Ashok Singhal was involved. But when the BJP lost the election in 2004, the absence of power had a natural effect. The secular lobby dominated from 2004 to 2014, but the Sangh continued its ideological campaign with committed *swayamsevaks*. Nevertheless, the centrists either fell silent or moved away.

Mission-2014 and Modi on the World Stage

But when the BJP's command was completely handed over to Narendra Modi in 2013, many professionals of Indian origin came from abroad to work during the elections, who contributed for the 2014 election campaign. Among this, Manoj Ladwa who lived in London became an important face; he was already campaigning for Modi in London. In the year 2005 Modi was the Chief Minister and he had to go to London. But due to the Gujarat riots, such an atmosphere was created that the trip had to be cancelled. The BJP had to face humiliation in many such cases while in opposition. In such a situation, there was a challenging situation for the Hindu Swayamsevak Sangh working around the world as well. Ladwa was also campaigning for 'Vibrant Gujarat'. Ladwa is said to be associated with the London chapter of the Sangh and is part of the Hindu Swayamsevak Sangh. Ladwa is also considered a trustee of 'Seva International', an organization working abroad on the lines of Sangh's *Seva Bharti*. In 2010, Ladwa founded 'India Inc' and became active as a strategist for Modi. In the campaign for the 2014 Lok Sabha elections, Ladwa was responsible for research, analysis and messaging and he campaigned for 'Narendra Modi for PM'. There were also many professionals who were part of Hindu Swayamsevak Sangh abroad and worked in multinational companies.

When Narendra Modi was successful in Mission 2014, interested professionals were given a place in the government and also in the BJP organization. But after Modi became the Prime Minister, a campaign to build India's strong image abroad started. America, which had once denied a visa to Narendra Modi, was also beginning to understand the growing power of India. When Modi went to America for the first time, his historic public meeting at Madison Square became a topic of discussion in the world. Another reason for the craze about Modi was that there are also a large number of people of Gujarati origin among the businessmen settled abroad. But after that, in Australia and other foreign tours, Modi's large public meetings with the people of the Indian community also became an important part, whose purpose was to establish the prestige of Indians and also to strengthen the ideology. Modi was recognized as a powerful head of state in the countries of the world.

The Strategy of the Meeting Abroad was Designed like this

The Sangh has reach in many countries of the world and is known by the name of *Hindu Swayamsevak Sangh* and it also has regular *shakhas*. That means, the Sangh had its own ideological base there. When Narendra Modi became the Prime Minister, the strategy was prepared with the coordination of the *Vichar Parivar* for the public meetings to be held during foreign tours. As a campaigner, Modi knew how such plan was executed. In such a situation, from the very beginning, he entrusted the responsibility of such meetings - from Madison Square to many countries - to BJP's National General Secretary Ram Madhav, who had come to BJP directly from the Sangh after the important victory of the year 2014. Later, Vijay Chauthaiwala also joined this plan, who is handling the responsibility of the head of the BJP's foreign department. Ram Madhav has been the spokesperson of the Sangh for a long time and he has also had the experience of closely watching the governance during the Vajpayee government. Ram Madhav's face was well-known in the Sangh established as a disciplined organization. In such a situation, Modi gave him the task of coordination by entrusting him with this responsibility. Madhav used to prepare an entire action plan before every meeting with the Hindu Swayamsevak Sangh of that country and the official working as a global coordinator. Presently, Soumitra Gokhale is working as

Global Coordinator of Hindu Swayamsevak Sangh and Dattatreya Hosabale as *Sahakaryavah* oversees Foreign Division. This type of public meeting is also a kind of demonstration of one's strength on foreign soil. In such a situation, mobilizing the crowd in the stadium was an important task, but the Hindu Swayamsevak Sangh was fully involved in it keeping in mind the prestige of India, as a result of which the voice of Prime Minister Modi was not limited to the country where the meeting was held. Rather, it became a topic of discussion all over the world, the effect of which was that Indians of other countries also started joining the Sangh rapidly.

World Sangh Camp-2015 at Indore

A five-yearly camp of Hindu Swayamsevak Sangh is also organized in India to connect Indians with their roots, which started in 1990, the year in which the foundation of 'Overseas Friends of BJP' to answer Congress propaganda politically was laid. Since then, the Rashtriya Swayamsevak Sangh started holding a camp of *the Hindu Swayamsevak Sangh* every five years. After forming a government at the centre under the leadership of Narendra Modi, who himself has been a RSS *pracharak*, this World Sangh camp was organized in Indore in December 2015 in which more than 700 delegates from 45 countries participated. Apart from *Sarsanghchalak* Mohan Bhagwat, people like then BJP President Amit Shah, Lok Sabha Speaker Sumitra Mahajan were involved. G Madhavan Nair, who was the Chief of ISRO, was the Chief guest of this ceremony, who mentioned the contribution from indigenous, science-technical, Indian scriptures mentioning about finding water on the moon to space science. For this camp, the then External Affairs Minister Sushma Swaraj was specially called so that the problems and challenges of Hindu families in the world could be understood and resolved. In the presence of Sangh's *Sarkaryavah* Bhaiyyaji Joshi, Sushma Swaraj brainstormed by forming a group of Sangh officials from countries like America, Australia, Myanmar etc. But the importance of such a meeting, the purpose of the event and how the Hindu society is waking up, was also quoted by Bhaiyyaji Joshi in his address. It is necessary to mention some excerpts from that address so that the script of this global expansion is understood.

He had said, "The thoughts entrenched in the blood, mind and brain of a Hindu never become weak. We are standing in the world with different type of thought process. We have considered the world as one family. We want to influence the world with our thoughts. If Hindus wake up, the world will wake up. Only Hindu society can give philosophy to end all conflicts in the world. We are Hindus, this is not ego, it is self-respect. Our (Hindu society) has started to wake up. The world will also wake up, it is our belief. In this alone the freedom of human life is guaranteed. The awakening of the world is the awakening of man." This address of Bhaiyyaji Joshi is present on the website of *Vishwa Samvad Kendra*, in which he further mentions the *Devasura* struggle, how truth was fought with untruth, justice with injustice, religion with unrighteousness and the demons fought with the gods, in which truth, justice, religion and the gods have always won. He said that the philosophy of Hindutva has been developed by Indian sages. This can be achieved only through love because we are the representatives of this culture.

Bhaiyyaji Joshi mentioned about Indian culture and Hindus not having the tendency to loot like foreign invaders, "*Sarsanghchalak* Dr Hedgewarji had said that we need people who would live, not die for the country and society. It is not ego; it is the language of principle. We are the representatives of Indian culture. We have to start from ourselves. If we wake up, then the world will also follow that path. Thousands of people from India went to many countries of the world, but we did not defeat or plunder any country. India has a tradition of giving, not taking. We took scriptures and values, not weapons. Indian thought does not believe in defeating, but in winning the mind. The task of the Rashtriya Swayamsevak Sangh or Hindu Swayamsevak Sangh is to make this journey visible. Swami Vivekananda had also said that if religion, duty, values will end in India, then they will not be seen anywhere in the world. Let us act from a humane point of view. We have to make the dream of the future come true." For which the Hindu Swayamsevak Sangh was working and the growing credibility of the Modi government abroad also contributed to this ideological expansion. But it also has to be understood how his activities take place.

The Work of the Sangh and the Victory of the World Religion

The Sangh carries out activities around the world under the name 'Hindu Swayamsevak Sangh' which is similar to the way it works in India. However, there is also flexibility in the structure in terms of the circumstances and legal provisions of those countries. But if we look at the number of Indians in the world then the data presented by the Ministry of External Affairs in Parliament show that the number of Indians in three categories in 208 countries is as follows - Non-resident Indians - 1 crore 31 lakh 13 thousand 360, number of people of Indian origin - 1 crore 78 lakh 82 thousand 369 and the number of expatriate Indians is 3 crore 99 lakh 5 thousand 729. If we understand it in a simple way, then India tops the category of countries going as expatriates to the countries of the United Nations. The number of people born in India who are living overseas as expatriates is said to be 1.75 crore.

Sangh thinks that a person of Hindu society, who is settled anywhere in the world, should be connected with India. With this spirit of '*Vasudhaiva Kutumbakam*', the Sangh is currently active in 39 countries of the world with a structure. The Sangh, which has taken its roots in India, has spread its branches on the map of the world to New Zealand in the east and Canada in the west. It is mentioned in detail in a presentation by Saumitra Gokhale, who is a coordinator of 'Hindu Swayamsevak Sangh' around the world. Apart from India, the 10 largest countries of the world, where there is a Hindu population, are Nepal, Bangladesh, Indonesia, Sri Lanka, Pakistan, USA, Malaysia, United Arab Emirates, UK and Mauritius. Apart from this, the countries which are known as 'indentured' and where people of Indian origin also have a major share in the governance are Trinidad, Guyana, Suriname, Mauritius, Fiji, Kenya etc. The purpose of the Sangh is to unite and organize the Hindus.

On the world level, Sangh's activity first began in Kenya in 1947 followed by Myanmar in 1950 and Britain in 1966. It started in the form of institution in the US in 1989. According to Gokhale, as of year 2016, there are 1,107 *shakhas* operating in 38 countries of the world, which are held once or twice a week. *Shakha* events also take place at the homes of Hindus in many countries. When KS Sudarshan went to the World Hindu Conference held in Trinidad in the year 2000 as Sangh Chief, the work of the Sangh was going on in about 32 countries.

Sangh's activities are not new in the world. But there is a natural effect of power and its leadership which cannot be denied. In 1995, Nelson Mandela participated in the World Hindu Conference in Durban, South Africa, where more than 30 thousand Hindus had gathered. People like British Prime Minister Margaret Thatcher have also attended the programmes of the Sangh. In fact, the Sangh does not expand only through the *shakhas*. For that, a calendar of communication and activities of the organization is prepared. How events are important in Hinduism, they are organized by Indian families in the countries around the world, in which people send their children to be introduced to Indian culture, such as the Guru Vandana programme. In this, the guru i.e. teacher sits on a chair in the front and students dressed in Indian traditional costume are made to stand and shown how the guru is respected in Hinduism. On the occasion of Raksha Bandhan, a large programme of tying 'Raksha Sutra' is also organized by the *Hindu Swayamsevak Sangh*, in which the local police or other organizations are invited and the importance of celebrating this festival is explained. Family activity through *Suryanarayan Yagya* and exhibitions related to Hindu tradition and culture are organized in schools, colleges and large auditoriums of the states. In Kenya, it is also included in the curriculum. In addition, as a service organization, *Swayamsevaks* come out to help during any disaster or adversity. In the *shakhas* held around the world, 'Vishwa Dharm ki Jai' (Victory to the world religion) is proclaimed. Just as '*Rashtra Sevika Samiti*' is the women's wing of Sangh in India, there is a '*Hindu Sevika Samiti*' for the world.

Growing Ideology-Propagation Activities in the World

The way the BJP came to power with a huge majority and Narendra Modi became its head, there was a tremendous craze among the people for *Hindu Swayamsevak Sangh*. Activities also increased in many countries of the world because the Sangh does its work abroad in the same way as in India. Apart from social programs, cultural festivals like Deepawali Milan, Rakshabandhan, initiatives were also being taken at the level of diplomacy with the aim of keeping in mind the conveniences of Indian Hindus. *Vishwa Sangh Shiksha Varg* (World Sangh Education Camp) is organized regularly and a prominent personality of that country is invited and made aware of their views through it. But how the enthusiasm increased after Narendra Modi became the Prime Minister was mentioned by Ravikumar working as Joint Coordinator in Australia; it was mentioned in several newspapers* during the '*Vishwa Sangh Shivir*' in Indore. Ravikumar had said, "Wherever Modi goes, he associates himself with the Indians there. We told him in Sydney that we have an Australian passport and whenever we go to India, it takes a long time to get a visa. Modi assured of help and in just 10 days he announced the facility of electronic visa not only in Australia but in 40 countries. Modi had a huge meeting in Sydney, in which the Sangh Parivar played an important role. Ravi Kumar had also given an example of the influence of the Sangh in foreign countries. He had said, "The work of *Hindu Swayamsevak Sangh* has been recognized by the governments of many countries. For example, in Myanmar, our *pracharaks* are given the facility of free first-class travel by railway for work related to orphans in the country. "

On January 9, 2018, the first conference of PIOs, i.e. people of Indian origin who play the role of parliamentarians or elected representatives in the countries of the world, was held in Delhi, in which 137 MPs-Mayors from 24 countries participated. The central government also started many important initiatives for the convenience of the Indian diaspora and made some of them more flexible than before. Under the 'Know India' (KIP) programme, the duration of this scheme, which was run to connect Indians settled abroad with their roots, was increased from 21 to 25 days and exemption of 2 to 6 programmes in a year was given. The data of the Ministry of External Affairs till the year 2018 shows that in the four years of the Modi government, 1,060 youth had taken advantage of this programme. *Pravasi Bharatiya Divas* held every two years was organized in Varanasi, the parliamentary constituency of Prime Minister Narendra Modi, on January 21-23, 2019, just before the Lok Sabha elections. Its purpose was to take all the delegates who came to the conference from there to Prayagraj Kumbh and then to participate in the Republic Day parade on 26 January. Apart from this, through several new initiatives, the Modi government also took the help of expatriate experts to make the events practical. The limit of scholarship for overseas students was also increased. However, the matter of giving voting rights to NRIs in India is long pending and there was a brainstorming on 1 February before the 2019 Lok Sabha elections, but the matter did not move forward. But in the coming time, this proposal is sure to be successful.

Modi's Foreign Travel and Elections

Prime Minister Narendra Modi had given the message of his foreign policy during his swearing-in ceremony. Inviting the heads of SAARC countries at the swearing-in, he drew a line for a friendly stance with the neighbours. However, the opposition also started accusing him of frequent foreign visits. According to government data released ahead of the 2019 Lok Sabha elections, till February 2019, Prime Minister Modi had visited 92 countries in 48 foreign tours. Modi would give importance to time in his travel plan and would do as many activities as possible in less time, as a result of which Modi enhanced India's prestige in the world. But the Congress and other opposition parties would constantly raise questions on Prime Minister Modi's visits and it was also ridiculed on social media. But Modi's roar and the way prominent countries like America, Russia, etc. also started respecting India's power and supremacy specially sent a good message to the Indian public. A few months before the Lok Sabha elections, many journalists who went on a tour for ground reporting realized that common people were angry with the opposition for questioning or ridiculing Modi's foreign travels because they believed that the powerful countries of the world were now looking at the Indian leadership with hope.

Certainly, after the year 2014, the world realized the power of India and gave full respect, in which the Indian diaspora settled or working abroad had a significant contribution and to unify these Indians abroad and promote Indian culture, *Hindu Swayamsevak Sangh* had worked. As a leader, Narendra Modi also attracted Indians living abroad and the global base of the Sangh proved to be helpful in enhancing his credibility after becoming Prime Minister. The Sangh expanded its work abroad to spread the ideology, but it was natural for the BJP to get its political benefits in India.

❑

19

CHAPTER

Vote for Nationality

Before voting in the Lok Sabha elections, 3.5 lakh villages were reached, how did the Sangh achieve 100% vote without directly naming Modi and BJP, saying no to NOTA and raising the spirit of nationalism.

The Sangh took unique initiatives in every field including expansion in the social sphere, intellectual world with better and wonderful coordination in a positive atmosphere of power and expanded the concerns of nationalism. The Sangh tried to touch every aspect through the affiliated organizations, for which the opposition has been attacking the Sangh. In the five years of Modi rule, the Sangh expanded itself and the year 2019 was also the time for repayment, where it was needed by the BJP, for which it was the turn of the Rashtriya Swayamsevak Sangh, which worked like a cadre for the BJP, to make the prepared land fertile. The BJP was running in step with its mother organization Sangh. But the defeat in the assembly elections in three states was naturally a concern. So, on one hand, the then BJP national president Amit Shah was galvanizing the workers by calling the 2019 elections as the fourth battle of Panipat, while on the other hand the *Sangh Parivar* was also preparing to send its *swayamsevaks* to the field to maintain the political change brought about in 2014. The Sangh had already decided its direction in the meeting of the *Akhil Bhartiya Pratinidhi Sabha* in Nagpur in March 2018. The meeting of the *Pratinidhi Sabha* is mandatorily held in Nagpur every three years because it is the election year of the office bearers of the Sangh, while in the remaining two years, one is in the north and one is in the south. Before this meeting, there was a lot of discussion that now Bhaiyyaji Joshi was not interested for this post due to age. In such a situation, the names of Saha-*Sarkaryavah* Dattatreya Hosabale and Dr. Krishna Gopal were being discussed for the post of *Sarkaryavah*. But the intention and direction of the Sangh leadership was very clear. The Lok Sabha elections were to be held in the year 2019 and the Sangh was working with a great coordination for the last four years, thereby widening the base of both Sangh and BJP. In such a situation, *Sarsanghchalak* Mohan Bhagwat decided to retain Bhaiyyaji Joshi and the *Pratinidhi Sabha* elected Bhaiyyaji for the fourth consecutive time for the post of *Sarkaryavah*. However, Sangh decided to increase the number of posts of Saha-*Sarkaryavah* from four to six. After this, the Sangh not only carried out the intellectual initiative, but also sharpened the ideological battle. But 2019 was purely an election year. So, Sangh did not want to leave any stone unturned to work on the already prepared system through public awareness campaign even at the last moment.

Upper Caste Reservation Stakes

But the defeat in the assembly elections in three states just before the Lok Sabha elections was not as big in terms of arithmetic as it was in terms of perception. In this defeat, the anger that arose in the upper caste society after the government overturned the Supreme Court's decision on the SC-ST Act was also coming to the fore as a major reason. Generally, this section has always been considered the traditional vote of the BJP. But after this defeat, it was natural to dread that the displeasure of this class might prove costly in the times to come. The Sangh continues to work on social issues and it gave feedback to the BJP about this displeasure. It was on the advice of the Sangh that the government took such a historic step, which was hanging in balance for decades. Even the opposition could not muster the courage to oppose it. On the advice of the Sangh, the government made a blueprint to implement the proposal giving reservation to the poor from upper castes. The whole process was kept very confidential. It was only after the approval of the Constitution Amendment Bill giving 10 percent reservation to the upper castes in the meeting of the Modi cabinet on 7 January, the media or other parties got the news about it. The government got it passed in the Lok Sabha on January 8, 2019 and in the

Rajya Sabha on January 9. President Ram Nath Kovind also gave his recommendation for the 103rd Constitutional Amendment on 12 January and the Personnel Ministry on behalf of the government also issued a notification to implement it from February 1, 2019. Without any tinkering or alteration in the existing reservation system, it shrewdly arranged reservation for the poor of the general category based on a criterion. Certainly, it was a stake that even the opposition could not dispute. But this campaign of BJP and Sangh had a direct impact on the ground. In Bihar, where the RSS Chief's statement regarding reservation had created a ruckus, the decision of the upper caste reservation had strengthened BJP's position for the 2019 elections. The party also made a comeback in those three states where it was defeated and which provided a ground for preparing the script for poor upper caste reservation. Often the Sangh's feedback on such issues has proved to be like a *Sanjeevani* (life-saver) for the BJP. So, after this wager, there could be no anger in the SC-ST community nor there could be any fear of resentment from the upper caste society. In such a situation, the Sangh gave push to its work through public awareness in the society.

The Sangh Reached Three and a Half Lakh Villages

Now was the time to cooperate with the BJP according to the policy of the Sangh. Though Sangh does not work for BJP or any party by taking the name directly, but it gives a signal to its people through the policies related to nation, issues related to society. With this thinking, the Sangh had formed village development teams in every province, whose two-day conference was also held in Awadh province in the year 2018. According to the plan of the Sangh, *swayamsevaks* were sent to work on connectivity in the villages. A massive public-contact campaign was launched in the villages, in which the Modi government's plan for social concerns and issues related to nationalism were shared with people. The BJP's booth committees mainly have Sangh's cadre. In such a situation, apart from the BJP, the Sangh was also doing the work of directly contacting the beneficiaries of more than 130 schemes of the Modi government. BJP's national general secretary Ram Madhav, who was a *pracharak* of Sangh said, "Sangh launched a public awareness campaign by reaching 3.5 lakh villages at the time of elections, that is, 60 percent of the country's part was covered by the Sangh under its campaign." He also adds that this time, since there was no option but crushing the Congress in the elections, a campaign to directly contact 23 crore beneficiaries of the Modi government's schemes, i.e. about 40 crore voters, was carried out. According to Ram Madhav, "There were many such schemes of the government for the election of the year 2019, which a common person must use in his daily life. Be it toilets built under the cleanliness drive or gas facilities for cooking or ATM-mobile work or schemes related to farming, the government was directly connected with everything." That is, the Sangh was giving a message by naming the schemes, while the BJP team was asking for votes solely on the basis of these schemes. The entire election campaign was revolving around beneficiary schemes and the beneficiaries who had benefited from them, thereby creating an atmosphere in favour of the present government. After implementing the decision of upper caste reservation, an order was given to implement it in central universities immediately. The BJP and the Sangh were encouraged by the decision of 10 percent reservation for the poor upper castes and the party entered election mode as soon as the interim budget session of Parliament ended on February 13. But after the beginning of the year 2019, the terrorist incident of Pulwama on 14 February pushed back all the issues. The Sangh also announced its decision to give push to the public awareness campaign in its scheduled meeting of the *Akhil Bhartiya Pratinidhi Sabha.*

The Development and Security of the Country is possible only in the hands of BJP

The meeting of *the Akhil Bhartiya Pratinidhi Sabha* of the Sangh was held on March 8-10, 2019 at Gwalior, Madhya Pradesh, just before the notification of the Lok Sabha elections was issued. In this meeting, the way *Sarkaryavah* Bhaiyyaji Joshi presented the report of the increasing credibility and progress of the Sangh in his annual report, the *swayamsevaks* were bound to be enthused. In this report, it was said that the election process is going to be completed in the country in the coming time. It is always expected that the elections should be conducted in a healthy and cordial environment. But for that it is necessary that the right of vote given by the constitution should be used by 100 percent of the voters. The Sangh also demanded that the administration assure the voters by making proper arrangements in this direction. Sangh's *Saha Sarkaryavah* Manmohan Vaidya also reiterated *Sarkaryavah*'s report and said that all the people should participate in the voting process and in order to ensure that there will be 100 percent voting in the election, the *swayamsevaks* will undertake public awareness campaign in the society. Amit Shah, the then national president of the party and Ramlal, the then national organization general secretary, were also present.

With the discussion of campaigning for 100 percent voting, the Sangh also gave direction to the *swayamsevaks* as to whose favor they have to create an atmosphere in though here also the name of Prime Minister Narendra Modi or the Bharatiya Janata Party was not taken. But the Sangh bluntly said, "The protection of development and self-respect of the country is only possible in the hands of a group that works honestly and with commitment in the interest of the country. Therefore, it is the national duty of all of us to be vigilant and discharge our responsibility in the process of voting." So, the *Sarkaryavah* of the Sangh, Bhaiyyaji Joshi mentioned in his report whom to vote for. It is just that Modi or BJP were not mentioned in exact words. But the appeal was for the same Bharatiya Janata Party, whose government had carried out 'Operation Balakot'.

After the martyrdom of more than 40 soldiers in the terrorist attack in Pulwama on February 14, 2019, the way the Narendra Modi government destroyed the camps of terrorists on the Pakistani soil through 'Operation Balakot' on February 26, the tide of nationalism was rising in the country. Therefore, the Sangh also mentioned it in Gwalior's *Pratinidhi Sabha*, "With the help of some internal anti-national elements, external forces are working to carry out violent incidents in the country. Attacks on Army-Security Forces bases, repeated attacks by Pak Army in the border area and just now the incident of Pulwama, the result of which is that civilians are being killed, Army and security forces personnel are getting martyred. No one should take India's tolerance for its weakness. We congratulate the Air Force and the Government of India for the indomitable courage of the Indian Air Force in Balakot on 26 February. During such incidents, all the social and political powers of the country have shown solidarity from time to time. The efforts being made by the present government are commendable." The Sangh also said that along with the alertness of the administration, the public should also be alert. Along with this, the Sangh also stressed that the traditional efforts of social awakening in the society, which were being made by religious centres or social institutions, should be effectively activated during the elections. For this campaign, the Sangh also said that educational institutions can also play an important role in awakening the society along with education.

Remembering Kabir's words in Gwalior's *Pratinidhi Sabha – Mann ke hare haar hai, man ke jeete jeet; kahe Kabir guru paiye, man hi ke partit'* (If a man is defeated in the mind, he is defeated, and if he is winner in the mind, he is a winner; God can also be found only by the faith of the mind.) the Sangh told all its *swayamsevaks* that there is a need to increase contact through the activities going on in various fields in a positive way because various forces working for the good of the nation with good motives should be successful. This will increase the effect of the power of good people. If you look closely at the paragraph on the national scenario in that report of the Sangh, it becomes clear what the Sangh wanted to say! The last lines went something like this – "We should have faith that we can do the work of uniting the power of good efficiently. If we move forward diligently in the favourable environment available today, we will experience progress towards our goal. Let us do this work in the form of worship and spiritual practice because the period of neglect and indifference is over. That is why we should move forward with courage and enthusiasm; this should be our resolve."

The above words by the Sangh can be defined in this way. It believed that the country and the world is going through a period of amazing change. The way the phase of fundamental change has started in the politics of India since the general elections of the year 2014, its glimpse is visible in 2019 as well. Generally, politics is considered to be divisive. But when the government works towards real achievements, the politics works to connect there. This is the message for the year 2019 as well, in which caste-sub-caste will not matter. A direct example of how politics can be done by connecting the society was the

2014 general election, where the BJP had prepared the bouquet of social equations, and strategically, the Sangh also played an important role in connecting people by going out of their purview. When the BJP entered the 2014 election season, it had three key issues—Narendra Modi's strong leadership credentials as Gujarat Chief Minister, the blatant failures of 10 years of Congress rule, and the Sangh Parivar's support, which directly benefited it. Indirectly, the Sangh believed that there was talk of anti-incumbency in the year 2019. But the leadership of Modi can beat it. That is, the creativity of the *Vichar Parivar* with the leadership of Modi was definitely going to prove to be important in the 2019 general elections.

Group of Teachers in Battleground

The Sangh's work of public awareness campaign and village-to-village connectivity continued. Meanwhile, the Sangh also planned to carry out the strategy of social harmony and intellectual impact. In February 2019 itself, an important meeting of about 200 teachers was held at Udasin Ashram, which was being used temporarily for the Sangh in Delhi. In this meeting, leaders like Sangh's *Sah-Sarkaryavah* Dr. Krishna Gopal, BJP leader Sudhanshu Trivedi, Union Minister Smriti Irani were also present. In this workshop, a blueprint was prepared that how the teachers would hold small meetings in the capital of the country so that the atmosphere created in favour of BJP could be converted into votes. For this, booklets about the work of government and facts were also made available to everyone; the data was to be presented during discussion in the meetings. A similar experiment was carried forward by the Sangh in all those places across the country where intellectual groups were aligning with the Sangh-BJP and it seemed necessary to do so strategically. In this chain, special focus was kept on Uttar Pradesh because there the SP-BSP had made a strategy to weaken the BJP-NDA's victory of 73 seats in 80 in 2014 by forming a grand alliance. But as the BJP was busy carrying out its plan, the Sangh intensified the work by forming a Dalit intellectual group of 25-30 teachers, especially in the Dalit-dominated areas where Mayawati had a base. 5 teachers were posted in a Lok Sabha constituency. The Sangh's focus, through the teachers, was to correct the figures by holding small meetings and respond to the confusion spread by the opposition.

'Academics for NaMo' begins

The Sangh-BJP believed that it had won the election battle in the year 2014 itself. Now the battle of 2019 was a battle of ideology, for which Swadesh Singh, Assistant Professor at Delhi University, carried forward the intellectual campaign under the guidance of Dr Krishna Gopal. The 'Academics for Namo' campaign was launched on March 5, 2019, with the objective of connecting professors, thinkers, writers, columnists and people engaged in dissemination of knowledge from across the country, who can contribute to this campaign. After passing out from JNU, he played an important role in the Yuva Morcha in the BJP. Currently working as a teacher in Delhi University, Swadesh Singh used his ability and contacts aggressively.

On March 5, at the 'Ambedkar International Centre' in Delhi, he laid the foundation of 'Academics for NaMo' along with 30 professors of Jawaharlal Nehru University (JNU), Delhi University (DU), Banaras Hindu University (BHU) and IIT and later conducted a workshop for 300 people. In a few weeks, more than 2,000 professors, thinkers, intellectuals from 50-60 cities became its official members on its website, after which about 3,000 intellectuals joined the entire campaign under the banner of 'Academics for NaMo'. To give edge to the ideological battle, getting professors, thinkers, writers, columnists to write articles on the functioning of the Modi government and making retaliatory attacks on issues like award-return, intolerance, not in my name, lynching were an important part of this campaign. 'Academics for NaMo' was working on a strategy to respond in a more aggressive manner than the opponents had tried to create a debate about the Modi government.

An essay competition on 'Modi 2.0 Idea of New India' was organized under its banner from March 19 to March 28, in which one had to write articles on the good work of Modi government, in which 10 young scholars were also honoured. After this, on April 2-3, 2019, this group held small meetings across the country. Throughout the election 'Academics for NaMo' worked more on creating a factual perception of when, what and why Prime Minister Narendra Modi was saying. Apart from this, it was also the job of this forum to give a befitting reply to the signature campaign being run by the opposition. This forum had also issued an appeal to all the other teachers, thinkers and intellectuals of the country, in which in the general elections of the year 2019, Narendra Modi was named as the first option and Rahul Gandhi was named as the second option and it was said that both the persons represented different views. Referring to the Congress's issues like familyism, corruption, appeasement, it was said in the appeal that now the people of the country do not want to accept the chains of the royal family. While on the other hand, there is the efficient leadership of Narendra Modi, who embodied the basic spirit of *'Sabka Saath, Sabka Vikas'*. Apart from this, Modi has set a target of building a new India by the year 2022 and has also talked about preparing a clear roadmap to fulfill the great Indian dream of making a developed and poverty-free India by 2047.

In such a situation, this election is not just a struggle of votes, but it is also a struggle of the ideas of two separate India. It was also said in this appeal that the narrative presented by Narendra Modi is certainly the best. So, all the intellectuals, teachers, researchers and thinkers of the country should come forward and give support to make Narendra Modi the Prime Minister again. Along with the appeal, more than 500 articles were written and published by these people under this campaign. Prime Minister Narendra Modi himself had expressed his gratitude by sharing this scheme on his Twitter handle on March 25 during the election. After the contribution in the Lok Sabha elections, this work is going on continuously.

After the election, Swadesh Singh gave a permanent form to 'Academics for NaMo' and named 'Academics for Nation' so that the intellectual campaign of nationalism / nationalism of the Sangh continues.

Third Party Intervention and 'Nation First' Campaign

For the Lok Sabha elections, different projects were going on in a formal-informal manner, in which the Sangh was contributing. When the opposition could not create an atmosphere against the Modi government and Narendra Modi as a leader, then an indirect campaign was started with NOTA. No one was affected by this campaign, but it was aimed at targeting people who liked Modi and the BJP so much that they would never vote for their opponents. The aim was to to put these people into despair on the basis of issues so that they press the button of 'NOTA'. Sangh Chief Mohan Bhagwat had already questioned the justification of NOTA. At a three-day function held at Vigyan Bhawan, Bhagwat had said on the question of NOTA that people should choose from among the available options because no one can get 100 percent best in politics. In such a situation, the Sangh not only campaigned against NOTA but it also intensified the campaign of 100% voting before every phase of voting. Officially, instead of campaigning under any Sangh banner, the *swayamsevaks* directly took over the responsibility. In simple language, it can be called 'Third Party Intervention'. Pamphlets were prepared with the hashtag 'Nation First', which were delivered door-to-door by the *swayamsevaks*. The people of the Sangh made a group and distributed this pamphlet. The Sangh did not mention the name of BJP or Narendra Modi anywhere in this pamphlet. But whatever issues were counted in the name of country and social schemes were all started during the tenure of Modi government.

First, the Sangh *swayamsevaks* appealed for '100 percent voting: Voting first', while the BJP was also running a 'Vote before 10.30' campaign. The 'Nation First' campaign run by the *swayamsevaks* of the Sangh was given the title 'Mera Vote Desh Ke Naam'. After this, a circular graphic was made at the bottom, in the middle of which was written 'My Sankalp' and around it five issues for the resolution in different colours were written like this - 'My vote, attack on terrorism', 'My vote, attack on corruption', 'My vote, attack on Naxalism', 'My vote, attack on familism', 'My vote, attack on NOTA'. Panch Sankalp (Five resolutions) was also reflecting the purpose of this campaign. This was followed by a frequently asked question-and-answer (FAQ) format – 'Who has my valuable vote?' It was followed by 17 points mentioned below. 'To those who'—

1. Gave strong and honest leadership to the country.
2. Give a befitting reply to Pakistan-sponsored terrorism.
3. Made India a space power.
4. Honoured the army.
5. Worked for the respect and development of all sections of the society.

6. Gave 10 percent reservation for the poor.
7. Provided financial freedom by giving 'Mudra' loan to crores of people.
8. Delivered health facilities even to the poorest person through 'Ayushman Yojana'.
9. Took steps towards eradicating poverty through schemes like Jan Dhan Yojana, Bima Yojana and Ujjwala.
10. Stopped infiltration and 42 lakh infiltrators identified by NRC in Assam.
11. Provided security and respect to women.
12. Under 'Swachh Bharat Abhiyan', 9 crore toilets were built.
13. Liberated Muslim women from triple talaq.
14. Took many steps to protect Hindu culture and tradition.
15. Nurtured the Gita-Ganga-Cow and village.
16. Made beautiful and effective arrangements for more than 20 crore pilgrims in Kumbh.
17. Raised the value of India in the whole world through yoga.

It was clear from the issues which political party was liked and disliked by this third party in the election. That is, under the 'Nation First' campaign, all the issues that were trying to inspire or shock the voters were related to the personality of Prime Minister Narendra Modi and the functioning of his government, which meant that the third party that was running the campaign of nationalism was asking for votes for the BJP and Modi. But the question arises that why Sangh was not taking it as a formal responsibility? The answer to this is mentioned in detail in the address given by Mohan Bhagwat in Vigyan Bhavan regarding the establishment of the Sangh. The Sangh does not directly talk about any political party, but it expresses its opinion about the society and policies of the country, even if any political party is benefiting from it. There was no doubt that the direct benefit of the campaign run by the *swayamsevaks* of the Sangh was going to benefit the Bharatiya Janata Party and its leader Narendra Modi. The interesting aspect is that the coordination in the *Sangh Parivar* was such that a similar paper was prepared by the BJP at that time, in which 25 points were included in the question-and-answer format. But its title was - 'Why do we want Modi government?' It also included all those issues, which were included in the pamphlet prepared by the *swayamsevaks* of the Sangh, which mentioned surgical strikes, social schemes, yoga to making country a space superpower.

Conclusion: In the last year, that is, in 2019, instead of directly taking the name of BJP or Modi, the Sangh did the work of public awareness in the name of the nation by raising the issues of the Modi government. Dr. Krishna Gopal, Sangh's *Sah-Sarkaryavah*, who played a role of coordinator between Sangh and BJP, himself went directly to 24 of the 39 provinces and held Lok Sabha-wise meetings. He talked to the people at the locations where he could not go through other means. The Sangh, while following its customs and policies, did not directly support any political party. But by undertaking social public awareness on the basis of issues, such an environment was created that the faith in Modi regime became stronger in the minds of the people. With the identity of Hindutva, the *swayamsevaks* of Sangh did the work of public relations among people in such a way that in the Lok Sabha elections such an atmosphere was created for the BJP that the blows of the opposition began to weaken and the balance tilted in favour of Modi speedily. With the coordination of Sangh-BJP, the ground was prepared in such a way that when the incident of Pulwama happened just a month before the election announcement and then 'Operation Balakot' was carried out as a decisive battle by the Narendra Modi government, the flame of nationalism was ignited in the entire country. It was as if Balakot which was carried out as a revenge for Pulwama, had spilled extra water on that spongy land and that sponge had absorbed that water. On the other hand, the then BJP President Amit Shah also managed the election in such a centralized manner that there was no scope for deviation/diversion. So, the proper management of the Sangh Parivar became a witness to the historic victory of the BJP under the leadership of Narendra Modi in the year 2019. With that the lack of coordination in the *Vichar Parivar* during the BJP government between 1998 and 2004 was forever buried in the pages of the past. Now under the rule of Narendra Modi, such a wonderful thread of coordination was woven from the very first day that in the last five years no knot was ever found, but its length is increasing.

And the most interesting aspect is that we reporters are still waiting for news of a newsworthy Sangh-BJP clash. But running on the highway of co-ordination, the *Vichar Parivar* prepared a sponge in the 2019 elections that can absorb all the issues that help the Modi government. The result was that in 2019, Narendra Modi registered a bigger victory than in 2014 and BJP got 303 seats. It was not a simple thing to get more seats than the majority compared to the last election and that too for the second time in a row. This election not only strengthened the Modi government, but also strengthened all the organizations of the *Vichar Parivar* and especially the ideology, whose acceptance increased rapidly.

The statements from the Sangh after the results were an expression of its role and happiness. How much the Sangh was relieved after this victory can be seen from *Sarkaryavah* Bhaiyyaji Joshi's statement immediately after the results on May 23, 2019, which said, "Once again the country has got a stable government which is the fortune of crores of Indians. It is a victory of the national power. Congratulations to all those who contributed in the journey of this victory of democracy. The ideal of democracy has once again been presented to the world. We express confidence that the new government will prove successful in fulfilling the wishes and aspirations of the general public. With the completion of the election process, all bitterness should end and public sentiments expressed should be welcomed with humility." The next day a statement from the Sangh's *Sah-Sarkaryavah* Manmohan Vaidya was released, in which he summed up the sentiments of the Sangh in this way, "This election was between two different concepts of India. On the one hand is India's ancient spirituality based integral, all-round and all-inclusive life-view or thought, which has been known in the world as Hindu life-view or Hindu thought; on the other hand, it was the non-Indian vision, which has been seeing India divided into many identities. The second concept has been working to divide the society in the name of caste, language, region or religion for its vested interests. Those who practice this divisive politics have always opposed the power that unites the society. An attempt has been made to create a misunderstanding by making various baseless and false allegations about it. This ideological battle going on since independence has now reached a turning point. This election is an important stage of this fight. When the society started to unite, then the ground under the feet of those who did politics by dividing started slipping. Therefore, all the divisive forces came together, supported each other and tried to face this uniting force, for which the well-informed, intelligent people of India have made the thought of development victorious by supporting a uniting and all-inclusive India. It is a day of great joy for the bright future of India. The people of India deserve congratulations for this. Hearty congratulations to the strong leadership that stands for India and all the workers in this ideological fight."

For the coordination to continue without any obstacle in the future also, initiative is going on in the entire Vichar Pariwar including Sangh and BJP. Not only in political, but also in socio-cultural and other activities, the coordination between Sangh, government and organization is setting a strong example. As a result, the BJP government was formed at the centre with a thumping majority for the second time, and with coordination, work started on ideological issues like Article 370, Shri Ram Janmabhoomi.

❑

20

CHAPTER

Operation – 370

Keeping the agenda of development paramount, the Modi government also sharpened the ideological agenda. The most important ideological issue in this was Article 370, which was realized immediately after the 2019 election results. But how was its script being drawn from Mission Kashmir, which was started three years ago, to bring the decades of struggle to an end with a happy outcome.

"धमकी, जेहाद के नारों से, हथियारों से
कश्मीर कभी हथिया लोगे, यह मत समझो,
हमलों से, अत्याचारों से, संहारों से
भारत का भाल झुका लोगे, यह मत समझो।

जब तक गंगा की धार, सिंधु में ज्वार
अग्नि में जलन, सूर्य में तपन शेष,
स्वातंत्र्य समर की वेदी पर अर्पित होंगे
अगणित जीवन, यौवन अशेष।

अमरीका क्या, संसार भले ही हो विरुद्ध
काश्मीर पर भारत का ध्वज नहीं झुकेगा,
एक नहीं, दो नहीं, करो बीसों समझौते
पर स्वतंत्र भारत का मस्तक नहीं झुकेगा।"

This poem by Late Atal Bihari Vajpayee, the former Prime Minister of India and a senior BJP leader, has become a symbol of the *Sangh Parivar*'s decades-long struggle for Kashmir and the resolution for the future. Even though this resolution was realized after the general elections held in the year 2019, Prime Minister Narendra Modi, who was an important link in the Kashmir movement as a *swayamsevak* of the Sangh, had prepared its script in such a way that Article 370 that was supposedly impossible to abolish became possible only with a determination.

With the result of the 2019 general election, both the ideological foundation of the Sangh and the political establishment of the BJP were moving forward on a new journey with a 'new resolution', which was named as 'New India'. The Sangh-BJP fought and won this general election as an important battle of ideology. In such a situation, now there was an opportunity to move forward on the unresolved issues of decades related to this ideology. Although there was an attempt to reduce the gap of six decades even during the Atal government, but due to the lack of majority of the BJP on its own, things did not work out. But in the year 2014, after the BJP came to the majority on its own, there was hope of realizing the dream. A poet has expressed in very beautiful lines as to what kind of Kashmir the Sangh and BJP wanted, -

स्वर्ग से सुंदर सपनों से प्यारा, ये कश्मीर हमारा है
गौर करो झेलम सरिता का, बहता नीर हमारा है
उपवन मय सारी सुंदरता, का जागीर हमारा है
सुंदर घाटी हैं सब अपनी, झील का क्षीर हमारा है
स्वर्ग से सुंदर सपनों से प्यारा, ये कश्मीर हमारा है।

The road to the abolition of Article 370 was not easy

August 5, 2019 has become a historic day for the country including all the organizations and cadres associated with the BJP and Sangh. Article 370 affecting the unity of the nation has become history. Prime Minister Narendra Modi became its important facilitator who along with the BJP President Amit Shah, who later became the Union Home Minister, had worked on a very 'secret screenplay' from 2016 onwards. It was an operation that only a few people at the top level were aware of. One of the most important characters was National Security Adviser Ajit Doval. It was up to Doval to ensure that the secrecy of the entire operation was maintained.

This task was not so easy as one had to go among the common citizens in Jammu and Kashmir, especially in the Valley region to prepare an accurate report that reflected the real condition of the land. Whether or not to abolish Article 370 depended on this. Actually, Prime Minister Modi was determined in this matter, but he wanted to know as to what was the stand of the people of Kashmir regarding Article 370. Prime Minister Modi was also trying to understand that if Article 370 is removed, then what can be the reaction of the public and what the common Kashmiri citizen thinks about this matter. For this mission, under the leadership of National Security Advisor Ajit Doval, a trusted team of people working in various security agencies was prepared, which included only trusted people associated with Intelligence Bureau

(IB), RAW and other organizations. This team had to go to the villages of Kashmir and first mingle with the common people and win trust. After that a real report was to be prepared regarding Article 370 after understanding the public opinion. However, the people involved in this operation were not told that its purpose is to remove Article 370 or that the government was making any preparations in this direction. People employed for this at the grassroot level were told that it was a part of routine feedback aimed at restoring confidence in the Kashmiri people.

Since Prime Minister Narendra Modi was a leader in the Kashmir movement, he was also well aware of the sensitivity of this issue. Narendra Modi was the prominent face among those who hoisted the Tricolour flag at Lal Chowk in Kashmir on January 26, 1992. He was at that time as a charioteer of the 'Ekta Yatra' from Kanyakumari to Kashmir under the leadership of BJP veteran Dr Murli Manohar Joshi. He was responsible for the success of that yatra. Even today the picture of Narendra Modi carrying the Tricolour flag at Lal Chowk ignites enthusiasm in the Sangh and BJP cadre. At that time when Narendra Modi was unfurling the Tricolour along with Murli Manohar Joshi at Lal Chowk, there were also bullets flying around. After that, the Tricolour flag was not hoisted at Lal Chowk for nearly three decades. Therefore, Narendra Modi did not want to make any haste on this issue. So, whenever any MP raised the issue of Article 370 in Parliament, the only reply came from the government that no work is being done in this direction.

It is well known that abrogation of Article 370 has been paramount in the agenda of the BJP and the Sangh Parivar. The Vichar Pariwar did not want to let the sacrifice of Jana Sangh founder Dr. Shyama Prasad Mookerjee go in vain because the ideological government was in majority on its own for the first time at the centre. But the slightest mistake could have created an atmosphere of unrest in the country on this issue as Article 370 had been made a matter of politics. While the BJP was in favour of removing it, the rest of the parties were against even touching it. But after being declared the Prime Ministerial candidate in 2013, Narendra Modi had strongly advocated starting a nationwide debate on Article 370 in a public meeting in Jammu. It was also an indication from his side that what would be his thought process about Article 370 if he came to power. As a part of this thought process, after the assembly elections in Jammu and Kashmir in the year 2014, despite the fragmented mandate, the BJP made up its mind to form the government in the state along with the Peoples' Democratic Party (PDP), whose ideology was totally opposite that of BJP's. This was part of the well thought out strategy of Prime Minister Modi.

In order to prevent the PDP from carrying forward its radical agenda in the government of Jammu and Kashmir, a common minimum program, that is, a common program of running the government, was prepared and a common government came into existence under the leadership of Mufti Mohammad Sayeed of the PDP. Sayeed was a seasoned political player and had been the home Minister at the Centre, too. He was the first Muslim person in the country to become the Union Home Minister—that too in Vishwanath Pratap Singh's government, which was supported by the BJP from outside. However, it was during his tenure that his daughter Rubaiya Saeed was kidnapped by terrorists and in return five terrorists had to be released, after which his daughter was released. The role of the BJP was strong in the government formed under the leadership of Mufti Mohammad Sayeed. But Prime Minister Modi was proceeding very cautiously. As the representative of the government, BJP leaders-Ministers were working on the ground so that the real situation there could be understood closely.

Suddenly on January 7, 2016, Mufti Mohammad Sayeed passed away in the All India Institute of Medical Sciences, Delhi due to illness. But after that PDP leader Mehbooba Mufti showed hesitation in government formation and Governor's rule was imposed in the state. But in April, Mehbooba Mufti met Prime Minister Narendra Modi and on April 4, 2016, she took oath as the Chief Minister. Narendra Modi, who was moving cautiously during the time of Mufti Mohammad Sayeed, stepped forward with political acumen. This is where Prime Minister Modi took the initiative to put his plan in action regarding the strategy to remove Article 370. Clearly, the work on the future of Article 370 had started three years before the 2019 Lok Sabha elections.

Mission Kashmir: History, Present and Future

This is how the communication between the local people and the team engaged in the secret mission took place

The biggest feature of Narendra Modi's regime is complete secrecy before the mission reaches its end. However, if someone gets to know about it, turning it in another direction is also another great feature. In history, there are few examples of keeping such an operation secret for a long time as was in the case of the removal of Article 370 from Jammu and Kashmir. Although many strategists of Narendra Modi believe that this operation started from December 2015 the work on it actually started from January 2016. It is pertinent to reiterate here that the BJP-PDP alliance in Jammu and Kashmir was beginning to see cracks as Mufti Mohammad Sayeed's daughter Mehbooba Mufti was hesitant to form the government after his death. But without worrying about it, Narendra Modi had started taking forward his mission.

A team of trusted officials from various security agencies led by National Security Advisor Ajit Doval was advancing. For this, the first task was to collect the documents related to the Sangh and Dr. Syamaprasad Mookerjee on Article 370. As per the instructions from the top level, these documents were translated into Urdu and other languages. Its purpose was to make available the thought process of the Sangh and Mookerjee regarding Article 370 in the local language. When the translation work was completed, a detailed questionnaire was prepared. The preparation of the questionnaire did not mean that the questionnaire would be filled out by the local people or a report would be prepared after filling it out. Rather, its purpose was that all the people involved in this mission should memorize all the questions and talk accordingly. The questions asked in the conversation with common Kashmiris were not of official type but of aggressive style, on which local Kashmiris could also debate and communicate with interest. For example, some of the questions were like this—what if Kashmir becomes a part of Pakistan? Do you know what is the condition of Muslims in Pakistan and Afghanistan? Conversations with facts about what is the true picture of Islam religion were also part of the questionnaire.

In fact, the purpose of such questions was to bring out the sentiments instilled by the extremists in the minds of the local people and then expressing their views by showing the correct picture. The major reason for doing this has been the history of the Kashmir Valley. Sheikh Abdullah formed a party called All Kashmir Muslim Conference to challenge Maharaja Hari Singh in Kashmir, but later he realized that doing so would not get him Hindu votes. So, later the name of the party was changed to 'National Conference'. But despite the long politics, till the year 1971, the impact of the National Conference remained more in the urban areas of the state. When Bangladesh was carved out of Pakistan in 1971, the fundamentalists started expanding their agenda in Kashmir. In the year 1971 itself, an organization named 'Jamaat-e Islami' entered the election. Earlier this organization worked as a socio-religious banner. After the year 1971, the influence of the National Conference was seen to be less and the Jamaat-e-Islami was seen to be a more effective organization. Now totally banned, the organization at that time tried to create religious frenzy by increasing its penetration in rural Kashmiri areas through a well-thought-out strategy as the National Conference was dominant in urban areas. This extremist organization tried to instill such feelings among the local people-'It is good for Muslims to stay with the Islamic country.' 'The solution to all problems lies in Islam'. 'Only an Islamic country can work for the welfare of the Muslims. Living with the infidels is not in our interest.' Panic was natural. Not only this, there were also incidents of killing those who gave information against terrorists to the local civil protection agencies.

But the team engaged in a secret mission to communicate with the local citizens used to confirm whether the infiltrators from across the border had come and taken shelter in any house. That means, it was only after complete preparation and confirmation that the team went out to talk to the people for its mission. Aggressive questions were prepared to bring out the sentiments filled in by the extremists. When people of various security agencies used to talk to the local people, the matter of Shri Ram Janmabhoomi also came up, which was infused in the minds of the people by the extremists. So, when members of the secret mission team used to ask complementary questions—do you want the whole world to be Islamic? The people of the team used to present the picture of the situation of common Muslims in Pakistan-Afghanistan with facts and then ask why despite being an Islamic country, the problem of Muslims there was not solved? The difference between soft Islam and radical Islam was shown by comparison with the situation in Pakistan. This dialogue went on for hours in the form of a debate. Indeed, the list of questions was so strategic and factual that in the end the common Kashmiri citizen agreed that the benefit for Kashmir lay in being with India.

Those People were Identified who could have been a Hindrance in Operation 370

Before carrying out its mission, the team of Modi government engaged in Operation 370 did a comprehensive survey of extent of the influence of *Jamaat-e-Islami* in various places. In this, the police force and the teacher community were specifically identified because it was in these two areas that *Jamaat-e-Islami* could cause internal harm by furthering its idea. The presence of the fundamentalists in the teaching community could have been disastrous regarding the flow of radical ideas and support for them in the police force could have been disastrous regarding the security. This group could work to instigate common citizens. So, this comprehensive survey identified all those people who were under the influence of *Jamaat-e-Islami* or worked for them. The purpose of this survey was not to see if any immediate action would be taken against them, but to find out how much potential these people have to cause damage to the entire operation.

In such a situation, Narendra Modi government started writing the script of development on radical ideas and started providing facilities like electricity, water, LPG to the people.

Local Problems and Solution Strategy

The fundamentalists and a select few leaders had given religious colour to the basic problems of the people of Kashmir, while the need was to solve the basic problems at the village level. Even after six decades of independence, the local people were facing problems regarding necessities, while the family of extremists and hardliners were living a life of luxury. When the team engaged in the mission interacted with the local people, it became clear that the problem of electricity and drinking water was of paramount importance to them. All the taps and other water sources used to freeze due to snowfall. If ice had to be melted for drinking water, then there was no fuel for it. In such a situation, during the Governor's rule, Narendra Modi government took the initiative of development at the Panchayati level. For this the Panchayats were taken into confidence.

'Confidential Report' became the Basis for Realizing the Resolution

After receiving this report of Operation 370 from time to time, the Central Government worked towards the empowerment of Panchayats. After the panchayat elections, the central government took the initiative to take the funds for development till the last point during the governor's rule itself, as a result of which the panchayat representatives started taking interest in development and felt that they could join the mainstream of development. If we look at the figures so far, then the central government has disbursed more than 12 thousand crore rupees to the panchayats in Jammu and Kashmir. To empower the Panchayats, for the first time, three-tier Panchayati system has been implemented there. The initiative of the central government at the panchayat level also gained the confidence of the people. Encouraging results were obtained at the panchayat level, but on the other hand, the radicals started trying to obstruct the democratic process. Then the central government tried to execute the strategy to remove Article 370 which gave special status.

The thinking of Prime Minister Narendra Modi and the BJP-Rashtriya Swayamsevak Sangh was strengthened again when in the general elections of the year 2019, the BJP won a bigger majority than in the year 2014, raising the spirit of nationalism. After this victory, there was no hindrance to take the ideological issues to fruition.

...and in six years, the gap of six decades was reduced

The number of people who voted for BJP also crossed 22 crores in 2019 compared to 17 crores in 2014. In such a situation, there was a need-to make the new voters and supporters who had come to the BJP with hopes, ideologically more committed. For this, it was necessary that at the ideological level, the issue which has been going on for six decades should be handled. But it is important to understand the background of this issue along with the BJP and Sangh before party prepares to remove Article 370. The BJP used to make Article 370 an issue before every Lok Sabha election for 20 years. The RSS cadre has been against Article 370 since the 1950s. Dr Shyama Prasad Mookerjee, the founder of Jana Sangh, went to Kashmir in 1953 and went on a hunger strike against it. Later BJP raised the issue in 1996, 1999, 2004, 2014 before the elections. But before the 2014 general elections, Narendra Modi started the debate on it in a different way. After being declared the Prime Ministerial candidate, when Narendra Modi held a rally in Jammu in December 2013 which was a few months before the Lok Sabha elections, he had sparked a new debate in the country on the issue. Modi had said in the rally that Article 370 of the Indian Constitution should be debated across the country. This provision has deprived Jammu and Kashmir of proper development and empowerment. At the same time, the then BJP President Rajnath Singh had said that there should be a debate in the Parliament whether this article has benefited the people of Jammu and Kashmir.

The BJP maintained Article 370 as an election issue across the country for six months before the 2014 Lok Sabha elections. The BJP manifesto also included issues like Article 370, rehabilitation of Kashmiri Pandits, Uniform Civil Code. In May 2014, the BJP government was formed with an absolute majority at the Centre, but publicly there was no effort was seen being made on this issue. Actually, the strategy of the BJP and government behind this was to first pursue the agenda of development and then find a solution to the ideological issue. But when about 11 months were left for the Lok Sabha elections, the BJP broke the alliance at its end with the PDP in Jammu and Kashmir and tried to send a message to the cadres that it will not compromise on issues like Article 370, Kashmiri Pandits, terrorism. In fact, here too the BJP had shrewdly carried forward its strategy. The BJP had received reports that the PDP could topple the government by October by making a human rights issue on the action taken on stone pelters in Kashmir. In such a situation, in the name of country's integrity and nationalism, the then BJP President Amit Shah had already played his card.

The BJP was moving ahead with a well thought out strategy. But the Pulwama attack stalled the party's preparations on Article 370 for some time. The tide of nationalism not only empowered the BJP politically in the 2019 elections, but also gave great support ideologically. The BJP was working on a strategy to remove Article 370 from Jammu and Kashmir for a long time. In the year 2019, when the Modi government was formed at the Centre with a huge majority which was larger than even 2014, the Prime Minister had a conversation with the then Home Minister Rajnath Singh for about 9 minutes in the *Rashtrapati Bhavan* on the day of oath, about the strategy to do something new in Kashmir. The command of the Home Ministry was handed over to Amit Shah. When the then National President of BJP Amit Shah took over the command of the Home Ministry, then Shah, who had become known for his unique working style, started work on removing Article 370 and 35 (A) from Jammu and Kashmir with firm steps. It is always said about Shah that before doing any work, he makes all kinds of estimations about its effect and makes all arrangements for vigilance. He did the same thing on this issue as well. Its hallmark was visible in late July 2019. The sudden deployment of 10,000 soldiers in Jammu and Kashmir gave impetus to the discussion that the central government was going to remove 35(A). But there was no official explanation from the BJP and the government. But the message was being given by the party that the jawans were feeling tired due to the first Lok Sabha elections and now the Amarnath Yatra. In such a situation, new deployment is being done only for the purpose of giving them rest. Apart from this, there were also indications of holding assembly elections there in October and the local security forces were also being talked about being given rest.

Meanwhile, a meeting was also held with the leaders of the party's core group of Jammu and Kashmir along with the BJP high command, in which the local leaders were bluntly instructed to work in the direction of diluting the discussions on the removal of Article 370 and 35 (A). After that meeting, Jammu and Kashmir BJP President Ravindra Raina started insisting that in the meeting of the core group, there was discussion about the security of the state and the assembly elections. Raina had said that BJP is ready for elections in the state and they wanted hat there should be an election as soon as possible. They were going to speed up the membership drive of the party there. Raina even said that the parties whose deposits have been forfeited are spreading rumours about the deployment of security forces. He even indicated to the journalists at the BJP headquarters that the election notification could be issued any time after the Amarnath Yatra. That means, every effort was being made to put an end to the speculation about Article 370 and 35 (A) at that time. But the whole script was ready in the mind of Amit Shah, who was known for a distinct working style.

In fact, after the Lok Sabha elections, when Shah became the home Minister, it was decided that the legal and political aspects of the abrogation of Article 370 should be prepared. This was done like a routine exercise, for which efforts were going on for decades. A senior party leader told me in an informal conversation after Shah became Home Minister that the legal aspects of Article 370 had been asked to be scrutinized. But then I also took it as a normal exercise because even at that time nothing concrete was visible and it was believed that there is no election yet, so the government will not take any immediate steps. But this work gained momentum on 26 July when the government decided to extend the session of Parliament by 10 days. Even the Ministers did not realize this change. But Shah was already preparing for it.

Amit Shah had explored what could be the legal options in view of the legal aspects. A floor management group was formed to collect data in the Rajya Sabha, which included Parliamentary Affairs Minister Pralhad Joshi, Minister of State for Parliamentary Affairs V Muraleedharan, Railway Minister Piyush Goyal, Petroleum Minister Dharmendra Pradhan and BJP's National General Secretary and Rajya Sabha MP Bhupendra Yadav. These Ministerial leaders were also not told which bill they had to garner support for. All they had to tell the parties they were talking to was that a bill necessary for the country was being introduced. A three-line whip was issued for BJP MPs till the Parliament session was on.

Strategically, the Narendra Modi government did not let anyone know about Article 370 and 35 (A) until the cabinet approved it on the morning of August 5 and a notification was issued by the President. After this decision, Home Minister Amit Shah introduced the 'Jammu and Kashmir State Reorganization Bill' in Parliament and presented a series of arguments as to why it was necessary to do so and for what political interests the previous governments had kept it pending till now. The preparedness of the government can also be gauged from the fact that the revised agenda for introducing the bill in Rajya Sabha was released at the last minute so that there should be no hindrance in the strategy of abrogating Article 370 in Jammu and Kashmir. Solicitor General Tushar Mehta had reached the room of Thaawarchand Gehlot, Leader of the House in Rajya Sabha at 10.30, half an hour before the proceedings of the House began. Gehlot's room was made a war room. The command here was handled by Home Minister Amit Shah. From there Tushar Mehta was sending legal details through chits to the speakers who were speaking on behalf of the BJP and the government in the House. Law Minister Ravi Shankar Prasad, Railway Minister Piyush Goyal, Minister of State for Parliamentary Affairs Arjun Ram Meghwal and MP Bhupendra Yadav kept going to and from the room. The Solicitor General and the Law Minister were sending legal details to the speakers of the BJP and the government through chit from the same room. While Mehta and Prasad were looking after the legal side, Goyal, Yadav and Meghwal were involved in floor management. Work was also going on regarding the strategy for the resignation of the opposition MPs. During the debate on the bill, Shah reached the war room four times. Shah kept on going back to the house after holding small meetings and had lunch also here. But the legal nuances of removing Article 370 had been told by Arun Jaitley to Prime Minister Narendra Modi. After Jaitley's death, when the Prime Minister interacted with some strategists to remove Article 370 from Jammu and Kashmir, he credited Jaitley for explaining the legal nuances of the issue. Then he had said that the issue of abrogation of Article 370 from Jammu and Kashmir was being considered very challenging as there were often talks like constitutional amendment to remove it, but the legal understanding of Arun Jaitley ji was so good that the issue of Article 370 could be handled only with a small legal change.

Thus, Article 370 was nullified and Ladakh was made a separate Union Territory after making Jammu and Kashmir a Union Territory. The Sangh had been demanding for a long time to make Ladakh a separate territory. For the Sangh, it was the realization of the ideological dream which it had been fighting for decades.

Thinking of what could be 'the best of the worst'

There is a saying - It is the best of the worst, that is, what can be the best in the worst. With this thinking, the abolition of Article 370 can be called a master stroke of the strong will of Prime Minister Narendra Modi. It was an initiative to secure the borders of the nation, about which a picture of terrorism and extremism always emerged in the mind. Whenever something happened, the army had to be brought to the fore; but now Kashmir is safe. However, during the first term of Prime Minister Narendra Modi, the initiative to realize this could not be completed because the sudden Pulwama attack had brought everything to a halt. So, when Narendra Modi again formed the government in the general elections of the year 2019 by getting an even greater majority than before, the responsibility of the Union Home Ministry was entrusted to Amit Shah. In the first three months after the formation of the government, the decades-old history of Article 370 became history in the true sense.

The most important thing in this was the efforts of Prime Minister Narendra Modi in this direction for three years. The report emanating from the secret mission paved the way for the abolition of Article 370 and today Jammu and Kashmir is on the path of peace, progress and prosperity. Truly bridging the gap of decades, the Narendra Modi government has ended 70 years of pain by abrogating Article 370 from Jammu and Kashmir and Ladakh, which had been left behind in the race for development. After liberation from these discriminatory provisions, Jammu and Kashmir and Ladakh, which are called 'heaven on earth', have now been brought at par with other states of the country by connecting them with the mainstream and in the last two years, this region is moving fast on the track of development along with the rest of the country.

"फजा ये अमन-ओ-अमाँ की सदा रखें कायम,
सुनो ये फर्ज तुम्हारा भी है हमारा भी"

—नुसरत मेहँदी

❑

21
CHAPTER

A Pleasant Feeling...

After the election results of the year 2019, the decisive battle of the Modi government on the ideological front won the hearts of the Sangh Parivar. Then with coordination, a step towards 'New India'.

The historic victory of the BJP in the General Elections 2019 had proved that now the BJP and the Sangh had come out of that bitter experience of the year 1998-2004 and written a new saga of coordination. When it had come to power at the Centre for the first time, the lack of coordination in the Vichar Pariwar was publicly visible, the brunt of which BJP had to bear in the 2004 general elections. But in 2014, Narendra Modi, along with the Sangh, drew a blueprint for coordination of which the 2019 general election became witness.

After this historic victory, the central government started taking steps in coordination with the family to strategically consider ideological issues. The legal consultation activities in the BJP had intensified before the 2019 general elections. All the legal aspects related to Article 370 were being brainstormed through the lawyers in the party. But it was being carried forward as a normal activity from the top level, while it was being decided by the top leadership that before the general elections, a tough decision should be taken on this and signal should be given to the ideological cadres so that enthusiasm and new energy could be infused. But in the meantime, the martyrdom of 40 CRPF personnel in the terrorist attack in Pulwama on February 14, 2019 changed the direction. The BJP changed the course of its election preparations, while the opposition was buoyed by the party's defeat in the assembly elections in three states-Chhattisgarh, Madhya Pradesh and Rajasthan earlier and attempts were being made to push the BJP back psychologically. But in the Parliament session before the general elections, based on the feedback of the Sangh, the BJP-led central government played the masterstroke of 10% reservation for the upper castes on economic grounds. The *Pradhanmantri Kisan Samman Nidhi* was started to allay the displeasure of the farmers, that is, the BJP was taking all measures to reduce the chances of loss in the general election. However, after the Pulwama attack, the country's trust in the leadership of Prime Minister Narendra Modi had grown so much that everyone seemed to say that 'Modi is no longer going to spare Pakistan'. He inaugurated the indigenous train

'Vande Bharat', which was going to be an example of the pace of India's development, from New Delhi Railway Station on 15 February, just the day after the Pulwama attack on 14 February. Modi's roar in every meeting and programme after that boosted the confidence of the country. Eventually, the Balakot air strike on 26 February changed the entire mood of the country and the election of the year 2019 was filled with the spirit of nationalism, i.e., the people who benefited from the development plans during the year 2014 to 2019, this feeling of nationalism also put an end to the natural resentment towards local MPs, the result of which was clearly visible in the results of the 2019 general election, and the BJP, while in power, set a record of winning the majority of seats for the second time. Then started the campaign to take the ideological issues to their logical end.

Shri Ram Janmabhoomi: The Wait of Centuries is Over

After coming to power for the second time, the abolition of Article 370 and then three months later, the Supreme Court's resolution of the ongoing dispute over Shri Ram Janmabhoomi in Ayodhya was certainly comforting for the *Sangh Parivar*. After the end of the decades-long judicial process, on November 9, 2019, Prime Minister Narendra Modi, in his message to the nation, termed it as a new dawn for India and said that now the country has to resolve that the new generation will be involved in the making of 'New India' a new. Taking forward the same message, the Prime Minister laid the foundation stone for the construction of a grand Ram temple in Ayodhya and said, "Just as the Dalits-Backward-Adivasis, every section of the society supported Gandhiji in the freedom struggle, in the same way today across the country, this virtuous work of construction of Ram temple has started with the cooperation of the people.

Traditional Costume: When Prime Minister Narendra Modi, wearing a dhoti kurta, reached Ayodhya, the birthplace of Lord Ramlala on August 5, 2020, the dream of hundreds of years had come true. The Prime Minister offered prayers to Ram Lalla and prostrated at the site of Ram's birth. With *bhumi-pujan*, the construction of the grand Ram temple started. The Prime Minister described it as a symbol of modern moment of Indian culture, faith and national spirit.

The example of how much satisfaction the decision on Shri Ram Janmabhoomi provided to the Sangh Parivar was clearly visible in the statement of *Sarsanghchalak* Mohan Bhagwat. He said, "The *Rashtriya Swayamsevak Sangh* welcomes the decision of the Hon'ble Supreme Court to give justice to the public sentiment, faith and belief of this country. This lawful final decision has been taken after a long judicial process which lasted for decades. In this long process, all the aspects related to Shri Ram Janmabhoomi have been carefully considered. The arguments put forth by all the parties from their respective point of view were evaluated. By patiently running this long brainstorming, we wholeheartedly thank and congratulate all the justices and advocates of all the parties who uncovered the truth and justice. We gratefully remember all the colleagues and people who made sacrifices who have contributed in many ways in this long endeavour. We also welcome the efforts made by all the people at the level of government and society to maintain complete order while maintaining the mood to accept the decision, brotherhood and congratulate them. The Indian people, who waited for justice with utmost restraint, also deserve to be congratulated. This decision should not be seen in terms of victory or defeat. The conclusion obtained from the churning of truth and justice should be seen and used as a decision to nurture the unity and fraternity of the entire society of India. The countrymen are requested to express their happiness in a restrained and calm manner by staying within the limits of law and constitution. We are confident that the initiative to end the dispute will be expedited by the government in accordance with the decision of the Supreme Court towards the end of this dispute. Forgetting all the things of the past, let us all fulfil our duties together in the construction of a grand temple at Shri Ram Janmabhoomi.

The flow of thoughts regarding Shri Ram Janmabhoomi was also seen in Prime Minister Narendra Modi's address to the nation. He called it a golden chapter in the history of the Indian judiciary. Like RSS Chief Mohan Bhagwat, Prime Minister Narendra Modi also said, "With today's verdict, the Hon'ble Supreme Court has given a message that even the most complex issues can be resolved within the ambit of the Constitution and the law. We should learn from this decision that even if it takes some time, we should be patient. It is in everyone's interest. In every situation, our faith in the Constitution of the country and the judicial system of the country should remain firm, it is very important.

The Sangh and the BJP in one voice called this decision a sign of the progress of the nation, the spirit of harmony, brotherhood, friendship, unity and peace. Due to Covid, there was a slight delay in the *bhumi-pujan* of the Ram temple. But on August 5, 2020, after reaching Ayodhya, Prime Minister Modi performed *bhumi-pujan* and said, "*Ram kaj kinhe binu mohi kahan bisram.*" His address was a reflection of how big an ideological success it was. The Prime Minister said, "Lord Bhaskar is creating a golden chapter today on the banks of Saryu. Every mind is thrilled, radiant. Entire India is emotional because the wait of centuries is coming to an end today. Now a grand temple will be built for our Ramlala, who has been living under sackcloth and tents for years. Ram Janmabhoomi has become free today from this centuries-long travail of breaking up and then standing up again. In the movement for the Ram temple, there was an offering, there was also a sacrifice; there was struggle, there was resolve. Today, I bow to all those people, whose sacrifice, renunciation and struggle is making this dream come true, whose penance is attached like a foundation of Ram temple." The Prime Minister exuded confidence at the *bhumi-pujan* ceremony, "We will all move forward, the country will move forward! This temple of Lord Rama will continue to inspire and guide humanity for ages."

The strength of the ideology and the spirit of service is the basic mantra of the Sangh, the example of which was also seen during the Corona period when the Sangh and BJP made service-spirit a means of public relations. Through this, again an attempt was made to send the message that even in times of crisis, the organization stands with the people.

Sangh-BJP's Service-spirit during Corona Period

During the difficult situation of Corona, when the opportunity came before the country to serve humanity, Prime Minister Narendra Modi gave the inspiration of *'Seva hee Sangathan'* (Service is Organization) while giving seven mantras. With this inspiration, lakhs of party workers set a wonderful example of service to the whole country under the efficient organizational guidance of BJP National President Jagat Prakash Nadda. The seven mantras were service spirit, balance, restraint, coordination, positivity, goodwill and dialogue. These were the mantras with which BJP workers were selflessly reaching out to needy people. By July 4, BJP workers had prepared and distributed food to more than 22 crore people and more than 4.5 crore face masks across the country under *'Seva Hi Sangathan'*. More than 5 lakh 40 thousand workers were involved in the service of the elderly. The Sangh was also leaving no stone unturned in reaching out to the needy through its subsidiary organization 'Seva Bharti'. To fulfil the needs of the people, along with food items, food packets, masks, sanitizers and mobile-iPad etc. were also provided to the needy students through the Sangh. This means of service was strengthening the sentiments of the people towards the BJP and the Sangh even during the Corona period. To convert this disaster into an opportunity, the Modi government gave a mantra of self-reliance which strengthened Sangh's call for *Swadeshi*.

The Path of Swadeshi through 'Self-reliant India'

Making the resolution of 'self-reliant India' during the Corona period, Prime Minister Modi gave new goals to India's self-power coming out of the epidemic. In May 2020, there was a definite discussion of a big package. But nobody had estimated that this package would be of 20 lakh crore rupees. Provisions had been made for every aspect including economy, infrastructure system, demography and demand in this *'Atmanirbhar Bharat'* (Self-Reliant India) package, which touched all the dimensions of country's infrastructure. The effect of this appeal was that the spirit of 'Vocal for Local' became a movement. The confidence of people to manufacture in their own country, to buy goods manufactured in their country and to promote it in the global market was strengthened and self-reliance in the country was brought to the centre of the debate. The mantra of self-reliance opened the way for *Swadeshi* and it was further strengthened when India joined the leading countries of the world by inventing two indigenous vaccines of Corona. BJP tried to give the message that today the country was moving towards defeating Corona completely. This became possible because the scientists in the country's medical field worked tirelessly under the able leadership of Prime Minister Modi. Between the Corona disaster and the invention of the vaccine, the Vichar Pariwar paved the way for a general victory in the Bihar elections as well.

Victory of Bihar Assembly Election through Coordination

The support of the Vichar Pariwar was very positive in the BJP's strategy for the victory of the Bihar assembly elections in the year 2020. The major reason for this was that the foundation stone of the Ram temple in Ayodhya, the prompt combat on the border with China and the unprecedented development of infrastructure in the border areas infused an energy and feeling in the minds of the *Vichar Parivar* and the people associated with them that why indeed having Narĕndra Modi only was necessary. The victory was also significant as the alleged controversy over the issue of reservation in the 2015 assembly elections created a ruckus. But with this victory, the pain of 2015 was erased. Apart from this, in the most important rural areas, the way the scheme of ration for the poor was delivered during the Corona period, Rs 500 in Jan Dhan, Divyang-elderly pension, Ujjwala cylinders etc. contributed positively at the ground level. Depositing Rs 2,000 of '*Kisan Samman Nidhi*' in the account of farmers immediately after sowing was the result of the party's strategic thinking, which left a deep impression on the mind of the people. In such a situation, in front of the public, on the one hand, there were attractive promises made by Tejaswi Yadav of RJD, and on the other hand, it was the delivery mechanism of the Narendra Modi government which had become a reality, which played a big role in the victory of BJP and in Bihar, the party achieved the figure suitable for the role of the elder brother in the alliance. Now the way forward was to make BJP self-reliant in Bihar like the Centre.

The Discussion of New India and Ideology Family

Reducing the gap of six decades, the Modi government abolished Article 370 within six years and Jammu and Kashmir was made a union territory according to the principles of the Sangh. The real integration of Jammu and Kashmir took place and now along with the development of the country, Kashmir also seems to be moving along. People have started getting the direct benefits of central schemes, due to which along with development, the thinking of the people of Kashmir is also in step with the change. Unprecedented opportunities have arisen for the youth of these regions. The government has taken steps to root out terrorism and poverty whereas in the 70 years since the implementation of Article 370, more than 41,500 Sikhs, Buddhists and people of other religions had to lose their lives in Kashmir. Ladakh was carved out of Kashmir through state reorganization with effect from October 31, 2019, for which the *Sangh Parivar* had been continuously fighting. Ladakh was a region with a distinct cultural identity and this demand was being made for 70 years, which was fulfilled by the Modi government. It got the status of a separate union territory. But keeping in view the challenges of the region, especially during the period of severe winter when it gets cut off from other areas of the state, no legislature provision has been made here. The central law now directly reaches the people of Jammu and Kashmir and Ladakh. The 170 laws of the Centre which did not reach there earlier, now came into force directly. It was an initiative which gave a pleasing feeling for the Vichar Pariwarand also for the BJP.

The wait of centuries was over. The historic verdict on the Shri Ram Janmabhoomi temple in Ayodhya, the move towards the construction of the temple after the *bhumi-pujan*, the Citizenship Amendment Act-2019—these were some of the issues that the *Sangh Parivar* had been demanding for a long time. Initiatives were being taken for this even during the Vajpayee government. But when that did not happen, the then *Sarsanghchalak* of the Sangh, KS Sudarshan had publicly targeted Atal Bihari Vajpayee. But now the Modi government implemented it in the first six months of the second term. Under this law, a provision was added to give Indian citizenship to the persecuted religious minorities i.e. persons belonging to Hindu, Sikh, Buddhist, Jain, Parsi and Christian communities in India's neighbouring countries-Pakistan, Bangladesh, Afghanistan. Along with this, special arrangements were also made to preserve the linguistic, cultural and social identity of the people of the Northeast. NRC was initiated in Assam. In order to end the problem of foreign infiltration, the long-standing demand that a National Register should be created was initiated in Assam on the orders of the Supreme Court. National Register of Citizens was published in Assam. The opening of the Kartarpur Corridor, the signing of the Bodo Accord, the solution to the Bru-Reang refugee crisis in Tripura was nothing less than the beginning of a new era.

Before the Bihar elections, India's strong position in the dispute with China on the Ladakh border and its action to give a befitting reply won the hearts of the country and the Vichar Parivaras well. After 50 years, China once again tried to infiltrate the Indian border, to which the Indian brave soldiers gave a befitting reply. Coming out of the mental pressure of 1962, the manner in which development activities were increased at the level of infrastructure in the border areas in the last six years certainly roused the anger of China. But the Modi government made environmental clearances related to defense and strategic sectors flexible and relaxed, giving a new impetus to infrastructure.

All the above examples, especially with the ideology family, have become examples of harmony and pleasant feeling. With the strength of ideology, both Sangh and BJP are writing a new chapter in society and politics. The journey of coordination continues with this pleasant feeling...

❑